COMRADES AT ODDS

COMRADES AT ODDS

The United States and India,
1947–1964

Andrew J. Rotter

Cornell University Press
Ithaca and London

This book has been published with the aid of a grant from the
Dean's Publication Fund of Colgate University.

First published 2000 by Cornell University Press
First printing, Cornell Paperbacks, 2000

Printed in the United States of America

Library of Congress Cataloging-in-Publication Data

Rotter, Andrew Jon.
    Comrades at odds : the United States and India, 1947–1964 / Andrew J. Rotter.
        p. cm.
Includes bibliographical references and index.
    ISBN 0-8014-3449-1 (cloth : alk. paper) — ISBN 0-8014-8460-X (pbk. : alk. paper)
    1. United States—Foreign relations—India. 2. India—Foreign relations—United
States. 3. India—Foreign public opinion, American. 4. United States—Foreign
public opinion, East Indian. 5. Public opinion—United States—History—20th
century. 6. Public opinion—India—History—20th century. I. Title.
    E183.8.I4 R63 2000
    327.73054—dc21

                                                            00-009283

Cornell University Press strives to use environmentally responsible suppliers and
materials to the fullest extent possible in the publishing of its books. Such materials
include vegetable-based, low-VOC inks and acid-free papers that are recycled,
totally chlorine-free, or partly composed of nonwood fibers. Books that bear the
logo of the FSC (Forest Stewardship Council) use paper taken from forests that
have been inspected and certified as meeting the highest standards for environmental
and social responsibility. For further information, visit our website at
www.cornellpress.cornell.edu.

Cloth printing   10 9 8 7 6 5 4 3 2 1
Paperback printing   10 9 8 7 6 5 4 3 2 1

For Padma

Contents

Acknowledgments

Acknowledgments should be more than lists, if for no other reason than that everyone reads them first. The danger is that if I wax lyrical about all the help I've had, about all the extraordinary ways in which friends, relatives, colleagues, and students have contributed to this project, this section will go on far longer than it should. So, quite out of character, I will economize, with apologies to those who deserve more fulsome thanks.

I begin with those who have helped me at libraries and archives in the United States, Great Britain, and India. The staffs at the National Archives in Washington and the Washington National Records Center in Suitland, Maryland, were courteous and professional. At the Truman, Eisenhower, and Kennedy presidential libraries, I was received with a spirit of generosity and a willingness to help that still takes my breath away. Librarians at Yale, Columbia, and Syracuse University libraries, and the Bancroft, Doe, and South and Southeast Asian libraries at the University of California–Berkeley, provided me with access to vital manuscript collections and one-of-a-kind sources that clarified my thinking about culture and Indo-U.S. relations; thanks especially to Ken Logan at Berkeley. At my home library at Colgate, Ellen Bolland, David Hughes, and Emily Hutton hunted down sources with awe-inspiring resolve and cheerfulness, making my problems theirs, and solving most of them. In London, I had good help from archivists at the India Office Library, and in Kew the staff of the Public

Record Office provided advice and files with its legendary efficiency. And I am very grateful to R. K. Perti and the staff at the National Archives of India and especially D. N. Panigrahi and the staff at the Jawaharlal Nehru Memorial Museum and Library, all of whom worked diligently on my behalf when I was in New Delhi some years ago.

People also gave me money to travel and write. Why they should do this has always baffled and delighted me, but I thank them very much for it. To the American Council of Learned Societies, the Truman Library Institute, and the Colgate Faculty Research Council, which has come to my aid more times than I can count, my deep gratitude. Jane Pinchin, my dean for most of these years, has supported this project in every way. The Gandhi Peace Foundation in New Delhi, and its director Shri Radhakrishna, and the Center for South Asian Studies at the University of California–Berkeley, headed most recently by Steven Poulos, provided me with office space and administrative help.

Over the past years—I'm afraid it's almost decades—I have tried out ideas on a host of unsuspecting victims, most of whom were nevertheless gracious enough to seem interested, and many of whom asked good questions and raised issues for me to think about. For arranging or attending my talks, wading through my prose, or hearing me out in hallways or restaurants or stuffy seminar rooms, I thank Susan Armeny, Tim Borstelmann, Dolores Byrnes, Tim Byrnes, Nathan Citino, J. Garry Clifford, Frank Costigliola, Carl Degler, Faye Dudden, Tony Fels, Lloyd Gardner, Sarvepalli Gopal, Carl Guarneri, Karen Halttunen, Deb Harkness, Gary Hess, Michael Hogan, Gene Irschick, Christopher Jesperson, Walter LaFeber, Doug Little, Doug Macdonald, Tom McCormick, Dennis Merrill, Janaki Nair, Arnold Offner, Thomas Paterson, Michael Peletz, David Robinson, Emily Rosenberg, Robert Shaffer, David Thelen, Peggy Trawick, Gary Urton, M. S. Venkataramani, Bill Walker, and Joanna Williams. My fine student assistants, Scott Mills and Brad Houston, soldiered through miles of microfilm.

I am particularly indebted to those scholars who read one or another version of the manuscript for Cornell University Press. The project was approved as a gleam in its author's eye largely because of the faith shown in it by Chris Appy, Kirin Narayan, and Michael Sherry. All three strengthened the manuscript with their perceptive comments and criticisms and their helpful suggestions, especially on the vexing relationship between culture and foreign relations. Mike Sherry and Robert McMahon read and commented on the full manuscript. I cannot thank them enough for their advice and support. Cornell University Press itself was again the best place imaginable to publish a book. It's been fifteen years since I met my editor, Peter Agree, and I still can't refrain from making a pun on his name. Roger Haydon gracefully ushered the book into print, Alja Kooistra was a patient manuscript editor, and John LeRoy was a careful and perceptive copyeditor. Thanks, too, to Dave Prout, who prepared the index, and to Julia Meyerson, who drew the digrams on pages 44 and 46.

Portions of this book are developed from material I previously published elsewhere. Chapter 5 is based on "Gender Relations, Foreign Relations: The United States and South Asia, 1947–1964," *Journal of American History* 81, no. 2 (1994): 518–542. An earlier version of chapter 6 appeared in September 2000 as "Christians, Muslims, and Hindus: Religion and U.S.–South Asian Relations, 1947–1964," in *Diplomatic History,* and chapter 7 expands on "Feeding Beggars: Class, Caste, and Status in Indo-U.S. Relations, 1947–1964," in Christian G. Appy, ed., *Cold War Constructions: The Political Culture of United States Imperialism, 1945–1966* (Amherst, 2000), 67–85.

I've been lucky in my friends, many of whom are named above. But whenever I needed a sensible word, a good laugh, unqualified praise or honest criticism, a pat on the back or a (usually figurative) slap in the face, I turned to my dear friends Carl Guarneri, Val Weller, Jerry Eisman, and Kathy Ward. They have always helped me to figure things out, and I am grateful to them beyond words.

Above all, my family has lived this book with me. My parents, Roy and Muriel Rotter, have shown me the awesome patience and unblinking support that I can only hope to emulate with my own children. Lorraine and Chandran Kaimal, my in-laws, have taught me about India, fed me, kept me almost up to date with the *New Yorker,* and inspired me with their wisdom and compassion. Sophie and Phoebe Kaimal Rotter are two naughty and delightful girls who have known about Daddy's book for as long as they have lived. They have waited good-naturedly for its completion, in hopes that he'll be able to wrestle with them more often. Watch out, girls. This book happened because of my wife, Padma Kaimal. Everything right about India in it is her contribution; everything wrong is the result of my stubborn refusal to listen. She has sustained me intellectually, emotionally, and in every way. The book is dedicated to her—the smallest of down payments on the greatest of debts.

Preface

> There is no such thing as human nature independent of culture.
>
> —Clifford Geertz, *The Interpretation of Cultures*

This is a book about relations between the United States and India from 1947 to 1964. I confess to feeling a slight urge to disavow that statement. A university press editor (not mine) once told me that the words "India" or "Spain" in a book title are death on sales, which tempted me briefly to remove "India" and substitute for it an ugly but provocative metonym, perhaps "snakes" or "burning bodies." I resisted, because in the end I insist on the intrinsic importance of relations between the world's two largest democracies, between people of such interest and diversity as Indians and Americans. Relations between the two nations had profound implications for hundreds of millions in the United States and India, and an impact as well on millions of others in countries affected by American and Indian behavior. During the period of the study, the United States was committed to fighting the Cold War, while Jawaharlal Nehru, the Indian prime minister and foreign minister, promoted "nonalignment," a path between the competing ideologies of the two Cold War camps. Partly because of this, the two nations were often at odds in their interpretations of world events: wars in Korea and Vietnam, the deployment of atomic weapons by the great powers, the legacies of colonialism and the meanings of nationalism in Asia and Africa, the danger of expansion by communist states, and so on. And Indo-American relations were marked by controversy—over the disposition of Kashmir state, the question of food aid for India, the American decision to supply India's rival Pakistan with arms and to enlist Pakistan in Asian military alliances, and the American approach to India's border war with China in 1962.

But the book is also something else: it is an attempt to apply cultural analysis to the study of relations between nations, in this case the United States and India. Its premise is that one can understand how peoples or nations relate to each other only with reference to cultures. While I do not denigrate the importance of studying Indo-U.S. relations for their own sake, they serve here rather as a means to the grander end of understanding the history of U.S. foreign relations, and international relations more generally, as a product in part of culture.

This unconventional argument makes for an unconventionally organized book. Unlike other studies of U.S.–South Asia relations during this period, this one does not offer a chronological narrative of diplomacy between the nations involved. That is not a postmodernist rejection of sequential history, nor is it meant to imply that there is no such thing as cause and effect. It is in the first place a recognition that several excellent narratives of the U.S.–South Asian relationship have already appeared, most notably those by H. W. Brands, G. W. Choudhury, Robert McMahon, and Dennis Merrill. A cultural approach is also more vivid and persuasive if it highlights episodes in the relationship that gained new clarity in the light of this kind of analysis. In each chapter after the introduction, I attempt to apply a particular aspect of culture broadly to the Indo-U.S. relationship, then to look closely at a specific policy encounter that reveals the influence of that cultural analysand. The result is a series of essays on Indo-U.S. relations, each of which is framed by a cultural category of analysis.[1]

What holds the essays together and makes them a book, apart from their focus on a particular relationship within a particular time period, is their common concern with culture. *Culture* is a vexatious word, "one of the two or three most complicated . . . in the English language" according to Raymond Williams, and when I use it I am the despair of my anthropologist friends, who argue that I insufficiently "problematize" it. But we have to start somewhere, and end up somewhere too, so we must make our definitions and forge ahead. I take as my definition of culture one developed by Clifford Geertz, by way of Max Weber: the "webs of significance" spun by human beings. At this level of generality, one can, for example, identify as filaments in the cultural web race, gender, and class (or caste)—the holy trinity of social historians. Religion is a thread of culture. Another, perhaps less common, is governance, the principles that guide human efforts to form political systems. And two more threads in the web are strategy and economics, the categories of analysis most familiar to diplomatic historians, though in my treatment they bear only partial resemblance to their traditional meanings. I examine one of these seven filaments of culture in each chapter of the book. The web metaphor also helps us understand that none of the filaments of culture exist independently of the others. The threads of a web intertwine and reinforce each other; in much the same way are such factors as race, gender, and religion interlocking and mutually supporting.[2]

This broad definition of culture is useful for a non-anthropologist who is less interested in exploring the endless mysteries of the word itself than in applying it to diplomacy. But there is a subset of culture that has particular resonance for foreign relations historians, and that is symbolic culture, or symbolic anthropology. The symbolic iteration of culture corresponds to what most laypersons think anthropology is about, lending it the distinct advantage of appealing to common sense. Interpreting symbols is something anthropologists have always seemed to do: Edward Tylor endorsed the exploration of symbols in *Primitive Culture* (1871); Franz Boas jettisoned the racist "evolutionism" of anthropology but kept the study of symbols; Talcott Parsons, who influenced Geertz, argued that culture "was above all the domain of symbols and meanings." Geertz's own definition has been summarized this way: "Symbolic anthropology views all acts and events as potentially meaningful, but also intrinsically ambiguous . . . not a cause to which events or institutions may be attributed, but a context within which they may be made intelligible." Use of symbolic culture allows, and requires, an analyst to take stock of rituals, stories and myths, games, food, folkways, habits, and customs. It also introduces ambiguity into interpretation, which seems to me sensible, and substitutes "context" for causation, which is potentially more troubling for a historian, though in the end not entirely at odds with historical epistemology, as I hope to show.[3]

I am aware of the controversy that surrounds the symbolic paradigm in anthropology. On one side, the postmodernists reject all paradigms, contesting, de-centering, and (naturally) problematizing virtually everything solid on which a concept of culture must rely. The practice of ethnography, and even language itself, merit no authority; as two anthropologists have put it, postmodern criticism has led to "a radical undermining of any assumption about the stability of particular cultural meanings." The result is that some practitioners have "abandoned the term [culture] altogether in favour of apparently less problematic terms like 'hegemony' or 'discourse.'" On the other side are critics, including some diplomatic historians, who are uneasy with Geertz's brief for context and troubled by his emphasis on ambiguity. Like most historians, frankly, they retain a reverence for cause-effect relationships. Insofar as culture matters, it is a variable dependent on other, firmer things, like economic need or national interest.[4]

My own view is that symbolic culture offers an exciting way to understand relations between peoples and nations. So much human interaction involves the interpretation (and misinterpretation) of one's own and others' experiences in symbolic terms. From webs of significance come images of others, amalgams of fact and fantasy, understood and expressed symbolically. People categorize whole groups of others according to the small things a few of them might do. In diplomacy, gesture, posture, facial expression, and verbal intonation can shape the outcome of discussion and negotiation. There is a content of diplomacy, but there is also a style, even a theater, to it. The symbolic, theatrical elements of diplomacy, conditioned as they are by culture, exert a subtle influence on the conduct of foreign relations.

Appearances matter: people react to the skin color, facial features, hair texture, and body build of others. How others smell is a crucial symbolic marker, often tied, in damaging ways, to the construction of race. People view space and time differently, have different religious stories and rituals, and have varying kinship patterns and family practices. Attitudes toward gender roles, the foods people cook and how they eat them, the clothes they wear, the games they play—all of these symbolic codes distinguish people from each other and affect relations between them.

Stereotypes—distorted images of whole groups of others—are built from symbolic materials. Americans and Indians began constructing stereotypes of each other from their first moment of encounter, and the inchoate images each side created crystallized with the onset of World War II in Asia. Hoping to understand their Japanese enemy, U.S. policymakers pressed anthropologists into service. "The concept of culture was drafted to help the war effort," Bernard Cohn has written, "and for the first time anthropological concepts were applied to nation-states." The American ascription of national behavior to culture was not confined to the Japanese. Beginning in 1942, American soldiers were stationed in India to help build the Ledo Road to China and to meet a possible Japanese invasion of India; by war's end, a quarter million had passed through the country. In letters, diaries, and conversations the troops registered their impressions of their Indian hosts, and Indians reciprocated. These impressions remained fresh when India became independent in 1947.[5]

While Americans believed that Indians shared a few attributes with the Chinese and Japanese, they found them more mystical, less disciplined, and altogether more exotic than their East Asian counterparts. Americans saw Indians as superstitious, unclean, diseased, treacherous, lazy, and pre-varicating. Indian society was stratified by caste, the source of shocking extremes of poverty and wealth. Indian men were effeminate, Indian women emasculating. While Indian civilization was old and decayed, the emergent Indian state was immature and therefore bumptious. American symbolic representations of India included beggars (poverty), fly-covered children with open sores and rheumy eyes (disease), Gandhians calmly taking beatings (passivity), burning brides or widows (depravity), and snake charmers, rope trick artists, and holy men recumbent on beds of nails (mystery or inscrutability). Indians, for their part, made references to the "Western mind," but they too distinguished among Westerners, frequently pointing out differences between the Americans and the British, most often to the detriment of the former. Indians saw Americans as arrogant, materialistic, uncouth, profane, and violent. Because American society lacked social boundaries, everyone in the country was rootless. Divorce was common, which proved that the family had little value. The only people in the United States who knew their place were blacks, shackled in subordination by white racism. American men were insensitive; American women were embarrassingly familiar with strange men. While American technology and economic might were unsurpassed, Americans were immature and lacked the wisdom and the will to control these forces. Indians represented Americans as smirking plutocrats (materialism, greed), grim-faced soldiers or cowboys (expansionism and militarism), lusty movie stars and scantily clad starlets (sexual license), and depraved, white-skinned crackers (racial intolerance).

Cases aside, this is not the first book on foreign relations history to use a cultural approach. Akira Iriye has long advocated the use of culture as an analytic tool alongside "power" and "economics." Iriye, whose definition of culture—"the sharing and transmission of memory, ideology, emotions, life-styles, scholarly and artistic works, and other symbols"—is essentially Geertzian, suggests that there are three ways in which historians might apply culture to the study of U.S. foreign relations. First, historians can interpret the state as a cultural expression, reflecting to some extent the "core values" and "basic ideals" of the people that constitute it. Second, the study of foreign relations need not be confined to the state. If it is difficult to find cultural elements in the writing of diplomats, it is not hard to discern values, attitudes, and prejudices in the discourse of novelists, traders, scholars, missionaries, and tourists. Finally, Iriye argues that cultural analysis can be brought to bear on issues of global importance "that transcend national boundaries." He has in mind such issues as human rights, the environment, and health care.[6] Michael Hunt's concern is with ideology. Approvingly quoting Geertz, Hunt finds ideology rooted in culture but ultimately distinct from it. Sustained and constrained by culture, ideology—"an interrelated set of convictions or assumptions that reduces the complexities of a particular slice of reality to easily comprehensible terms and suggests appropriate ways of dealing with that reality"—is nevertheless autonomous. In Hunt's formulation, ideology seems to process culture, condensing and crystallizing its fluid forms and rendering them useful instruments for the state's foreign policymakers. A Freudian might compare Hunt's version of culture to the dream material, ideology to the dream work that compresses and sharpens the material, shaping it into images that are (potentially) comprehensible to the dreamer. The result of this process, Hunt claims, is an ideology of U.S. foreign policy that consists of three "core ideas": a belief in liberty, an embrace of racial hierarchy, and a suspicion of revolutions.[7]

Neither Iriye's nor Hunt's discussion of culture gives me quite what I am looking for in my analysis. Iriye's definition, including as it does emotions, lifestyles, memory, and artistic works, seems to me to jumble together as "symbols" signifiers (like paintings) and things signified (like memory). Equally puzzling is Iriye's idea that culture is itself a process, the "sharing and transmission" of ideas. Whereas Iriye cannot avoid a sprawling definition of culture that fails to resolve into a coherent mechanism of policymaking, Hunt is perhaps too eager to give precision to an approach that may be, by his own account, "conceptually fuzzy and interpretively messy." For one thing, Hunt's "core ideas" do not encompass several webs of significance that I believe have influence on U.S. foreign policy—gender and religion, for instance. Moreover, unless one assumes that these American core ideas are universal categories, their relative specificity makes it difficult to compare American ideology to that of another country. Broader categories of culture, not condensed by ideology, allow for greater freedom in analyzing the behavior of other nations; while I do not think, for example, that Indians have a meaningful national attitude toward revolution, their political institutions embody a culturally conditioned idea of what government should be.

Without placing their work firmly and explicitly in a foundation of culture, a number of other diplomatic historians (and an occasional enterprising international relations specialist) have in recent years explored categories of analysis that fit into Geertz's symbolic universe. To demonstrate that ideas matter at all to policymakers has been the considerable contribution of Bruce Cumings, Frank Ninkovich, and Anders Stephanson, though among these three Nietzsche is more likely to be cited than Geertz.[8] Building on the work of Jack Snyder and others, Alastair Iain

Johnston has developed the concept of "strategic culture" and applied it imaginatively to the history of China's foreign relations.[9] In a series of innovative articles and commentaries, Emily Rosenberg has pioneered the use of gender to interpret episodes in U.S. diplomacy, and she has been joined by Geoffrey Smith, Laura McEnaney, Michelle Mart, Frank Costigliola, Robert Dean, and Kristin Hoganson.[10] The impact of race thinking on American foreign relations, as well as the role of the Civil Rights movement in shaping diplomacy, have been examined by Gerald Horne, John Dower, Mary Dudziak, Paul Gordon Lauren, Alexander DeConde, Thomas Borstelmann, Penny Von Eschen, and Brenda Gayle Plummer. All of these approaches fall within the realm of culture, and all have been useful to my exploration of Indo-U.S. relations.[11]

If Iriye and Hunt take diplomatic historians to the threshold of cultural analysis, and if those scholars just mentioned illuminate several pathways into the realm of foreign policymaking, how do we show finally the relationship between culture and diplomacy? By what process do webs of significance influence policymaking? In the general absence from diplomatic discourse of direct evidence concerning such things as religion, race, and gender, how do we know that culture is translated into the operating assumptions of policymakers? How can we prove to a skeptical audience, one most familiar with the policymaker's language of power and money, that culture matters?

To answer these questions, let me begin by echoing Iriye and subscribing to an expanded definition of U.S. foreign relations. The term "diplomatic history" is now widely seen as archaic because it implies the study only of what one diplomat said to another. The people who used to be called diplomatic historians increasingly regard their task as the investigation of encounters between peoples of different nations, whether or not these people represent their nations officially. This suggests that contacts between private citizens can be interesting and significant in their own right. It also indicates a renewed appreciation for the role that interest groups or influential individuals play in the formulation of foreign policy. These groups and individuals may be more susceptible than policymakers to the influence of culture. More likely, they may be more willing to express their feelings, attitudes, and values than an embassy official who is writing for the secretary of state, or an assistant secretary who is talking to representatives of another country. In part, then, this book finds culture by circumambulating policymakers.

But only in part, for in the end I will argue that culture shaped the thinking of policymakers too. And I'll make a statement that sounds cranky but is not, I think, unfair: it is surprising that the burden of proof falls on those of us who think that culture is a determinant of U.S. foreign policy. The current popularity of cultural history, its incursion into the fields of intellectual, social, and political history, should leave historians of U.S. foreign relations expectant that their time, too, has come. While common sense is rarely as common as one supposes, it is reasonable to assume that what affects the outlooks of most of us also affects the outlooks of those who make foreign policy. We think about race, and so presumably did the Missourian Harry S Truman, the Kentucky-born ambassador to India John Sherman Cooper, and that cautious advocate of civil rights John F. Kennedy. Truman's secretary of state, Dean Acheson, was the son of an Episcopalian bishop; Dwight Eisenhower's secretary of state, John Foster Dulles, the son of a Presbyterian minister, called himself a "Christian lawyer"; Dean Rusk, secretary of state during the Kennedy and Lyndon Johnson administrations, nearly became a minister himself. Those who made U.S. foreign policy between 1947 and 1964 no doubt shared with their fellow citizens, who farmed or sold insurance or took dictation or taught history, some fundamental beliefs about gender.

Decision makers are creatures of culture, not just policy wonks who shed their images of others like raincoats at the office door. Even the sophisticated men and women at the White House, the State Department, and the Pentagon, and their sophisticated counterparts in New Delhi (and in Pakistan) were affected by long-standing images of the others with whom they dealt. "No one who has even been involved in these relations," Nathan Glazer has written, "can doubt that [they] cannot be reduced simply to pragmatic calculations of interest, or to staked-out ideological positions. Something more is involved: how we see and feel about them, and how they see and feel about us." This would seem particularly true of United States–South Asia relations. I would establish here the principle (if political scientists have not already done so) that the less people know about each other, the more likely it is that they will fall back on long-standing stereotypes when they interpret each other's behavior—and I would add the corollary that where national interest is less than fully engaged, symbolic images are especially meaningful. In this way, it seems to me that Geertz's definition of culture as context and the historian's pursuit of cause- and -effect relationships are not altogether antithetical.[12]

Still, like Michael Hunt, I find it necessary to give some kind of shape to the cultural impulses, the Geertzian context, present among policymakers. I think, however, that the process of condensation by which culture becomes ideology removes too much of the culture. Weber's image, "webs of significance," offers a better description of how culture affects foreign policy. Webs are structures, but soft ones. They have shape, sym-

metry, purpose, and limits, so they do not include every human phenomenon. Like all people, foreign policymakers spin webs. They share them
among themselves, and they maintain more than one at a time. Some they
bring with them to public office; others await their arrival, to be inherited,
elaborated, and extended. People are not only the makers of webs but
their subtle victims, because they can become enmeshed in the filaments
they or others have made and become dependent on the sustenance and
security that their webs provide. All of us see the world through these networks of meaning. And, no matter what others' webs look like, we perceive them through our own.

Borrowing and adapting from the work of political scientists Gabriel Almond, Sidney Verba, and Lucian Pye, I will call the network of webs at the
policymaking level a "political culture." This consists, according to Verba,
"of the system of empirical beliefs, expressive symbols, and values which
defines the situation in which political action takes place." Emerging in
the late 1950s, political culture theory used insights from anthropology,
sociology, and psychology to make judgments about "national character."
The theory was stigmatized as conceptually soft by structuralists, insufficiently serious about class by Marxists, and verging on racist for its implication that the "wrong" culture might impede democracy and what in the
West is termed modernization. For a time the theory had few defenders.
Lately, however, it has shown signs of a comeback, as structuralism and
Marxism in particular have lost favor among social scientists, and as inter-
est in culture has revived.[13]

The theory of political culture has not generally been used to examine
U.S. foreign relations, but its employment by comparative government
and area studies specialists suggests that it might be of interest to foreign
policy historians as well. Political culture can illuminate the study of U.S.
foreign relations in several ways. First, the term itself associates popular
perceptions of others with official thinking. The source of political culture, writes Pye, is "both collective history of a political system and the life
histories of the individuals who currently make up the system"; it is thus
"rooted equally in public events and private experiences." The concept
thus unites seemingly opposite entities—the popular and the elite, the individual and the institutional, the attitudinal and the intellectual, even
the emotional and the rational—the cultural on the one hand, the political on the other. All people spin webs of significance, and all become enmeshed in them.[14]

Second, the term's equation of the cultural and the political assumes a
more thorough infiltration of the latter by the former than one would expect to find in an ideology. Political culture is a subset of culture gener-

ally. It thus requires that we take symbols seriously at the policymaking level. The prominence of culture in political culture also enables us to include at the level of policymaking more analytic categories than is possible with an ideological approach, even one, like Michael Hunt's, that is rooted in culture but does not find expression in cultural terms.

The prominence of politics in political culture is the concept's third strength. Despite their skepticism about structure, political culture theorists are ultimately interested in power. To say that allegedly soft presences such as beliefs, attitudes, and images affect politics is not to claim that foreign policy is made by *Zeitgeist*, nor by rabbis, novelists, or comic book illustrators. Policymakers are influenced and constrained by webs of significance, but they are human beings with agency, and they do what they are supposed to do—they make policy decisions. There is also room in political culture for the pursuit of national interest. Foreign relations is an encounter of images and symbols, through which rational vectors such as national interest must play.

Finally, political culture is an attractive concept because it borrows ideas from several disciplines. The interdisciplinary foundation of political culture gives the concept richness and broad appeal, in part because it can be approached from a number of access points. One can explain the operations of political culture only with reference to psychology, anthropology, sociology, and political science. And who better than a historian to place these unruly disciplines in the necessary perspective of the *longue durée*?

How can one identify the culture in political culture? One way is to find in the language of policymakers indication of cultural influence. The language can be spoken or written. As Frank Costigliola has noted, language is powerful; what one says, and how one says it, matter a great deal. When, for example, the U.S. ambassador to India, Loy Henderson, once characterized Nehru as "vain, sensitive, emotional, and complicated," his words carried a special valence, redolent of gender. Henderson could have said, "Nehru is a difficult man to deal with," but the vocabulary he chose meant something more. The language of the body, mentioned earlier, is also meaningful in diplomacy. One needs to interpret posture, gesture, and facial expression, as revealed in photographs or recorded, intentionally or inadvertently, by someone present during a conversation. An Indian waggling her head from side to side would seem to an American to be saying no, but in fact the gesture indicates agreement. While an American consular official in Calcutta would consider it polite to blow his nose into a handkerchief, then stash the cloth back in his pocket, an Indian would find the act revolting, though would probably say nothing.[15]

There may also be associative evidence that culture influences diplomacy. By this I mean that policymakers from time to time take actions that seem consistent with stereotyped attitudes and inconsistent with apparent national interest. For example, the Eisenhower administration chose to make the United States a military ally of Pakistan in 1954. Some, including the members of the administration, argued that the decision was in the interest of the United States, which sought the containment of the Soviet Union. Others, then and subsequently, objected that national interest could not possibly be served through the alliance, since Pakistan had next to nothing to contribute to the defense of Asia, and that the policy would outrage India, ultimately the more important country in South Asia. In fact, the Americans favored Pakistan because they were impressed with the allegedly manly, martial qualities of the Islamic nation's political leaders and soldiery.

Culture is encoded in language, but it resides in the minds of those who make foreign policy. Here we enter the realm of psychology, a place where it is necessary for historians of diplomacy to go. "An individual's cognitions, the processes by which he perceives and evaluates his physical and social environments . . . contribute to his conclusions and recommendations," the diplomatic historian Richard H. Immerman has written. If we are to understand the policies people make, we must understand, in some deep way, what makes them tick, what goes on in their minds as they assess situations and think their way toward policies. We must understand how Americans and Indians perceive themselves and others. The psychoanalyst Alan Roland, who has worked in the United States and India, writes that "the intrapsychic self varies significantly . . . according to the social and cultural patterns of societies so civilizationally different. I find that people have a very different experiential, affective sense of self and relationships, as well as vastly different internalized world views that give profoundly different meanings to everyday experiences and relationships." These relationships, of course, include those with people—even diplomats—of other nations, other cultures.[16]

Self-other theory is the cord attaching political culture to the study of U.S. foreign relations. Much has been made recently of self-other theory—indeed, too much. The theory has become a trope; one of its leading exponents, Edward Said, has complained that "the word [others] has acquired a sheen of modishness that has become extremely objectionable." A cultural interpreter of foreign relations, however, cannot help but find self-other theory useful, since it emphasizes fundamental perceptions of difference that must inevitably influence how people treat each other diplomatically. Perhaps we can escape from the trap of "modishness" if we place self-other theory in historical context and apply it to peoples involved in a particular relationship. We must also recognize the theory's subtleties. It is not meant sharply to dichotomize different peoples, but to show how selves create their own identities in part by projecting onto others their own worst traits. Unwilling to countenance a self-image that includes characteristics that are shameful, depraved, or even criminal, and unwilling to control behaviors that spring from these undesirable traits, selves preserve their integrity by imagining that others are the ones who are (for example) depraved. Others are in some sense the malevolent alter egos of selves; what the self cannot abide, it ascribes to the other. Exaggerating, misinterpreting, or falsely generalizing from cultural or even physical characteristics that others may in fact have, selves accuse others of their own worst sins. People with dark skins harbor some darkness within. Those who move away from home must lack affection for their families. And so forth.[17]

The matter is more intricate yet. Relations would have been easier had Americans and Indians seen each other as polar opposites. There is nothing especially discomfiting in knowing that a counterpart will behave in every situation exactly as you would not. Such behavior has the virtue of predictability. It is much more troubling when a counterpart *seems* completely unlike you, an absolute other, while at the same time seeming to share some of your most important characteristics. That was the case with Americans and Indians. Foreign to each other, the two peoples nevertheless had a common history of having lived under British colonialism and having liberated themselves from it. Americans spoke English, as did most educated Indians. Both peoples believed in democracy, and both inherited political and legal institutions from the British. Both countries were socially heterogeneous, and both have struggled to resolve internal tensions caused by ethnic, racial, and religious differences. Americans and Indians were incomplete others, or even selves seen in a distorting mirror. To confuse the issue further, American and Indian images of each other were not static over time. While the core values constituting both cultures remained in place, changing historical circumstances destabilized perceptions of the self. Since the representation of others is conditioned by perceptions of the self, others changed as selves required them to, in order for selves to maintain their own sense of balance.

Selves also recognize that others contain part of them, undesirable as that part may seem. There exists an ongoing struggle between rejection of one's worst qualities and a desire for reconciliation with them, an understandable longing for wholeness. Relations between selves and others are thus fraught with ambiguity, as selves are torn between loathing self-made others and recognizing elements of their own identity in them. The identity fragments projected onto others are still too much *us* to be jettisoned forever. This means that relations between selves and others, between different cultures, or peoples, or nations, will not always be bad. When there were points of commonality, as there were between Americans and Indians, there were opportunities for harmony and accord. During the Nehru period, Americans and Indians were comrades at odds.

This emphasis on the duality of identity requires us to write diplomatic history from both sides of the relationship. The time span of this book, which corresponds to the period of Nehru's prime and foreign ministries in India, deliberately signals my interest in India's foreign policy. Until recently, U.S. diplomatic historians have tended to write books from the American perspective exclusively, assuming that, for the twentieth century at least, American power was greater than that of any counterpart nation and thus that only U.S. policy was worthy of study. But power does not always translate into influence. As Robert McMahon has written, South Asia "was an environment that would repeatedly wreak havoc with even the most carefully formulated of American policy initiatives." Nehru often appealed successfully to public opinion in Asia and Africa, frustrating American attempts to warn nationalists on those continents against co-optation by world communism. The Pakistanis used American Cold War arguments to obtain U.S. military assistance, in spite of American fears, wholly justified, that Pakistan's real target of concern was India, not the Soviet Union. It is also important to write on all sides of the relationship because of the crucial similarities and differences in culture between Americans and South Asians. Interaction among Americans, Indians, and Pakistanis profoundly affected the evolution of relations between their nations. Ideas about space, economics, religion, race, class, gender, and modes of governance differed in ways that colored perceptions on all sides and conditioned the ways in which all sides made policy. When one takes culture seriously, one must look at all versions of it in a diplomatic relationship.

Speaking of Pakistan, a word of explanation is order. I emphasize in this study Indo-American relations, and that is plenty to cover. One cannot, however, write a history of this encounter without reference to Pakistan, and I have not attempted to do so. The histories of India and Pakistan are entangled so completely that disaggregating them is not just undesirable but impossible. Neither nation acted without considering the impact on the other. India felt deeply betrayed by the partition of the subcontinent, and suspected Pakistan of scheming constantly to subvert it, even to the point of introducing the Cold War into the region. Pakistanis were convinced that India had never reconciled itself to the division and hoped to surround the Islamic state with hostile neighbors, then pick it apart, province by province, beginning with Kashmir. Whenever the Americans took an initiative toward one of the two nations, they had to anticipate the inevitable and often baneful consequences for their relationship with the other. Still, I have written less on Pakistan than on India. Pakistan is not as accessible to me, for linguistic and especially personal reasons. And it was hard enough for a somewhat parochial Americanist to learn about India sufficiently to write the book I did; trying to learn more about Pakistan would have delayed this much-delayed project even longer.

The novelty of my culturalist approach demands that I be more explicit about methodological matters than is customary. My use of political culture, conjoined to the theory of selves and others, requires me to use unusual sources and to read the usual sources in unusual ways. Since I argue that policymakers shared with the public a symbolic universe, a context within which to assess foreigners, I rely on evidence drawn from the cultural record of the Indo-American encounter: plays and movies, novels, stories, songs, cartoons, games, photographs, and the writings of tourists or missionaries for Christianity and Hinduism. But I have not discarded the documentary evidence on which foreign policy specialists normally rely. I have consulted the State Department volumes *Foreign Relations of the United States*, read the speeches and memoirs of policymakers, squinted at microfilmed newspapers, visited archives and libraries in India and Great Britain, and done the rounds in the United States: the National Archives, the Library of Congress, the Truman, Eisenhower, and Kennedy presidential libraries, and several collections of relevant papers. To these primary sources I have added books and articles by historians, political scientists, anthropologists, sociologists, and psychologists.

I must add that American primary sources are more abundant and more accessible than Indian ones, at least to an American researcher. During my time in Delhi, there were few post-Independence records open at the Indian National Archives. The availability of private papers at the Jawaharlal Nehru Memorial Museum and Library is sporadic, in part because many collections that have been accessioned have not yet been organized. (Nehru's papers are slowly being opened to scholars.) Books by Indians, especially ordinary Indians, about the United States are relatively rare. Before 1965, few Indians were permitted to immigrate to the United States; casual travel to the United States was limited by the expense of the trip and possibly the Indian perception that white Americans would abuse them. As a result, my discussions of Indian views of Americans are not as finely wrought as I would like, and I am forced to rely heavily on second-hand versions of Indian attitudes—of the sort one finds in American or British memoranda of conversations, for example. I have done what I could to corroborate second-hand Western accounts of Indian attitudes with assessments by Indians and some (usually Western) anthropological data.

I anticipate criticism of two main varieties. From some of my colleagues in the Society for Historians of American Foreign Relations, I expect to hear that the cultural analysis lacks rigor, treating too much the context of diplomacy and not enough the cause-and-effect relationship between foreign policy decisions and historical events. Culture is contingent, a variable dependent on the operation of other, more salient matters, especially strategy and economics. Culture is also formless, which makes its influence impossible to either verify or disprove. I would respond that cause and effect, while critically important, is perhaps not so easy to discern as my colleagues would claim. I would say also that I have tried, often at some length, to show a correspondence between culturally conditioned ways in which selves made others and specific events in the Indo-American relationship, which I reconstruct using evidence of the type most diplomatic historians regard as sound. And I would argue that culture is finally embedded in history. My research has impressed me with the depth of the roots of the Indo-American relationship. What happened between the United States and India after 1947 had origins not in the use of the atomic bomb, the Iron Curtain and Zhdanov speeches, or even the partition of the subcontinent, but in the symbols and myths Americans and Indians created about each other many decades before the Cold War, and in events that occurred as far back as the early nineteenth century.

Others, who are likely to sympathize with my efforts to apply a cultural analysis to foreign relations history, might nevertheless take issue with the amount of generalization I employ here. Nations and cultures are not coterminous, particularly when the nations in question are made up of as many cultures as are India and the United States. To assume that one can write of an American or an Indian (or even Hindu) culture is to reduce the culture concept to meaninglessness or to engage in gross stereotyping of the sort I claim to deplore. I am "essentializing" others—that is, reducing their complex cultures to a small handful of elements that can be grasped, and condemned, by Westerners.

There was a time when "lumping," as John Lewis Gaddis has called it, was admired as an antidote to "splitting" the foreign relations field into numerous detailed monographs. At least it was tolerated as innocent. I would suggest that generalization need not be essentializing if it is carefully undertaken, and would point out that I generalize as ruthlessly about the United States as I do about India. It is of course true that in societies as diverse as those in the United States and India, it is unlikely that a single set of values, beliefs, and attitudes can be made to stand for everyone's. But I would nevertheless contend that Americans on one side and Indians on the other shared a culture that gave them a common identity, if not a full-fledged national character. My political culture model suggests that policymaking elites in the United States and India were most influential in shaping national political identity. In the United States between 1947 and 1964, the political culture was formed by well-off, white, Protestant men. In India, the issue was more complicated. While those in power worked hard to include in government religious minorities (especially Muslims), women, and members of the lowest caste, by and large the nation was dominated by Western-educated Hindu men. And yet, as I have argued, these powerful men were strongly affected by images of others held by their constituents.[18]

To both camps of potential critics I say: read and consider. Whatever criticism might be made of the culturalist approach to diplomatic history, it is unlikely to include the charge that the method lacks ambition. As I write I have in mind Bruce Kuklick's admonition: "Theories that extrapolate explanations from tiny amounts of evidence are not powerful; they are empty." I hope I have marshaled enough evidence to prove my case here. But I cannot quite let it go at that, so I counter with some advice of my own, though it is purloined from William Appleman Williams: play the course yourself. Research a nation's ideas about space (try Russia or China), then test the hypothesis that these ideas predict strategic conceptions. Wonder about economics as a cultural system, not just an exchange of goods and services detached from the perceptions of those doing the exchanging, and wonder whether terms like "market," "protectionism," and "debt" mean different things to different people. (They do.) Does a nation's system of governance affect its prevailing ideology? If so, and if ideology in turn influences foreign policy, diplomatic historians must take it into account. Follow John Dower and those who have linked race and international relations, for race has had a powerful political valence in the twentieth century, and ideas about race have shaped the identities of foreign policymakers. Follow Emily Rosenberg and others who have discovered the gendered elements of diplomacy. Did Americans, for example, underestimate their male Vietnamese enemies in the 1960s because they were smaller and less hirsute than Westerners, and because they sometimes held hands when they walked down the street? To what extent did religious difference inform U.S. policy toward Catholic countries in the nineteenth century? Look carefully at references diplomats make to status, pride, or prestige. These are indicators of class, caste, and status, and it would be surprising if they failed to condition the attitudes a nation's representatives held toward others. Above all, write foreign relations history from the bottom up and from both sides now. Clifford Geertz is right: there is no such thing as human nature independent of culture. Last I checked, diplomacy was a human activity. It is time for its history to acknowledge that.[19]

A. J. R.

Introduction
Americans and Indians, Selves and Others

> I'm in love with the country. I find the heat and smells and oils
> and spices, and puffs of temple incense, and sweat and dark-
> ness, and dirt and lust and cruelty, and above all, things won-
> derful and fascinating and innumerable.
> —Rudyard Kipling

> That was what we were taught—*the lower classes smell*. And here,
> obviously, you are at an impassable barrier. For no feeling of
> like or dislike is quite so fundamental as a *physical* feeling.
> —George Orwell, *The Road to Wigin Pier*

N o single book about India written for adult Americans had more
influence than Katherine Mayo's *Mother India*. Statistics tell part of
the story: by the mid-1950s the book had gone through twenty-
seven American editions and sold well over a quarter of a million copies
in the United States alone. When Harold Isaacs asked 181 prominent
Americans their impressions of India in 1954 and 1955, forty-six of them
mentioned Mayo's book as a source of their views, and many more offered
opinions about the country that could hardly have come from another
source. Only the collected stories of Rudyard Kipling were cited by
Isaacs's subjects more often than *Mother India*.[1]

In 1927, when *Mother India* was published, Katherine Mayo was a reasonably well known muckraker who had made her reputation with books
exposing corruption among the New York state police, investigating alleged YMCA mismanagement of the army canteen in France during the
World War (*That Damn Y*), and criticizing the U.S. administration of the

Philippines for its leniency. She and her companion, M. Moyca Newell, traveled to India by way of England, arriving in Bombay in December 1925, and touring the country for four months. Everywhere she went she was escorted by British officials. She dined with them at the Bombay Yacht Club; she watched a session of the Indian Assembly from the private box of the commander in chief. She bombarded her hosts with requests for information: what were the chief causes of mortality among Indians? What was the average age of women at marriage? How frequent was animal sacrifice? Understanding fully that Mayo was compiling a "brief . . . against India," one, that is, that would endorse the continuation of British rule, the officials provided her with the best intelligence they could muster. By the time Mayo and Newell left for home, they had watched Hindus pray in their temples, witnessed death rituals at Benares, seen goats slaughtered at the Kali *ghat* in Calcutta, visited hospitals and huts, and studied reservoirs—nearly all in the company of the Europeans responsible for governing the peculiar and unruly land.[2]

Mother India was a scathing indictment of Hinduism. Mayo charged the religion, first of all, with the abuse of girls and women. Though Mayo's figures were incredible in their magnitude and their extraordinary precision, it was certainly true that there were child brides in India, that baby girls were deprived of food and sometimes killed outright, that women often perished during childbirth, and that new widows committed suicide—*sati*—by throwing themselves on their husbands' funeral pyres. Mayo recounted all of this, and much more, and blamed it all on Hinduism. Hindu men were somewhat better off than women, but the exactions of the caste system, combined with the males' natural cowardice and sexual depravity, left them sorry and contemptible creatures. Moreover, India was filthy. Its people were disease ridden. Its animals, even the supposedly "sacred cows," were horribly mistreated. The high-caste Brahmins were deceitful, arrogant, and cruel. There could be no blinking in the face of harsh reality; "spades are spades," as Mayo titled one of her chapters. It was not, as many Indians claimed, the British administration that was at fault, but the character of Hindus: "Inertia, helplessness, lack of initiative and originality, lack of life-vigor itself—all are traits that truly characterize the India not only of today, but of long-past history." Given the debasement of the Hindu people, independence for India was a fanatic's dream.[3]

There was no doubt that the book was tendentious. Mayo was an Anglophile convinced that Western liberal supporters of the nationalist leader Mohandas Gandhi had misplaced their sympathies, and she fabricated evidence in order to prove India's lack of fitness for self-rule. But it is unlikely that disclosure of Mayo's dishonesty would have made any difference to those thousands who embraced her conclusions. Not only did the book sell rapidly in the United States: it was, according to two of Mayo's correspondents, "the most discussed book of the last ten years" in London, and "the topic of conversation at every dinner party" in Simla, the hill station capital of the raj during the hottest summer weather. A man named Edgar Allen Woolf wrote a play based on *Mother India*—it starred Madame Alla Nazimova as a twelve-year old Indian mother of two—and Mayo was inspired to write three more books about India over the next eight years.[4]

The book had its critics, some British and American, most of them Indian. Gandhi, who shared a good deal of Mayo's disgust with the Indian sewer system, nevertheless titled his review of *Mother India* "The Drain Inspector's Report," and attacked the book as one-sided. Dhan Gopal Mukerji accused Americans of reading *Mother India* for its "sex and Indian pornography." "Excuse me," an Indian journalist wrote Mayo, "you have written a low thing for a low purpose. . . . You have greatly injured the feelings of Indians." Another Indian correspondent sarcastically thanked Mayo for her "most Christian intentions" but urged that they "be directed to your own America, where even a blind man can point out things to make a cannibal shudder." There issued forth a torrent of books refuting *Mother India*'s claims. Most of them played on Mayo's title. Mukerji wrote *A Son of India Answers*; others included *Sister India, Father India,* and *Uncle Sham: Being the Strange Tale of a Civilization Run Amok*, in which author K. L. Gauba claimed to do to the United States what Mayo had done to India.[5]

Years later, long after the controversy sparked by *Mother India* had calmed down, Harold Isaacs's subjects recalled Mayo's indictment of Hinduism, not the remonstrations of her critics. Mayo's description of India took hold among Hollywood filmmakers—increasingly referred to as "movie moguls" by the 1940s—who told Isaacs's associate Dorothy Jones that *Mother India* influenced them more than any other single source about India. Small wonder, then, that the films they produced exploited stereotypes first popularized by Mayo. Journalistic treatments of India focused on the country's extremes of wealth and poverty, the cruelties of caste, natural disasters, or a variety of bizarre practices from consorting with cobras to relaxing on beds of nails.[6]

Katherine Mayo's India was a place of destructive superstition and sexual perversity. In that way it became a repository of Americans' projected fears about their own society. During the 1920s, many Americans felt that their version of Christianity was under attack, either from the freewheeling secularism of the period or from other, heretical religions. One of the most successful of these so-called heresies was Hinduism. Initiated by the appearance of the charismatic Swami Vivekananda at the 1893 Chicago

World's Columbian Exposition, and the Swami's subsequent establishment of several American centers for the instruction of yoga, a "Hindu craze" swept the country, involving particularly well-off, white women in cities. This was connected in turn to an American fear of sexual license, which Mayo also projected onto India. Very young Indian women, Mayo claimed, were forced to have repeated sexual intercourse with men. Appendix 1 of *Mother India* was a grisly list of injuries suffered by girls who came to a hospital for treatment: "Aged 9. So completely ravished as to be almost beyond surgical repair. Her husband had two other living wives and spoke very fine English." Mayo's readers were grateful for these revelations. "I, myself, feel indebted to you," wrote L. Louise Haas, "for so courageously dragging this adder of sensuality from its dark fetid nest of satiation."[7]

Troubled by fears that apostasy and sexual promiscuity were weakening their own society, Americans welcomed the projection of their maladies onto a far-off place. It was reassuring to pretend that these problems belonged to someone else, someone seemingly "less civilized" than they. Projection seemed to promise that the problems could be solved if others, not themselves, corrected their behavior. Needless to say, this made problem solving a good deal less painful. It is also likely that Americans, revolted as they might have been by Mayo's description of India, nevertheless found the alleged libertinism of Hindus fascinating, even titillating. Indian behavior, as Mayo reported it, seemed to contrast so sharply with the kind of discipline that was expected of Americans that it generated in the United States some of the excitement of the forbidden. In spite of themselves, Americans felt drawn to India.

Mother India was not the only literary source of American impressions of India, and not the only one that cast stereotypes or projected Americans' peccadilloes onto Indian Others. Harold Isaacs's subjects referred more often to Kipling than to Mayo, remembering, presumably, the novel *Kim*, the stories in *The Jungle Book* and *Plain Tales from the Hills*, and the poem "Fuzzy-Wuzzy," with its classic line: "Yore a poor benighted heathen but a first class fighting man." American perceptions were influenced as well by other British authors on India, among them E. M. Forster, George Orwell, John Masters, and most notably Helen Bannerman, whose children's book *Little Black Sambo* had a profound effect on American racial attitudes toward Indians and African Americans. American writers who treated India included Louis Bromfield, whose popular novel *The Rains Came* (1937) was turned into a popular movie, and the journalist Louis Fischer, who published a breathless biography of Mohandas Gandhi in 1951.

It might have been embarrassing for sophisticated men and women to have mentioned it, or perhaps they forgot, but it is likely that the Americans in Isaacs's sample also learned about India from sources less exalted than literary ones. There was, for instance, the magazine that Kirin Narayan has called "that venerable institution of pop-anthropology": the *National Geographic*, source of schoolboy fantasies. Narayan cites a 1913 article by a "Reverend Zumbro," in which fifty-one of fifty-six pages are devoted to pictures of men lying on beds of nails, hanging upside down over fires, sporting horribly long fingernails, and so forth. How many influential Americans saw Hollywood's adventure films about India, those—like *The Black Watch* (1929), *The Lives of a Bengal Lancer* (1936), and *Gunga Din* (1939)—that depicted Muslims as tough but treacherous, Hindus as craven but treacherous, and the British as brave and well meaning and determined to bring order to a savage land? Did future U.S. policymakers play the Milton Bradley Company's "Game of India" while growing up? Based on the Indian game *pachisi*, a 1930s version of the "Game of India" had on its cover a picture of two camels, in vaguely Indian rig, posed in front of an Egyptian pyramid. The game board featured four triangular sections, which loosely refer to India's four major religions. Buddhism is represented by a large Buddha figure with his hand Napoleonically inserted in his robe and with someone (seemingly a confused Muslim) *salaaming* before him. Islam is a camel, a crescent moon, and a Mughal-style door; a Sikh man wears a turban. The fourth triangle probably means to symbolize Hinduism; its chief referent is an elephant.[8]

In their own ways, with varying degrees of intensity, all of these sources contributed to the process by which American selves fashioned Indian Others. The terminology of "self" and "Other," and indeed the nature of the images produced by Western literature, films, and objects of popular culture, suggest initially that Americans believed the worst of Indians and saddled them with relentlessly negative stereotypes. As Sander Gilman has put it, the construction of Others, the assignment of stereotypes to those who seem foreign, exotic, unfamiliar or simply odd, is the recourse of selves who feel anxious about their "inability to control the world." When the self's "sense of order and control undergoes stress, when doubt is cast on the self's ability to control the internalized world it has created for itself, an anxiety appears. . . . We project that anxiety onto the Other, externalizing our loss of control. The Other is thus stereotyped, labeled with a set of signs paralleling (or mirroring) our loss of control." As a result, the "bad self" becomes the "bad Other." A sense of self-control can be regained if the bad Other is controlled—or so hoped religiously and sexually anxious Americans in the 1920s and 1930s.

Like the definition of selves, writes Gilman, the definition of Others incorporates the three "basic categories" of "illness, sexuality, and race." Others are assigned the most malign or threatening features of these categories. Sickness embodies the loss of control; disease itself, Gilman points out, is regarded as a " 'thing' lying outside the self that enters to corrupt it." Nor is it just the sickness of the body that selves fear. Mental illness, associated particularly with the "loss of language," represents a loss of control that is at least as threatening as that caused by physical illness. Sexuality by definition seems beyond the grasp of the self: "For a secure definition of self, sexuality and the loss of control associated with it must be projected onto the Other." Finally, racial difference becomes a way of distinguishing Others from selves, and, in ways that are metaphoric, those who are racially distinct from the self become a repository for impulses that are "dark," as in hidden or evil. For white Westerners, dark skin represents a darkness within, projected from a guilty self onto those bearing physical manifestations of darkness, and often linked to pathology and hypersexuality—a point to which a later chapter is dedicated.[9]

The process of constructing Others on the basis of illness, sexuality, and race had serious implications for American perceptions of Indians. Americans and most Westerners represented India as a disease-ridden place inhabited by sexually perverse, dark-skinned people. Indians were the opposites of us. Go to Persia, wrote Hegel, and the European "will find himself still somewhat at home," among those with "European dispositions, human virtues and human passions"; but "as soon as he crosses the Indus . . . he encounters the most repellent characteristics, pervading every single feature of society." More recently, as Lloyd and Susanne Hoeber Rudolph have observed, "India seen as a mirror image of the West appears otherworldly, fatalistic, unequalitarian and corporate. It is as though we would be less ourselves, less this-worldly, masterful, egalitarian, and individualistic if they were less what they are." We would in fact be more ourselves, but a good deal less stable for the tensions in our identities. And let us remember that the reason for projection, for creating Others in the image of the failed self, is to regain control of the self, and that the way to achieve this is to dominate the Other. This was the mission of Orientalism, as Edward Said has described it. It lay behind British imperialism in India, and when the United States inherited from the British the role as defender of the West following World War II, it inherited as well the strategic and psychological investments of a great power.[10]

Language was one of the ways in which Westerners sought to control India. In an effort to discipline their multilingual colony, the British made English its official language and thus a prerequisite for advancement in the civil service. Millions of Indians learned English, though rarely to the satisfaction of their British rulers or American visitors. Westerners were scornful of what they called "babu English"—a babu being an Indian civil servant or factotum who (the British implied) was pompous and rather laughable. Westerners made fun of Indian-English malaprops, the singsong inflections of Indian speech, and other aesthetic gaffes by Indians who used the language. At the same time, Western users of English selectively borrowed terms from Indian languages, especially Sanskrit. These terms were generally of two types: those denoting wealth or effeteness, and those suggesting danger. In the first category were "Brahmin," usually preceded by "Boston" and indicating old money; "mogul" (the moguls, or Mughals, ruled India from 1526 to 1857—one of their kings, Shah Jehan, built the Taj Mahal); and "nabob," from the Hindi word "nawab," meaning a deputy or governor. In the category suggesting danger were the words "thug," "goon," "juggernaut," and "monsoon."[11]

Indian words were sources of amusement and objects of ridicule for Westerners. "I shall arrive next January," Mark Twain wrote Kipling in India in August 1895, "and you must be ready. I shall come riding my ayah [a nurscmaid] with his tusks adorned with silver bells and ribbons and escorted by a troop of native howdahs [boxy chairs carried by elephants] richly clad and mounted upon a herd of wild bungalows; and you shall be on hand with few bottles of ghee [clarified butter], for I shall be thirsty." In 1952, Harry S. Truman received a letter from a Narayanhity Durbar of Kathmandu. The president sent the letter to his secretary of state, Dean Acheson, with the attached note: "I think he has a couple more initials after his name, which I think makes him the king." The *New York Times* chief foreign correspondent C. L. Sulzberger recorded with amusement the names of four South Asian tribal leaders—the Wali of Swat, the Wong of Bong, the Faqir of Ipi, and Nono of Spiti—while the authors of Donald Duck comics, not content with actual funny names, made up their own: the Rajah of Footsore, and the Maharajahs of Backdore, Swingingdore, and Howduyustan.[12]

If it were only that Westerners believed the worst of Indians and found them dangerous, perverse, disgusting, and ridiculous, we would expect relationships between Americans and Indians, and between the United States and India, to have been unrelievedly awful. But it was not this way. There were times when Americans admired Indians and got along well with them, and at times the feeling was mutual. United States–India relations during the Nehru period were not always bad, as one might expect if the two peoples simply did not like or understand each other. In the end, the relationship between peoples and nations was an ambivalent one, buffeted by deep cultural differences and yet sustained by some common attitudes and interests. "We can move from fearing to glorifying the Other," Sander Gilman has written. "We can move from loving to hating. The most negative stereotype always has an overtly positive counterweight. As an image is shifted, all stereotypes shift. Thus stereotypes are inherently protean rather than rigid." To this critical point we will return at the end of the chapter.[13]

American Images of India before 1947

American images of India changed over time, but a number of stereotypes remained relatively constant, from the arrival in India of the first American clipper ships in the late eighteenth century to the birth of independent India and Pakistan in 1947. At the foundation of all other American perceptions was the view that India was a land of mystery, exotic and inscrutable. A veil seemed to hang over the country, preventing observers from seeing its features clearly. Perhaps all Asia was inscrutable to Westerners. Even those who understood East Asia, however, confessed themselves baffled by India. "It seemed to me," wrote the Japan expert Edwin O. Reischauer, "that almost to the extent I understood East Asia, I was incapable of understanding India." Tear away the veil and one glimpsed all manner of wondrous and horrible things: a land of the fabulous and the occult, filled with "amazons, monsters and devils," maharajahs and maharanis, snake charmers, rope trick artists, fortune tellers, holy men on beds of nails, yogis with amazing powers, terrifying idols—a *National Geographic* India. The earliest Western accounts of India described one tribe "with heels in front and toes turned backward, who have no mouths and live on the smell of roast beef and the odors of flowers and fruits"; another group had "ears that hang down to their feet and are used as covers at night"; in a third, girls "conceive[d] at age five and [were] old at eight." During his first summer in the United States in 1934, Krishnalal Shridharani unexpectedly found himself the guest of honor at a tony Long Island dinner party, hosted by a woman he hardly knew. His position was clarified after the meal, when his hostess hushed the room and announced: "And now, our distinguished guest from India, that land of mystery, will perform the rope trick." "India, as every one knows," concluded Kipling, "is divided equally between jungle, tigers, cobras, cholera, and sepoys."[14]

Those who hoped to know India better—who were perhaps more curious than revolted—got on a ship and went there. Frequently, a Westerner's first impression of India was established even before he or she laid eyes on the place: India had a distinctive smell. British travelers described the last few days of a voyage to India: "[There was] a difference in the air or in the atmosphere or in the way the wind blew or possibly even the smell," one "difficult to pinpoint, partly the populace, partly the different vegetation, partly the very rapid fall of dusk and the cooling off which leads to the most lovely scent just after sundown." While many commented on the characteristic odors of India, few described them as "lovely." Sir Richard Francis Burton, the British adventurer and linguist, was accosted by "a close-faint, dead smell of drugs and spices" in Karachi, while a visitor to the nearby Sind plain encountered "an ammoniac odour which more or less grips you by the throat." Sydney Greenbie, an American who visited India in the late 1920s, recoiled at "the smell of fresh blood pouring down the streets of Delhi, the sweetish odor of human flesh decayed." Most of what Westerners smelled, or thought they smelled, was feces, animal and human. The old India hands called India "the land of shit and shankers." The French Abbé J. A. Dubois, whose *Hindu Manners, Customs and Ceremonies* was cited frequently by nineteenth-century visitors, was fascinated and repelled by the Indian relationship to feces. He described in detail the common sewer in the middle of South Indian village roads, "which receives all the rubbish and filth from the houses. This forms a permanent open drain, and gives off a pestilential smell, which none but a Hindu could endure for a moment." The abbé also noted the "wretched stench" of Indian huts, women who made pyramids of their feces in the hope of curing sterility, and a group of high-caste Brahmins who engaged "in a sort of competition as to who shall give vent to the loudest eructations"—that is, a farting contest.[15]

The odors of India registered profoundly with Westerners and contributed to the process of making Indians Others. "Odours," writes the novelist Patrick Süskind, "have a power of persuasion stronger than that of words, appearances, emotions or will. The persuasive power of an odour cannot be fended off, it enters into us like breath into our lungs, it fills us up, it imbues us totally." The prevalent smell of feces in India persuaded Westerners that Indians were essentially uncivilized. By the nineteenth century olfaction had dropped to the bottom of the hierarchy of the senses. People who smelled strong were considered primitive, and those who insisted on sniffing others became, in Alain Corbin's phrase, "objects of suspicion." (According to the Abbé Dubois, Indians had a keen sense of smell.) Many of the worst and most threatening smells came from India. Foul-smelling water, especially ponds in which hemp was cured, was alleged to be particularly dangerous. Europeans recalled the apocryphal story that Alexander the Great had been poisoned by the reeking breath of an Indian girl. And there was a "persistent anxiety aroused by excrement," because feces reminded the upwardly mobile Western bourgeoisie of its sordid past among the animals, where instinct and not rationality reigned. Indians, surrounded by stool, were made recipients of Westerners' projected anxieties—about who they had been, and who they might be still.[16]

Smells and other features of India were intensified because India was so crowded. Voyagers who stepped off the boat, usually in Bombay harbor, were enveloped instantly in the tumult of the Indian crowd. Bearers jockeyed for position, food vendors chanted advertisements for their wares, and beggars pressed close, respecting none of the personal boundaries of the body to which Westerners were accustomed. The crowd was a frightening thing to a Westerner. The French sociologist Gustave Le Bon, who published *The Crowd* in 1895, thought crowds caused disintegration of the family, a rise in crime, and an overload of the senses that led to nervous breakdowns. When Harold Isaacs asked his subjects to describe India, he elicited the following: "teeming masses, teeming cities, teeming population, teeming millions; swarming masses, great masses, vast, tremendous, enormous masses; . . . mobs of people, sea, hordes, millions of people; nobody knows how many there are on this human anthill." The population biologist Paul Ehrlich first experienced the horrors of overcrowding in Delhi:

> As we crawled [by taxi] through the city we entered a crowded slum area. The temperature was well over 100, and the air was a haze of dust and smoke. The streets seemed alive with people. People eating, people washing, people sleeping. People visiting, arguing and screaming. People thrusting their hands through the taxi window, begging. People defecating and urinating. People clinging to buses. People herding animals. People, people, people, people. As we moved through the mob, hand horn squawking, the dust, noise, heat, and cooking fires gave the scene a hellish aspect. Would we ever get to our hotel? All three of us were, frankly, frightened.[17]

India would not have seemed so overwhelming if it had not been so bright, hot, and wet. The Indian climate exhausted people, made them ill, and not infrequently killed them. The American Price Collier speculated that India seemed inscrutable mainly because people there "had to assume concealing expression[s]" to protect themselves from the powerful sunlight. "When you walk out . . . into the sun of India it hits you like a blow," reminisced a former British officer. "Every time you walk out of doors during the middle of the day you feel as if you've been hit by some-

thing. It's a mistake to think that people get used to heat—they don't."
Nor did they find the monsoon season much of a relief. During the "wet"
the rain coursed down, causing rivers and sewers to overflow, disrupting
transportation, encouraging mildew and mosquitoes, and turning well-
trod paths to mud. Then the storm would pass, the sun would come out—
and once more it would be oppressively hot.[18]

Some Western travelers sought relief from the odors, crowds, and even
the climate of the Indian city by venturing into the countryside, or what
they usually referred to as "the jungle." The word "jungle" comes from the
Sanskrit "jangala," meaning uninhabited or uncultivated ground, and in
its original sense it described the land outside the towns with reasonable
accuracy. To Westerners, however, the jungle was a wild and forbidding
place. It contained occasional villages, but for the most part the jungle
was filled with terrifying animals. These were not the ordinary beasts who
inhabited the forests of Europe and North America—they were monsters,
whose most frightening features were said to be accentuated by the tropical environment in which they lived. Indian animals were allegedly bigger
than others. Herodotus claimed knowledge of three-hundred-foot-long
eels in the Ganges, dogs big and tough enough to fight lions, and enormous snakes. Nineteenth- and twentieth-century visitors spotted monkeys,
tigers, elephants, buffalo, colorful birds, crocodiles (called "muggers"; an
early Thomas Cook travel guide encouraged the "sportsman" to shoot
them at will from the windows of the Darjeeling train), insects, and
snakes. These last two most disturbed Westerners in India. In the spring,
wrote Henry M. Field, "the insect world . . . comes forth. All the insects
that buzz and sting fill the summer air; and then the reptile world creeps
abroad. Out of millions of holes, where they have slept all winter long,
crawl cobras and other deadly serpents, and all slimy things." Many travelers reported chilling encounters with cobras, though their stories were often second hand.[19]

The presence of these animals gave credence to the Western perception that India was an exotic place. More than that, the characteristics of
Indian animals, whether genuine or exaggerated by Western imagina-
tions, came to stand for features of the Indian people. Observers could
not help comparing Indians to animals. The streets were beehives, the
bazaars "ant-hills." Sydney Greenbie thought that "the native of Madras
moves like a lithe thing of the jungle" and was appalled by the "beastlike-
ness" of Indian society. To Price Collier, the animal qualities of the Indian
people made them "no more fit for representative government than are
the inmates of a menagerie. . . . Were the British to leave India for three
months, India would resemble a circus tent in the dark, with the

menagerie let loose inside. . . . I can see no advantage," Collier concluded, "in opening the doors of the cages for many years to come." Particular animals represented particular aspects of the Indian personality. Indians were annoying, like insects, treacherous like snakes (recall Kipling's treatment of the cobra Nag in "Rikki Tikki Tavi"), violent and dangerous like crocodiles and tigers, mischievous children (like monkeys), and passive, willing to accept their fate as stoically as elephants, buffalo, and cows.[20]

What emerges from nineteenth- and early-twentieth-century Western accounts of India and Indians is the conviction that this was a disorderly place, these an unruly people. Modern Westerners believed in the need for self-discipline and self-control. Their lives were governed by rational processes and they moved in linear fashion, from point A to point B. They tried to control their bodies, with their clothes and hygienic and medical practices and sexual self-denial. And they tried to control others' bodies too, by isolating the ill, confining the insane, and punishing the criminal. By their science they classified things; in Michel Foucault's terminology, they structured "discourses"—work, language, life itself—into disciplines. What they could not abide in themselves they projected onto others, especially in the categories of illness (or death), sex, and race. Westerners found in Indians the very opposites of their rational self-images, exemplars of the undesirable and forbidden.[21]

Indians' alleged lack of self-control came through emphatically to Westerners who observed Indian violations of hygiene. Mary Douglas has written that "there is no such thing as absolute dirt: it exists in the eye of the beholder." Dirt is a problem in that it "offends against order"; uncleanness is "matter out of place . . . that which must not be included if a pattern is to be maintained." If order is the desideratum of the post-Enlightenment Westerner, the dirt and disorder of India was for the Westerner an object of loathing. And it was not just any dirt that one found in public in India, but the kind that Westerners ranked as most defiling: corporeal excreta, and their stains and smells. These included spit, snot, perspiration, blood, urine, and feces, most of which are encountered with some frequency on Indian streets.[22]

Indians, who bathe more often than Europeans and brush their teeth with fierce regularity, did not subscribe to Westerners' codes of public fastidiousness. "They hawk, spit, pick their noses, wipe them on a corner of their *dhoti*, or belch, all quite without embarrassment," observed an American traveler in the 1920s. A former British officer based in Dehra Doon was once asked by an Indian doctor to nominate him for membership in the elite, local club. The officer agreed, and invited the doctor to the club for dinner: "He was quite nice to everybody but halfway through he cleared his throat, turned round and spat on the floor." That did it; the doctor was blackballed. Indian thoroughfares were splotched with the dark red stains of expectorated betel nut juice, often mistaken by alarmed visitors for puddles of blood. Open water tanks and rivers were used for bathing, washing clothes and animals, and drinking. The best evidence that Indians were unable or unwilling to control their bodies was their propensity for public excretion. Westerners were disgusted by the presence of human excrement in public places, and the willingness of Indians to touch fecal matter (cow dung was patted into cakes, dried, and used as fuel or building material) or even consume it (some Hindus drank a potion made of milk, ghee, curds, dung, and cow urine) horrified them beyond measure.[23]

The public presence of feces and other unsanitary substances was not simply an affront to the Western sense of order or a violation of socially conditioned taboos. Public filth, along with high population density and a tropical climate, contributed significantly to the spread of serious diseases. Until at least Pasteur's work in the 1870s, neither Westerners nor Indians fully understood how diseases like smallpox, cholera, bubonic plague, typhus, leprosy, dengue fever, and malaria were transmitted, but they knew that all of them were present in India and were potentially deadly on an epidemic scale. Some sensed that there was a correlation between dirt and disease, among them U.S. consuls stationed in India during the late nineteenth century. Bombay, Calcutta, and Madras, the cities in which U.S. consulates were located, were hardship posts, and Americans who served in them faced illness constantly. The sources of disease, the consuls wrote, included "a cordon of cess pools" that surrounded even the healthiest neighborhoods of Calcutta, wet soil "teeming with malaria and luxuriant with rank grass," and rats that infested the stables adjacent to the consulate in Bombay. Benjamin F. Bonham, consul in Bombay during the late 1880s, moved his office "to get as far away from the native quarters as I could without being inconveniently remote from business." Consuls were forced to take long leaves of absence to recuperate from illness, or in some cases driven to resign out of fear for their safety. In 1904 the Bombay consul William Fee lost his ten-year-old daughter to bubonic plague.[24]

There was epidemiological wisdom in some of this thinking about the causes of disease. Plague was borne by fleas on rats, like those in the Bombay stable. Malaria is carried by mosquitoes, which congregate near pools of stagnant water. The cholera bacillus, identified in Europe in 1883 and endemic in parts of India, lives stubbornly in polluted water. Disease was prevalent and virulent in India, and poor sanitation contributed to it. Americans also came to believe that Indian diseases could be exported to the United States, even by apparently healthy individuals, and even on inanimate objects. In the late nineteenth century there were periodic scares that Indian hides, a leading export to the United States, were contaminated with plague. Katherine Mayo claimed that the United States might be infected by a horde of superficially healthy carriers of cholera. Mayo was concerned about the trickle of Indian immigrants to the United States during the first two decades of the twentieth century, and so were West Coast whites who encountered them. Like the Chinese and Japanese who came to America in much greater numbers, Indians were greeted with alarm and disgust. The San Francisco-based Asiatic Exclusion League reported in 1909 that "Indians were being admitted with exotic Oriental diseases." The turbans worn by Sikh men, who made up the great majority of Indian immigrants in California, became special targets of the exclusionists. "The outside is usually rather clean," warned the San Francisco *Call*, but "it would take a bacteriologist to write the story of the inside."[25]

Following Erving Goffman, the immigration historian Alan Kraut has pointed out that people with diseases, or those alleged to have them, are frequently stigmatized by others. "The abomination of the body," writes Kraut, is "the most essential form of stigma." Disease is insidious because it cannot always be detected; and because it can be contagious, those who are healthy are inclined to shun or isolate those suspected of infection. What is mysterious about the Other may be contained within his or her cells, out of sight of the most attentive observer. The wildest fantasies are possible about those of whom nothing is known, emigrants from faraway places over which the healthy have little knowledge or control.[26]

Faced as they often were with their own mortality, Americans in India were fascinated but generally disgusted by the Indian way of death. Muslims, like Christians, typically buried their dead, but the noisy funeral procession that preceded the burial was much remarked upon. Visitors commented with astonishment on the death rituals of Parsis. Originally from Persia and followers of the religious teacher Zoroaster, the Parsis migrated to India in the seventh and eighth centuries, settling for the most part in Bombay. Parsis believe that the burial of the dead defiles the earth and the burning of them defiles the air, so they expose their dead on the roofs of buildings called the Towers of Silence. The corpses are picked clean by vultures, and the bones are disposed of by specially appointed workers. No American traveler to Bombay missed the Towers of Silence. Some sympathized with Parsi practice. Most were horrified.[27]

Benares, a city on the Ganges River, is the most significant pilgrimage point for devout Hindus. People come each day to worship in its temples, to bathe in the river, and to die, for many believe that death in Benares will free them from the dolorous cycle of reincarnation. Should one die in Benares, one may be cremated (the usual Hindu practice for disposing of the dead) on one of the burning *ghats*, series of steps set into the riverbank. Western visitors took in the scene from a boat on the river, and the guides on these boats were quick to point out any incompletely burned corpses that drifted by. Observers always noted the foul look and stench of the water, the sight of people drinking from the river just steps away from a sewer outlet or a floating corpse, and the acrid smoke billowing up from the burning *ghats*. "We lay off the cremation ghat half and hour and saw nine corpses burned," wrote Mark Twain. "I should not wish to see any more of it, unless I might select the parties."[28]

Persistent Images: American Views of Independent India

The India of Kipling, Twain, and Mayo, the seemingly undisciplined subject of British rule, became independent on August 15, 1947. In a radio broadcast from New Delhi, the new prime minister, Jawaharlal Nehru, told his compatriots: "We are a free and sovereign people today and we have rid ourselves of the burden of the past." It was not to be that easy. The burden of religious division was most immediately felt, as the ghastly Hindu-Muslim-Sikh riots of the late summer took hundreds of thousands of lives and threatened to destroy both India and Pakistan. Nor would the threat of famine disappear with freedom. There was the psychological weight of past subjugation to a white nation; the insults and humiliations of colonialism could not be quickly jettisoned. And Western images of India remained in force with surprisingly few modifications. Indians and Pakistanis were free after 1947, but in the West they were still Others, and still encumbered by Westerners' continued anxieties about themselves.[29]

In the political culture of Washington during the early Cold War, India remained an exotic and bizarre place. One day in 1951 Chester Bowles, a former governor of Connecticut and a leading liberal Democrat, cornered President Harry Truman and asked if he might be appointed ambassador to India. Bowles recalled Truman's reaction: "The President was appalled at the thought of anyone wanting to go to India and he said, 'Well, I thought India was pretty jammed with poor people and cows wandering around the streets, witch doctors and people sitting on hot coals and bathing in the Ganges, and so on, but I did not realize that anyone thought it was important.' " Other officials had similar impressions of India. Truman's secretary of state after 1949, Dean Acheson, remarking on Indian efforts to bring to an end the Korean War in July 1950, confessed: "I have never been able to escape wholly from the childhood illusion that, if the world is round, the Indians must be standing on their heads—or, perhaps, vice versa." An officer at the U.S. embassy in New Delhi in the late 1940s found in South Asia "a culture strikingly different from ours. There was a British veneer, but the sights and sounds and smells, the people's dress and language, the horse-drawn tongas, the crowds in the native bazaars, the ancient monuments—all were alien to us." There was for Americans an Alice in Wonderland quality about the subcontinent, as University of Pennsylvania president Harold Stassen discovered in late 1950, when he thought he had boarded a plane for Delhi but found himself instead in Karachi. Vijayalakshmi Pandit, the Indian ambassador in Washington from 1949 until late 1951 and Nehru's sister, told the ambassador-at-large Philip Jessup that she had seen her brother "freeze up" whenever he spoke to Loy Henderson, her counterpart in New Delhi. Jessup thought the two nations should be closer, "but . . . there seemed to be some barrier."[30]

American and Indian policymakers had no doubt that there was something fundamentally different about the others, and that whatever it was interfered with the establishment of altogether friendly relations. In fact, U.S. officials saw culture as a powerful and intractable presence, a feature so essential to India at least that it was futile to think of circumventing it, much less dislodging it. U.S. policymakers had discovered culture during World War II, when anthropologists had explained the "fanaticism" of the Japanese with reference to Japan's national character. They had claimed that elements deep within the Japanese psyche made the Japanese who they were; to hope that the adversary might change was to take quixotic aim at the unyielding fact of culture. In a similar way, young officers who came to India after 1947 hoping to change the country for the better were disabused of their optimism by the older hands. In a more sober moment than the one that prompted his comment about Indians standing on their heads, Acheson told a pair of senators "that there was a fundamental difference in values that was responsible for the great gap between the thinking of our leaders and the thinking of Nehru." At bottom, though they may have shared the American dreams of freedom and prosperity, the Indians just were not like us.[31]

Nineteenth- and early-twentieth-century travelers had come to India by ship. After 1947 visitors, including officials, usually arrived by plane, and it was a somewhat different experience. It was harder to anticipate India when one could not see it coming, and the smell of India remarked upon by seagoing travelers was concealed from those who flew into Indian airports until the very last minute. The airport itself was a profound jolt. Westerners were disoriented by the crowding and pushing, the heat, and the slowness with which things seemed to move. The biggest shock for first-time visitors was the ride from the airport into the center of town, where most hotels and official residences were located. The Bombay ride was particularly difficult, "a disheartening introduction to the new Indian Republic," wrote Chester Bowles on arriving in 1951. "The strange new smells, the grim miles through one of the world's worst slums, the sidewalks covered with tens of thousands of sleeping people . . . most of them lying on the hard pavement, the ever-present poverty, misery and squalor, were impressions which we absorbed silently and apprehensively." Now visitors smelled India. The odors were an "assault . . . on the senses of those who are habituated to a more muted experience." In a poor Gujerati village in 1947, John Frederick Muehl noted the intensity of the "smells of spice and urine, of garlic and curry powder and dysentery stools, all the assorted smells of the Indian village, all the smells of life, decay, and death." Ten years later, the writer Arthur Koestler, on a self-described "pilgrimage" in India, caught a whiff of the Bombay sewers just as the door of his plane was opened: "As we descended the steps I had the sensation that a wet, smelly diaper was being wrapped around my head by some abominable joker." In September 1960, President Dwight Eisenhower mentioned to Nehru ("in a humorous vein") the "odors he [had] encountered between the airport and the city of Karachi" when he had visited South Asia the previous December.[32]

Independence did not change other Western impressions of India either—the place was still crowded, hot, and vaguely foreboding. Official documents echoed Katherine Mayo on the "faceless mass" that was the Indian population: "torpid, ill-fed, highly susceptible to disease and shackled by their own poverty and superstition," as the State Department described it in October 1949. Air conditioning came slowly to India, so "the heat and humidity were oppressive, nearly unbearable." Westerners learned to expect erratic or violent behavior in India during the hottest months of spring and summer. And rural India still seemed a jungle. In the late 1940s and 1950s, the Indian "jungle thriller" became a genre of Hollywood film. American theaters featured such movies as *Man-Eater of Kumaon* (1948); *Song of India* (1949), which concerned a prince and a princess who go hunting in a forbidden preserve; *The Jungle* (1952); and *Eyes of the Jungle* (1953). The animals remained in India too, and they persisted as metaphors for alleged aspects of the Indian personality. Like the passive poor, cows still wandered stupidly and miserably through the streets. "You know how ingenious and tireless the Indians can be when they set themselves to cause trouble," wrote a British official, evoking images of primates and children. Westerners also castigated Indians for coddling their beasts. *Life* magazine published, in October 1951, an article by the former ambassador to the USSR William C. Bullitt; the piece was titled "The Old Ills of Modern India." Writing in the context of a Congressional debate over whether to give surplus foodgrain to India, Bullitt claimed that protected or sacred cows, birds, insects, and monkeys were gorging themselves on cereals while millions of people starved. Monkeys alone, wrote Bullitt, ate over one million tons and destroyed more than two million tons of grain and other foods each year. "Tell me," Groucho Marx asked an Indian contestant on his television quiz show, "is [India] still all snakes, elephants, jungles, or sacred cows?"[33]

Americans who encountered India after 1947 continued to find it a disorderly place. Despite the demands of the postwar world Indians refused to be rational. "India is Asian and Indians, no matter how westernized, are Asians and often totally unpredictable to Westerners," advised a document prepared in the New Delhi embassy for the State Department. This unpredictability revealed itself in a variety of ways. It served, for one thing, to explain the otherwise inexplicable horrors that followed partition in 1947. The mass bloodletting, shocking and horrible as it was to Indians and Pakistanis, was to Americans simply insane. *Time* magazine's cover story on the bloodshed proclaimed that "the genius of India has ever been for myth, not rationality." The authors of the piece could not pinpoint the cause of the violence. When six million Jews had been killed by Hitler's Germany there had been a state to blame, but in this case "the appalling fact is that most of the killing was unorganized and spontaneous"—precisely what one would expect from an unpredictable people. The writers could only conclude that India's sin came "from the dark and universal fear which rests in the slime on the blind sea-bottom of biology."[34]

Nearly every American official who visited India reported an incident that illustrated the Indians' apparent inefficiency, irrationality, or simple peculiarity. George McGhee came to South Asia in December 1949, in his capacity as assistant secretary of state for Near Eastern and African Affairs. The morning before his meeting with the deputy prime minister, McGhee and his wife had breakfast at the embassy with Ambassador Loy Henderson and his wife. The McGhees had put in an order for eggs the previous night, but the servants brought no eggs, just "trimmings." The McGhees repeated the order, asked for coffee, and waited. "Bearers kept coming in to rearrange forks and perform other tasks." Some porridge arrived; the Americans sent it back because they had not ordered it. The eggs came just as McGhee and Henderson were leaving for their appointment. The coffee never did come. In April 1961 Ambassador John Kenneth Galbraith wrote to President Kennedy about a recent soccer match played between Indian and Indonesian teams in Djakarta. The Indonesians got a medicine man to the stadium early to consecrate the place for an Indonesian victory. Did it work? Galbraith asked the Indian friend who was telling him the story. "Of course not," the Indian replied. We had the better team and anyhow our astrologists had picked the day."[35]

Once more, the clearest evidence that India was disorderly was the dirtiness of the place. There was, as ever, dirt in the streets, dirt on the trains, dirt in the air, and dirt in the food and water. Much of the dirt, as ever, was feces. Americans who romanticized Indian villages were frequently shocked when they actually entered them. In Halvad, John Frederick Muehl wrote, "there are the usual disillusionments, the rubbish and the feces and the garbage underfoot." Americans in India found the filth hard to get used to. "Sanitation is [a] highly secondary matter in food handling and preparation," wrote one. "The Indian appears to me to be sensitive about his native dishes, and it is almost with maliciousness that he thrusts them upon a visitor." A Fulbright lecturer based in Madras was "disgusted at the sight of women going along the main thoroughfare with a handful of freshly expelled cow dung, and the intimate living with cow dung was equally revolting." So was the sight of lepers with "open red sores" standing next to "a cart filled with dates for sale, although covered with flies." Often of necessity, Americans in India talked obsessively about their intestines, for they found themselves losing control of their own excretory functions. Everyone laughed when, in December 1952, an Indian university official introduced the American ambassador as "Chester Bowels," but one suspects that Bowles at least winced with recognition. During the early 1950s, a lecture series in India was known to Americans as "the dysentery circuit." An officer at the embassy in New Delhi described a luncheon for John and Robert Kennedy in 1951 during which the brothers, "having the usual tummy trouble . . . kept pushing pieces of the curried chicken and the papaya underneath the lettuce so they wouldn't have to eat it."[36]

From dirt came disease. By 1947 the causes of India's most serious diseases had been identified, and there were prophylactics or cures for all of them. Americans in India took regular doses of chloroquin, a quinine extract, to ward off malaria, and antibiotics and sulfa drugs were effective against dysentery and typhus. There were vaccinations against smallpox, boiling one's drinking water prevented the transmission of cholera, and leprosy could not be contracted by touching a leper, despite a considerable mythology to the contrary. But Westerners still got sick in India, and they continued to associate the place with disease. When Bowles and his family went to India in 1951, they brought with them a formidable personal pharmacy, and provisions: "all kinds of canned goods and powdered milk and . . . clothes to last for five years." The Bowleses had been frightened by the State Department's designation of India as a maximum hardship post, and by the New Delhi embassy's "Post Report," a document given to all new officers in India. Bowles recalled that "every page dripped with gloom and discouragement." The report implied "that there was practically no decent food available," and it "talked ominously of strange new diseases, blistering heat, cobras, sneak thieves and red tape." The report, Bowles told his successor, George V. Allen, "seemed almost designed to prove to people that they could not live in India and stay well and happy." Bowles revised the report, but he also established a medical service in the chancery run by an American doctor.[37]

These common perceptions of India did not necessarily mean that all Americans found all Indians distasteful. There were Americans, Chester Bowles prominent among them, who liked the people and loved the country. The interviews done by Harold Isaacs indicate, however, that in general mid-twentieth century Americans had negative feelings about Indians. Of the 181 people surveyed by Isaacs, 28 percent had predominantly favorable views of Indians, 40 percent were predominantly unfavorable, and 24 percent were mixed. Americans and other Westerners assigned to Indians a number of negative personal characteristics. Indians were hypersensitive and tended to get emotional when aroused. Indians had a kind of "moral arrogance," sustained by the Hindus' smugness over their self-proclaimed spirituality. It was apparently impossible for Indians to stick to a particular set of principles; they were inconsistent at best, and often they were guilty of hypocrisy and prevarication. Nehru preached nonviolence, but when he thought India's interests were directly threatened he sent in the troops, as he did in Kashmir in 1947, in the princely state of Hyderabad in 1948, and in Portuguese Goa in late 1961. Indians were hypercritical, petulant, insincere, and sanctimonious. It was difficult to like them, and even harder to trust them.[38]

What was perhaps a vague feeling of distaste for the "Indian personality" came into sharper focus when Americans contemplated Jawaharlal Nehru. The prime minister was of course a man of international stature, so his views were frequently reported in American newspapers and magazines. Leading Americans went to India and met Nehru: Vice President Richard Nixon in 1953, Secretary of State John Foster Dulles the same year, President Eisenhower in 1959, Vice President Lyndon Johnson in

1961, and others. Three times during his ministry—the fall of 1949, December 1956, and November 1961—Nehru made official state visits to the United States. These visits in particular gave Americans the opportunity to examine the Indian leader closely, and while some came away admiring Nehru for his intelligence and independence of mind, many more concluded that he exemplified all that was wrong with Indian society.

Americans tagged Nehru with a variety of epithets that reflected their impressions of Indians in general. Nehru was vain; he wore a hat not because it was an emblem of nationalism but because he was bald. He was, according to a CIA sketch, "volatile and quick tempered." Critics charged that he was "naive," "evasive," "surly," and "fluffheaded." He was not an idealist but "just another practical politician keeping himself on top of his big dung heap," "an arrogant, anti-American, pro-Communist, high class, aristocratic, stiff-necked Hindu." William Bullitt characterized Nehru as "an exquisite and ineffectual dragonfly flashing his iridescent wings above a swamp."[39]

Nehru's 1949 visit was a disappointment. Let it be said that the Truman administration tried to be accommodating. The president even sent his private plane to London to pick Nehru up. (One wonders at the impression created by this gesture, for the plane was called *The Sacred Cow*.) But things just did not work. A welcoming dinner in the prime minister's honor proceeded for the most part in uneasy silence. Acheson tried to salvage the evening by inviting Nehru to his home after hours and urging him to talk about anything at all he wished. Nehru went on until 1:00 A.M., at which point, Acheson recorded in his memorandum of the conversation, "either due to the lateness of the hour or the complexity of the subject, I found myself becoming confused and suggested that we adjourn the discussion." Nehru "was one of the most difficult men with whom I have ever had to deal," Acheson wrote in his memoir.[40]

Some Americans thought that Nehru's visit had been a triumph. Adlai Stevenson called him "one of the tiny handful of men . . . who wore a halo in their own lifetimes," and when Nehru departed, wrote Elsie Morrow in the St. Louis *Post Dispatch*, he "[left] behind clouds of misty-eyed women." But few in Washington or New Delhi shed tears. "A visit from a man like Nehru inevitably attracted Pacifists, friends of Asia and well-meaning cranks, and this group of people were vocal and received perhaps undue publicity," Loy Henderson told his British counterpart in India, Sir Archibald Nye. "But the general impression left in America was that India was making no contribution to [solving] world problems, was unlikely to do so so long as the present policy persisted and that Nehru displayed little sense of practical realism." Nehru had been "both wooly and eva-

Truman listens, Nehru speaks. Nehru found the president vulgar; Truman later reported his impression that the prime minister "just didn't like white folks." White House Files, Courtesy Harry S. Truman Library.

sive." Elbert Mathews, who at the time of the visit was chief of the State Department's Division of South Asian Affairs, thought that "it was just almost impossible" for Nehru "to take an objective look at the United States. Every time he looked . . . all of these stereotypes that he had acquired or these perceptions that grew out of his own cultural background just came down like a veil between himself and the United States. And we never did break through; I just don't think there was any way we could have broken through." The platitudes that had been uttered by both sides during the visit could not disguise their mutual distaste.[41]

Nehru's return to the United States in December 1956 was somewhat more successful. The State Department and President Eisenhower still believed that the Indian prime minister was too sensitive, emotional, and volatile, and thus the very personification of his country. But Eisenhower got along better with Nehru than Truman had, and other officials, including Dulles (whom Nehru disliked), were largely kept away. The atmosphere was good in part because the United States and India were on the same side of two recent events: the Anglo-French-Israeli attack on the Suez Canal and the Soviet invasion of Hungary, both of which had occurred the previous October. The United States and India deplored the drive on Suez, and both nations condemned the crackdown in Hungary,

Friendly, but not too close: Eisenhower and Nehru, 1956. Courtesy Dwight D. Eisenhower Library.

though India had done so somewhat belatedly. Still, it was Eisenhower's personality that won Nehru over. The prime minister later said that the president was "thoroughly honest," that he had "a certain moral quality" and was "a fine person." The *Nation* celebrated all the good will with a story titled "The Twain Have Met," while a columnist for the *Times of India* praised Eisenhower for "his informality of manner which puts a stranger at ease." And yet, there remained signs of disagreement and misunderstanding. Prior to a speech in Chicago, Nehru was introduced as "the mystical man in the middle"; the Indians in the room winced noticeably. A *Times of India* cartoon showed Nehru pinning an "I Like Ike" button to his coat, where it joined buttons proclaiming "I Like Nasser," "I Like Mao," and "I Like Me." Eisenhower (and, oddly, a bull) look on, worried. Eisenhower's discussions with Nehru on substantive issues recalled Acheson's conversations of seven years earlier. The two men had obvious differences on Pakistan, Kashmir, and the relative strength of nationalism and communism. Evidently lost in the fog of Nehru's rhetoric, the president forgot key points the prime minister had made. Even temporary agreement on foreign policy and a happy personal relationship could not erase long-standing suspicions.[42]

That became evident during Nehru's third official visit to the United States, in November 1961. Nehru had looked forward to meeting President Kennedy, whom he associated—along with Chester Bowles, John Kenneth Galbraith, and Adlai Stevenson—with the liberal wing of the Democratic party. The preparation and protocol for the visit were excellent,

Kennedy and Nehru review the troops, Washington, 1961. Kennedy would call the meeting "the worst head-of-state visit I have had." Courtesy John F. Kennedy Library.

but Nehru and Kennedy were uncomfortable with each other. The issue of nuclear testing tormented their discussions. Nehru believed that all forms of testing were dangerous and immoral, while Kennedy argued that the American tests, held underground, could not be equated with the atmospheric blasts conducted by the Soviets, who in any case had resumed testing first. It did not help that a month after returning home, Nehru ordered Indian troops to seize Goa from the Portuguese, over Kennedy's strong objections. If Nehru, as Harold Isaacs wrote, had "come to personify India in its . . . relations with the rest of the world," then it was likely that the Kennedy administration viewed India with the same suspicious ambivalence with which it regarded Nehru.[43]

America in the Mind of India

All of this looked very different from the Indian side.

Indians, suspiciously ambivalent about the United States, constructed stereotypes of Americans that neatly complemented American stereotypes of them. While Americans regarded Indians as hypersensitive, arrogant, unrealistic, mired in superstition, indolent, irresponsible, and disorderly, Indians believed Americans were hypersensitive, arrogant, overly rational, materialistic, racist, vulgar, shallow, hasty, and violent. In an essay widely read in India, Swami Vivekananda summarized the Indian view of American men:

> Intoxicated by the heady wine of newly-acquired power, fearsome like wild animals who see no difference between good and evil, slaves to women, insane in their lust, drenched in alcohol from head to foot, without any norms of ritual conduct, unclean, materialistic, dependent on things material, grabbing other people's territory and wealth by hook or crook, without faith in life to come, the body their self, its appetites the only concern of their lives.

Things had changed very little by the mid-1950s, when an Indian psychologist asked a group of Indian students in the United States to describe Americans. Their list of adjectives included "materialistic, arrogant, smug, frivolous, condescending, intolerant, self-righteous, insular, morally loose, [and] lacking in family institutions."[44]

Like Americans, Indians constructed Others in their own images. To Others Indians imparted those characteristics they disdained or feared in themselves, features with which they had themselves been saddled (hypersensitivity and arrogance, and later violence), and especially those features that seemed to them too "Western" and thus anathema in the context of their own struggle against British colonialism. Partha Chatterjee has argued that Indian nationalists attempted to create for their movement an identity that distinguished Indians from Westerners, even while they adopted, at least implicitly, Western ideas about progress and modernization. Drawing on the discourse of Western imperialism, the nationalists made a distinction between the materialist West and India-the-spiritual. In the realm of the spirit, India "considered itself superior to the West and hence undominated and sovereign." Indian nationalist leaders routinely contrasted the secular West to religious India, even if they were not themselves religious men and women—as indeed, few were.[45]

Adopting the mantle of spiritual superiority suggested that Indian nationalists should divest themselves of the taint of materialism. Admitting that their pursuits were as rational and materialistic as any Westerner's would have undercut the nationalists' uniquely spiritual identity, and would have invited the humiliating conclusion that the oppressed had accepted life lessons taught by the oppressors. Indian nationalists purified their purposes by projecting any characteristics of rationality, the trappings of Western-style modernity, onto Westerners themselves. America in particular came to represent the excesses of the modern, the repository of features the nationalists could not admit they had themselves. America also represented the excitement of the modern, with its technology, its speed and efficiency, and its frightening and alluring license.

In the years before independence, even highly educated Indians had few sources of information about the United States. Diplomatic contacts between the United States and India were limited, and filtered at both ends by the British. Restrictive American immigration laws, especially after 1924, made it difficult for Indians to emigrate to the United States, and casual travel to the United States was uncommon. The historian M. S. Venkataramani recalled that he read unflattering descriptions of the United States in British newspapers and journals. Before 1947, no public or university library in India subscribed to the *New York Times*, and by 1946 only one Indian newspaper bureau received the *Nation* and the *New Republic*. Venkataramani remembered that *Time* and *Life* "were somewhat better known," making available to Indians such articles as *Time*'s partition cover story and William Bullitt's attack on Hinduism. In general, before 1947 "a young Indian graduating from a university would have had . . . very little opportunity to acquire any meaningful knowledge of American history and institutions."[46]

The key word in this passage is "meaningful," for there were other ways for Indians to learn about the United States, before and especially after 1947. Indian newspapers contained stories about America, though generally of a particular sort. "Racism, snobbery and material ambition are over-exposed," wrote the *New York Times* India correspondent Robert Trumbull. "If the average Indian's impression of the United States is formed by the newspapers, he must think of Americans as a race of hustling dollargrabbers, fantastically efficient during working hours but obsessed in leisure with comic books, night clubs, the cruder sports and vicarious sex." Probably more important sources of Indian impressions of the United States were American movies. The great Bengali filmmaker Satyajit Ray got his start watching American films: "Westerns, gangster films, horror films, musicals, comedies, dramas and all those other species which Hollywood served up with such expertise, came tumbling my way to be lapped up with ever-increasing appetite." In the relative chill of a Bombay theater—"every seat a cool retreat"—Indian audiences could see the latest offerings. In 1953 a self-described "British observer in India" complained to Chester Bowles that Indian students "take their whole picture of Western life from films. As the most startling, spectacular, voluptuous or brutal films tend to draw the largest audiences, they are the main influence." Kissing on-screen produced "yelling in a kind of orgiastic excitement"; from the film *Samson and Delilah* viewers gained the impression that Delilah was "ONE OF OUR RELIGIOUS HEROINES." The movie page of the *Times of India* on May 12, 1961, listed the following possibilities: *Bells Are Ringing, Abbott and Costello Meet Frankenstein, Legions of the Nile*, two Elvis Presley films, *The Scarface Mob, Samson and Delilah* (still running or re-released eight years later), and *Seven Ways from Sundown*, starring Audie Murphy as "the man who shook Texas like a pair of dice," evidently a reference to a crucial scene in the Indian epic *Mahabharata.*[47]

These sources, along with the testimony of increasing numbers of private and official Indian visitors to the United States after 1947, provided an abundance of images of America and its people. Like Americans who encountered India, Indians often remarked on the smells of Americans. Indians who are vegetarians, as many Hindus are, claim that they can smell meat in the body odor of carnivores. When one Hindu father learned that his son was planning to marry an American woman, he wrote to remind the young man that the odor of an Anglo-Saxon should provide reason enough to end the arrangement. There is some evidence that smell has greater significance to Indians than to modern Westerners. Indian primers on care of the body contain advice about the nose, including an injunction to "free" the nostrils each morning with drops of salted water or oil. Smell is an important theme in Salman Rushdie's novel *Midnight's Children*, in which the main character, the "cucumber-nosed" Saleem Sinai, has a highly developed sense of olfaction. In South Indian poetry and literature, smells act as "markers of identity," indicators of profound memories and experiences. Proust was inspired when he bit into a madeleine. Indians know who they are when they smell certain odors.[48]

Americans who went to India expected to see a steaming jungle. Indians had no such illusions about the United States, and indeed worried that they would freeze to death during the winter. But the United States was a different kind of jungle to an Indian visitor: it was an urban jungle, where the chief danger was anonymity. Indians know who they are in relation to others. At home, among a nuclear or extended family and able to identify fellow members of a *jati*, or subcaste, Indians are fully at ease, so much so that "they make Westerners look stiff, masked, and uncomfortable both in themselves and with others," according to the anthropologist Stephen Tyler. Remove Indians from their own secure networks and they are lost, until they can map out the new situation. What Westerners experience as crowded chaos on arriving in India provides Indians with precisely the sense of comfort they miss when they come to the United States. The Parsi P. E. Dustoor, who arrived in San Francisco in the late

1940s, found the street "deserted," with none of the "human swarms, on and off the pavement, one sees in Bombay or Calcutta." Cars sped past in both directions, but "the traffic was noiseless." Silent machines provided the only presence on the street; America was literally a jungle, an uninhabited place. A letter writer to the *Times of India* blamed cars, along with trains and airplanes, for the "nomadic state" of Americans. Because Americans moved so quickly they were not "rooted in the soil, and true culture can grow only with intimate association between nature and man."[49]

Unlike the jungle of India, the urban American jungle was not the preserve of wild animals. Indians nevertheless commented on what they considered to be the peculiarities of the American relationship with animals. Indians regarded the idea of keeping a house pet as bizarre, especially if the animal was a dog. In India most dogs are scavengers, usually dirty and dangerous, and until recently no respectable person would contemplate domesticating them. Alleged American promiscuity led some Goans to charge, in the 1960s, that visiting hippies were suckling and mating with the monkeys who lived in the local temples. Hindus were most appalled at the American appetite for beef. No amount of abuse meted out to Indian cows could be worse than their wholesale slaughter by Westerners. Several Indians ate meat by accident in the United States. R. L. Sharma got over it: "The thought of a Brahmin boy eating of the holy cow tore me apart. . . . But when I observed that many Americans were tall, healthy, and vigorous, a voice within me told me, 'To hell with the India of holy men and holy cows!' " Others could not suppress their revulsion. "To a high caste Hindu," wrote Krishnalal Shridharani, "an assortment of sliced meat is about as appealing as an array of sliced babies." The first time he saw "naked meats" in a cafeteria, Shridharani had to put a scented handkerchief over his nose to avoid becoming ill.[50]

Indian nationalists argued that the unique virtue of their nation resided in its spirituality, its moral sensibility, and significantly its restraint. Gandhi was perhaps an exaggerated version of the abstemious patriot, shunning as he did flavorful food and sex, but denial of the body was an important rite of passage for many nationalist leaders. Nehru spent many years in jail, where he refused special privileges and gifts from friends on the outside. This was not the way Americans behaved. The modernity embraced by Americans rejected spirituality; their faith in capitalism placed the accumulation of things above the quest for morality. Indians saw themselves as a people of self-control, Americans as a people of license. For one thing, Americans drank alcohol, often to excess. A story in the Bombay *Current* of December 5, 1951, told of the arrival in the city of a baseball team from the American Men's Club of Calcutta, which had come to Bombay for a game with some Americans there. The team was received at the airport by Bombay's mayor, S. K. Patil, and according to the story, the Americans had been drinking throughout the flight. Now they "serenaded" the mayor, whose city was under an edict of prohibition, with an off-color version of "How Dry I Am," as they held aloft an enormous whisky bottle and beer tankard. Mayor Patil stomped off in a fury, and an official from the local U.S. Information Service office destroyed incriminating photographs of the episode.[51]

Indians also claimed that Americans showed no sexual restraint. Whether in the United States or India, American men and women embraced in public without embarrassment. In 1943, just before her daughters left to go to college in the United States, Vijayalakshmi Pandit received a book of statistics on divorce, crime, and venereal disease in America, along with a warning not to let the young women go off unchaperoned. The American movies seen by Indians often reinforced the notion that Americans were promiscuous. Cynthia Bowles, the daughter of the ambassador, felt uncomfortable watching *Come Back Little Sheba* with an audience of Indians, especially the scene in which a boy tried to seduce a girl and "was not very firmly repulsed." George McGhee's wife Cecelia, ignoring a hint from Elise Henderson, wore to a formal dinner in New Delhi an evening gown that revealed her shoulders and got "a disapproving look" from Nehru. At university in England during the 1950s, Deepak Lal and his Indian friends "lusted after the seemingly loose young American women who came our way," though without success.[52]

American perceptions of India were shaped by the presence of dirt in India, especially feces. Because filth offended against the modern Westerner's need for order, its prevalence made India seem the most disorderly place imaginable. A brief explanation of the Hindu attitude toward bodily functions might be worthwhile. It is not just a perception—the turds are undeniably there. The Hindu idea of *dharma*, or right conduct, is suffused with the urgency to avoid pollution. Almost everything in the universe defiles to some extent, but there is a hierarchy of pollution that determines which substances are relatively more or less polluting than others. The strongest pollutants are dead things and the secretions or excreta of the body, including spit, snot, phlegm, urine, and feces. To contain these substances inside the body is most harmful. There is nothing edifying about public deposits of these excreta, and many Indians are disgusted by the presence of human feces on the street, but public cleanliness matters less than the avoidance of personal contamination. "In India we are keen on defecation," says Gita Mehta. "Unfortunately, our concern with purification does not extend from the body to the street." Cow dung, too, defiles things above it in the pollution hierarchy, including images of the gods. Even the least pure part of the cow, however, is relatively more pure than the most exalted human being. The *panchgavya*, that mixture of the five products of the cow, can remove the impurities of a Brahmin. It should also be noted that dried cow dung, used by the poor for fuel and building material, has little odor.[53]

Once more inverting the Western stereotype, Indians believed that Europeans and Americans were disgustingly dirty. Indians made a distinction between Western social hygiene, which they generally praised, and the personal cleanliness of Westerners, which they deplored. Swami Vivekananda found Westerners so embarrassed about excretion that they refused even to mention it, and women in particular "would rather die" than go off to the bathroom in the presence of men. Such delicacy, Vivekananda thought, was unhealthy. Indians of all classes bathed frequently, Americans less so, and Europeans still less. Westerners retained snot in their handkerchiefs. When Brahmins drink from a glass they avoid putting their lips to the rim, instead pouring straight into their mouths. To them saliva is polluting; as Gordon Allport has observed, while no one (except a Brahmin) would think twice about swallowing saliva with a beverage, one would not spit into a glass and drink it. Shoes that have been outside defile homes and temples and must be removed. Visitors to India learn that Indians prefer not to shake hands, fearing that a touch might spread illness or pollute them. "It is a strange and ironic paradox," noted Krishnalal Shridharani, "that many Westerners, after having been to India write about the unclean habits of the Indians, while homeward-bound Hindus speak of the careless hygiene of Europeans and Americans."[54]

Criticize an American, or simply mention to one that cleanliness was in the eye of the beholder, and one risked an explosion, for Americans were hypersensitive—or so Indians said. Americans reacted with vehemence when Indians denigrated their culture or criticized their foreign policy. Americans were also arrogant and self-righteous. Indians were aware that Westerners charged them with the same vices, but they had a hard time taking the accusation seriously, coming as it did from a people so manifestly convinced of their own rectitude. The Indians frequently complained to the British about their sanctimonious allies. Sir Girja Bajpai, the secretary-general at the Ministry of External Affairs, told a British official in 1948 that "the Americans, by their mixture of self- righteousness and arrogance, had made themselves thoroughly disliked in India." Indians resented Americans for their "superiority and condescension," reported J. D. Murray of the British Foreign Office, "and they find very irritating the assumption that what is good for the States is equally good for

India." Arrogance made the Americans stubborn and unwilling to listen to others. Following Dulles's visit to India in 1953, Nehru reportedly told associates, "the most we can expect out of his visit here is that he has got some idea into his rather closed head as to what we feel about various things."[55]

There was one more charge that Americans and Indians applied to each other with equal vigor, and that was the accusation that the others were inclined to violence. As we have seen, Americans associated Indians with dangerous wild animals, and more to the point regarded with horror the religious violence that occurred after partition. While Indians did not excuse the violent acts of their compatriots, they nevertheless responded, first, that America's independence had been bought with blood too, and, second, that violence in American society was an everyday affair. Certainly the impression Indians got from watching American movies was that the United States was a land of gangsters and cowboys, and that both groups were careless with firearms. Indian newspapers carried sensationalized accounts of actual events and actual accounts of sensational events, especially lynchings of blacks in the South. Soon after arriving in New York, Krishnalal Shridharani was "reminded of the kidnappers and gangsters America is famous for in India." That prompted a discussion of whether the United States was "infested with gangsters," which, Shridharani admitted, "gave me no comfort at all." The prevalence of violent crime in America, claimed Indians, could be explained by the rootlessness of the people and the resulting shallowness of their culture.[56]

Other stereotypes applied to Americans by Indians were the opposites of what Indians prized most in themselves. While Westerners believed that Indians lacked linearity, Indians contended that Americans were rational to the exclusion of emotion and matters of the heart, and most especially that they were materialistic. Let us concede that Americans had accomplished many things, Indians would say. The standard of living of Americans was high, their machines were efficient, they could make war and movies and paper cups with remarkable facility. What they lacked was warmth, sincerity, and fine feeling. Americans had lost their souls. The president of the All India Newspaper Editors Conference insisted that cubist art, among other things, proved that modernity had "produced a type of mind, devitalized in its outlook, insulated in its methodology, moved and motivated by legal rather than ethical values, material rather than moral values. The art of life, savouring the joy of life, eludes [the Americans'] grasp." By the 1950s Indian visitors were shopping eagerly in American stores, but they wondered whether all the convenience they provided would lead to "mental laziness and haziness" in shoppers and clerks alike.

Vijayalakshmi Pandit recounted the experience of buying a few sundries at an American department store. After waiting ten minutes for the bill, Pandit asked what was taking so long. The sales clerk apologized: the cash register was broken and she was having trouble adding up the prices.[57]

Indians nevertheless believed that Americans were obsessed with money and material things. The average educated Indian, wrote the journalist Kusum Nair in 1961, identified America with "brash materialism, fabulous luxury, softness; bikinis, night clubs, television sets, giant automobiles, machines, and gadgets; quantities of liquor and frozen and canned foods of every kind." Nehru also believed this. He came to the United States in 1949 "with the greatest misgivings, since all his life he had regarded Americans as imperialist materialists." At a dinner given for him in New York City, one of a group of prominent business leaders leaned over to Nehru and said, "Mr. Prime Minister, do you realize how much money is represented at this table? I just added it up, and you are eating dinner with at least 20 billion dollars." The remark appalled Nehru, confirming all of his suspicions about the crassness of American culture. Nehru reportedly told his cabinet "that he had come back from his American visit convinced that India had not a single friend in America and that she would be foolish to rely upon America for any help," and confided to his private secretary: "Americans think they can buy up countries and continents."[58]

What suffered most from the materialism in America was culture, in its old fashioned sense. American culture, if it existed at all, was shallow, vulgar, and excessive. Indians who wished to come to the United States for study should go without illusions, Nehru cautioned in July 1954: "I am all for broadening the outlook of the person. But mere breadth is not enough; there must be some depth also. As far as I can see, there is neither breadth nor depth about the average American. . . . The United States is hardly a place where one could go at present in search of the higher culture."[59]

There was so much that was cheap and tawdry in American life: the "vulgar radio advertising," Hollywood movies, comic books "and the other trash and worse than trash that they wallow in by way of reading"—even men's ties. Americans tended to "vulgarize everything, disregarding both the dignity of public life and the sanctity of private joys and griefs." With their "philistine's contempt for the finer things in life," the American had in India a reputation as "gum-chewing [and] loud-voiced . . . a mixture of Babbit[t] and Diamond Jim Brady, spewing into spittoons when he was not spewing dollars over all and sundry." Directly tied to their vulgarity was the Americans' alleged penchant for extravagance. The "satisfaction of appetites is their true God," declared Vivekananda. "They [are] given to excess in all their habits of consumption." These habits rankled with Indians, especially when they involved food. When India suffered from famine in 1946, the newspapers criticized Americans' wastefulness and the seeming reluctance of the U.S. government to share abundant foodgrain with those who needed it. Prakash C. Jain, who came to study journalism at the University of Minnesota in 1951, was taken aback by the splendor of an ordinary cafeteria, in which no less than fifteen dishes were made from potatoes.[60]

Jain was also surprised by the speed of life in the United States, the haste with which Americans did things. Even before he came to America he pictured a place of "streamlined limousines whizzing past at breakneck speed" and "cancans with blue-eyed blondes kicking heels over heads in frenzied gymnastics—an opulent society with abandon and excitement as its principal motto." Not all of Jain's stereotypes of America were confirmed, but this one was. American haste was both physical and mental. "Americans live too fast," asserted G. P. Hutheesing, Nehru's brother- in-law. "They do not have time to think. They feel that they must be on the move every moment and as a result never take time out for reflection and meditation." Nehru agreed, and said as much to Chester Bowles. Indians described Americans as "mercurial"; they changed their minds so often (said Vijayalakshmi Pandit) "that one never knew from one day to the next what [they] thought of a country."[61]

Others, Not Others: Comrades at Odds

If this was all there was to say about American and Indian views of each other, the conclusion would be obvious: the subjects of years of mutual misunderstanding and misrepresentation, Americans and Indians despised each other and could not get along. No one who believes that another's nation is a noxious, hot, crowded, disease-ridden jungle, full of people who take after their animals and are disorderly, arrogant, prickly, violent, irrational, and sanctimonious, can possibly appreciate the other. No one who holds that another's nation is a cold and alienating urban jungle, full of people who are immoral, rigid, hyperrational, violent, personally unclean, arrogant, vulgar, materialistic, and hasty, can have any respect for the other. And yet at times, Americans and Indians, the United States and India, did get along. While the abiding condition of the United States–India relationship was discord, there was "accommodation amid discord," in Gary Hess's phrase. The story that follows in these chapters is not just a chronicle of failure. Sometimes good intentions were enough to override cultural or personality conflicts; sometimes the interests of the two nations coincided; sometimes, as in the case of the Wheat Loan of 1951 or the border war with China in 1962, the Indians needed help so desperately that they swallowed their pride and accepted it from the vulgar materialists. Most of all, there were ways in which Americans and Indians were not so different, and there were ways in which their differences offered opportunities for the reintegration of American and Indian selves.[62]

On the American side, there were moments of admiration for what seemed to be the essence of India: the spirituality and reverence for tradition that twentieth-century Indians themselves would turn to the purposes of nation building. The first of these moments occurred in New England during the 1830s and 1840s, when the Transcendentalists Ralph Waldo Emerson and Henry David Thoreau became infatuated with Hinduism. They read the *Bhagavad Gita*. Emerson wrote a poem called "Brahma"; Thoreau's *Walden* extolled a Hindu-style of renunciation. A second moment came in the late nineteenth century, when Americans ambivalent about (or hostile to) modernity sought refuge in Asian religions, and Bostonians William Sturgis Bigelow, Percival Lowell, and George Cabot Lodge searched for "nirvana," though for the most part in Japan. The excited reception given Swami Vivekananda at the Chicago Exposition in 1893 testified to the attraction of India for the antimodernist as well. Most familiar to Americans living today was the passion of the 1960s counterculture for Indian clothes and music and pop versions of Indian religion.[63]

There were moments of appreciation for the United States in India as well. From the 1920s on, Indian nationalists' impressions of the United States wavered. Some were wary of American support for Great Britain and of America's own imperialist indulgences in Latin America and the Philippines. Others were inclined to accept at face value American rhetoric about the importance of self-determination. (Nehru felt both ways.) During World War II, many Indians thought that President Roosevelt was trying to prod the British toward granting independence. Key figures in the Roosevelt administration, including FDR himself, made clear their opposition to colonialism, and the president sent emissaries to India in the hope that they could negotiate some kind of arrangement between the two sides. The Americans were not successful, and the Indians' highest hopes were temporarily dashed.[64]

Still, a reservoir of good will remained, to be tapped in times of need or particularly friendly relations between individuals. There were, after all, similarities between Americans and Indians. Each was labeled arrogant, hypersensitive, and violent by the other, and each denied these charges.

From their vantage point, British officials observed that both countries seemed to have an "ineradicable addiction . . . to lecturing the rest of the world," and that "neither the Indians nor the Americans seem to accept criticism with any equanimity." At times Americans and Indians admitted to common foibles. Chester Bowles noticed that the apparent Indian tendency to be petulant, arrogant, and moralistic was very much like American behavior soon after the republic was founded. An Indian editor admitted that Indians were "aggressively frank" and "extremely sensitive"—just like the Americans, who were "extremely candid and extremely touchy." The problem, some claimed, was simply that the two peoples didn't know each other very well. There were no real barriers to understanding, cultural or otherwise, for people all over the world were more alike than different. The mystery Americans ascribed to India and Indians ascribed to the United States would vanish when Americans and Indians could visit each other's countries and come to understand each other as people.[65]

What finally kept the flame of accommodation flickering amid the murk of discord, however, was not the similarity between the two peoples but their most profound differences. Similarity is no guarantee of harmony; two peoples given to pontification, for instance, are unlikely to be friendly, and to perceive similarity in an Other is to fear that one's unique identity is at risk. As Paul Berman has rendered it: " 'Our resemblance threatens to obliterate everything that is special about me.' " To understand why things between the United States and India were not worse than they were, it is necessary to return to the process by which selves construct Others. Recall that selves project onto Others those features that cannot be reconciled with self-image, or which, in Freudian terms, are impermissible to the superego. American selves, operating largely within the categories of sexuality, race, and illness, projected onto Indian Others traits that seemed loathsome or illicit: Indians were, among other things, unsanitary, disorderly, promiscuous, and primitive. Indian selves projected onto American Others those traits that seemed to violate the values of traditionalism and spiritualism, family, and community: modernism, secularism, materialism, and footloose individualism. Superficially, both peoples felt better for having divested themselves of these qualities. And yet, the act of projection left selves incomplete. The constructed American self was constituted mostly of intellect, while the Indians personified pure instinct. It could not be. Ultimately, selves must reintegrate their identities, reconciling the stuff of intellect with the stuff of instinct.[66]

O. Mannoni has written, "Civilized man is painfully divided between the desire to 'correct' the 'errors' of the savages and the desire to identify himself with them in his search for some lost paradise (a desire which at once casts doubt upon the merit of the very civilization he is trying to transmit to them)." Americans were not about the business of imperialism in India, and they did not literally regard educated Indians as "savages." They did consider themselves far more civilized than Indians, further advanced along what they assumed to be a common path toward social development. They also felt, at some level, that India had something they needed in order to achieve personal fulfillment. India was bizarre and threatening to Westerners, but it was also beautiful and alluring, a paradise. The Transcendental movement was, in Perry Miller's words, "a protest of the human spirit against emotional starvation," and it hoped to find sustenance in the spiritual values of India. Those who revolted against modernism in the United States used India as a source of an alternate vision of society, one that seemed closer to the yearnings of the soul. Many believed that Hinduism brought to its adherents an inner peace. This appealed to some Americans during the war in Vietnam.[67]

For Indians, similarly, what made America a place to be reviled rhetorically also made it a place to be admired, albeit quietly and at some remove. Americans seemed so precise! Most of the time their institutions worked; one could buy postage stamps, cash a check, or make a long distance telephone call with a minimum of fuss. The trains and airplanes usually ran on time. Even working-class families had a degree of material comfort— enough food, a house, a car, and by the mid-1950s a television set. The frenetic mobility of Americans, criticized by Indians as the reason for American inconstancy and impatience, was also understood to coincide with Americans' ability to adapt to changed conditions. That was not at all a bad thing for Indians to learn. Nor was some measure of bumptiousness. Ironically, while some Americans admired Hinduism as a philosophy of pacifism, Hindu revisionists in the late nineteenth century sought to recast their religion as one that was every bit as militant as Christianity, and thus capable of standing up to the British in the struggle for independence.[68]

In *Midnight's Children*, Salman Rushdie tells of Indians visiting American warships in Bombay harbor following World War II. It was embarrassing for a young man to take a tour, writes Rushdie, because there were always hordes of very pregnant Indian women lingering on board, hoping to give birth and thus deliver their babies into automatic American citizenship. The story may well be apocryphal, or simply more magical than realistic, but it tells a truth: riven as they were by cultural differences and misunderstanding, Others as they were to each other, Americans and Indians might occasionally be connected, too, by the bonds of magnetic difference or grudging admiration.[69]

1

Strategy: Great Games Old and New and Ideas about Space

Eyeless, noseless, and lipless, asking a dole at the door.
Matun, the old blind beggar, he tells it o'er and o'er;
Fumbling and feeling the rifles, warming his hands at the
    flame;
Hearing our careless white men talk of the morrow's game;

Over and over the story, ending as he began:—
"There is no truce with Adam-zad, the Bear that looks like a
    man!"
                        —Rudyard Kipling, "The Truce of the Bear"

The last living thing that I attempted to shoot was a bear 37
years ago. Since then I have not [shot at anything] because I
have no desire to do so and the very idea is somewhat repugnant to me.
                        —Jawaharlal Nehru, 1954

The terrible war was over, the aggressor at last defeated. Exhausted after years of fighting and horrified by the bloodshed, the Western nations were tempted to turn away from the moral and strategic demands of the world system and resume their relative solipsism. But the
danger on the horizon was too great to be ignored. And the expert, writing anonymously (though practically everyone knew who he was),
sounded the alarm: Russia, the erstwhile ally on whose soil the enemy had
come to grief, whose people had fought with a bravery so compelling as to
inspire once-suspicious Westerners to hymns of praise, was "intoxicated"
with its newfound power and bent on conquering the world. Having ex-

panded their borders to absorb Asians and Europeans, the Russians would aim next at Turkey, long the target of tsars. They would pressure the Near East, then India, looking to control Europe and Asia. (The author included with his tract a map indicating Russia's past and present frontiers, the former in green, the latter in red.) Russian expansionism was not much motivated by ideology. Instead, the late war had thrown off the balance of power in Europe, and the Russian dictator, who was in several ways worse than the despot he had recently helped defeat, had been allowed to accumulate power by Western nations that were insufficiently vigilant or unconvinced by stark evidence of their peril. "Ability and audacity have guided the engine," the author wrote. "Fortune, and the errors of enemies, have contributed to its action . . . [and] political morality has been no check on the councils of Russia." Somehow, the balance of power must be restored.

I confess: this tract was written not by the American diplomat George Kennan (Mr. X) in 1947, but by the British soldier-diplomat Sir Robert Wilson 130 years earlier. It refers to the Napoleonic Wars, to the balance of power conceived at Vienna in 1815, and to the Russian empire of Tsar Alexander—though the most recent Russian borders *were* colored red on Wilson's map. I thought the trick worth playing because the similarities in Western assessments of Russian ambitions in 1817 and 1947 suggest one of the two main points of this chapter: that the Cold War, the conflict between the United States and the Soviet Union after World War II, was predicated on a historic contest for empire, what Wilson grandly called "the operation of power since the world began." Nowhere was this more true than in South Asia. There, beginning with warnings from Cassandras like Wilson, Great Britain and Tsarist Russia played the Great Game, seeking to thwart what each saw as the expansionist schemes of the other. The start of the Cold War, coincident with the creation of independent India and Pakistan in 1947 and the simultaneous retreat of British power, brought a new conflict to the region, in which the chief contestants were the United States and the Soviet Union. Theirs was not for the most part a shooting war but a contest of economic and military aid, of alliance building, and of rhetoric and propaganda. It was, in these ways, much like the Great Game.[1]

This chapter concerns the Cold War great power struggle over South Asia as a strategic matter. It differs from most other accounts of the subject in its rendering of strategy as a phenomenon with nineteenth-century antecedents. Historians have sometimes referred to the British-Russian duel in Central and South Asia as the Victorian Cold War. Equally, one might describe the twentieth-century contest as the New Great Game. The assumption that the strategic formulae of the post-1945 period emerged suddenly and only in response to global conditions following World War II is rather like a schoolboy's supposition that his elementary school didn't exist before he got there. That is not to say that the two Great Games were identical. The New Game was more ideologically charged than its predecessor. Because of the total nature of the Cold War and the increasing destructiveness of the weapons that accompanied it, it was more frightening than the First Game; no Kipling emerged to romanticize it. The powers that played the Game in the 1850s were not the same as those who clashed in the 1950s. Russia had become the Soviet Union, Great Britain had largely retired to Nestor's role, and the United States had emerged as the strongest nation on the scene, albeit one distracted by obligations it created for itself elsewhere. Most significantly, the twentieth century's Game differed from the nineteenth's because India and Pakistan were independent countries and no longer "the playthings of others," as Jawaharlal Nehru put it—though this difference was sometimes forgotten by the powers. Yet, none of these features invalidate the essential continuity of the two Great Games.[2]

Mention of India and Pakistan as participants in the New Game brings me to a second point, one that also distinguishes this account of strategy from others. I use the capacious definition of strategy provided by John Lewis Gaddis: "the process by which ends are related to means, intentions to capabilities, objectives to resources." Strategy is no fixed concept. The word has different meanings for military planners, business people, and historians. More fundamentally, it means different things to different nationalities and states because it is shaped by culture. Embedded in the concept of strategy is a set of beliefs about space: what is in it, how it is measured and configured, and how people exist in relation to it. As Gaddis has written, "there is no reason to assume that all nations—or all individuals within nations—perceive space and time in precisely the same way on all occasions." Indeed, they do not. American and Indian—that is to say, largely Hindu—ideas about space are basically different, and this makes American and Indian strategic thinking different. One cannot understand Indo-U.S. relations during the Nehru period without accounting for strategic definitions that are shaped by profoundly different cultures.[3]

Lest readers think that I am jumping to the deterministic conclusion that a nation's strategic behavior is fixedly and inevitably a result of its citizens' perception of space, I would offer several qualifications. For example, there may be a disjunction between how a state "thinks" about the world in strategic terms and how it operates in world affairs, a difference between what Alastair Iain Johnston terms its "strategic- culture language" and its "body language." Culture is partly contingent; the specific choices made by foreign policy elites are to some degree determined by realities of power that exist in a realm that overlaps with culture but is not altogether coincident with it. A nation may dream of empire, but it can only capture and hold one if it is economically and militarily powerful. Conversely, there is nothing quite like economic and military weakness to make a nation strategically modest. To return to cases, the postwar United States was powerful not only because it was culturally disposed to seek influence beyond its borders but because its economy and armed forces were the strongest in the world. India's power was limited not only because its ambitions were culturally constrained but because the country was impoverished and had the misfortune to share a continent with the Soviet Union and China. Fear is a powerful solvent of desire.[4]

Still, as long as "strategic culture" is understood as shaping or predicting and not determining behavior, as "the body of attitudes and beliefs that guides and circumscribes thought on strategic questions, influences the way strategic issues are formulated, and sets the vocabulary and the perceptual parameters of strategic debate," it seems to me a valuable concept. Unlike definitions of strategy that assume all nations will respond in the same way to external opportunities or threats, the addition of culture to strategy takes into account different webs of significance that exist in various places, and different perceptions of space. Strategic culture is also more sensitive to history than a neorealist definition of strategy. The will to power is not universal. It does not everywhere trump a people's perception of their place in the world.[5]

Most Westerners see expansionism as the logical extension of power; if you have it, you use it. In this syllogism resides a particular understanding of space. Westerners imagine space as available, beckoning those outside to occupy it, settle it, master it. "The history which Europeans constructed for themselves was part of a growing process of control over space," writes Bernard S. Cohn. How much the allure of space bewitched Americans has been well documented. Beginning with the seventeenth century, European settlers saw space as an opportunity. Americans moved west if they failed in the east, for the West would allow them to start life over again. Space was a necessity, preventing the United States from developing too quickly over time and becoming corrupt, luxurious, pathetically European. Space was exciting—more democratic, more liberated, and more dangerous than what passed for civilization in the East. Space was a white American right, and Native Americans, Europeans, or Mexicans who challenged the right of a white American to move west must be removed or destroyed. "Expansion lies at the center of the American *Weltanschauung*," wrote William Appleman Williams. It was and remains the key to resolving the visceral problems created by the sense of uniqueness, the commitment to mission, and the way out of being isolated—of being alone." The frontier historian Frederick Jackson Turner "truly understood the American idiom: the only way to preserve the Present is to recreate it into infinity. . . . And to do that, one needs first a continent, then a hemisphere, next the world, and finally the universe—or at least a galaxy."[6]

Whenever there seemed a threat to the frontier, Americans grew anxious, worried that they would be physically restrained, or that the closure of the West would mean the end of imagination, and with it a loss of energy and virtue. They worried about this prior to 1812, and hoped that war would remove at last the British obstacle to their expansion. They worried in the 1840s that the Indians, Mexicans, and (still) the British were hemming them in. They worried in the 1890s, when the superintendent of the census announced that the West had been settled and the "free lands" taken up. And they worried again, after World War II, that depression would return if the nation lost access not to free lands but to free markets, another version of the frontier.[7]

At each of these moments in history there were voices raised against expansion into space, Americans who urged political leaders to concentrate on domestic reform rather than territorial aggrandizement. Each time they were overruled. People kept moving west, and the nation kept growing. Even the census superintendent's judgment that the West had been settled failed to change the commitment to expansion, or at least to alter the belief that space was an opportunity. When Americans weren't actually expanding the polity—"extending the sphere," James Madison had called it—they were traveling, exploring, testing themselves in barely known places. Space seemed in calmer periods a marvelous place to go, actually or vicariously. In times of crisis it could be the salvation of the republic.

What Indians thought of space requires a bit more to explain. Of course, no more than all Americans did all Indians think alike. Men and women (of both nationalities) likely saw space differently, and so did different racial, ethnic, political, and religious groups. The makers of Indian foreign policy following independence, including Nehru, were British educated, and their having gone to Europe at all suggests that influential Indians traveled when they had good reason and the means to do so. And Nehru recorded in his autobiography: "I dreamt of astral bodies and imagined myself flying great distances. This dream of flying high up in the air (without any appliance) has indeed been a frequent one throughout my life."[8]

It is also worth noting, however, that Nehru apparently did not start having this dream until Westerners introduced him, at age eleven, to theosophy. There is in Hinduism, and thus among a large majority of Indians, a tendency to view space as uninviting, perhaps uninteresting, and almost certainly threatening. Space is not the exciting temptation it is for Americans but the disturbing unknown, where more bad things can happen than good. There are practical, historical reasons for these different perceptions. By the beginning of the nineteenth century, the lands that lay beyond the borders of the United States were sparsely populated or weakly held. Power moved from inside out. India remained a British colony until 1947. Its weakness, its susceptibility to invasion, was manifest every day in the presence of white men in pith helmets ordering Indians about. The British were the latest in a long line of invaders, which included Mahmoud of Ghazni, the Mughal Babur, the Portuguese, and the French. Where South Asia was concerned power flowed from outside in. Space, the lands that lay beyond the borders of India, was threatening; expansion was never an opportunity and seldom a possibility. Frontiers are not always positively charged. Analyzing the experience of China, Owen Lattimore argued that frontiers face inward as well as outward, defining the size of the polity in accordance with the power held by the state. "To reach out too far beyond the periphery of this manageable whole is wasteful," Lattimore wrote—a lesson discovered by the British in India in the nineteenth century.[9]

The psychologist Sudhir Kakar has emphasized Hindus' reliance on *samskaras*, or "innate dispositions," to explain human behavior. He recounts the story of a Hindu holy man, meditating on the bank of the Ganges, who suddenly has a female mouse drop into his lap. Taking pity on the creature, the holy man transforms it into a girl, and he and his wife raise her as their daughter. When it comes time for the girl to marry, the man provides several attractive prospects. First comes the sun god, whom the girl rejects as "too plump and redfaced." How about the god of clouds, powerful enough to cover the sun? "Oh, father," the girl protests. "He looks much too morose." The man next summons the mountain god, strong enough to stop the cloud, but the girl thinks him "massive and clumsy." Nearing despair, the holy man asks the mountain if he knows of someone better. The mountain replies: "The mouse can bore as many holes in me as it wants to. Considering that, it must be stronger than I am." When the man produces a male mouse, his daughter excitedly proclaims that here is a husband she can be happy with—whereupon father changes daughter back into a mouse, and the furry lovers run off happily. As Kakar explains, the presence of *samskara* makes irrelevant any need to assure that a "child's potentialities . . . be boundlessly fulfilled." Because Hindus believe in "inner limits, there is not that sense of urgency and struggle against the outside world, with prospects of sudden metamorphosis and great achievements just around the corner, that often seems to propel Western lives." This is not fatalism, but instead a recognition that people are heavily influenced by an unconscious that is metaphysical in origin, and thus powerful enough to discourage pointless quests into space.[10]

Along with *samskara,* Hindu cosmology generally indicates that space should be approached with suspicion. According to Hindu (and, broadly speaking, Buddhist and Jain) texts, the earth lies at the center of the universe. It is shaped like a disc, and divided into a series of concentric land masses and oceans. The central continent, called Jambudvipa, consists of four countries that sprawl away from Mount Meru at the center, the southern one being India (Bharat). Jambudvipa is surrounded by a ring-shaped ocean of salt; beyond it are six other continents, all ring-shaped, and all separated from each other by oceans consisting, progressively, of sugarcane juice, wine, ghee (clarified butter), milk, whey, and fresh water. Beyond the last ocean is a circle of mountains, then "a realm of darkness that extends to the uttermost bounds of the universe." The accompanying diagram indicates the pattern.[11]

The configuration of the Hindu cosmos does not necessarily predict apprehensiveness about space. After all, it might be pleasant to sail on an ocean of sugarcane juice. But there is more to it than that. The salt ocean enclosing Jambudvipa was "filled with sea-monsters, whirlpools, treacherous rocks, and unpredictable storms," and islands in it were populated by creatures with one leg or with their heads planted in their chests. Beyond the first or second continent—the texts vary on the matter—no proper human being can live. Perhaps for these reasons, orthodox Hindus tended not to travel beyond India's borders much, especially by ship; their presence on the *kalapani,* or "black waters," would make them ritually unclean. The brilliant South Indian mathematician S. Ramanujan, invited in 1913 to study at Cambridge, hesitated to go because he was a Brahmin, and thus proscribed from crossing the sea. The punishment for defiance was exclusion from caste. Ramanujan resolved to leave India only after he had a vision that he received divine permission to travel abroad. Five years later he returned having contracted tuberculosis, and when he died in April 1920, most of his Brahmin relatives skipped the funeral. (In 1953 India's ambassador to the United States, G. L. Mehta, explained that Indian students rarely came to America before the First World War because it "seemed very distant to us—it is at the antipodes in

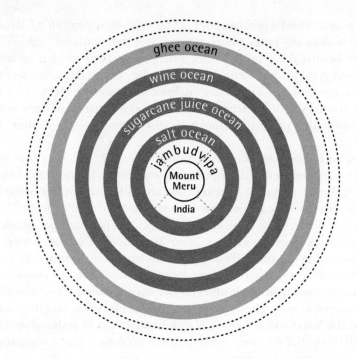

our ancient literature . . . we call it the 'Netherworld'!") Hindu epics do involve travel and adventure in alien places. The hero Rama and his brother Lakshman go to Lanka in the *Ramayana*—but only after the nearby island has been connected to India by a bridge, and indeed it is populated by demons. In an old South India song, Yasoda calls her son Krishna home, warning that he "must not stay at the crossroad when it is twilight" and invoking rumors "that an ogress with red hair and poisonous breasts is on her way to harm you." Friedhelm Hardy points out that the crossroad and twilight are "areas of transition from one boundary system to another," places where Indians are least comfortable.[12]

These cosmological principles make comprehensible several sociological practices having to do with space. Observers have noted, for instance, that Indians, who are normally fastidious about personal cleanliness and grooming and whose houses, no matter how modest, are tidy and well swept, live with a degree of filth in public areas that is startling by contrast. Alan Roland suggests that respect for self and family explains the well-scrubbed private spaces, while "outside the family space is a no-man's land" that commands little interest. And there is a suspicion among orthodox Hindus that eating a meal away from home—"taking food outside"—is a certain invitation to disease. This explains why India's restaurants have often been luxurious establishments for foreign tourists, or somewhat seedy places considered suitable mainly for single men.[13]

Space and Cold War Strategy

Ideas about space shaped the strategies of the United States and India during the Cold War. Quickly abandoning hope of resisting communism selectively, in places where they could marshal their strength and in which they had compelling interest, American policymakers embarked on a crusade to confront the menace everywhere it appeared. Louis Halle has perceptively described the Cold War as having a "total character," such that "there could be no geographical limitation to it, and it could properly end only when one side had, at last, destroyed the other." The totality of the conflict was underscored by the authors of National Security Council document 68 in early 1950: "The assault on free institutions is worldwide now, and in the context of the present polarization of power a defeat of free institutions anywhere is a defeat everywhere." Four years later, President Dwight Eisenhower bemoaned the situation to Congressional leaders: "Where in hell can you let Communists chip away any more?" he wondered. "We just can't stand it." In 1961, John F. Kennedy promised that the nation would "pay any price," and so forth, in pursuit of universal liberty. The protection of the entire free world was at once a solemn responsibility and an exhilarating opportunity, consonant with the expansive American world view that nearly always won out over a blinkered focus on limits. Space beckoned again; the Cold War was the New Frontier.[14]

With limited power and with a strategic culture founded on a suspicion of space, independent India was born into the Cold War with assumptions very different from those of the United States. Western observers tried often to characterize India's foreign policy. They labeled it "neutralist," quixotic, or "wooly" when they could not divine its purposes. Nehru most often used the term "nonaligned" to describe his strategy. The most perceptive outsider analysis of Indian foreign policy was that of Sir Archibald Nye, the British high commissioner in India. Nye had served as vice-chief of the Imperial General Staff during the Second World War. He had been governor of Madras state (later Tamil Nadu) from 1946 to 1948, then became high commissioner, the Commonwealth equivalent of ambassador. In a six-page, top secret letter sent to the Commonwealth Relations Office in London on May 17, 1951, Nye acknowledged that India had not played a positive and forceful role in South and East Asia. Its pusillanimous attitude toward China was "perverse," its policy toward the disputed state of

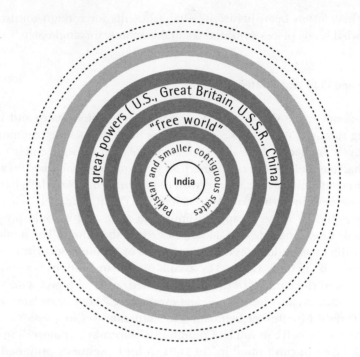

Kashmir intransigent. As a result, India had "failed to provide a rallying point for the protection of democracy in the East." It was tempting, Nye understood, to give up efforts to "wean" India to the free world side and a more responsible position on the Cold War.

Nye urged his colleagues to resist this temptation, for it remained "essential to deny India to Russia." The Great Game had resumed; as "in earlier days . . . any weakening of the South-Eastern perimeter of the Soviet Orbit would have a disastrous effect on our whole position in the Middle East." The question was how to keep from communist hands a people whose foreign policy seemed torn by inconsistencies that frustrated the noblest intentions of Western governments. It would help, Nye suggested, to see Indian policy "as operating in three concentric circles, the principles governing each of which bear little or no relation to the principles followed in the others." The innermost circle consisted mainly of contiguous states—Afghanistan, Ceylon, Nepal, Tibet, and Burma—where India had "vital" interests. In the second ring, including the so-called free world minus the United States and Great Britain, India's interests ranged in strength from moderate (in Southeast Asia) to minimal (South America). Toward the "outer ring" of the four great powers, India practiced "nonalignment." Pakistan, Nye argued, was unique. Here, to a much greater extent than elsewhere in the inner ring, India's policy was "hard-headed" and based on a "narrow calculation of self-interest" that India would defend, if necessary, by force.

Within the first circle, India played "power politics." India might moralize about the behavior of the great powers in Korea or South Africa, but the government's performance in the former princely state of Hyderabad, in the lingering internal colonies of Pondicherry and Goa, and in Nepal, which India ultimately turned into a virtual colony of its own, was derived from a strain of *realpolitik* that Bismarck would have recognized. (The previous spring, the American ambassador-at-large, Philip Jessup, had complained to Nye that Indian leaders would barely talk to him about foreign policy "because they were so obsessed with [the] East/West Bengal situation," a border dispute with Pakistan.) In the second circle Indian policy was characterized by anticolonialism and support for nationalism, with perhaps a smattering of realism in Asian countries, like Malaya and Iran, where India's interests were engaged. Finally, in the outermost ring, containing the United States, Great Britain, the Soviet Union, and the People's Republic of China, India's relations were "to a great extent determined by her passionate desire to keep out of conflict and to stand aside from Great Power struggles." Here nonalignment was most evident. India refused to "face the facts of Soviet expansionism," exhibited an "almost pathological" dislike of the United States, and had "yielded . . . to [the] self-deception" that the Chinese had no aggressive designs, despite their "invasion" of Tibet seven months earlier.

Nye's analysis appeared to make a discouraging picture. India seemed hypocritical for bullying weaker neighbors while scolding the great powers for practicing imperialism. Its steadfast refusal to negotiate with Pakistan over Kashmir burst any Gandhian pretensions about loving peace above all else. Indians could turn their heads when the Soviets and Chinese meddled in affairs beyond their borders, but ignoring the meddling would not make it go away. Yet Nye remained hopeful. There had been some progress in Indian attitudes, he thought. It bore remembering that the United States had been "isolationist" for many years, and that Great Britain had been slow to respond to the dangers presented by Nazi Germany and the Soviet Union. Britain, linked to India by an intimate past and through membership in the Commonwealth, still had special influence in India, where a "great fund of genuine goodwill, confidence and even affection towards the United Kingdom" persisted.

A diagram of Nye's spatial model of Indian foreign policy looks strikingly like the map of Hindu cosmology shown earlier. There is no ocean of ghee on the Nye diagram, and no one-legged monsters, in the literal sense. Still, Indian caution about space is clearly reflected. Within familiar (and familial) boundaries Indians are secure and confident, with ample scope for ego development and realization of identity. The borders of Nye's inner ring are roughly those of ancient Bharat and thus, to many Indians, part of the nation's natural sphere of influence. The second ring encompasses nations beyond safe space, though perhaps not those beyond the reach of civilization. India was disinclined to venture forth on an expansionist policy. Because of the "negative" principles of Gandhism, wrote Nye, "India has no inspiring positive belief," and "is not, and never through her history has been, disposed of her own accord to use her manpower outside her own territory." India had some interest in this sphere. Nehru spoke his mind on colonialism, nationalism, and racial discrimination in Asia and Africa, and he was deeply concerned for the safety of Indians living abroad. These matters involved projection of interests internal to India onto situations abroad. Colonialism, for instance, was a live issue for Indians whose political identities were formed by resistance to it, and it remained salient as long as the Portuguese clung to colonies on the subcontinent and in Africa. Concern for Indians overseas was an expression of anxiety for family members who had left the security of home. Beyond, in the third ring, were nations by which Indians wished only to be left alone. The great powers were not populated by aliens, mysterious and terrible, but by dangerous men whose capabilities and intentions portended no good. They were expansionists who coveted space, and their conflict with each other threatened to engulf India even as it stood peacefully within its borders. It was wisest not to side with any one or two of them; it was best not to get involved with them at all.[15]

Great Games and the Cold War in South Asia, 1947–54

When Kipling's old Indian beggar, "eyeless, noseless, and lipless," warned against "the Bear that looks like a man," he meant the Russians who intrigued in Central Asia and menaced the high passes of the Hindu Kush during the second half of the nineteenth century. But well before the British government took formal control of India following the Sepoy Rebellion in 1857, intrepid young men in the employ of the military or the East India Company were meeting the Russian threat by exploring the rivers Indus and Oxus, cultivating or bribing or negotiating with potentates from the Punjab to Persia and the khanates east of the Caspian Sea, and masquerading as Muslim pilgrims oddly ignorant of simple Islamic rituals. One of these, Arthur Conolly, first called the contest "The Great Game," though

Kipling would popularize the phrase in his 1901 novel *Kim.* (Conolly was beheaded in 1842 by the Emir of Bokhara.) The phrase understates the seriousness with which the British and Russians vied for influence in Asia, but it accurately conveys the sense of adventure shared by the principals on both sides and the absence of open warfare between them most of the time.

The Great Game originated with fears that the tsars hoped to extend their reach to India. Even Aurangzeb, the last of the powerful Mughal emperors (r. 1658–1707), refused to allow a Russian mission to Delhi for fear it would subvert his regime. The British inherited Mughal concerns. Rumors reached London in 1807 that Napoleon, having defeated the Russians, had proposed to combine forces with Tsar Alexander and conquer Turkey, Persia, and India. The partnership failed to gel, and it dissolved entirely with Napoleon's ill-fated invasion of Russia in 1812. But Russian appetites only increased after the French were beaten, at least as far as the British were concerned. Robert Wilson sounded the tocsin in 1817. There followed a century of moves and countermoves between agents of the two powers. St. Petersburg was undeniably, though sporadically, expansionist wherever it could muster its forces. The Russians sought influence in the Balkans and quarreled with the Turks. They fished in troubled waters in northern Persia, mapped Afghani mountain passes, and, late in the century, made clear their intention to dominate China, Mongolia, and Korea. They absorbed, after 1865, the Central Asian khanates of Khiva, Bokhara, and Khokand, including the great silk road cities of Tashkent and Samarkand. Russia had no choice, wrote the Foreign Minister Prince Gorchakov, for its position in Central Asia was "that of all civilized states which are brought into contact with half-savage nomad populations possessing no fixed social organization. In such cases it always happens that the more civilized state is forced . . . to exercise a certain ascendancy over those whose turbulent and unsettled character make them undesirable neighbors." [16]

Some in Britain and India saw Russian actions as defensive, or at least limited in scope. These observers, most of them associated with the Liberal Party, favored a strategy called "masterly inactivity," meaning that the British should husband their strength in India, watchfully waiting to see what the Russians would do and preparing to pounce on an invader with stretched lines of supply and communications and weakened by a debilitating march through the mountains. Others, however, were convinced that Russian seizure of the khanates foretold a pattern of expansion that had India as its ultimate target. This view was favored by the Tories and most of those in the military. "I solemnly assert my belief," wrote Sir Charles MacGregor, head of the Indian Army Intelligence Department, in 1884, "that there can never be a real settlement of the Anglo-Russian question *till Russia is driven out of the Caucasus and Turkistan.*" Advocates of this "forward policy" proposed that Britain secure a glacis of buffer states between Russia and India. Not only would the forward strategy give the Russians pause; it would convince the allegedly warlike peoples of Central Asia that the British were tough and willing to fight.[17]

Generally, the "forward school" got much of what it wanted by the end of the nineteenth century. As early as 1832, following a series of moves and countermoves in Turkey and Persia, "the wily hand of the czar was seen behind every minor uprising, behind every rumor out of a bazaar." Beginning in the late 1830s, Afghanistan became the chief front in the Game. Sent in 1888 to Gilgit, in the mountains of Kashmir just north of the Indus, Colonel Algernon Durand grimly monitored the movements, or rumors of movements, of Russian soldiers said to be in the area. Durand had no doubt that the Russians were coming. "The Great Empire," he wrote, "is expanding in many directions; . . . her tentacles creep cautiously forward towards our Indian frontier." "The Battle for Armageddon" was approaching. Three years later, Durand seemed confirmed in his prediction when the British agent Francis Younghusband encountered a small force of Cossacks in the high Pamirs, 150 miles south of the established border of Russia and well within the British sphere of influence. The leader of the Cossacks, a Colonel Yanov, invited Younghusband to dinner and cordially showed him a map indicating Russian claims to Afghan, Chinese, and Indian territory. Younghusband told Yanov that the Russians "were opening their mouths pretty wide." Yanov laughed and said it was "just a beginning." The Russians later escorted Younghusband out of the area; the British responded by sending forces north to secure several frontier towns.[18]

The first Great Game ended with Russia's defeat in the Russo-Japanese War in 1905. The loss meant the end of the tsar's dreams of an East Asian empire, and political troubles at home now demanded his attention. The British, meanwhile, who were becoming apprehensive over the growing power of Germany, concluded that Russia might be a counterweight to German power in the east, and when a Liberal government came to power in London in late 1905 the time had arrived for a deal. The Anglo-Russian convention was signed in August 1907. It called for both sides to refrain from intrigue in Tibet, marked Afghanistan as a British interest, and divided Persia into two spheres of influence, the northern dominated by Russia and the southern by Great Britain. The victory of Bolshevism in Russia in 1917 revived the Game briefly, though in changed circumstances: subversion, not invasion of India, became the Soviets' goal. But they made no headway with nationalist leader Mohandas Gandhi, and when independence came to India and Pakistan in 1947 it was not associated with communism or much Russian help at all.[19]

But 1947 brought the Cold War, and with it a New Great Game in Central and South Asia. Precisely what the Soviets had in mind during the later 1940s, 1950s, and early 1960s, under Josef Stalin and Nikita Khrushchev, remains in dispute. Recently opened documents from Moscow's archives do not settle the issue. Certainly the Soviets had ambitions beyond their borders. But were these ambitions open ended, part of a plan to take over the world by invasion and subversion? Were they inspired by revolutionary communist ideology or by historic forces that ran deeper than ideology and had endured much longer? Did the Soviets genuinely feel threatened by the West, fearing encirclement, or was that argument just a smoke screen designed to conceal aggression?

Only cautious answers to these questions are possible. Soviet postwar planning memoranda written in 1944 and 1945 indicate that influential leaders saw the world not in ideological but geopolitical terms. They presumed the emergence of what Maxim Litvinov called "zones of strategic predominance" and did not propose to confront the West in an ideological global struggle. This was also Stalin's view. "Soviet documents," write Vladislav Zubok and Constantine Pleshakov, "reveal not a trace of revolutionary romanticism in the Soviet leader" after 1945. He had sought a great power accord with the United States and Great Britain, but having in his view been denied that he resolved to assemble his own bloc, including countries in spite of their revolutionary commitments, not because of them. The lack of clear vectors in Soviet policy as revealed by the documents suggests to Melvyn Leffler that Stalinist policy overall "was erratic and contingent"; in East Asia, writes Odd Arne Westad, "Stalin could not make up his mind" how to avoid confrontation with the United States; and in Germany, according to Norman Naimark, Soviet goals "remained unreconciled" for the length of the occupation. Zubok concludes that Stalin wanted "to transform the internationalist communist ideology into an imperial, statist one, rooted more in Russian history than in the Comintern slogans." This dictated a "cautious expansionism," not merely defensive in nature but irregularly, even haltingly, implemented. With the reservoir of history came a culture of expansionism, complete with derisive images of others (vicious Germans, backward Chinese) and a notion of "Russian exceptionalism" that justified the process of conquering and civilizing the frontier.[20]

The thesis that the Soviets probed cautiously, and for historical and cultural rather than ideological reasons, applies especially well to the Middle

East and South Asia after 1945. Stalin sought joint management of the Turkish Straits and a military base at the Dardanelles. The Soviets occupied northern Iran, then established a puppet regime there, hoping to pressure the government in Tehran into providing them with oil concessions comparable to those long accorded the British. (In both instances, U.S. and international pressure caused Stalin to back off.) The Soviets moved more carefully in Afghanistan. They made a border agreement with Kabul in 1946, and the following year built a telegraph line connecting the Afghan capital and Soviet Tashkent. But when in the late 1940s Soviet agents were infiltrated into northern Afghanistan to radicalize the inhabitants, they met with a stubborn refusal to cooperate. Long interested in the affairs of India, the Soviets nevertheless kept a low profile there into the early 1950s. Soviet attitudes toward Nehru and his Communist Party of India (CPI) opponents shifted several times from 1945 to 1954: Nehru was a bourgeois who had sold his country out to Wall Street, until he became a heroic advocate of nonalignment in the Cold War, while the CPI was first adventuristic, later the courageous follower of the Chinese revolutionary path, and finally obstructionist in its resistance to Nehru's enlightened foreign policy. All of the Soviet initiatives in the area echoed tsarist strategies during the first Great Game. The Russians in both games meddled and probed, sought influence wherever they could, ascribed imperialist designs to their adversaries, threatened to use force but rarely did so, and backed down in the face of warnings by equivalent or superior powers.[21]

By 1945 Great Britain was no longer the power it once had been, lacking economic and military reach. The British conceded independence to India and Pakistan in 1947 and Burma in 1948. As if by instinct, however, they moved to reassert their authority in the Near East and South Asia. Empire is, to some extent, a habit. Emotional ties held Britain to its former colonies, bonds of affection that cannot entirely be dismissed as the romantic invention of colonialists unhappy with the loss of their large houses and servants. Like the Americans, the British were worried about Soviet expansionism. The heirs of Robert Wilson and Francis Younghusband knew their history, and were at first more concerned than the Americans about Russian intentions, even while they were less convinced of their basis in communist ideology. Above all, the British retained economic interests in their former colonies. "The great thing was," recalled Lord Gladwyn, the undersecretary of state at the time, "to try to establish a new and, if possible, an intimate relationship with old dependencies which, in our weakened state, it was impossible to hold down by force, even if that was desirable." It was the particular mission of the Labour gov-

ernment of Prime Minister Clement Attlee, elected in July 1945, to transform the nation from colonial policeman to banker of the Commonwealth sterling area. But even if the British were able to pull this off—and
given their tenuous economic status this was by no means assured—it was
clear to officials in the Foreign and Commonwealth Relations Offices that
they would need help from the United States. The Great Game had resumed. India was "the only possible buttress" against Soviet expansionism
in Asia, Archibald Nye told Raymond Hare of the State Department in
May 1949. The British would educate the Americans about the fine points
of Asian gamesmanship: London would supply the brains, Washington
the money and the muscle needed to hold South Asia.[22]

British policymakers attempted to implement, through American sur-
rogates, a strategy of masterly inactivity. The British lacked the means to
create a forward policy in buffer states surrounding Soviet Asia, and they
assumed that the Americans lacked the will to do so. The Trans-Caspian
area, where the first Great Game was played so vigorously, was a lost cause,
as was China by 1949. The British had an unhappy history with
Afghanistan. Even Pakistan scarcely seemed worth much trouble, given its
lack of resources, though it could not be abandoned altogether. The
British hoped to direct American attention to India, setting for their
pupils two delicately balanced tasks: first, stabilize India economically and
secure it against expansion or subversion; and, second, do not attempt to
interfere with time-honored British prerogatives. Since the British knew
India better than the Americans, they would call the shots.

The Indian response to British plans was initially wary. The British
could not help seeming to condescend to their former subjects. Nehru hit
back from time to time. In a March 1948 speech he reminded the British
of their imperialist record and castigated British journalists for reports
that "offensively misrepresent us." ("The speech was fundamentally unfriendly to this country," fumed a British official. "It will be a long time before the Indians learn that it is not always true that the more they kick our
bottoms, the more we shall give heed to them.") But usually relations
were better than this. As two historians have written, "India was prepared
to judge its former rulers magnanimously" by 1947. It chose to stay in the
Commonwealth at independence and reaffirmed the decision two years
later. Many Indians admired the way in which the British had departed,
with the notable exception of the partition decision, and Nehru's personal friendship with Lord Mountbatten, the last viceroy, and with Mountbatten's wife Edwina helped ease the transition to independence and prepared the ground for cordial relations.[23]

The more difficult problem was to enlist the Americans in the Game. It was not that American policymakers were at cross-purposes with their British counterparts. The Americans were accustomed to following the British lead in South Asia, and frictions that developed between the two sides during the war over the disposition of India vanished with the British decision to grant independence. It was rather that the Americans, heavily occupied elsewhere in the world, were if anything too deferential to the British on Indian issues and thus initially unwilling to put themselves forward. At least before 1949, British officials worried that the United States had no India policy and hardly thought about the place at all. It was difficult, for example, to persuade the Americans to take the lead in sorting out the dispute between India and Pakistan over Kashmir, which erupted into war in the fall of 1947. The Americans heard the British out on the issue, admitted "that they were short of background information" and expressed a willingness to cooperate; British experts took pride in the degree to which the Americans accepted their interpretation of events. "But," wrote a British official in November 1948, "when it comes to our asking them to take the job over from us they are inclined to retort: 'well who started the British empire?' " And P. F. Grey of the Foreign Office reported that "Americans had very little interest in India and they remembered how many Viceroys and other Englishmen of great reputation had tried and failed to solve the communal problem" there.[24]

In the fullness of time the Americans accepted the British view. Lobbying by British officials helped. More important were changes in world conditions in 1949 that rekindled a sense of crisis in Washington and brought increased American attention to South and Southeast Asia. The Marshall Plan, passed by Congress in March 1948, had brought temporary relief from the economic difficulties of Western Europe, but by the middle of 1949 it was clear that aid alone, no matter how extensive, would not solve abiding structural problems with the world economy. The West Germans suffered from low production resulting in part from a "security psychosis," living, as they were, unarmed and in close proximity to the Red Army. In France there was political instability and economic malaise, both exacerbated by the debilitating war to keep Vietnam in the French empire. A slight recession in the United States precipitated a hemorrhage of dollars from Great Britain, already reeling from a parlous trade balance between the sterling and dollar areas and in debt to several former colonies, especially India. Things were no better in East Asia. The communists were sweeping to power in China; occupied Japan had become a laboratory for American social experimentation but remained economically frail; Indochina was convulsed in war. As the Truman administration, led by its sophisticated secretary of state Dean Acheson, began to address these hardships, it came to understand that economic recovery and security were global problems requiring global solutions. What had seemed the periphery of the world system now appeared as fundamentally important to the so-called core. Japan would not recover without the markets and resources of Southeast Asia. The materials for building atomic bombs were available in Africa. And the extension of Soviet power to the Indian subcontinent would discourage democracy in Asia and the free world generally, jeopardize British economic standing in the region, and, as U.S. policymakers declared in April 1949, "gravely affect the security of the United States."[25]

The phrase came from a report written by the Near and Middle East Subcommittee of the State-Army-Navy-Air Force Coordinating Committee (SANACC), which had been charged to study U.S. interests in South Asia and to recommend measures that would best serve them. The subcommittee concluded that South Asia was worthy of U.S. attention, that it must be turned "toward the U.S. and other Western democracies, and away from the USSR." The United States should consider providing economic aid, which would help stabilize democratic governments in the area. Military materiel might also be needed if these countries were to maintain internal security and prevent "Communist domination." Continued collaboration with the British was desirable. The United States should encourage "cooperation among the nations for constructive purposes." With the Kashmir conflict still festering, India making clear its intention to control events in Nepal, and Pakistan and Afghanistan trading threats over the Pushtun area adjoining their border, it was hard to imagine what the subcommittee had in mind. In any case, the report was approved by SANACC on May 31 and referred to the National Security Council (NSC), which used it to help prepare a study on U.S. policy toward Asia generally. That study, NSC 48/1, called for the United States to "exploit every opportunity to increase the present Western orientation" of South Asia, "and to assist, within our capabilities, its governments in their efforts to meet the minimum aspirations of their people and to maintain internal security." Failure to undertake this policy could have serious consequences: "Should India and Pakistan fall to communism, the United States and its friends might find themselves denied any foothold on the Asian mainland." The paper was approved by President Truman on December 30, 1949.[26]

The crises of 1949 restored the Americans to their traditionally expansive vision of the world. When space is a requirement for social peace, economic growth, and national security, there can be no respect for limits, and thus no distinction between center and periphery. When space in addition provides an opportunity to do good, to satisfy an impulse to make things better through reform, it dissolves into the atmosphere breathed by the reformer: a stranger is just a friend you didn't know you had. So went U.S. Cold War policy into the new decade. Gone was any cautious desire for a "strong point" defense of American interests. It was replaced by a strategic doctrine that presumed all areas equally vital to American security. NSC 68 was the signature document of this "perimeter" strategy, but by including South (and Southeast) Asia among the nation's critical concerns NSC 48/1 also gave impetus to the ambitions of Cold Warriors. And what better place than India for those who wanted a chance to make the world better? Given the poverty in which most Indians lived, the Western belief in their backwardness, and even their dark skin (which seized the sympathies of American liberals who sought racial equality at home), India seemed the perfect space in which to do good.[27]

The U.S. Strategic Commitment to South Asia

And so, at the behest of the British and for reasons of their own, the Americans committed themselves to South Asia. At first they tried to be evenhanded—"there was no question of trying to enter into any sort of alliance with anybody," recalled Elbert Mathews, director of the State Department Office of South Asian Affairs from 1948 to 1951. Nor were they inclined to be generous. India had not come into the American Cold War camp, and Nehru's seeming equivocation on the rectitude of the powers exasperated U.S. policymakers. But given the weakness of South Asia and the apparent Soviet threat, the Americans believed that something had to be done. Mathews and his boss, George McGhee, who was assistant secretary of state for Near Eastern, South Asian, and African affairs, spearheaded efforts to supply economic and military aid to India and Pakistan. U.S. economic aid for South Asia, which began with a trickle in 1951, would eventually grow to a formidable level. Military assistance was a more complicated matter. The British, while welcoming U.S. help in South Asia, were not convinced that arming the parties in the region would contribute to its security, and even those who accepted the wisdom of modernizing Indian and Pakistani armed forces were unhappy at the prospect of replacing British arms with American. When India and Pakistan fell out over Kashmir, the United States embargoed arms sales to both countries from March 1948 to March 1949.[28]

During that time the Kashmir issue remained stalemated, but U.S. relations with India nevertheless improved. Nehru's anger over the activities of the Indian Communist Party fell on the Soviet Union as well, and insist as he did that he welcomed Mao Zedong's revolution in China, the prime minister privately feared what it might mean for India's security. Nehru's occasional praise for the Soviets and his continued embrace of what the Americans disdainfully called "neutralism" were represented by Indian diplomats as necessary for "home consumption." There was "no doubt at all as to which side India would take should there be a third world war—the United States could count absolutely on having India at its side in such a conflict," I. S. Chopra of the Indian Embassy assured the State Department in May 1948. If this were true, providing arms for India might be a judicious down payment on a future friendship. The Indians wanted American weapons and military help. They sought consultation and training with American officers, spare parts for their tanks, recoilless guns and ammunition for them, and modern fighter jets. The United States, pleaded Elbert Mathews, should be responsive: "With the downfall of China to the Communists and with the emergence of India as an anti-Communist leader in Asia," he wrote McGhee in early March 1949, "the importance of U.S.-India relations is increasing rapidly and it would no longer appear too early to listen at least to whatever the Government of India might have to say on the subject of Indo-US military cooperation." Following up on the SANACC report of that same month, Secretary Acheson urged his counterpart at the Defense Department, Louis Johnson, to "give urgent consideration" to Indian requests for military help. Hampered by tight budgets, the advocates of military assistance for India were stymied throughout 1949, though India did purchase from the United States just under $900,000 worth of equipment during 1949–1950. There seemed reasonable promise of further cooperation.[29]

Then, in late June 1950, came the Korean War. India supported resolutions condemning the North Korean attack and calling for aid to South Korea, but Nehru was unconvinced that the invasion confirmed American fears about communist expansionism worldwide and tried to broker a settlement predicated on the admission of the People's Republic of China to the UN. The breach in "free world" defenses, if only temporary, worried U.S. policymakers enough to make them more attentive to India's economic needs; Americans increasingly saw India as Asia's democratic alternative to China. But Nehru's Cold War inconstancy soured policymakers on the prospect of arming Indians who, it seemed, could not predict which way they planned to shoot. McGhee, who had fought hard for military aid, now became disillusioned, arguing that "Mr. Nehru's foreign policy of 'neutralism,' . . . in the final analysis, is favorable to the Soviet Union." Before Chester Bowles left Washington in late 1951 to become the ambassador in New Delhi, officials told him "that India's friendship would be a liability in case of war." Bowles doubted that; he would become the leading advocate for India in the Truman and later the Kennedy and Johnson administrations. Early in 1952, he tried to reassure the State Department's John Hickerson that while "Nehru had burned his fingers on the Chinese Communists," this was "part of the learning process." Hickerson replied that he "hoped Mr. Nehru would learn about the Communists while he still had some fingers left to burn."[30]

Like nations on a seesaw, poised over a fulcrum of American approval, India and Pakistan took turns rising and falling out of U.S. favor. With the Korean War, Pakistan began a prolonged period of ascendancy. Convinced that the contest with the Soviet Union had emerged on every front by late 1949, U.S. policymakers concluded that something must be done to shore up South Asia. If, as most of them thought, India had grown fickle, efforts must be made to enlist willing Pakistan in the struggle. The resumption of the Great Game pleased the British, who had worked hard to tutor the Americans in their new responsibilities to this persistent competition, but the American nomination of Pakistan to serve as the South Asian frontline state in the struggle was less enthusiastically received in London. It was greeted with anger, derision, and fear in New Delhi.

From the moment of independence in August 1947, Pakistani leaders felt insecure about their nation's place in South Asia and the world. India had more land, more people, more money, more prestige, and more soldiers. Pakistanis felt most of all neglected by the British, who seemed to regard the Islamic state as the necessary but unfortunate offspring of their withdrawal from South Asia, barely tolerated, never favored. British officials noted, in early December 1947, Pakistani "bitterness" over Britain's lack of friendship, and speculated that the Pakistanis were already preparing to make overtures to the Americans for assistance. Or to anyone else, for that matter: with the U.S. arms embargo in place in 1948 and 1949, the Pakistanis did nothing to discourage rumors that they were exploring arrangements with the Soviet bloc. These reports got the Americans scrambling, and by the end of summer 1949 they had sold Karachi large quantities of tank ammunition and mines. Along with the requests for arms came intimations that Pakistan would consider making alliances designed to deter Soviet probes, especially in the Middle East. Prime Minister Liaquat Ali Khan pursued arms avidly on a visit to the United States in May 1950. There existed the 1937 Saadabad Pact between Turkey, Iran, Iraq, and Afghanistan. Pakistan might be interested in joining, an official hinted to George McGhee, if the treaty were strengthened and if Pakistan "could be assured of arms."[31]

Perhaps this sounded like blackmail to the Americans. They nevertheless saw advantages in following up. Friendship with an Islamic country
could in part deflect Muslim criticism of U.S. support of Israel. It would
also give a beneficial jolt to what Americans construed as India's arrogance. A Department of State report suggested that India might become
"Japan's successor in Asiatic imperialism," to which "a strong Muslim bloc
under the leadership of Pakistan, and friendly to the U.S.," might provide
a counterweight. With U.S. military support, perhaps the Pakistanis would
offer the Americans bases and "other facilities" that would allow closer
monitoring of Soviet activities in the area. Most of all, the Americans persuaded themselves that arming Pakistan in this way and underwriting a
Pakistani alliance with other Middle Eastern states would dissuade the Soviets from renewing the tsarist pursuit of the Great Game. The concern
was not so much that the Russians themselves would invade Pakistan's
part of the world, though infiltration by Russian agents was as distinct a
possibility as it had been in the 1840s. Rather, U.S. policymakers came to
believe, especially in the aftermath of Stalin's occupation of northern
Iran in 1945–46, that the oil fields of the Persian Gulf area, access to
which was critical to the West in time of war, could be cut off by a Russian
military thrust south from the Soviet republics. In this view they adopted
the logic of Sir Olaf Caroe, the British former governor of India's Northwest Frontier Province and a future mediator of the Kashmir conflict. In
his book *Wells of Power*, published in 1951, Sir Olaf argued that, prior to
independence, the Persian Gulf had been under the implied protection
of the Indian army, officered by Englishmen and including Muslims, Hindus, and Sikhs. The British withdrawal from India, and partition, meant
there was no longer a credible deterrent to Russian expansion into the
Gulf. "The chain of continuity has been snapped," Sir Olaf wrote. "There
came a parting of the ways in the long comradeship between Englishmen
and those others, Pakistanis and Indians, who had long dealt together
with affairs arising beyond their frontiers. These men had been brought
up in a great Service, and their field of action lay mainly in the . . . west
and north-west of the old India."[32]

But the requirements had not changed. It was imperative to safeguard
"the sources of fuel on which these populations equally with the Western
world depend." And the way to do this, Sir Olaf thought, was also clear:
the West must encourage Pakistan, the most Western of Islamic nations,
to take the lead in organizing a "Northern Screen" that would protect the
area. He suggested using the North Atlantic Treaty as a model for this Persian Gulf pact.[33]

Chester Bowles considered Sir Olaf's argument claptrap, a "superficial

analysis" that "totally ignored Pakistan's internal instability and her uneasy situation with her neighbors." Most U.S. policymakers disagreed. By
early 1951, the State Department had begun seriously to discuss creating
a Middle East defense group that would include the Saadabad Pact nations and Pakistan. At separate meetings in February, U.S. diplomats in
the Middle East and South Asia concluded that the participation of Pakistan was essential to the defense of both regions. McGhee told British officials in early April that Pakistan was "vital to the defence of the Middle
East" because of its (unusually) "efficient Army and Air Force." And a revised Department "Policy Statement" on Pakistan, dated July 1, 1951, was
straight out of Olaf Caroe: "Pakistan has the military manpower which
could assist Near East countries in blocking Russian aggression especially
through Iran. The Pakistan army, properly equipped, would be in a position to send troops to Iran's assistance and so to fulfill one of the traditional functions of British-Indian troops in past wars."[34]

The American position presumed a connection between providing the
arms the Pakistanis wanted and enlisting Pakistan's help in defending the
Middle East. In the short run, this presumption was naive. While Karachi
hinted that the two actions were related, it hoped to gain the benefits of
the first without paying the costs associated with the second. Over the
summer of 1951, Prime Minister Liaquat sent his foreign policy advisers
off to London and Washington with a shopping list of weapons. To P. C.
Gordon-Walker, the secretary of state for Commonwealth relations, Foreign Minister Sir Zafrulla Khan professed himself "very frightened that
the Russians would come through into Persia to the East of the Caspian
and it would be very hard indeed to resist them." Pakistan had the manpower to send up to three divisions "abroad"—if they had the needed
equipment. On October 18, two days after Prime Minister Liaquat was assassinated, former foreign minister Mohammed Ikramullah and Pakistan's ambassador to the United States, M. A. H. Ispahani, met first with
McGhee, then with officials of the Office of South Asian Affairs, including
its director Donald Kennedy. Ikramullah told McGhee bluntly "that he
was here to get as much military equipment as he could." McGhee explained that the United States already had heavy commitments to supply
other parts of the world. Then he probed: did Pakistan have in mind participating in Middle East defense? Ikramullah turned vague. Pakistan followed a policy of "moderation," which it would be happy to promote
throughout the region once assured of a "sound position." Thus enlightened, McGhee turned Ikramullah over to Kennedy, to whom the former
minister repeated the request for arms. Kennedy observed that Pakistan
was already to receive seventy American tanks, and rehearsed McGhee's

comments on commitments elsewhere and McGhee's question about Pakistan's role in Middle East defense. Ikramullah replied that "Pakistan can play a part in such a program." Yes, said Kennedy, but "it was important not only to learn that Pakistan could participate but also that it would participate"; there was a good deal of difference. At this point, Ikramullah apparently lost his temper. Both countries knew what they wanted, he said heatedly. "The time was past for words; Pakistan wanted action." He could make no commitment to Middle East defense—only his government could. But "you must make up your mind about Pakistan." The Kashmir situation was festering, the Russians were stirring up trouble, and discontent with the West was spreading in Pakistan and throughout the Middle East. Pakistan must have American arms.[35]

Eventually, Ikramullah calmed down. He met with Secretary Acheson on October 22, repeating once more his request for arms, receiving once more a litany of other American commitments, evading yet again the matter of Middle Eastern defense. Ikramullah saw Kennedy again on November 16, and this time told him flatly that his government's policy was "to refrain from attempting to assume a position of leadership in the Middle East" in order "to keep from being called names," presumably by other Muslim states. This briefly put to rest the prospect of a Middle East defense pact. The Americans did come through, in late November, by selling a small amount of military equipment to Pakistan. Karachi's Cold War loyalty and relative moderation on the Kashmir problem were worth something to the United States, even if grander plans had foundered. The Pakistanis emerged from the fall negotiations with far less than they had hoped, but they were better armed than before, and no one, save the Indians, was likely to call them names.[36]

The British observed these discussions with apprehension. Heirs of the foremost players of the first Great Game, they were not averse to enlisting Pakistan to secure the northwest frontier and the Persian Gulf, especially since Great Britain was more dependent on Gulf oil than was the United States. The Pakistanis, wrote J. D. Murray of the Foreign Office, "have no religious or other aversions to war, like the Indians. Therefore, they want to be in on the ground floor" of a Middle East alliance. Deeply concerned, however, about the negative Indian reaction to any plan that involved strengthening Pakistan militarily, the British rejected, in late November 1951, the American insistence on building up Pakistan. The British were thus jettisoning the "forward strategy" in favor of a form of "masterly inactivity." The first option required a militarily vigorous Pakistan, the mere fact of which threatened India as long as the two sides remained at loggerheads. The second implied a low profile policy that honored the status quo and thus favored India, the stronger party of the two. Privately there was greater sympathy in England for India's case. And attaching Pakistan to the defense of the Middle East could create more problems than it would solve.[37]

But despite the disappointments of late 1951, the Americans would not be denied; the State Department, a Foreign Office man recorded sourly, "apparently find it hard to take 'No' for an answer" from Pakistan. Already the United States was growing impatient with a British policy that seemed skewed toward India. Burton Y. Berry, standing in temporarily for McGhee as assistant secretary of state in February 1951, criticized Great Britain's "cynical policy of flattering the most powerful government in the region." The British were "unimaginative and disturbingly opportunistic," and "their dog-in-the-manger attitude in South Asia [was] inexcusable." Acknowledging the difficulties of fabricating a defense organization on the NATO model for the Middle East, the Truman administration now contemplated a pact that would commit Muslim countries only to consult together on defense matters of mutual concern. The arrangement was christened the Middle East Defense Organization—MEDO. The Americans hoped it would attract the Pakistanis without frightening them with a long list of new responsibilities, would meet British objections that the West was already overcommitted, and above all would calm Indian opinion, understandably nervous at the prospect that Pakistan would be formally involved in Middle East defense, but perhaps susceptible to the argument that, in a region "without any defense, there most certainly should be some defense planning," as Acheson told Indian ambassador G. L. Mehta. When the Pakistanis returned to Washington in July 1952 with further requests for military equipment, the State Department invited them "to participate in planning arrangements for the defense of the Middle East." It went no further, as time ran out on the Truman administration, a lame duck after November. Still, as Robert McMahon has written, the administration's "vision of Pakistan assuming a central role in Western defense planning for the Middle East would form the basis for the alliance between Washington and Karachi forged by Truman's successor," Dwight Eisenhower.[38]

The new president was fiscally cautious and disinclined to militarize problems that might have diplomatic solutions. He also appreciated India's policy of nonalignment more than his predecessor. But he did not obstruct the plans of his secretary of state, John Foster Dulles, to construct a system of "free world" military alliances that would ring the Soviet empire, containing communist expansionism and raising the possibility of liberating communist nations. To prevent global war, the secretary told the NSC in March 1953, the United States needed "a firm policy to hold the vital outpost positions around the periphery of the Soviet bloc." Examples of these outposts, said Dulles, were Indochina, India, and Pakistan. He soon recanted his interest in India, which proved unwilling to involve itself in any of Dulles's pacts. As for Pakistan, Dulles and military strategists quickly decided that MEDO, as a planning organization, would be inadequate to protect the Middle East in the event of a general war. The Americans endorsed instead the idea of a formal defense alliance with Turkey and Pakistan as its axis and Iran and Iraq as future members—the "northern tier" concept. This would be an alliance with teeth, relying as it did on those who professed their willingness to fight, not merely consult, in the presence of a threat to their security. With assistance from the United States, the martial leaders of Turkey and Pakistan (where, in April 1953, the military had deposed the indecisive prime minister Khwaja Nazimuddin) would build their armies, promise mutual support, and pledge themselves to resist Russian encroachment. The British reacted with dismay to this decision. The Indians were of course furious, as we will see. But the Americans went ahead anyway. Eisenhower approved a package of military aid for Pakistan in early January 1954, announced it the following month, and the two countries signed a Mutual Defense Assistance Agreement in May. The alliance itself evolved more slowly. Turkey and Pakistan made a bilateral defense agreement in April, but Pakistan first joined the Southeast Asia Treaty Organization, in 1954, signing on to the Baghdad Pact, with Great Britain, Turkey, Iran, and Iraq, only in June 1955.[39]

The benefits of the Middle Eastern alliance were a good deal less than the signatories had hoped; the fallout was far more toxic than they had feared. The British, who had resisted the northern tier idea, found themselves pulled into it via the Baghdad Pact. They came to see it as the lesser of evils, the only way to maintain influence in the Middle East in light of Egypt's intensifying nationalism, the only way to maintain access to Iranian oil, the only way to protect their military bases in Iraq. The addition of Pakistan to the pact three months after the British joined it was not altogether a surprise, but the British did not welcome it. Nor were they pleased as American arms shipments gradually weaned the Pakistanis away from British equipment. The decision to arm Pakistan came over Afghani objections as well. Since partition, Afghanistan had disputed the location of its border with Pakistan—the British-made Durand Line—and in particular the disposition of the Pushtun people, who had been placed on the Pakistani side of the boundary but whose loyalties, the Afghani government insisted, belonged to Kabul. Angered by Pakistan's refusal to negotiate on the "Pushtunistan" issue and frightened by the prospect of a disagreeable neighbor armed with American weapons, the Afghanis drew closer to the Soviet Union, eventually accepting economic aid and establishing a relationship that the tsars had only dreamed about during the days of the first Great Game. In 1953, Dulles had noted Afghanistan's "disapproval" of U.S. aid to Pakistan, but he did "not think the Afghan attitude need be given great weight." By 1959, Chester Bowles unhappily quoted what a British officer had recently told him: "For more than a hundred years Afghanistan served as a buffer state between Czarist Russia and British India. I do not know how many thousands of young Englishmen and Indians died in the three Afghan wars to keep the 'Bear that walks like a Man' behind his border. But I do know that in five years the Russians have accomplished there what they had failed to accomplish in the previous century without risking a single soldier."[40]

Nor were the Americans entirely satisfied with the policy they had wrought. Those in the Eisenhower administration responsible for India diplomacy criticized the decision to ally with Pakistan. U.S. diplomats in Pakistan were not always enthusiastic either. When a Defense Department mission visited Pakistan to evaluate the military aid program in early 1955, "it was perfectly obvious," the head of the mission wrote, "that no member of Country Team [i.e., the embassy staff] had any clear idea of the part Pakistan was expected to play in the defense of the Middle East." Eisenhower grumbled that the U.S. decision to make a military ally of Pakistan "had been proved costly," and that the decision to give the Pakistanis military aid but virtually nothing else was "the worst kind of a plan and decision we could have made. It was a terrible error, but we now seem hopelessly involved in it." Worse yet, the Pakistanis themselves were unhappy with what they considered to be American parsimony and pressure to attach themselves to the Baghdad Pact. What the Pakistanis wanted all along had been clear to themselves and the British. As Neville Maxwell observed: " 'Joint defence' . . . was never more than a Pakistani ploy, angled at those Westerners, particularly Americans, who liked to visualize linked defence pacts making strong, containing chains" along bloc borders. Pakistan was arming against India. Compelling Karachi to join the northern tier pact amounted to calling its bluff.[41]

For all its problems, the U.S.-Pakistan military relationship proved durable. U.S. military aid grew through the 1950s and beyond. The Baghdad Pact was succeeded in 1958 by the Central Treaty Organization (CENTO), without Iraq, but with an increasingly active United States serving on most of its committees. By 1962 the Americans talked of supplying tactical nuclear weapons to CENTO forces. Still, in light of its limited results, it is worth asking why the Truman administration began moving toward an alliance with Pakistan, and why Eisenhower and Dulles consummated the arrangement. No doubt there were policymakers who expected Pakistani forces to respond to aggression in the Persian Gulf. The chance to secure air bases near the Soviet border was surely a major reason for creating the alliance, and these the Americans got: in May 1960, Frances Gary Powers took off in his U-2 aircraft from a base near Peshawar—a spot on the map Soviet premier Nikita Khrushchev had reportedly circled in red, marking it for annihilation. But if there was some hope of using Pakistani troops to protect the oil fields, this was never spelled out in the dozens of reports on the region generated over the years by the State and Defense Departments and the National Security Council. Instead, a joint intelligence group acknowledged in June 1953 that "even with substantial Western military aid, Pakistan could probably furnish few if any troops for early employment outside the subcontinent" unless a settlement was reached with India, and over four years later the U.S. ambassador in Pakistan called the military aid program a "hoax," pointing out that Pakistani "concentration on India is such that a considerably larger Pakistan arms program would not yield a division for use to the West within the Baghdad Pact area." Robert McMahon, who assumes strategic motives for U.S. policy toward the region, nevertheless admits: "One searches through the voluminous American planning documents in vain for a more concrete explanation of the role that Pakistan was expected to play in the containment of Soviet influence and power, in war or in peace." That Pakistani air bases were highly desirable to the United States is not in doubt, but to argue that obtaining them was the main purpose of forging an alliance and inducting Pakistan into CENTO is to put the cart before the horse.[42]

To explain the American decision, one must return (at last!) to the twin theses of this chapter, to the argument that U.S. strategy toward South Asia during this period was predicated on history and culture. Instructed by the British, the Americans came to think of the Cold War in Central and South Asia, and in the Middle East, as a reprise of the Great Game. They assumed that the Russians would expand to the south if left unchecked. Like all bright and willful students, the Americans refused to accept their lessons in every detail. The British worried that the application of the "forward strategy," that is, the mobilization of Pakistan, would burden the politically fragile country while antagonizing India, a more valuable strategic asset in the long run. Until 1955, when for reasons of their own they joined the Baghdad Pact, the British therefore sought the return of "masterly inactivity" by the Western powers in the region, the implication of power rather than its projection. The Americans, beginning in 1949, moved fitfully toward military support for Pakistan. They were convinced that a "northern tier" defense was needed, even if it wasn't clear precisely what it was needed against. Shoring up Pakistan would reestablish in the area a strong Western presence missing since the heyday of the raj. It would show resolve and commitment to Muslims, encourage nationalism to shed its communist skin, and give pause to potential invaders from the north—just as the largely Muslim Indian army had done in the second half of the nineteenth century.[43]

The American decision to arm Pakistan was also influenced by culture. Inheriting not only British strategic planning but British stereotypes of South Asians, the Americans convinced themselves that the Hindu men of India were effeminate and thus passive, incapable of standing up to a determined foe. Pakistani Muslim men, by contrast, were tough, courageous, and usefully belligerent. Because Hinduism was polytheistic, its adherents were unable (and unwilling) to distinguish truth from falsehood, right from wrong; theirs was a situational morality that was inappropriate in the polarized atmosphere of the Cold War. Like Christianity and Judaism, Islam was monotheistic, which meant that its followers believed in a single truth. As long as it was the right truth—that the Western nations were good and the Communist bloc evil—the Muslims of Pakistan could be counted on to take a stand in the ideological struggle. I will elaborate on ideas about gender and religion in future chapters.

I am most concerned here with strategic culture, and most immediately with ideas about space. Recall the argument: that Americans tend to view space as an opportunity to explore, to exploit, to do good. The totalization of the Cold War was in some measure a projection of that view. No place was off-limits because there could be no limits. All places were of interest and concern because the imagination of Americans rendered frontiers spaces, not lines. These ideas about space, coupled, after 1945, with the power to actuate them, led logically to a "forward strategy" in South Asia, and everywhere else. There was no need to define a specific threat to the region—to show, for example, that the Russians or Chinese had plans to invade India. Americans brought to their South Asia policy a habit of mind, initiated by the British experience of the first Great Game and blended with a potent cultural tendency, a way of thinking about space that presupposed an assertive foreign policy. The habit was nurtured by the optimistic view that a venture into space would solve problems. When it apparently did not, there was confusion and consternation in Washington.

For all of the difficulties the alliance created for Great Britain, Afghanistan, Pakistan, and the United States, the nation that it outraged was India. Since independence, many Indians had regarded the Americans suspiciously, as the heirs of British imperialism. American sympathy for Pakistan seemed to Indians to confirm the historical pattern of Western favoritism of Muslims. When rumors of U.S. military aid to Pakistan first surfaced in November 1953, Indian politicians and the press reacted with disbelief and anger. The secretary-general of India's Ministry of External Affairs, N. Raghavan Pillai, told the British high commissioner that such an alliance could damage India's relations with the West. "The Americans," he said, "had much to learn[,] particularly in relation to the East. . . . If they persisted in pursuing this policy over Pakistan it would be one of the biggest mistakes they could make." When Vice President Richard Nixon visited on December 2, Nehru cautioned that any Pakistani aggression that followed a military agreement with the United States would inevitably be blamed on the Americans. (Nixon, unmoved, became a strong advocate of Pakistan.) Throughout December, Nehru's Congress Party mobilized huge anti-American demonstrations, and an editorial in the *Times of India* warned that if the military alliance came to fruition "the ultimate and disastrous consequences will be incalculable." The ambassador in New Delhi, George V. Allen, who had opposed military aid for Pakistan, had the task of breaking news of the decision to Nehru on February 24, 1954, the day before it was publicly announced. Nehru reacted calmly, to Allen's relief, not questioning American motives but describing possible negative consequences of the decision. He was sharper before the Lower House of Parliament (Lok Sabha) the next week, declaring that U.S. aid "created a grave situation for us in India and for Asia," and saying pointedly that "India has no intention of surrendering or bartering her freedom for any purpose or under any compulsion whatever."[44]

About a week after the Eisenhower administration announced its intention to ally with Pakistan, a timely cartoon appeared in the *Hindustan Times.* Signed by "Ahmed," it depicts four men on a park bench. Left to right are a rawboned American soldier; a short, swarthy man dressed like a woman and labeled "Pak"; Nehru, who holds on his lap a briefcase containing "Blueprints of lasting peace in Asia"; and a sinister- looking Asian marked "China," reading the *Moscow Observer.* The American's arm is draped over the shoulder of the Pakistani, and the soldier is saying to an obviously unhappy Nehru, "Say, Bud—shove over a bit, will ya!" The Chinese looks on with interest, anticipating Nehru's arrival at his side of the bench.[45]

The cartoon is a comment on space. The bench is South Asia. The American has horned in on it, while the Chinese waits, at leisure, at its far end. By allowing himself to be seduced by the soldier (U.S. military aid), Pakistan has prostituted himself to an outside power and invited war into

The Hindustan Times *cartoonist Ahmed on the U.S.-Pakistan military alliance, 1954. Nehru, and India, will find space increasingly limited.* Hindustan Times.

the region. The misalliance of the United States and Pakistan encroaches on India's reasonably safe space, and will force India to move closer to the Soviet bloc in order to maintain a balance of power in the area. Far from protecting South Asia from communist penetration, U.S. aid to Pakistan will provoke conflict there, drawing the Cold War to the region like filings to a magnet by making Pakistan strong enough to attract the attention of its enemies but not strong enough to resist them. The proposed pact would bring war "right to our doors, to the frontiers of India," Nehru said in early January 1954; after U.S. aid was announced, an Indian diplomat declared that it had "brought [the] Cold War nearer in space and time." As Archibald Nye had written in 1951, India saw itself in world affairs at the center of a series of concentric rings. Beyond its own circle India would confine itself to diplomacy and moral suasion. Within its own circle—concerning, that is, its own autonomy and security—India was as assertive as any nation. "European and some other great countries," Nehru told delegates to the Asian-African Conference at Bandung in April 1955, "have got into the habit of thinking that their quarrels are the world's quarrels and that, therefore, the world must submit to them. I do not follow that reasoning. I do not want anybody to quarrel in Europe, Asia or America, but if the others quarrel, why should I quarrel and why should I be dragged into their quarrels and wars?"[46]

The United States projected its own perceptions of space onto India, seeing the Indian strategic conception as an extension of its own. The Americans assumed that, like them, Indians had global ambitions. Or at least enormous regional ones: according to Loy Henderson, who was U.S. ambassador in New Delhi from 1948 to 1951, Nehru believed "that India as an independent state had inherited a position in Asia roughly equivalent to that of British India; that India had the right and duty to maintain the kind of law and order which it considered to be most advantageous to . . . all of Southern Asia." (It wasn't so, Indian diplomats insisted. As one of them told the skeptical Henderson in April 1948, "India feels that its first task is to develop itself.") When India refused to venture beyond its circle of interest, Westerners wondered what was wrong with it. At the height of the Korean War the Americans and others asked whether "India is really after all very much of a factor in world affairs," and the British undersecretary of state, M. Esler Dening, wrote Nye that "it is very difficult to lay one's hand on one's heart and to say that India shows signs of making a major contribution to the progress of human affairs in these particularly dark and tortuous times." India was not "a rallying point for anything or anybody." Nor could the Americans credit what seemed to them the Indians' absurd sensitivity about foreign influence in their midst. When he tried, for example, to negotiate an aviation agreement with India in the fall of 1954, George Allen attributed his difficulties in doing so to the Indian "inferiority complex" and the "latent xenophobia" that existed "among even the most sophisticated Indians."[47]

The Indians for the most part knew better than to project their own perception that space was threatening onto Westerners, whose history belied this possibility. But projection was not entirely absent from Indian foreign policy thinking. In 1958, Allen recalled a conversation he had with Chakravarti Rajagopalachari, the governor-general of India from 1948 to 1950. Rajaji (as he was known) "twitted" Allen about the ubiquity of the U.S. military. "You Americans," he told Allen, "are an amazing people. For 150 years you were isolationists. Now you've suddenly become interventionists and are intervening all over the world everywhere." Indian analyses of U.S. policy often targeted a richer irony. "What we fear," Indians told Allen, "is that you Americans are not quite aware yourself how deeply, and perhaps inextricably, you are becoming involved. You are not imperialists in the orthodox, nineteenth- century style, but perhaps, without being really aware of it, you have created a new, streamlined version of imperialism." Maybe, "unconsciously or absent-mindedly," and in an effort to contain the Russians, Americans would come to control South Korea, Taiwan, Vietnam, Japan, and the Philippines: "You may intend to leave, but how and when? The pattern of your acts looks disturbingly familiar." When Allen responded that the United States was obliged to respond to communist aggression, Indians pointed out that the only foreign military they saw in Asia was American.[48]

There was a way in which Nehru extended to the great powers, including the United States, the Indian concept of space: maintenance of a sphere of influence more or less contiguous to a country was an acceptable means of self-defense. Just as India demanded no interference with its efforts to absorb colonial enclaves within its borders (princely Hyderabad, French Pondicherry, and Portuguese Goa), to dominate nearby states (Nepal, Burma, Sri Lanka), and most of all to overmatch Pakistan, so was India willing to look the other way when the powers sought to keep control of their own spheres. The Soviet Union's establishment of satellite states next to itself might be regrettable but it was understandable. The Soviets, Nehru thought, wanted "friendly and dependent or semi-dependent countries near" their borders. Nehru's strategic thinking was on vivid display in October 1956, when British, French, and Israeli forces launched an attack on Egypt's Suez, and the Soviets crushed an uprising in Hungary. Nehru condemned the first as a return to colonialism, but on the second he remained quiet for several days, even abstaining on a resolution condemning the Soviet use of force. Eisenhower was dismayed by Nehru's apparent hypocrisy—"It is our duty to mankind," the president wrote Nehru, "not only to bring before world opinion the facts with respect to the deplorable situation in Hungary, but to make it clear that the leaders of free and democratic countries cannot remain silent in the face of such terrifying pressures upon our fellow beings"—but Nehru's reticence was consistent with his geopolitical views, whatever one might think of them. Ultimately, they worked to American advantage. In April 1961 the United States sponsored an abortive invasion of Fidel Castro's Cuba by anticommunist Cuban exiles. The new Kennedy administration, which had authorized the attack, was sharply criticized around the world, but Nehru muted his remarks, noting that the United States had good reason to be concerned with events in Cuba and professing "complete faith" in Kennedy's assurances that no U.S. invasion was contemplated. Ambassador John Kenneth Galbraith, who had arrived in New Delhi just a week before the attack, observed in a letter to the president: "We did not escape unscathed but it was no disaster." Nehru had remained true to his principles.[49]

Nehru's attitude toward China was more complicated. The two nations share a long border, of course. During Nehru's years as prime and foreign minister, China developed into a great power, possessing far more military wherewithal than India and, as events in Korea demonstrated, a willingness to use it. China occupied India's innermost strategic circle as a neighbor, and the outermost as a world power. Nehru's policy toward the People's Republic was mostly predicated on a wish that China would keep to itself. "I don't think that Nehru was ever naive about what was going on in China," recalled Chester Bowles. "He was just hoping and hoping and hoping that the Chinese would let him alone, that they had enough problems in China, and if he had a fair approach to China and did not annoy China, that she would stick with her problems of internal development." What Loy Henderson read in late 1948 as Indian "smugness" at the prospect that China was "destined to disappear for some time as a world force" was in fact wishful thinking. When Donald Kennedy of the South Asia Office wrote two years later that "Mr. Nehru has been trying to persuade himself that the Chinese Communists are merely agrarian reformers . . . who harbor no aggressive intentions," he was right: Nehru hoped it was true.[50]

Nehru sympathized with China's security concerns. He regarded China as a past victim of Western imperialism, like India. The Indians were dismayed when, in 1950, the Chinese sent troops into Tibet to bring the rebellious state—or province, depending on how one looked at it—under central government control. India had quietly encouraged Tibetan autonomy, and the return of Chinese power to Tibet promised to complicate border disputes between China and India. Yet Nehru chose a pragmatic response, simply keeping quiet. "We were inclined to think," recalled K. P. S. Menon, then the foreign secretary, "that the autonomy of Tibet was, at any rate for the last half a century, the outcome of one of those imperialistic forays into China. . . . Now, we thought, we would forget the past when both India and China suffered from imperialism . . . and start afresh." The Indians took a captious tone when Americans challenged their defense of their authoritarian neighbor. K. M. Panikkar, India's ambassador to the PRC, wrote an American official in early 1951 that "the essential fact about New China is that it is not frightened." It had legitimate security needs ("Korea and Vietnam to the Chinese are not mere territorial names"), and a bitter memory of a time when "the mere demonstration of naval might in the Yangtze was sufficient to bring the Chinese to their knees." "A great power has risen in the East, whether you like it or not, and that power is not prepared to be recognised as a great power at the sweet will of other nations," Panikkar declared. "If other nations are to deny to China the position which she claims, then China will fight—and fight like hell."[51]

But India would attempt to placate the Chinese only if its own vital interests seemed not to be at stake. Nehru had always insisted that India's northern border extended to the Himalayas, with the specific boundary having been negotiated by none other than the British imperialists. Because of British involvement, the Chinese never accepted the borders as fixed. There were two areas in dispute. In the northwest were two mountain ranges, the Karakoram and the Kuenlun, and between them a desolate plateau called Aksai Chin ("Desert of White Stones"). In 1873 the British Foreign Office had drawn a boundary along the ridge line of the Karakoram. Twenty-four years later, however, Sir John Ardagh, of the British General Staff, proposed extending the border all the way north to the Kuenlun, thus incorporating Aksai Chin and providing an extended buffer against the Russians. The Chinese resisted this claim, and even British officials in India found it extravagant. But over time, with activity in the area insufficient to force the hand of either side, the British and Indians came to regard Aksai Chin as theirs. In the northeast, the British boundary was drawn in 1913 by Sir Henry McMahon, the foreign secretary of the Indian government. Hoping to separate Tibet from China, which had just embarked on an extended period of political tumult, McMahon proposed a boundary between India and China that ran at several points over a hundred miles north of the existing border. The Tibetans were induced to agree to the adjustment by whispered British promises of help in their quest for autonomy. The Chinese indignantly refused to accept the change. Yet, even more than the Ardagh border in the west, the McMahon Line, despite its provisional status, gained standing in India through its unilateral assertion by the British.

When Zhou Enlai, foreign minister of the People's Republic of China after 1949, approached Nehru to discuss the borders, Nehru, to Zhou's surprise and displeasure, put him off. Nehru staked India's claim to a border in the west that gave India most of the Aksai Chin and to the McMahon Line in the east. In July 1954 he directed, in a secret memo, that "a system of checkposts should be spread along this entire [northern] frontier. More especially, we should have checkposts in such places as might be considered dispute areas." Zhou of course had no knowledge of this statement, and he continued to press for negotiations, any time and any place. The borders, he insisted, had never been legally demarcated. Nehru responded that he would "talk," not negotiate, for (he claimed) there were no real disputes, only boundaries established since time immemorial. Neville Maxwell has characterized this position as " 'What we claim, is ours.' "

In 1959 an ongoing revolt in Tibet intensified. The Dalai Lama fled to India, which harbored him, and the Chinese accused the Indians of granting sanctuary to other "rebels" south of the McMahon Line. There were armed clashes on both frontiers, in which the Indians were bloodied. Meanwhile, China concluded mutually satisfactory boundary negotiations with Burma in 1960 and Pakistan in 1962, evidently without the kind of "bullying" of which Nehru accused the Chinese in their contacts with Indian diplomats. India stiffened its position. Public opinion ran hotly in favor of punishing Chinese "aggression" in the mountains, and the government decided, in November 1961, to establish posts in Aksai Chin and even *north* of the already disputed McMahon Line, up to a place called the Thag La Ridge. The decision ratified what the Indians called, without irony, their "forward policy." In June 1962 an Indian detachment set up a picket on the south bank of the Namka Chu River, within view of Thag La. The officer in charge, evidently worried about the implications of his decision, called the post Dhola, after a pass several miles south of the McMahon Line. This was to be the first stage of an Indian offensive, codenamed Operation Leghorn.

India's adoption of the forward policy was unacceptable to the Chinese. They outfitted seasoned troops with mountain gear and sophisticated weapons, and carefully planned a counterstroke. On the morning of October 10, 1962, the Chinese, in battalion strength, overwhelmed an Indian outpost just northwest of new Dhola. As the mortars crashed down on Indian positions the regional commander, General B. M. Kaul, turned to Brigadier John Dalvi and exclaimed: "Oh my God, you're right, they mean business." Kaul immediately left for New Delhi to brief Nehru on the situation.

The Chinese paused, awaiting a concession, but there was none. Instead, Nehru asserted on October 12 that the Chinese would be evicted from "our territory," though he could not say when. Thus, on the 20th, the Chinese attacked again, pushing south of the McMahon Line, overrunning post after post, thrashing Indian forces who fought bravely but were undersupplied, outmanned, and often badly led. (A smaller Chinese offensive in the west simultaneously pushed the Indians out of Aksai Chin, though here the Indians suffered fewer casualties.) So swift was the Chinese assault that American rifles, which had been rushed to the scene, were captured still in their crates. Indian battalions broke up and scattered; their remnants were killed, captured, or, if they were lucky, escaped to the south. There was panic in Assam, the state adjoining the war zone, and there was panic too in India's cities, where some expected bombing by the Chinese air force. Mao Zedong and Zhou Enlai were burned in effigy, Chinese in New Delhi and Calcutta were set upon by angry mobs, while Japanese diplomats stuck rising sun insignia on their cars so there would be no mistaking their loyalties, and legislators in Punjab turned up for a session in military uniforms. Nehru requested more American arms, though with such excruciating indirection that the Americans weren't certain they had been asked.

Abruptly on November 21, the Chinese halted their advance. They declared a unilateral cease-fire and withdrew their troops to positions twenty kilometers north of what they termed "the illegal McMahon Line." As Maxwell puts it, "China had been engaged not on an invasion of India, but on a giant punitive expedition." The Chinese sought a favorable boundary settlement. As they withdrew, they arranged the return of all materiel captured from the retreating Indian forces, including the crate of American rifles, for which they demanded a receipt. The Chinese got what they wanted from the war: the return of Aksai Chin and the removal of the Indians from the Thag La area. India refused to accept this outcome, and still refuses to accept it.[52]

To those who regarded India as a nonaligned state, devoted at least rhetorically to the pacifism of Mohandas Gandhi and chary of inviting the Cold War into South Asia, Nehru's refusal to negotiate with the Chinese about the northern border seemed at first glance puzzling. One finds an explanation in Archibald Nye's description of India's policy within its innermost strategic circle. Here Indian ambitions were anything but meek. That the northern boundary ran to the Himalayas Indians had no doubt, for it said so in ancient Hindu texts, the Hindu epics *Ramayana* and *Mahabharata*, and much of Hindu literature. (That the Himalayas, the Kuenlun, and Thag La Ridge were coterminous there could also be no doubt.) India was not looking for trouble outside its sphere, but inside its proper place Indian space was inviolable. As I will argue in a later chapter, Nehru found it necessary to represent the people of independent India as a family. He and others had tried to include the Chinese as metaphorical members of the extended clan with the mid-1950s slogan "Hindi-Chini Bhai-Bhai"—"Brother-Brother." The Chinese action, reasonable as it seemed to its perpetrators, and even, in retrospect, to others, was in fact a betrayal of familial trust, a fracturing of what Indians hold most dear. It was no coincidence that during the border war the finance minister, Moraji Desai, urged genetic families to sacrifice for the national family by contributing money and jewelry for defense; "ornaments for armaments," Desai called the campaign.[53]

Convinced of his nation's rectitude, and assuming that the Chinese would in the end heed his logic or at minimum refrain from using force, Nehru was shocked by the Chinese attack. If he did not share the popular view that the Chinese feared the Indian military, he nevertheless felt sure that, somehow, matters on the border would resolve themselves in India's favor. After the war, Nehru ruefully remarked that "we were getting out of touch with reality in the modern world and were living in an artificial atmosphere of our own creation." The border war changed him. He was disabused of the fiction that there existed an Asian solidarity, that China would leave India alone because the two nations had similar histories of injustice at the hands of Westerners. He seemed weary, subdued; fatigue was "etching rings under his deeper set, sadder eyes." Forced by popular outrage to fire Krishna Menon as defense minister, he would never again have a confidant in his cabinet.[54]

Nehru's, and India's, relationship with the United States changed too. President Kennedy wrote Nehru in late October, offering "support as well as sympathy." The Americans were concerned with India's fate, and while they doubted the Chinese would try to conquer India and shied from offering "unqualified support to all of the Indian border claims," they dramatically increased their military aid and agreed to train Indian pilots and to supply mobile radar units to help protect Indian cities. Kennedy told the NSC in May 1963 "that it was obvious we would defend India if [it was] attacked," likening the commitment to India to those to Korea and Thailand. But American support was qualified. The Kennedy administration hoped to use military aid to leverage India into settling the Kashmir conflict with Pakistan. The State Department suggested that a somewhat protracted conflict between China and India might not be a bad thing because it would demand "the absorption of Chinese energies," and in the end, with the dispute over boundaries unresolved, "we would be less likely to hear the Indians plead the Chinese case in the United Nations and elsewhere." Lingering war would also prolong the delightful agony of the Soviet Union, forced to choose between its powerful communist rival and a nonaligned country it had spent years cultivating. And the Americans couldn't help gloating over India's predicament. When an Indian MP, in Washington to lobby for more aid, asked Congressman Wayne Hays about the American attitude toward India at the time of the Chinese attack, Hays replied: "It couldn't happen to a nicer bunch."[55]

In his nation's time of trial, Nehru swallowed some of his pride and with it the gall that accompanied U.S. aid. The two countries' air forces conducted joint training exercises. American U-2 spy planes, engaged in surveillance of Tibet, were allowed to land and refuel in India. In early 1964, Nehru permitted the Americans to attempt to place a nuclear-powered sensor at Nanda Devi, a Himalayan peak, in order to monitor Chinese missile development. But Nehru would not compromise on other issues. He rejected the American effort to bring him around on Kashmir unless the Pakistanis met certain "preconditions." When Ambassador Galbraith tried to discuss this with Nehru, the prime minister "got very angry, shouted and pounded the table," and demanded to know "why we assumed the Pakistanis were right and the Indians wrong." Nothing was settled. Nor was Nehru willing to create a military alliance with the United States. That was going too far, for it would destroy any vestige of non-alignment and acknowledge the arrival of the Cold War in South Asia, impinging on India's modest but precious space—Bharat, the middle of the universe. As arrogantly and desperately as Nehru would defend his version of India's borders, he would never concede that their disposition was an excuse for permanent great power involvement in the region, any more than he would admit the necessity of arming Pakistan against communist encroachment.[56]

In what would be the last eighteen months of his life, Nehru discovered that it was a dangerous world, even if India's ambitions were limited and even if it renounced great power conflict. India may not have been interested in the Great Game, old or new, but the Game was interested in India. By 1963, space had proved threatening, constantly contracting in volume, and thereby offering less and less room to a country seeking safe withdrawal.

2

Economics: Trade, Aid, and Development

An economic system, like a nation or religion, lives not by bread alone, but by beliefs, visions, daydreams as well, and these may be no less vital to it for being erroneous.
—V. G. Kiernan, *America: The New Imperialism*

Time, in my experience, has been as variable and inconstant as Bombay's electric power supply. Just telephone the speaking clock if you don't believe me—tied to electricity, it's usually a few hours wrong. Unless we're the ones who are wrong . . . no people whose word for "yesterday" is the same as their word for "tomorrow" can be said to have a firm grip on the time.
—Salman Rushdie, *Midnight's Children*

Visitors to the southwest coast of India, which stretches from the town of Quilon to Kanyakumari at the country's southern tip, are often struck by the color and quality of the sand on the beaches. Much of it is fine and glows golden in the sun. The gold is speckled with patches of coarse, black sand, dramatic by contrast. According to a local myth, the colorful sands are the result of a divine marriage foiled. The god Shiva had announced that he would marry the virgin goddess Kanyakumari. This disturbed the other gods, who believed that if the goddess lost her virginity she would also lose her ability to battle demons. The gods urged Shiva to reconsider, but he dismissed their concerns and set off for a midnight wedding with his lover. To disrupt the proceedings one of the gods turned himself into a rooster and crowed as if to herald the dawn. Shiva, fooled into thinking that he had missed his rendezvous, turned back, leaving his bride at the altar. Kanyakumari waited until dawn, and when her groom failed to show up she cursed her colorful wedding feast and scattered it across the beach, turning it to crushed seashells and gold-black sand.[1]

There is, regrettably, also a scientific explanation for the colors of these Travancore sands. The black sand contains ilmenite, which holds 55–60 percent titanium oxide, a valuable ingredient in paint and a substance widely used in weapons production. The golden hue of the other sand indicates the presence of monazite, a phosphate containing a rare earth element called cerium—used to make high-grade abrasives and illuminating arcs for searchlights—and thorium oxide, which is used in gas mantle lanterns found throughout South Asia. More important, thorium has the atomic number 90 and an atomic weight of 232.1; it is two steps down the periodic table from uranium, and like uranium it is radioactive. From the mid-1940s to the mid-1950s, Western scientists and policymakers believed that uranium was a rare commodity and that thorium might be a substitute for it in the manufacture of atomic bombs. The monazite sands of southern India held a greater concentration of thorium than any others in the world, so their fate was a subject of great interest in any number of countries.[2]

This chapter describes the economic relationship between the United States and India from 1947 to 1964. Like the other chapters in this book it does its job selectively and episodically, taking from a complicated history of economic relations a few examples that seem illustrative of the whole. There are more systematic studies of United States–India economic relations. None of them, however, begin with a discussion of a South Indian religious myth, and that should offer a clue—if readers still needed one—to the way in which this book treats the subject of economics.[3]

Economics, like strategy, would seem to be a reasonably straightforward matter: it is the production, distribution, and use of income, wealth, and commodities. There were three economic elements in United States–India relations during the Nehru years: trade—the exchange of goods and services between countries; aid for India from the U.S. government; and investment in India by private companies based in the United States. All three of these involved reciprocity. Even in its aid programs the United States was not engaged in charity, and far less so in its efforts to encourage trade and investment. From the economic relationship the Americans sought material benefits, including the procurement of scarce raw materials and a profitable return on loans and investments. The Indians also hoped for material benefits: freedom from hunger and overall improvement in agricultural productivity, industrial growth, a higher per capita income, a stable currency, and so forth. All of these desiderata could be quantified.

But something renders impossible a strict, cost-benefit analysis of American-Indian economic relations: economics is a cultural system. Economics, the domain of the material, is at the same time an element of political culture, like strategy a filament in a web of significance. It is possible to measure how much monazite one nation sold to another, how much the buying nation paid for the shipment, and how the transaction affected each nation's overall balance of trade. One cannot so easily measure the thinking that went on in both countries during the negotiation of the purchase. But one can assume that how the negotiators behaved toward each other, or how at least they perceived each other's behavior, shaped the results of their talks. At the core of Americans' and Indians' perceptions of each other as economic men and women was a collection of images, drawn from history and personal contact. To be sure, policymakers were concerned about access to raw materials and rates of return and yield per hectare of land. As they thought about these material matters, however, the images they held of their counterparts as economic actors inevitably influenced their calculations.[4]

American Ideas about the Cultural Obstacles to India's Development

Western thinking about India as an economy began with the belief that India was a vast treasure-house, a land of precious metals and priceless gems. Fabulous India contained the cave of Ali Baba, Aladdin's lamp, the world's largest diamond, buildings (like the Taj Mahal) studded with jewels, and even the enormous ruby affixed nonchalantly to the head of Bibi in Walt Disney's *Little Lost Elephant.* Because of these marvels, wrote Hegel, "from the most ancient times downwards, all nations have directed their wishes and longings to gaining access to the treasures" of India. Longings were never enough. Westerners claimed that Indians stubbornly refused to yield up much of their wealth: they were (it was said) hoarders of the first magnitude. Wealthy Indian princes refused to buy, sell, or swap their valuables, preferring to let them lie idle while they lived parallel lives of indolence. In 1927 the American trade commissioner in Bombay complained: "Vast reserves have been accumulated . . . estimated as amounting to more than five billion dollars—but they have been jealously hoarded in the form of unproductive precious metals. . . . The traditional wealth of the Indies is there, but in such a form that it yields nothing to its possessors." India's gold—40 percent of the world's annual production—was never coined; its huge supply of silver was put only to "ornamental uses." Americans eager to put all this wealth into circulation fantasized about stealing it, and this became the theme of scores of stories and films about India. Western thieves were performing the important service of liberating captive riches from the clutches of skinflint princes, and they were depicted as heroes or, at worst, lovable rogues. This perception carried over into official discourse. In October 1950, Elbert Mathews, director of the State Department's Office of South Asian Affairs, despaired that India lacked the capacity for significant capital formation because "indigenous savings are traditionally solidified in land or precious metals and jewels." The United States therefore had no choice but to allow India to acquire capital from "extra-regional sources."[5]

Westerners also claimed that Indians were lazy by nature. This became particularly evident when Indian workers were compared to Chinese. "The Chinese is active, industrious, enterprising, and independent—the native of India idle, living only for the day, never wishing or hoping to change his conditions, always irretrievably in debt, and never able to work without a master," Robert Minturn observed in 1857.[6] A half century later, Katherine Mayo echoed these conclusions about Indians. "The masses," she wrote, showed "little ambition" to improve their lives:

> Their minds as a rule do not turn to the accumulation of things. They are content with their mud huts. Given windows and chimneys, they stop them up. Given ample space, they crowd into a closet. Rather than keep the house in repair, they let the rains wash it away, building a new one when the old is gone. Rather than work harder for more food, they prefer their ancient measure of leisure and just enough food for the day.[7]

The stereotype of the idle Indian persisted after 1947. Philip Jessup, President Truman's ambassador-at-large, once asked an Indian official to confirm that "the Indian worked only as long as it was necessary to earn a sum sufficient for his immediate needs." A British official concluded blandly in 1949 that "the average Indian does not work very hard." In July 1961, President Kennedy's ambassador to India, John Kenneth Galbraith, arrived for a visit in the southern Indian city of Madras. He recorded the event in his diary: "Municipal employees gathered by the hundreds to see me come and go. The damage to public business may not have been irreparable. In India, the difference between working and not working is not always decisive."[8]

Indians may have been hoarders and slothful according to Westerners, but those among them who did seek economic contact were notorious for their cunning, their dishonesty, and their insistence on tortuous bargaining. Nineteenth-century American consuls in Indian ports, men responsi-

ble for looking after U.S. commercial interests, blamed the sharp practices of local merchants for American traders' general lack of success in
the country. Indians in business shunned free enterprise and tended to
conspiracy. Robert Minturn noted that nearly all Westerners looked down
upon the Jew "as the embodiment of the lowest and most absorbing from
of avarice." In India, however, the Jew was "nowhere. . . . In every department of business . . . he is completely beaten out of the field."[9]

By the Cold War decades, these images of Indian merchants had been
translated into more benign language, but were no less tenacious for that.
Indians were fond of "oriental bargaining" and were "extremely shrewd in
negotiations." Eugene Braderman, the acting director of the Far Eastern
Division of the Commerce Department, described in early 1953 "the nature of business" in India. Businessmen, he wrote, "ordinarily enter into
agreement only after protracted negotiations have resulted in the best
possible agreement." There was little that was predictable about doing
business with Indians. Everything was "personal" or "individual," and
there was no "common standard among businessmen in India as to what
constitutes ethical and unethical business practices"—*caveat emptor*. Indian merchants abroad, especially in Africa and Southeast Asia, had repu-
tations for greed and unscrupulousness that fit closely with Western constructions of them.[10]

In the years after 1945, Western economists came increasingly to evaluate nations according to their level of development. A nation was "developed" if it was industrialized and had extensive trade with other nations.
A nation was "undeveloped" or (more charitably) "underdeveloped" or
(more charitably still) "developing" if it had not *yet* achieved developed
status—if its resources were insufficiently exploited, if its industrial base
was limited, and if it traded only fitfully. Economists assumed that all nations would follow the same path to development. It was universally desirable to industrialize, to increase productivity and the size and diversity of
the economy through trade. Economists thought of themselves as psychologists and the nations they studied as children or patients. Raymond
Williams has noted "the parallel sense of *development* and *developmental* in
psychology, describing processes of 'growing-up.' " Like a fully developed
person, a developed economy is described as "mature." An "underdeveloped" economy is by contrast "immature," "backward," or even "retarded." If industrialization is "a natural state to be reached," as George
Lakoff has written, then "underdeveloped" countries become "immature
children, to be taught how to develop properly or disciplined if they get
out of line." The economies of "underdeveloped" states and the people in
them had some growing up to do.[11]

Metaphors of maturity connected economics to psychology, and conditioned Indo-American economic relations. Understand how a child becomes an adult, and you will understand how an economy of struggling farmers will grow into a modern, industrial one. In the nineteenth century, the people of India were not yet ready, by American standards, to mature. They were "children of the soil," as the U.S. consul in Calcutta wrote in 1882, children most assuredly because they were dependent on the products of the earth and on Great Britain, a mature mother country, to sustain them. Over seventy years later, the National Security Council thought it unlikely that India was ready to become an adult. The newly independent nation was threatening to fly apart because of the imposition of "western ideas, religious beliefs, moral values, and productivity upon the folkways and mores of a society in which the masses are plodding, illiterate, sub-marginal farmers." The NSC's skepticism was not shared, however, by the MIT economists Walt W. Rostow and Max Millikan. In 1957 the two men published a short book called *A Proposal: Key to an Effective Foreign Policy*. Anticipating by three years Rostow's famous "stages of growth" argument, *A Proposal* contended that nations needed assistance to nudge them along toward the desirable goal of development. The book became a primer on development for Massachusetts senator John F. Kennedy, who in 1958 cosponsored a resolution to provide India with extensive U.S. economic aid. Along with Rostow and Millikan, Kennedy believed that by the late 1950s India was an adolescent nation; it had reached the point of "take-off" and was therefore on the verge of economic maturity.[12]

But that was not the whole story. While India was a young state with an underdeveloped economy, its new structures rested on the foundation of an old civilization. India was, therefore, at once callow and decrepit, both very young and terribly old. American statesmen were frank about the schizophrenic nature of India's state of maturity. After a visit to India in December 1959, President Dwight Eisenhower said good-bye in a broadcast over All India Radio: "You are a very old civilization, with an ancient tradition and culture. We are a young country. . . . But, in another sense, in the sense of your independent nationhood, you too are young." Ambassador Galbraith made his grand statement on comparative maturity when he arrived in India in April 1961. "It is a privilege," he said, "to be for a few years an interpreter between the oldest of the great democracies and the youngest and between the young and mercurial culture of the United States and the old and stable culture of India. We have heard often in these last years of the underdeveloped countries. As regards economic matters, the phrase has meaning. But economic and cultural development need to be sharply distinguished. We need always to remind ourselves that some countries which have far to go in economic development have come far in their larger knowledge of man and life. I have come to such a country."[13]

Eisenhower's and Galbraith's assessments of India's development were by no means negative, and this point will be taken up further on. And yet, there is something condescending about depicting a society as old, as if its glories were attached to a civilization long past. For many years, Westerners coming to the study of India for the first time were handed A. L. Basham's *The Wonder That Was India*, a title that was equal parts reverence and lamentation. India *was* marvelous once, but it was now played out. Westerners described India and its people in language that evoked old age. People in India could not think straight, and could not move logically from one point to another. They were disorderly: "My observation of the turbulent and challenging scene in that old, old country," wrote a historian who lectured in India in 1946, "made me realize with a start that youthful America is a fairly orderly, settled country." The land itself was tired from overuse. Elbert Mathews told a television audience in 1951 that "Indians were crowded into an old country which is striving to produce enough food" for its huge population and was so far failing to do so. Yet this failure might not matter: India, wrote Marie Buck during a drought in 1952, "is so old, and famine and devastating epedemics [sic] so frequently her lot, this is just one more to be stoically endured." Eternal India! Though its history was "blotted with famine . . . always it has endured. A heritage of courage and hope has come down through the centuries of trial."[14]

Like the teeth of an old person, India's economic infrastructure was rotting or decayed; like an octogenarian's joints the bureaucracy was ossified. Hindu minds moved slowly, and Indians were poor listeners, subject, a high-ranking American official claimed, to "a fixed pattern of thought somewhat removed from the realities of the situation." Old civilizations, like old people, had difficulty changing their minds. Their complexes were also of long standing. Responding to a 1950 analysis of Indian opinions critical of the United States provided by Ambassador Loy Henderson, Secretary of State Dean Acheson wrote that the department "believes attitudes you have described have been latent and submerged for a n[umbe]r of years.[15]

Sometimes descriptors of India-the-old applied as well to India-the-new. Like the elderly, for example, young children lack control of the excretory function, which could explain the alarming amount of human feces found on India's streets. Children are no more organized in their thinking than are old people, and both can be emotional and naive. The inefficiency of India, commented on by many Westerners in the nineteenth and twentieth centuries, could be attributed to a society so aged that it could no longer keep track of things, or a state so young that it hadn't yet learned to do things precisely and punctually.[16]

Of relevance here is the Indian concept of time. It may be true that the very old are less concerned than others about punctuality, the need to be places (like work) by a certain time. But in focusing on Indian perceptions of time and the Western understanding of those perceptions, we are really confronting stereotypes of Indians as children. For children, more than other humans, utterly lack interest in time, and the way most Indians regarded time and handled numbers more generally reinforced Western views that Indians were children.[17]

There are differences between modern Western and Hindu understandings of time. For Westerners time is linear, moving inexorably forward from the past and bearing with it human progress. As moderns, Westerners believe in what Mircea Eliade called "the irreversibility of events"—things happen, and time marches on. Time is also a commodity, an item to be valued and a currency to be used prudently: time is money, time is spent, time is budgeted but sometimes runs out. In Hindu cosmology time runs not along a line but in cycles, and it is ahistorical in Western terms. Time is not a commodity that can be used up or exchanged for something else. While Westerners believe in "consistency, regularity, and integration," Hindus inhabit a world of elements and "essences" (*guna*) that are liquid. Time is fluid; it flows through a universe that is itself characterized by flux. For that reason, according to G. Morris Carstairs, "punctuality and precision" are "wholly foreign to village life" in India.[18]

It is unlikely that American and Indian foreign policymakers ever undertook even such a rudimentary excursus into the subject of time. Possibly they had no need to. Gandhi and Nehru, for example, were hardly representatives of what Eliade termed "archaic societies." The Mahatma was very careful about time, and one of the few objects he owned at the time of his death was a watch. Nehru kept appointments. And yet, Western discourse on India highlighted the imprecision of Indians about numbers, their faith in astrology, and their overall lack of respect for time as a precious commodity not to be wasted. Hindus "take no thought for the morrow," wrote the Abbé J. A. Dubois. Indians could never properly estimate distances or the time it took to cover them, Hindus had no sense of history, and there was no Hindi word for "punctuality." On his way to India in 1909, Price Collier reflected on his departure from a comprehensible, Western universe: "It is already becoming evident that many things that I have considered of fundamental importance have no significance here at all. All the clocks and yardsticks, and weights and measures are different, or do not exist at all. We are going into a world where the best of us, no matter what our education and experience, can only grope about." The nonfunctional timepiece was for Westerners both a metaphorical device used to represent Indians' apparent disdain for time and an actual object, the inaccuracy of which Westerners felt acutely in India. Western watches often break down in the Indian climate, and Indian-made watches bought to replace them are notorious among Indians and Americans for their erratic behavior.[19] For Westerners, the abuse of time or timepieces characterized Indians and children. Katherine Mayo compared Indian politicians during the 1920s to children playing with a watch:

> An outsider sitting through sessions of Indian legislatures . . . somehow comes to feel like one observing a roomful of small and rather mischievous children who by accident have got hold of a magnificent watch. They fight and scramble to thrust their fingers into it, to pull off a wheel or two, to play with the mainspring, to pick out the jewels. They have no apparent understanding of the worth of the mechanism, still less of the value of time. And when the teacher tries to explain to them how to wind their toy up, they shriek and grimace in fretful impatience and stuff their butterscotch into the works.[20]

Making children of others over whom one wishes to rule is a feature of colonialism, and it intersects with cultural filaments of race and gender that are also put to the purposes of control. Westerners claimed that dark-skinned others were intellectually incapable of self-rule, and that women or effeminate men were flighty and helpless and needed the protection and stability that only they could provide. Children were naive, impetuous, quarrelsome, physically and emotionally immature, and unable to manage tasks (like trade) requiring numbers, because their thinking was not linear and they failed to understand time. As Ashis Nandy has argued, colonialists projected their post-Enlightenment ideas about individual maturation onto other societies that were supposedly more primitive than theirs. The lack of progress of individuals became a way to explain inadequacies of less "developed" cultures. "What was childlikeness of the child and childishness of immature adults," Nandy concludes, "now also became the lovable and unlovable savagery of primitives and the primitivism of subject societies." Colonialism and imperialism were construed as positive goods because they led to the tutelage, guidance, and discipline of young pupils by mature teachers. The British in India believed this. "Never forget," wrote Rudyard Kipling (with his usual irony), "that unless the outward and visible signs of Our Authority are always before a native he is as incapable as a child of understanding what authority means, or where he is in danger of disobeying it." The efforts by the British to bring about a settlement between Muslims and Hindus prior to granting them independence was described by the viceroy as an "attempt to induce the children to play together." Americans used similar language to rationalize their empire. Filipinos, Latin Americans, and Vietnamese were "babies of the jungle" or "children," and not always of wholesome parentage. They needed United States help to achieve political and economic maturity.[21]

The Western view of Indians as children did not disappear with the independence of India and Pakistan in 1947. The vast majority of Indians were farmers who remained as dependent on the land as their ancestors had been. Westerners claimed that the rulers of Indian princely states behaved like spoiled children. Westerners also depicted India's political leaders as immature. In the days before independence, Westerners dismissed Congress Party demands for liberation because (they said) Indians were not yet mature enough to handle freedom. Mahatma Gandhi's simple *dhoti* became a diaper in Western representations. A 1932 cartoon in a Pittsburgh newspaper showed John Bull, dressed in a nightshirt and clearly at wit's end, holding Gandhi by the back of his diaper and "walking the floor again"; Gandhi clutches the nipple of a bottle of goat's milk while a cradle marked "India" rocks nearby.[22]

U.S. officials considered prime minister Jawaharlal Nehru insufficiently mature to lead a great nation. Writing for Secretary of State George Marshall prior to Marshall's meeting with Nehru in October 1948, Joseph Satterthwaite, head of the State Department's Bureau of Near East and South Asian Affairs, explained that India's foreign policy was "indicative of its political and international immaturity and a feeling of self-righteousness," characteristics that were "shared and epitomized by Prime Minister Nehru." Ambassador Loy Henderson had an idea for Nehru's first visit to the United States in the fall of 1949: if "some Indian tribe could make him 'Big Chief' with feather bonnet and take appropriate photographs and if in some western town a group of cowboys—or dudes dressed like cowboys—could present him with a ten-gallon hat and chaparejos and put him on a calico pony, he might be really pleased. With all his complexity," Henderson concluded, Nehru "still has in him the makings of a small boy." The following February, the Nehru visit having occurred without the Saturday matinee theatrics, Henderson seemed less charmed by the prime minister's boyishness. He wrote to Secretary of

Walking the Floor Again
—Hungerford in the *Pittsburgh Post-Gazette*.

1932

The British are at wit's end with Indian nationalism, and especially with its leader. Gandhi is both infantile and superannuated in this 1932 cartoon. Harold R. Isaacs, Scratches on Our Minds: American Images of China and India, 1980 edition. Reprinted with permission from M. E. Sharpe, Inc. Publisher, Armonk, N.Y. 10504.

State Acheson that Nehru was "vain and immature. . . . Indian leaders, particularly Nehru, have been cajoled and treated as spoiled children so long by other members of the Commonwealth that they have tendencies to become outraged when they encounter opposition on the part of Western countries to any of their cherished schemes. They must eventually become sufficiently adult to recognize that disagreements of this character are an inescapable part of international life."[23]

Advice given Western governments by their representatives in India was predicated on the view that Nehru and India lacked maturity. Be firm but gentle in explaining U.S. policies to Indians, because the Indian government was "inexperienced" and the country "politically immature," which led to "inordinate sensitivity and suspicion" on the part of Indian leaders. Indians were "childish," "spiteful," and "excitable"; a U.S. Senator recently returned from India and several other Asian countries decided that some nations were "not mature enough for the responsibility of complete freedom." Chester Bowles, who served as ambassador in New Delhi from 1951 to the early spring of 1953, got along well with Nehru and wrote sympathetically and perceptively about India. But Bowles, too, accepted the argument that India was immature, and thus urged patience on the Truman administration: "We should never assume that this part of the world will act logically or reasonably. On the contrary, we should be prepared for the fact that on a short-term basis it will often act emotionally and sometimes irresponsibly. We must be mature enough to reject the 'tit-for-tat' kind of reaction which could only make the situation worse." This was shrewd advice, even if its rationale was unsound. It was, in any case, rarely heeded.[24]

Indians and Cultural Obstacles to Economic Understanding

The construction of economic others, of culture-bound images of foreigners, was a bilateral process. Indians, too, generalized about Americans as economic actors: Americans were allegedly greedy and materialistic, which led them to a number of behavioral excesses. And Indians saw Americans as immature. India lacked the power to act on these perceptions. But the images nevertheless complicated economic relations between the two countries, assuring that issues surrounding trade, aid, and investment would be far more troubled than policymakers in both nations would have hoped.

There was a popular American comic strip during the 1950s called "Elmer." Written and illustrated by Doc Winner, "Elmer" was widely syndicated, and one of the places it appeared was the *Hindustan Times*, published in New Delhi. Elmer was an impetuous boy, perhaps twelve years old, who had a fondness for get-rich-quick schemes. In a strip that ran in the *Times* on January 3, 1954, Elmer sells his dog, Spot, for a dollar, which he spends immediately on four ice cream sodas. Once the sodas are gone, however, Elmer has second thoughts—"Crim-a-neutlies!! Mebbe I shouldn't have sold him"—and he cries remorsefully: "Oh, boo-hooo! He's gone and for a measly dollar!" But Spot escapes his new owner and runs back to Elmer, who is overjoyed to see him. In the last panel of the strip, Elmer ties his dog to a peg under a sign reading, "Dog for Sale—$1.00 or best offer." "You're worth your weight in gold baby," Elmer tells Spot, "so long as you keep coming back."[25]

"Elmer" was created for an American audience, but the Indian editor who chose the strip knew what his readers expected. Indians commented frequently on American materialism. Educated Indians in the 1950s and early 1960s accused Americans of "brash materialism, fabulous luxury, [and] softness;" Americans coveted "bikinis, . . . television sets, giant automobiles, machines, and gadgets." The death of Henry Ford brought a dismissive obituary in the *Indian News Chronicle.* "As a pioneer in the field of mass production he virtually revolutionized modern industry, but this is hardly an achievement which will establish for anyone a claim to immortality." It was the alleged American pursuit of wealth without regard for status that particularly amused Indians, who if given a choice between the two tended to prefer the latter.[26] The *Times of India* shared with its readers a famous American joke:

> "My family can trace its ancestry back to William the Conqueror," said one American to another.
> "Next you'll be telling me that they came over with Columbus."
> "Certainly not! My people had a boat of their own!"[27]

Prime Minister Nehru liked some Americans, but throughout his life he remained convinced that Americans were "imperialist materialists" who "think they can buy up countries and continents." Nehru worried publicly about the effect of wealth on the values of ordinary Indians. American capitalists were dreadful role models. Nehru, Loy Henderson explained to Dean Acheson in early 1949, believed that the United States "was an overgrown, blundering, uncultured and somewhat crass nation, and that Americans in general were an ill-mannered and immature people, more interested in such toys as could be produced by modern technique and in satisfaction of their creature comforts than in endeavoring understanding great moral and social trends of this age." (Years later, Henderson clung to his assessment of the prime minister. He wrote that Nehru had been contemptuous of American "commercial mindedness" and thought Americans "a vulgar lot too deeply interested in making money as the key to success.") In October 1949, Nehru told a New York audience: "You will not expect me to say that I admire everything that I find here in the United States. I do not. The United States has got a reputation abroad . . . of being materialistic and of being tough in matters of money." George V. Allen, who succeeded Bowles as ambassador in 1953, observed that Nehru was "instinctively opposed" to "private businessmen whom he considers by and large to be tradesmen, money lenders and exploiters. Like his Brahmin forbears, he considers accumulation of large personal wealth to be crude and even wicked."[28]

The materialism, crassness, and boorishness of Americans were blamed by Indians on the immaturity of the United States. (Indians did not believe that the United States was simultaneously old and young, as Americans believed of India.) The "cult of youth" in the United States, claimed Krishnalal Shridharani, made Americans volatile, credulous, and sometimes foolish; ironically, Americans provided Indian fakirs with a better audience than Indians did because "so long as your act gives them a 'kick,' they do not care about the facts." "I am convinced by this time that Americans are very like children," wrote the traveler P. E. Dustoor in 1947. He offered as evidence: "(a) their fondness for sweets and candies . . . ; (b) their infatuation with the comics, the more blood-thirsty the better . . . ; (c) their love of ice-cream and ball-games; (d) their naive worship of film stars; (e) their insatiable curiosity and inquisitiveness; (f) their excessive fondness for gadgets . . . ; (g) their love of . . . first-name-calling and backslapping; (h) their passion for bright colours, with red predominant, and their abandonment to the craziest of ties and polychromatic shirts." American childishness seemed to be reflected in U.S. foreign policy. The Korean War appeared to Indians to be an example of this, especially when the involvement of Chinese forces in the late fall of 1950 prompted President Truman to say that the United States would use "every weapon we have" to end the war. Clement Attlee, the British prime minister, flew to Washington to try to calm things down, a move applauded by an editorialist for the *Times of India* as necessary "to curb American impetuousity and exuberance. . . . The Korean disaster will continue . . . if the more sober counsels of the Old World fail to check the uncalculating exuberance of the New." An Indian intellectual approved the "moralistic lectures" that Krishna Menon and Nehru gave the Americans on Korea and other subjects, which "seemed to us an appropriate response by members of an older and wiser civilization to the bumbling and fumbling of unsophisticated parvenus who had fortuitously been given great power in the affairs of the world."[29]

Menon and Nehru agreed with this assessment of American immaturity. Menon confided to the British high commissioner in India in late 1953 that the Indians would have to "make allowances" for U.S. policy in South Asia because the Americans were "naive, impulsive and inexperienced" and would therefore make mistakes. Nehru called the Americans "naive," "lacking in intelligence," "immature," and "very impatient." "It is only their money and their power that carries them through, not their intelligence or any other quality," he declared. As he told a British reporter, "what can we do but wait for America to grow up?"[30]

We are faced—not for the first nor the last time in this book—with a seemingly logical conclusion: given the negative images Americans and Indians made of each other as economic men and women, cooperation between the two peoples in economic matters should have been impossible. Indians, according to Americans, were slothful hoarders of wealth and manipulative businessmen, the representatives of a spent civilization and an unruly, immature state. Americans, claimed Indians, were unlettered boors intent only on making money, the undisciplined offspring of a society with no respect for history and one that managed to combine naiveté and hubris in equal measure. The two peoples ought to have scorned and despised each other. And yet, while problems and misunderstandings troubled United States–India economic relations, during the period 1947–1964 American trade with India grew and United States aid for and investment in India increased. How could this have happened?

There are two answers. The first is that each side's construction of the other corresponded to some extent to what we may gingerly call "reality." The Hindu concept of time, for example, differs from the Western one. American newspapers have astrology columns, and some readers may take them seriously. But no American paper devotes a whole page to astrology, as does the *Times of India,* and it is unlikely that any American astrologer would advise against selling for an entire week, as a *Times* columnist did for the week of May 21, 1950. The relentlessness with which Americans equate time with money makes it hard to deny that Indians are to some extent right about Americans' materialism. The leading exponent of the theory that India was at once old and young was Jawaharlal Nehru himself. In letters to his close American friend Frances Gunther, Nehru praised the "vitality" of Gunther's epistolary style and lamented that his own language was burdened by "thousands of years of tradition" that clung to him like "decadent putrid matter." With the approach of independence the young India emerged alongside the old—there is "something of the sparkle of youth in her eyes"—or *from* the old, as in the words of Nehru's independence eve "Tryst with Destiny" speech: "A moment comes, which comes but rarely in history, when we step out from the old to the new, when an age ends, and when the soul of a nation, long suppressed, finds utterance." Other Indian leaders took up the metaphor. India was "a Baby Dominion . . . an Infant in arms with a [need] for great care and minute nursing;" Indians were people of "immaturity and inexperience" who were still in early 1950 undergoing "growing pains" and inclined to be somewhat "childish." No American official would have quarreled with these self-characterizations. Indeed, they doubtless reinforced the American belief that India was an immature state that needed the wisdom of a more advanced people to help it develop properly.[31]

The second reason why United States–India economic relations were not an unmitigated disaster was that each country's negative image of the other had a positive counterweight. Take hoarding, for example. While holding wealth out of circulation was reprehensible to Americans, it could at the same time be seen as prudent, and might even indicate a determination to invest—depending on where the hoarded wealth was held. The sharp business practices of Indian merchants could be called unscrupulous, but could also be understood as shrewd and enterprising. A British intelligence officer once compared the Brahmin approach to business to that of Yorkshire and Lancashire businessmen, "with an eye always open for the main chance, intensely shrewd, practical, conservative and respectable." (John Kenneth Galbraith was amused to find an "enterprising" street vendor in Delhi wrapping spices in surplus copies of President Kennedy's inaugural address.) Nor did Americans always regard the extreme age and youth of India as a bad thing. Old India was not just ossified India but a place where the tradition of craftsmanship was respected. Young India was foolish and bumptious, perhaps, but it had an admirable exuberance, and in their allegedly childlike qualities the Indians had an innocence that romantically inclined Westerners longed to recapture.[32]

Indian images of America had positive sides, too. The relentless pursuit of wealth was not an ennobling endeavor, but it could be a handy one if it was successful. India needed food and financial help, and rich Americans were best equipped to provide them. While immature Americans were no pleasure to be around, America the youthful could be invigorating to Indians. Swami Vivekananda thought Americans "full of fresh energy and ever ready to welcome anything new." Krishnalal Shridharani associated youth with American "vigor" and "big-heartedness." These redeeming qualities might well be envied and even sought after by a nation hoping to become modern, hoping to round out its identity. Let us see how the culture-shaped images formed by both sides worked in trade, aid, and investment.[33]

Trade

The United States and India have had a long but sporadic history of trade. It began officially on the day after Christmas in 1784, when the American ship *United States* arrived at the east coast port of Pondicherry and "caused much speculation to the inhabitants." Commerce picked up quickly after that. Vessels out of Boston, Salem, and Plymouth carried tobacco, copper, naval stores and pine board to India and returned with tea, sugar, hides, spices, and textiles, especially the prized "blue cloth" dyed with indigo. George Washington sent an American consul to Calcutta in 1792. By 1807, U.S. trade with India was valued at over $4 million, more than twice the value of trade with China. The carrying trade, by which American ships transported Indian goods to third countries, was particularly lucrative until the British largely put a stop to it. By the mid-nineteenth century, Americans were shipping great quantities of New England ice to India—the American "Ice King" Frederick Tudor sold over 80,000 tons of the stuff in 1860—and at century's end kerosene was the new wonder export, most of it sold by Standard Oil, whose employees routinely staffed the consular offices in Madras, Calcutta, and Bombay.[34]

American commercial ambitions in India were at all times constrained by the British, who discriminated against American exports, entangled U.S. merchants in skeins of red tape, and denied American companies the right to search for raw materials. Even before the creation of independent India and Pakistan in August 1947, however, the relative economic positions of the United States and Great Britain in South Asia began to shift. Beginning in 1943, the United States shipped large amounts of war materiel to India to help American, British, and Indian troops fight the Japanese. By the time the war ended, it was clear to many in the British government that India could not be maintained as a colony. The British owed huge sterling debts to their dependencies, with India due £1.4 billion. This, along with the overall weakness of the postwar British economy, undercut British hopes of reestablishing even their economic power in South Asia. The Nehru government's decision to stay in the British Commonwealth gave rise to optimism in London that India would remain loyal to its former masters. But Nehru was not operating on sentiment. "I predict," he said in June 1945, "the gradual decline of British political influence in Asia and the growth of American economic influence." The winds were shifting. "It is naturally our desire to develop friendly relations and contacts with the United States," Nehru wrote. "We are likely to have dealings with them in many spheres of activity, industrial, economic and other."[35]

The Americans did not move immediately to corner the market in India and Pakistan. The United States was far more concerned with events in Europe than with those in South Asia, which was not a Cold War cockpit in 1947. Nor was the United States unsympathetic to the revival of a profitable bilateral relationship between Great Britain and its former South Asian colonies. By the late 1940s, American policymakers had concluded that only world trade would assure the permanent economic recovery of the noncommunist world. The developed nations, particularly those in Western Europe but also Japan, depended on their colonies and former colonies to supply them with food, raw materials, and markets in return for manufactured goods. The CIA noted, in September 1948, that India and Pakistan provided "an important market and a source of raw materials, investment income, and carrying charges for the U.K., thus strengthening the U.K.'s and Western Europe's efforts toward the economic recovery essential to U.S. security." Citing British experience in South Asia and believing for the most part that their interests in the region and those of the British were the same, the Americans allowed themselves to remain for the time being "Great Britain's junior partner," as Robert J. McMahon has written. Between 1948 and 1953, U.S. exports to India averaged $294 million annually, while imports from India averaged just over $260 million. (The comparable figures for Pakistan were $47.5 and $29.6 million.) These were substantial but not enormous figures, and trends in trade were fickle over the six-year period.[36]

Yet there were things that the United States wanted from India, items for the pursuit of which they were unwilling to spare British feelings. These were strategic materials that American policymakers believed vital to the success of the U.S. economy and the defense of the free world. During World War II, the United States had depleted its mineral resources, and policymakers worried that the country would become a "have-not" power in this regard. In July 1946, Congress established a stockpile of strategic materials, to include such substances as copper, lead, zinc, bauxite, and manganese. These items, among others, would be critical to the United States should war come with the Soviet Union. And the Soviets seemed determined to deny the United States the resources it needed to maintain a strong economy. "We must again prepare for a showdown with the forces of totalitarianism and conquest," warned an official. If the Soviets gained control of "the Eurasian Continent," the United States would lose access to raw materials in Africa and Asia. The Truman administration bought up what foreign resources it could, gave the CIA the mandate to protect several vital extraction facilities abroad, and began to use economic aid as a way to inoculate poor countries against communism and, more directly, as currency with which to purchase strategic materials. This policy was continued by President Eisenhower, who encouraged what he liked to call "the exchange of perishables for durables."[37]

Manganese

One of the critical materials in India was manganese. Steelmaking was the backbone of the American economy as it moved off wartime footing after 1945, and steel could not be made without manganese. For many years the United States had imported manganese from India—at the turn of the century manganese rivaled carpets as the leading Indian export to the United States—and what was a satisfactory trade arrangement before 1941 became a serious dependency after the war. There were manganese deposits in the United States and elsewhere, but they produced ore of such low quality that the costs of excavating and refining it were prohibitive. The Soviet Union held vast deposits of high-grade ore, and as late as 1950 the United States bought some of it. This was not, policymakers recognized, a strategically sensible reliance. More and more, the United States turned to India, where the supply and quality of manganese were so great that the ore could be delivered for less than half the cost of refining the inferior domestic product. In 1948 India surpassed the Soviet Union as the United States' chief supplier; by 1952 India provided 35 percent of the manganese used by the United States. "Our steel," an official told a Senate subcommittee, "comes from India (where we get our manganese), and not Pittsburgh."[38]

The Americans went to some lengths to acquire Indian manganese. Policymakers proposed to exchange economic assistance for the ore, a straight barter deal. In the spring of 1951, Truman sent the former ambassador to Brazil William D. Pawley to India to "open negotiations on certain strategic materials of great interest to our Government," including manganese. But obtaining manganese from India was never simple. Exports of the mineral to the United States fluctuated throughout the 1950s, and the Americans could never get all they wanted.[39]

There were two reasons why India's manganese proved elusive, and both confirmed American images of Indians as economic actors. In the first place, the Americans believed that India was hoarding its manganese, purposely making it difficult for others to buy it. They charged that the Indian government, despite its professions to the contrary, opposed the development of its extractive industries by foreign capitalists. As of 1949, India required that anyone seeking even to prospect in the country must first be approved by a provincial government, with permission to be granted only to qualified geologists representing firms that were registered or incorporated in India. American officials also noted a split within the Indian government on the matter of selling manganese abroad. Some sought to use the export of manganese as a "bargaining device," designed to ratchet up prices and earn much-needed foreign exchange. That was a tactic worthy of the shrewdest Bombay merchant. On the other hand—and here is where hoarding came in—a number of industrialists, including officials of the powerful Tata Iron and Steel Company, argued that reserves of manganese should remain in India, not be sold abroad. India would establish its own manganese refining industry, the product of which (ferromanganese) would be used in domestic steelmaking. This was hoarding with a purpose, for eventually Indian steel would compete with American, especially in Asian markets. The outcome of this disagreement was a combination of price bargaining and withholding manganese sales, which were not after all incompatible. In late 1948 the Indian ambassador in Washington, Sir Benegal Rama Rau, told Commerce Secretary Charles Sawyer that India's government was placing manganese exports "under control" so that they might bring "the best possible returns in foreign exchange." When Sawyer wondered whether it would not be more sensible "to export as much manganese to the United States as possible," the ambassador replied that, with controls, it was "not possible to export to any one country as easily as it is when no controls exist." It was this sort of logic that later prompted an official in the Eisenhower administration to observe that "the Indians must be taught to sell."[40]

The second cultural inhibitor of India's willingness or ability to sell manganese to the United States was India's advanced age. The country was simply too old to satisfy the requirements of a modern world economy. This image applied in part to the musty government bureaucracy, which made a nightmare of foreigners' efforts to operate within the Indian economy. Worse still was the country's ancient infrastructure, especially its transportation system. Even if Indians had not been sharpsters and hoarders, Westerners asserted, they could not have provided the United States with sufficient manganese because their roads and vehicles, their railroads and rolling stock, were in such terrible shape. Transportation in India was not like it was in the West. Manganese ore, mined by hand, was carried in bullock carts from mines to railheads. There were constant delays on the railroads. The central government allocated scarce freight cars on a weekly basis, making it hard to predict how much space would be available for manganese. There was no standard gauge in India: at state borders, workers unloaded one train and packed its freight onto another, causing "delays and inconveniences," as an American document understated it. Storage facilities in port cities were too small.[41]

What vexed Americans most about this situation was the apparent unwillingness of the Indian government to do anything about it. Prior to his negotiating trip to India in the summer of 1951, William Pawley received a background memo on strategic materials from Harold Linder, of the State Department's Office of Economic Affairs. The problem with transporting India's manganese, Linder wrote, was not so much a shortage of equipment as "the inability of Indian managers to achieve traffic density comparable to American practice. Repair of bad order cars and locomotives takes too long," and Indian workers were "notoriously undependable." While several new track sidings "might be helpful," what India needed more was the "skill to get an average of ten trains per day over the road." It was infuriating that, despite conversations between American and Indian officials in which U.S. assistance was explored, the Indian government "has not suggested any help is necessary or wanted on the railroads." The Indians seemed incapable of understanding the obvious benefits of improved transportation. As a result, it was unlikely that even a price increase for manganese would inspire greater production. India itself, stuck in its premodern ways of thinking and doing things, was the problem.[42]

Monazite

United States–India negotiations over Indian supplies of monazite sands called forth pejorative images of the economic other even more vividly. Recall that monazite, with which India's Travancore coast was richly endowed, contains the radioactive element thorium and a number of rare earths, cerium most prominent among them. By 1945, American officials were very much interested in getting their hands on the world's supply of thorium. Working with the British and the Belgians, General Leslie Groves, head of the Manhattan Engineer District, tried to corner the market in thorium. Uranium was scarce; thorium, Groves wrote, "will be the ultimate means of producing what we are after." During the war, the Germans had obtained thorium in France, and Groves was sure that Soviet physicists were "fully aware" of thorium's value. It was thus imperative that the United States and its friends monopolize fissionable materials. There was thorium in Brazil, a country then susceptible to U.S. influence but one with an unstable government. The biggest prize was India, with deposits many times richer than those in Brazil. "We, the British Empire and ourselves, can get control of the Indian supply at any time," Groves observed confidently.[43]

While Groves fixated on the thorium content of monazite, other U.S. officials contemplated the capture of monazite's rare earths, especially cerium. As a practical matter, no one had used thorium as a fissionable material in 1945, and as it turned out no one ever would. But cerium was essential for the construction of jet engines, which made the element, according to the U.S. Atomic Energy Commission, "of direct and immediate importance to the defense effort." The felt need for thorium would come and go; cerium and other rare earths found in monazite would remain vital to the United States for many years.[44]

India had other plans for its monazite. Atomic energy was a gleam in official eyes at the time of independence. India's immediate need was not fissionable thorium but processed thorium nitrate, needed in the production of the incandescent gas mantles widely used in lanterns throughout South Asia. In the past, India had sold monazite to U.S. firms, which then processed the material and shipped thorium nitrate to Indian mantle companies. This created precisely the kind of relationship that Indians associated with colonialism: the subject nation produced the material of value, the material was refined by the colonialist nation, and the refined material was sold back to the subject nation at an artificially high price. The way out of this cycle of exploitation was for the subject nation to stop selling the material to the colonialist (or neocolonialist) country and then to open its own processing plant. This is what India tried to do. India embargoed monazite in 1948, and the government hoped to contract with a Western concern for a monazite processing plant, to be built somewhere near the sands in Travancore. As refiners of their own strategic mineral, the Indians could avoid importing expensive American thorium nitrate, could sell rare earths like cerium to the Americans and West Europeans, and could develop nuclear power without having to rely on others to provide them with fissionable materials.

The chief Indian negotiator on issues involving nuclear power was Sir S. S. Bhatnagar, secretary in the Department of Scientific Research and member-secretary of the Indian Atomic Energy Commission. Bhatnagar was not particular about which Westerners helped India build its processing plant. He turned first to the British. In early 1947 India and Great Britain agreed that India would sell the British nine thousand tons of monazite over the next three years in return for a British government effort to persuade a private company, Thorium Ltd., to build a processing plant in India, and a British promise to buy all the surplus thorium nitrate produced by the plant in its first five years of operation. Some monazite was shipped to Great Britain, but ultimately the deal fell through. Thorium Ltd. saw no profit in constructing a factory of the size wanted by the Indians, and Indian officials became convinced that the British were leading them on, hoping to acquire all nine thousand tons of monazite and then to back out of the deal. So Bhatnagar tried the Americans. The leading American processor of monazite was the Lindsay Light and Chemical Company, and U.S. government officials urged the firm to take Indian overtures seriously. But this campaign, too, proved fruitless.

The Indians turned finally to a French firm, La Société des Produits Chimiques des Terres Rare (STR). The French were anxious to launch their own atomic program and believed that a special arrangement to buy Indian thorium and rare earths, such as a joint processing plant would provide, would give the effort a boost. The Americans were scornful of the project. Charles Lindsay III of Lindsay Light and Chemical thought the French, like the British, only wanted as much monazite as they could obtain and had no intention of building anything in India, while U.S. Ambassador Loy Henderson warned the Indians that the French atomic energy commission had been infiltrated by communists. The Indians ignored these objections, the project went forward, and in December 1952 Nehru dedicated the French-Indian processing plant at Alwaye, near the port of Cochin on the Travancore coast. The plant could produce 1500 tons of thorium annually.[45]

Needless to say, on the monazite issue the United States and Indian governments were at cross-purposes. The Americans were dismayed at the Indian embargo, for they could hardly expect to monopolize atomic materials if they could not buy monazite at will. Because the United States processed almost all of the thorium nitrate needed by India before 1953, it could strike back: in 1948 the Truman administration embargoed shipments to India. When the Indian government objected, Secretary of State Acheson and Ambassador Henderson, urged on by officials at Lindsay Light and Chemical, were clear about their expectations. The embassy wrote Bhatnagar in December 1950, "informing him that no change in the export policy affecting shipments of thorium nitrate to India from the United States is contemplated for the present and apprising him of the dissatisfaction we feel at the maintenance of the Government of India's embargo of monazite exports to the United States." Henderson hoped that the firm policy would prompt the Indians to treat U.S. concerns more seriously.[46]

Inadvertently but very quickly, Henderson's hopes were fulfilled. By

1951 there was famine in India, and Nehru swallowed his pride and requested American help. Several members of Congress urged that U.S. aid be made contingent on India's willingness to release several strategic materials, including monazite. The State Department seemed to resist this suggestion. Assistant Secretary Jack McFall wrote one Congressman that "it is the Department's belief that the hunger of the Indian population is not a matter with which to bargain, but rather a fact which should be dealt with to the best of our ability on its own merits," and Acheson testified before the Senate Foreign Relations Committee that the United States had all the thorium it currently needed (this was untrue) and that the Indian embargo kept the dangerous element away from the Soviets and Chinese.[47]

The State Department, however, was not above using Congressional disenchantment on the monazite issue to promote U.S. interests. While no department official ever told the Indians that a more flexible position on the embargo was a prerequisite for U.S. aid, neither did the department determinedly dissuade those who sought a quid pro quo. To his disclaimer of bargaining over hunger McFall added: "a humanitarian measure such as this [food aid] would not be without effect on the general political and economic climate in India where our continuing negotiations looking to the increased availability of strategic materials to the United States are being carried out." Virtue need not be its own reward. Indeed, the State Department took an interested view of efforts by others to tie food aid to an end to the monazite embargo. James S. Murray, the assistant to the president at Lindsay Light and Chemical, boasted to State Department officials on March 13, 1951, that he "had been stirring up the present considerable publicity concerning the proposed shipment of wheat to India and India's embargo on monazite shipments." Replying for the department, science adviser R. Gordon Arneson insisted that Murray's campaign gave the public "only half the story." It was, nevertheless, a useful half. Three days later, Arneson, over Acheson's name, wrote about the subject to Loy Henderson in New Delhi. He took note of the Lindsay Company's lobbying and admitted its effectiveness: the department faced criticism for "being too ethical in resisting effort to link monazite with wheat." In Congress, a proposed amendment to the wheat bill would require that India allow the export of strategic materials, including monazite, if it wanted American wheat. The department would resist this "use of starvation as a bargaining counter," in part because its "humanitarian gesture . . . would not be without beneficial effect" in India, and also because the stratagem might backfire and fail to bring in more monazite. Having said that, Arneson wondered whether the embassy might think it propitious to approach the Indian government once more on the monazite issue. James Murray had brazenly told Ambassador Vijayalakshmi Pandit that food aid was being held up because of the monazite embargo, so Nehru himself was doubtless aware of this possibility. Any approach "should of course be on merits of monazite problem alone. However, it may not be inappropriate [to] refer to Department's staunch and continuing resistance to considerable pressure in US for linking monazite to wheat and state that US continues [to be] hopeful that GOI will find it possible soon to permit shipments of monazite to US."[48]

This suggested demarche may have been soft blackmail, but the Indians felt it was blackmail just the same. The administration denied that it sought the linkage of wheat and monazite while nevertheless using Murray's lobbying campaign as a cat's paw to make the Indian government reconsider its embargo. To an extent the stratagem worked, and negotiators tacked toward a compromise. Henderson followed up the Arneson telegram by meeting with Bhatnagar. Henderson said nothing about the troubled wheat bill but focused on the monazite problem, eliciting from Bhatnagar a philippic against Lindsay Light and Chemical. Indian policymakers nevertheless began to yield. On April 3, 1951, Bhatnagar offered to sell the United States small amounts of "monazite derivatives," without specifying what those substances might be. Elbert Mathews, director of the State Department's Office of South Asia Affairs, helpfully pointed out that the end of the monazite embargo need not require the sale of radioactive thorium, since the United States was more interested in buying monazite's rare earths. This clarification of the U.S. position allowed Nehru to save face. Speaking in Parliament on May 10, the prime minister insisted that "it is a fundamental part of our policy that such material as is particularly related to the production of atomic or like weapons should not be supplied by us to foreign countries." That did not mean, however, that India would refuse to sell nonradioactive monazite products to the United States. If American wheat came to India as a loan, raw materials could be used to repay part of it. Satisfied, Congress stripped the food bill of any mention of specific minerals, and the bill finally passed in early June. Truman signed it on the 15th.[49]

There was an apparent burst of goodwill after that. William Pawley went immediately to India and stayed into July, negotiating on monazite and other strategic minerals. He tried to convince the Union Carbon and Carbide corporation to build another monazite processing plant in India, for which Bhatnagar fervently hoped, never mind the French, and the Indians reciprocated by shipping five hundred tons of monazite to the United States, despite the embargo. But discussions soon foundered, and the good feelings dissipated. Union Carbide did not wish to get involved in processing monazite in India, and Lindsay Light and Chemical claimed that it would not buy any of the semiprocessed monazite products of the pending Alwaye plant. The Indians, for their part, injected into the negotiations a request that the United States help build a processing plant for ilmenite, the black sand that shared the Travancore beaches with monazite. This was an unlikely possibility. At the same time, faced with the prospect that the products of the Alwaye plant would have no market in the United States, Indian officials warned that they might look elsewhere, even to communist nations, for buyers.[50]

That was the last thing the United States wanted. In October 1951, Congress approved the Battle Act, requiring the termination of U.S. aid to any country selling embargoed items to communist countries. Thorium nitrate appeared on embargo List A, containing the most strategically sensitive items. No Indian official, least of all Nehru, had ever embraced the Battle Act, but the New Delhi embassy had assured Washington that the Indian government was nevertheless complying with its terms. The situation changed on July 17, 1953, when a Polish freighter left Bombay carrying just over a ton of thorium nitrate, bound for the People's Republic of China. India's finance minister, C. D. Deshmukh, told Ambassador George V. Allen that the thorium shipment had been authorized by Nehru himself because of the changed "international situation"—the armistice in Korea—and, more pointedly, because the United States refused to buy India's thorium nitrate. Nehru himself told Allen "categorically and with some vehemence that India . . . would never submit to derogation of its national sovereignty in permitting United States law to determine with whom and in what commodities India could trade." Allen protested that India understood the provisions of the Battle Act and had under its conditions agreed to accept American aid. Nehru retorted that "India had never agreed to attachment of political strings to aid" and "that he could not accept the conditions of [the] Battle Act as binding on India."[51]

If the Truman administration had used Congressional anger over the monazite embargo to complicate the Wheat Bill in 1951, now the Indians would get their own back against Dwight Eisenhower's State Department. The Indians were taking a chance that the Americans might cut off aid over a ton of misdirected thorium nitrate, but it was not a big chance, for the administration had committed itself to the success of the first Indian five-year plan, and an aid cutoff would have confirmed communist propaganda, both in and outside of India, that U.S. assistance came only with strings attached. The State Department, Battle Act administrator Harold Stassen, and Ambassador Allen decided that the Indian government had not "knowingly permitted" the thorium shipment and thus had not violated the Battle Act. The thorium bound for China was most likely to be used for gas mantles; if it was designated for atomic energy experiments, it was of insufficient quantity to do much harm. The key was to prevent such shipments from happening again. Would India promise to respect the Battle Act in the future? Allen asked Nehru in late August. In response, "Nehru stared at [the] ceiling for [a] full minute, smiled, turned to Ambassador [-designate to Thailand William J.] Donovan, who was present, and asked if he had ever been to Thailand before." And it did happen again: in November, 3328 pounds of thorium nitrate were indirectly shipped to Poland. The purchaser was the British firm Polychemia, which had earlier handled the China consignment. Bhatnagar denied that the sale had been willful, and the Americans, though angry, were grudgingly inclined to agree.[52]

In the end, U.S. policymakers decided that the only way to guarantee that no thorium nitrate would be shipped from India to the communist bloc was to buy it all themselves, placing any surplus in the strategic stockpile. This promised the Indians a predictable and lucrative market, which of course was what they had wanted all along. The American offer, Bhatnagar observed, meant that India "could now deny inconvenient importunities" from communist countries because "no thorium nitrate would be available." The two sides haggled over price—on which more later—the amount of thorium nitrate to be purchased, and its quality, but a commitment was finally made in April 1954 and a contract for 230 tons of thorium nitrate was signed on December 14, 1955. It was a "preclusive" purchase by the United States; while thorium nitrate was no longer very useful to the Americans by the mid-1950s, policymakers were willing to spend over $2 million to keep the substance out of communist hands. The agreement also allowed the United States and India to avoid conflict over possible violations of the Battle Act and thus assured the reasonable safety of Indian aid appropriations.[53]

The history of Indo-American sparring over monazite is partly the story of a great power trying to dominate a postcolonial state. Americans believed almost by instinct in an international division of labor, whereby developed nations did what they did best—manufacturing, refining, and processing—and underdeveloped nations, like India, grew crops and pulled raw materials from the earth. U.S. foreign aid programs, beginning with Truman's Point Four in 1949, had as their premise the improvement of agriculture and extractive industry in Asia and Africa. Sales of raw cotton, oil, monazite, and the like would generate the foreign exchange the poor nations needed to buy goods that were produced more efficiently abroad. Thus, when India decided that it would build its own processing plant for monazite, the Americans reacted with skepticism and scorn. Countries like India were not supposed to refine their own raw materials. The Indians would never get their processing plant running: they were incompetent, and no self-respecting Westerner would help them. (The French, U.S. policymakers believed, had no self-respect.)

India's insistence on processing monazite suggested a stubbornness that defied economic logic. The embargo meant that India was hoarding, refusing to make its mineral wealth available to the world. Congressman Charles J. Kersten, who led the effort to make U.S. food aid contingent on an end to the embargo, saw no reason why the United States should pay for India's food. The Nizam of Hyderabad, he insisted, the "world's champion miser—can put his hands on $500 million in gold bullion and $1.5 billions in jewels without moving out of his palace. . . . Why not order the wheat and send Nizam and some of his fellow princes the tab?" Representative John Rankin jeered that in India "they wear more diamonds than anywhere else in the world," while John Vorys thought the embargo a clear example of Nehru's hypocrisy, which Vorys denigrated in metaphors of age: "Nehru says to us, 'We Indians are a young nation and you should be kind to us and make allowances for our youth.' Then out of the other side of Nehru's mouth: 'You Americans are so adolescent. We Indians are an ancient people with a culture thousands of years old; we had a rich civilization when your ancestors were running around in bearskins. You really ought to revere and venerate the ancient wisdom that comes from us.' "[54]

In American discourse, Indians who were not hoarders were hagglers. Indian business executives were notorious for their sharp practices, especially their efforts to force buyers to pay high prices for their wares. Cheating in the bazaar, it seemed, was readily extrapolated to the international marketplace; buying strategic minerals from an Indian could be as harrowing an experience as buying a carpet or a curio. Loy Henderson explained that the Indians wished to maintain their embargo on monazite and build their own processing plant in order to prevent the accumulation of unrefined monazite abroad and increase the demand for Indian processed monazite products, thereby raising prices. This tactic, coupled with India's implicit threat to sell thorium to the communists, proved successful when the United States agreed to buy thorium nitrate preclusively. Negotiations to do this took over two years to complete, evidently because the Indians kept raising the price. In mid-January 1954, exhausted State Department officials gave in. They would pay India's asking price, an exorbitant $3.50 per pound, "to stop further haggling on price which might also permit GOI to open discussion on other points." The two sides then quibbled for three more months over the amount of thorium nitrate to be sold.[55]

American behavior during the monazite discussions corresponded to long- standing Indian views of the Americans as grasping materialists, uninterested in ethical practices when it came to money and willing to subordinate human concerns to the pursuit of profits. Nehru, Bhatnagar, and other Indian officials failed to distinguish between private U.S. companies and the U.S. government, believing, with some justification, that in matters involving strategic minerals the government served the interests of the corporations. In September 1950, Andrew Corry of the New Delhi embassy probed Bhatnagar on the progress of talks with Union Carbon and Carbide aimed at the construction of a monazite processing plant. Mention of the corporation "set Bhatnagar off." Representatives of U.S. companies, Bhatnagar charged, were "arrogant, interested only in dollars, and unwilling to treat except at arms-length." Corry remonstrated; Bhatnagar must understand that private firms needed to make profits. Bhatnagar agreed, but said he had the "impression that the profit-making side was overshadowing all other considerations in the minds of American businessmen." He added that "Nehru also seemed disposed to form a similar judgment." The machinations of Lindsay Light and Chemical during the Wheat Bill debate were viewed with bitterness by Indian officials. "I do not want that the American companies treat us like poor cousins," Bhatnagar told Corry in the midst of Lindsay's propaganda campaign. And yet when they persisted in doing so, the U.S. government proved all too willing to pressure the Indians to end the embargo of monazite.[56]

Beryl

A similar situation emerged with regard to the mineral beryl and its core element, beryllium. Like cerium, beryllium was useful to the defense industry, particularly as an alloy with copper. Like thorium, beryllium might in theory be used in the production of atomic power: beryllium oxide could be placed in a nuclear pile to slow the reaction. India treated beryl as a strategic commodity, embargoing it, as it had monazite, in 1946.

The Indians were willing to sell some beryl to the United States, under certain conditions. The Indians wanted, at various stages of the discussions, American steel, caustic soda, 0.75 percent of the world's oil production, or a processing plant that would enable the Indians to refine beryl and make beryllium oxide. An agreement was made in 1950, under which India would sell the United States 25 percent of all beryl ore mined in India each year for a five-year period in return for United States help with beryl mining and processing and "certain information and assistance in the atomic energy field."[57]

The arrangement ended in 1955 because beryl seemed less important to U.S. policymakers than it had five years earlier. Like thorium, it never came to much as a constituent of an atomic reaction. Added to this were the frustrations felt by Americans and Indians over each other's behavior during the beryl negotiations. Once again, the Indians seemed to conform to American stereotypes of them. They were hoarding beryl as they hoarded other strategic minerals, and they refused to end their embargo, agreeing only to "relax" it "in exchange for special concessions which they believe they cannot obtain through the regular channels of trade or by normal business procedures," Andrew Corry complained. Cooperation so blatantly had a price for Indians. It was beryl for steel, or oil, or phosphate, or the " 'know-how' in processing beryl and compounds including the 'master alloy' " (with copper), spoken of as if it were the secret of fire. Loy Henderson rendered his judgment on Indian bargaining habits in the midst of negotiations in June 1949. The talks had great symbolic importance. Indian officials, Henderson wrote, "are deeply interested in what the attitude of the United States will eventually be" toward the beryl issue. Will it be "strictly commercial or even of a haggling character, or will it demonstrate a desire on the part of the United States to assist India in its efforts to develop new fields of industry and to aid struggling Indian scientists to stand on their own feet?" Nehru, ever wary of " 'American dollar imperialism,' " remained "mistrustful of American motives." Even while restricting the freedom of his own negotiators, Nehru was planning to blame the Americans if the talks failed to produce an agreement. " 'We told you so,' " Nehru would tell his people. " 'The Americans are not really interested in assisting India. Such aid as they might give us would be only under conditions . . . so onerous that we could meet them only with great difficulty.' "

It was no mystery to Henderson why the Indians saw things this way: they had a child's understanding of international affairs. "With their lack of international experience, and in their ignorance of the ways of the world, they had assumed that the appearance in the family of nations of an independent India would arouse universal sympathy and enthusiasm," prompting offers of aid from nearly everyone. Like a precocious child who finds himself performing before an apathetic audience, India was hurt and "disillusioned" by the West's seeming disinterest in its welfare. When the Indian economy deteriorated, Indian leaders, "accustomed for many years to placing the blame for India's troubles upon foreigners," held the West responsible for their own failures. During the beryl talks, U.S. negotiators had not haggled but had instead proposed a straightforward deal: Indian beryl for American expertise. This was apparently too loaded an offer for the "unbusinesslike" Indian negotiators, especially given Nehru's "suspicions of American imperialism" and his desire not to make "concessions" to it. Henderson urged the State Department to be generous but firm in negotiations. Seek India's "good will," he advised, while refusing to give in to every petulant request. "I feel that it would be bad for the Indians psychologically," Henderson concluded, "if we were to give them something for nothing at a time when they have something which we need and which they could let us have without any great sacrifice on their part."[58]

Henderson's was not a wholly unfriendly sentiment, but it smacked of paternalism in its analysis of Indian psychology. The Americans also felt annoyed at what they saw as haggling by the Indians over the amount and price of beryl to be sold to the United States. The Indians, Henderson told Bhatnagar, had reneged on a hard-won compromise over how much beryl to sell. They quibbled over price, too. When the negotiations began in 1949, the world market price for a ton of beryl was $26. By the time the arrangement was ready for signatures in October 1950, the price, claimed G. S. Bajpai, the secretary general for external affairs, had risen to $35. Henderson asked if Bajpai's observation of this fact meant that India wanted the United States to pay the higher price. Bajpai said no. "He did not wish [to] make any request. He merely wanted attention of U.S. Government brought to change in prices as compared with last year with thought that U.S. Government could decide for itself what would be fair thing to do." This is a style of bargaining familiar to any Westerner who has visited India: an inquiry to a shopkeeper or taxi driver about price often elicits a shrug, and the response: "Pay what you like." The burden of decision is placed on the buyer, who must decide what is fair; a sense of guilt is presumed to prevent a very low offer from being made. (If a low offer is made, it is laughed off.) In the case of beryl, Henderson checked and found that Bajpai had misstated the price, which was in fact $28 a ton, and that was what the United States agreed to pay.[59]

Indian officials saw in the beryl negotiations evidence of American duplicity in economic affairs and materialism overall. At the outset of the discussions in early 1948, the Americans refused to admit that they wanted beryl for the development of atomic energy, claiming instead that the element had only "industrial" applications. The Indians knew this was untrue, and eventually the Americans conceded as much. Again, the Indians failed to distinguish between efforts by private U.S. companies and the U.S. government to obtain beryl. They were confused for good reason, for the U.S. AEC was directly involved in discussions between the Indians and American companies, and officials in the U.S. embassy in New

Delhi lobbied Indian officials on behalf of American corporations, with a determination reminiscent of that shown by the Standard Oil consuls during the 1880s.[60]

U.S. Aid for India

We move next to consider United States aid programs for India in the period 1947–64. This segment can be brief because the subject has been studied by W. W. Rostow, Charles Wolf, and most recently Dennis Merrill, to whose work interested readers are referred. The history of U.S. aid for India—and by that is meant direct financial aid, low-interest loans, technical assistance, and donations or loans of food—was not altogether a chronicle of hostility and recrimination, not just a wrangle between two peoples who disliked each other because of their differences. The United States did not aid India immediately after independence because South Asia was on the periphery of the Cold War. The frontline states in Western Europe, apparently menaced by the Soviet Union (and critical trade partners of the United States), received billions of dollars under the Marshall Plan; there was nothing left for India. The situation changed in 1950, following the communist takeover in China and the eruption of war in Korea. The Cold War had come to Asia, and the Truman administration responded by extending funds to hungry India during the fall of 1950. The following year brought the controversial wheat bill. Struck by the difficulties of convincing lawmakers to help India economically, Truman and his two successors tried to institutionalize an aid program for India. They never quite managed this, but aid nevertheless increased substantially through the 1950s and into the early 1960s. The Agricultural Trade and Assistance Act, approved in 1954 and better known as PL 480, provided India with more than $2 billion in surplus farm commodities between 1956 and 1963. Aid from other government sources also rose throughout the Eisenhower and Kennedy years, reaching a high of over $465 million in 1962. By this time, as Merrill notes, India received more aid from the United States than did any other nation.[61]

For some Americans, the aid was never enough. Chester Bowles protested bitterly when Congress cut proposed appropriations for India, and he was joined at various times by other ambassadors to New Delhi and Adlai Stevenson, Hubert Humphrey, and John F. Kennedy. These advocates for extensive aid argued that an inadequate U.S. response to India's problems would confirm communist claims that the capitalist world was uninterested in the woes of people of color, or simply unable to cope with massive rural poverty. The Indian communist parties would benefit from American neglect: "the situation here can rapidly deteriorate," Bowles warned in September 1952, "and we may find ourselves with a new China on our hands." Truman and Acheson, Eisenhower and Dulles, and those in Congress who endorsed aid to India but in smaller quantities, also made their arguments with reference to the fight against communism. Opponents of aid to India claimed that giving money to Nehru would discourage loyal friends, like the Pakistanis, who had declared for the United States in the Cold War. Nehru was some kind of socialist, the argument ran, so support for his country was implicitly support for an undesirable economic system. In 1962, Democratic Senator Stuart Symington asked, "Where is the logic in providing such multi-billion dollar assistance to a country whose Secretary of Defense [Krishna Menon] constantly attacks us, whose military plans and programs build up the Soviet economy at the expense of our allies and ourselves, and whose chief leaders constantly threaten with military aggression some of the steadfast and loyal friends the United States has in the free world?"[62]

It is no surprise that anticommunism was put to use by policymakers as a rationale for their divergent goals. Indeed, it says a good deal about the limited political vocabulary of the Cold War that men as different as Bowles and Symington invoked the fear and loathing of communism in defense of both giving India millions more and cutting India's aid to the bone. There was something missing from the American-Indian dialogue on aid. Mutual high-handedness was part of the problem. Designing its pitch to Congress for aid to India in 1952, the State Department concluded, "we want India to be stable—to be self-supporting. To do this they will have to 'change their ways.' " The Indians routinely challenged the sincerity of American concern for their welfare.[63]

Americans discussed aid for India using metaphors of maturity. As ever, Americans believed that India was simultaneously too old and too young, at once decrepit and underdeveloped. The traditions, habits, rigid bureaucracy, and ancient infrastructure of India made it difficult for the United States to get economic assistance to those who most needed it. The caste system had been abolished by the Indian constitution, but Americans noted that it remained in place, especially in the villages, and that high-caste Brahmins tried to obstruct the distribution of aid to their alleged social inferiors. Americans also claimed that as a result of caste privilege their aid lined the pockets of government officials and reinforced timeless patterns of nepotism. Some Indian businessmen, wrote Bowles, clung "to the old traditions of monopoly," keeping prices artificially high and wages unconscionably low, despite the influence of U.S. aid. Bowles and others worried that U.S. food aid in particular, off-loaded in major ports like Calcutta and Bombay, would fail to reach the inland villagers who needed it most. The archaic transportation system, the tardy trains and crumbling roads that caused bottlenecks in the selling of manganese, threatened to inhibit the distribution of grain in the countryside.[64]

At the same time, India's government and economy were too young and underdeveloped to absorb large amounts of aid effectively. It took responsible adults to handle money wisely; Indians were "spoiled children," in Loy Henderson's view. It would not be a favor to an immature country to overburden it with assistance. Policymakers in the late 1940s and early 1950s believed that India was not ready for massive outside aid, which would inevitably create a parallel demand for scarce Indian capital and, in the case of Western loans, stretch India's dollar reserves beyond capacity. Some help, of course, was necessary, and advocates of limited aid to India invoked the supposed immaturity of the Indian economy to bolster their arguments. In February 1952, Dean Acheson urged an increase in U.S. aid for India because "the economic resources of South Asia are underdeveloped and the area is industrially and technologically retarded." Five years later, John Foster Dulles still was not sure India was ready for an economic takeoff. "You have to achieve a certain minimum speed to take-off," he cautioned the Senate foreign relations committee. "It would not be prudent to invest our resources in development programs which are too small to offer any hope of eventually achieving a self-sustaining rate of growth." Walt W. Rostow and his colleague Max Millikan were more optimistic. The MIT Center for International Studies (CENIS), founded by Rostow and Millikan, opened an office in New Delhi in 1959, which devoted its energies to India's economic problems. The Indian economy was young, and its architects were overly fond of socialism, but Rostow and Millikan believed that the takeoff was at hand. There was paternalism in their attitude; there was a misplaced faith that all nations behaved according to models fashioned on the banks of the Charles River; and there was, at the same time, enthusiasm for the youthful vigor of India—suggesting, once more, that the metaphors of maturity did not always have negative applications.[65]

United States Investment in India

The U.S. government was willing to provide economic assistance to India after 1950, but policymakers preferred that aid come from private sources in the form of investment. While British capital dominated the Indian economy during the nineteenth and early twentieth centuries, American corporations had not been idle. U.S. oil companies entered India during the late 1800s, and in 1906 the General Electric Company helped finance a dam on the Jhelum River in Kashmir. Following Indian independence U.S. private investment rose steadily, from $27 million in 1949 to $68 million by 1953 and $225 million in 1959, by which time the United States had supplanted Great Britain as India's major source of private capital. American and Indian economists were nevertheless disappointed with the figures. A developing nation as large as India should have attracted more outside money. The government of India tried to improve the climate for investment during the late 1950s, offering foreign investors tax incentives and rebates on the cost of machinery or plants. The government also created the All India Investment Center to "help guide potential investors through the bureaucratic mazes of New Delhi," as an American bureaucrat put it.[66]

Yet "bureaucratic mazes" were precisely the problem, from the standpoint of American investors. Here was old India again, with obstacles strewn in the path toward growth. Reforms designed to make foreign investment easier were undercut by onerous requirements, demands by bureaucrats for bribes, and levies on capital that seemed a throwback to colonial days. The result of these restrictions, concluded Eisenhower's Treasury Secretary Robert Anderson, was "to scare off private investment," and Dulles criticized the Indian government for "their internal condition which impedes the flow of private funds." There were progressive businessmen in India, men like J. R. D. Tata and G. D. Birla, and the Sarabhai textile families of Gujarat state. These progressives succeeded not because of the India system but in spite of it; for experimenting with work incentives and "scientific management" the Sarabhais were thrown out of the Gujarat mill owners' association.[67]

Indian suspicions of American investors limited the flow of U.S. capital to India. There was not much to do about the presence of profit-hungry capitalists on Wall Street, but the Indian government could at least try to curb their influence in Bombay, if not keep them out altogether. In April 1947, Asaf Ali, the first Indian ambassador to the United States, told an audience of businessmen in New York that "the door is wide open for American investment" in India, then listed various conditions and restrictions on the open-door policy. (Quoting Ali extensively, the New York *Times* used the verb "warn" five times in its story on his speech.) "We are anxious to industrialize India as rapidly as possible," Nehru told a U.S. official two weeks later. "But we are equally anxious to prevent any foreign control of Indian industry." What Nehru had in mind became apparent the following year, when Parliament approved the Industrial Resolution. The act stipulated that certain industries—munitions, atomic energy, and railways—would be owned by the government, placed various restrictions on private firms, and set a ceiling of 30 percent on foreign capitalization of enterprises. The various prohibitions of the act seemed to reflect Indian hostility to avaricious Americans. Ambassador Vijayalakshmi Pandit told Dean Acheson that "it was difficult [to] convince Indians [that the] US [was] not trying [to] buy India," and a letter writer to the *Times of India* in late 1953 compared the American to a landlord attempting "to tighten his grip on the village economy." "The PM," an Indian labor leader said of Nehru, "is very sensitive about receiving dollars."[68]

American officials and potential investors saw these Indian attitudes as irrational prejudices. In February 1950, Loy Henderson had a brisk exchange of views on this and other economic issues with Sir Benegal Rama Rau, now director of the Reserve Bank of India. U.S. investors, said Henderson, were "not inclined to come into India" because they doubted they would be "welcome." Recent concessions made by the Indian government were not good enough; "American investors had the impression, probably with considerable justification, that they were not really wanted in India and that those concessions . . . had been granted with reluctance and in the spirit that in this stage of India's economy foreign private investments were perhaps a necessary evil which Indian must tolerate for the time being at least. American investors," Henderson concluded, "were not to be tempted to go into a field where they were likely to be considered as a temporary necessary evil."

Sir Rama, who knew the American scene, made a shrewd reply. He told Henderson that he thought it unlikely that Americans would invest much in India even if his government instituted a more liberal investment policy. Americans had, he said, an automatic "suspicion of the real attitude of India toward foreign investments which could not be removed by mere announcements." The suspicion ran deeper than that: it was the outcome of competing images, ideas bred in the bone about how peoples and nations should behave in economic terms. The Indians, claimed the Americans, were incapable of opening their old-fashioned economy to vital outside capital, and were jealous about their nascent enterprises. The Americans, responded the Indians, were too greedy to consider an economic proposition that denied them less than the lion's share of the profit. Under these circumstances, substantial U.S. private investment in India was unlikely.[69]

The Puzzle of Economic Success

There is no doubt that Indo-U.S. cultural differences, or mutual perceptions of these differences, soured the economic relationship between the countries. In truth, however, relations were not wholly miserable. The United States and India did trade with each other. The Americans secured most of the strategic raw materials they sought from the India, and the Indians generally agreed not to sell thorium and beryllium to communist countries. While both nations complained about various aspects of the U.S. aid program for India, by the early 1960s India was receiving abundant U.S. aid, at least when one contrasted with the microscopic level of U.S. help just a decade earlier. It will not do to say that the Indo-U.S. economic relationship was a failure between 1947 and 1964.

Can it be both ways? Can cultural difference explain both failure and success? It can if one remembers that others are projections of selves, and repositories not only of revulsion but desire. Selves constitute others of characteristics that selves find insupportable; these features are the dark places in the soul to which selves cannot admit. Americans saw Indians as representatives of an old culture and a new state. Indians were disorganized, disrespectful of time and enumeration, slothful and corrupt, a people who hoarded their wealth, refusing to distribute or sell it—unless they could make a very good bargain. Indian selves were built from a spiritualism that rejected the base concerns of the modernized West. Indians regarded Americans as grasping materialists, too mesmerized by the dazzling cheap light of profit to care about matters of the spirit or human suffering.

The making of others also involves the projection of the self's desires. Others become to some extent what selves wish to be. Self-fulfillment, for Americans, depends on admiring the attributes of others that selves seem to lack, on romanticizing the exotic in others and on incorporating, if only vicariously, exotic elements into the self. What is loathed and feared in others is offset by positive counterweights that can inspire admiration, or are themselves inspired by a need to admire something about the other: the rational, modern Western self found emotional fulfillment in exotic qualities perceived in Indians. Indians' negative images of Americans also carried positive counterweights. Indian selves did not need to exoticize Western others to be fulfilled. They needed instead to understand the value of those core Western qualities they exaggerated and scorned: the saturnalian, loathsome, yet strangely enviable characteristics of materialism.

Each of the items on the list of what one people disliked about the other's economic behavior therefore carried a positive charge. Indian civilization was old, but that did not mean it was altogether decrepit or ossified, for age could be associated with wisdom. The mid-nineteenth-century American poet William Rounseville Alger wrote:

> Young and enterprising is the West;
> Old and meditative is the East.
> Turn, o youth! with intellectual zest,
> Where the Sage invites thee to his feast.[70]

Old India had a tradition of craftsmanship; artisans, working as their admirable ancestors had, were "patient, enduring, and accurate." New India, with its youthful government and economy, was by contrast bumptious and careless and stubborn, but it also had freshness and energy. Its caprices could be forgiven by a United States that had been young once. India was a developing country, not a developed one, so it was necessary to make allowances. Emanuel Celler, congressman from New York, met Prime Minister Nehru in India in late 1953 and was much impressed. "I had once characterized him as reserved and aloof," Celler told the India League of America. "I take it all back. There is a quality of boyishness about him, an engaging openness of expression, coupled with vigor and exuberance." The final two adjectives in particular were complimentary flip sides of Nehru's so-called naiveté and volatility.[71]

Were Indians sharpsters? Not necessarily—they might just be good at business. An amateur Indian poet—a twentieth-century counterpart, perhaps, of W. R. Alger—nicely captured this puzzled American admiration in October 1961:

> We look upon your noble nation
> The ancient land of Budh
> With deep and lasting admiration—
> As any stranger should.
>
> Your culture we do glorify
> Your well-known sanctimony.
> But why must you become so sly
> Each time it comes to money?
>
> Your rituals have without a doubt
> Great meaning to the scholar.
> How has it therefore come about
> This worship of the dollar?
>
> Impressed with all your learning, wow!
> We're simply thunderstruck.
> But who would think you'd teach *us* how
> To make an easy buck.[72]

Did Indians hoard their wealth? It was possible to see hoarding as saving, which was not a vice. A study published in 1961 revealed that Indians saved at a rate comparable to that of Americans and most Europeans, a trend that, "if continued, augurs well for the future growth and health of the Indian economy." Indians weren't hoarding: they were merely frugal, putting their money aside for a rainy day.[73]

Negative Indian views of Americans as economic actors were also offset by positive counterweights. American youthfulness brought with it an energy similar to that admired by Americans in youthful India. Nehru was a severe critic of American culture, which he regarded as superficial, but he could not help praising the United States as "a land of new ideas, new vigour and new power." (Nehru loved children.) The precision of Americans, their fussiness about punctuality and numerical accuracy, the very speed at which they moved, indicated an unhealthy obsession with getting ahead—unhealthy, that is, unless your people were hungry and your economy needed help. The pursuit of material gain was a logical response to material deprivation, and while the Americans failed at introspection they were good at producing wealth. The Americans were "lacking in spirituality," decided Swami Vivekananda. So, "I give them spirituality, and they give me money." It was a reasonable exchange for the swami and his twentieth-century heirs, who saw themselves as long on religious values but rather short of cold, hard cash.[74]

3

Governance: The Family, the State, and Foreign Relations

> There is one ubiquitous theory which may be detected in political thought from Confucius to Rousseau, from Aristotle to Freud. It is the idea that family relations—those between parents and children, between husband and wife—provide a model for political systems and serve to define the relationship between the individual and authority.
>
> —Emmanuel Todd, *The Explanation of Ideology*

> The strain of looking after a family is great!
>
> —Jawaharlal Nehru, 1927

An American who arrives in India for the first time, without the benefit of an Indian family or good local contacts, is inevitably bewildered and sometimes overwhelmed. She has jet lag for one thing, and to compound her disorientation international flights ordinarily arrive in India in the middle of the night. The sights and sounds and smells of the place slide with distressing ease into the categorical stereotypes that Westerners bring with them: the paradox of a rigid bureaucracy and hopeless mass confusion, the crush of people (among whom only the Americans seem willing to wait in line), the heat, the insects, the argument over taxi fare into the city, and then, on the roads from the Delhi, Madras, or Bombay airports, the appalling poverty of thousands of men and women asleep in the open air, children running naked in the rubble, the odor of cooking fires fueled with dried cow dung. More confusion awaits at the hotel: "Reservation, madam? Sorry, we are full up"—though in the end, a room somehow appears. After several hours of sleep, an

American awakens to the noise of the street, the blare of music from a Hindu temple loudspeaker, or the strenuous cleansing rituals of a Brahmin in the next room, and, feeling stunned, she asks, as Americans in spite of themselves always seem to: "Where am I?"

After this, Americans' paths diverge. Some continue to be outsiders, seeing India as tourists but never breaking through the surface realities of the country. They take in Rajasthan and the Taj Mahal, the temples in Tanjore or Khajurao, the shopping in Delhi or Bombay, then return home to wonder, "Where was I?" Others, however, by prior arrangement or good luck, are taken in by an Indian family. This association draws the visitor deeper into Indian society. Patterns may emerge from the apparent chaos of everyday life. Relationships of caste and gender are revealed during family meals, when men, and women visitors, are served first, female family members next, and servants the leftovers. Families often include aged parents and grandchildren, cousins and widowed in-laws, all of whom interact with ease and warmth. Children, especially boys, are barely disciplined. And, very quickly, American visitors are brought into this circle and treated with gratifying affection. Children sit comfortably on Westerners' laps, and refer to their guests as "auntie" or "uncle." Mother brings out the wedding pictures; guests are briefed, often in mind-numbing detail, on the genealogy of the extended family. Water is boiled for tea, advice is given, transportation to the railway station is offered.

Then, just as a visitor begins to worry that such apparently unqualified affection can never be returned, there emerges another side to the intimacy. Favors, it turns out, are to be reciprocated. If you are receiving help in India, it is natural that you should offer to help Indians who might visit the United States. Since you can easily buy another tape player back home, you ought to sell the one you are using in India to nephew Raju, who could use it in his studies—for a fair price, of course. But most of all, since family members have revealed so much of themselves to you, it is your obligation to share with them the important details of your life. And so, matter-of-factly, come surprising questions: "How much money do you make?" "Why no children yet?" (Or, "Will you keep trying until you get a boy?") "Why do you live so far from your parents/siblings/children?" "How big is your house? Your car? Your wardrobe?" Moreover, if you are staying with a family, or in a flat they own, you are subject to visits at all hours of the day and night, which are both helpful and intrusive. The family wants to know if you are feeling better, if the mop was left in your room, if you received your train tickets yet, or if the man came by to fix the toilet. As the psychologist Alan Roland puts it, "the normal separation, privacy, and autonomy of Western-style relationships and the psychologi-

cal space around oneself disappear into the more symbiotic mode of giving and asking, of caring for and depending on, of influencing and being
influenced, of close, warm, emotional connectedness and interdepen-
dence." Americans living with a family in India might put it less gener-
ously: they have no privacy, and they have no time, and indeed nothing
else, that is fully and only theirs.[1]

Now turn the tables, and consider an Indian who has just arrived in
New York City. Accustomed to clear markers of rank in his own country,
socially at ease there, an Indian in the United States for the first time is inevitably bewildered and sometimes overwhelmed. "One of the world's
most pathetic sights is the lone Indian in some large Western city,"
Stephen Tyler has written, and any American who has borne witness to
this unhappy spectacle can confirm the truth of Tyler's observation.
Raised in a close-knit and doting family, often an extended one, Indians
(especially men) expect to be looked after. Someone should provide for
their needs, offering food and shelter, a folded towel, an extra pillow.
Emotional requirements should also be met, through good conversation,
and with sympathy—for missed relatives, lost luggage, a toothache. "In India," notes Tyler, "one's family and kin are a constant in an otherwise dangerously variable world," and as there is nothing more dangerously variable than an unfamiliar American city, someone must step forward as a
surrogate family member to help the Indian visitor overcome his sense of
isolation. There is no settled life beyond the bounds of family. All the relationships an Indian forges, even professionally, are modeled after familial ones.[2]

Indians in America don't wish to seem presumptuous or intrusive, but
that is how Americans often see them. An Indian asks no more than what
he and his family would unhesitatingly provide a visitor to his home. But
most Americans fail to appreciate this, and they are astonished at what
seems the visitor's gall in asking for so much without any recognition of
how much it really is. At the end of the day, when dinner is over and conversation spent, American couples wish to bid their guests goodnight at
the front door—or at least the bedroom door—and have some time to
themselves. If a guest's stay in the country is to be protracted, his American hosts hope he will seek invitations elsewhere, or venture out on his
own for meals and entertainment. Americans value their privacy. No matter how much they might enjoy an Indian visitor's company, they do not
generally regard him as a member of the family, with whom intimacy must
be shared. Chester Bowles, the sensitive U.S. ambassador to India during
parts of the 1950s and 1960s, recounted in his memoirs a conversation
with an Indian student. "I have been to both America and Russia," the

young man told Bowles. "In your country I simply drifted around by my-self. I was very lonely. . . . In Moscow I was met at the airport by a friendly guide who did not leave my side until I started back to India. He took me to parties and meetings and into many homes. I had a wonderful time."

Bowles shook his head over that one. The student had "completely overlooked the fact that in America he had been free to come and go as he chose, while in Russia he had been given a rigidly guided tour with a policeman at his elbow." On the contrary: the young man preferred a gov-ernment escort to a freedom he regarded as rootlessness, the signature of an uncaring people. He wanted to be guided because it reminded him of family life back home. Relatively few Indians joined the Communist Party. But socialism nonetheless appealed to many Indians, and less for ideolog-ical than for behavioral reasons. In its promise to look after people, even at the expense of freedom, socialism resembled the Indian family.[3]

American children, when grown, frequently move away from their natal families, and it is rare to find first cousins clustered in a neighborhood, at least among the middle class. In India, writes David Mandelbaum, "the family is at the core of a man's allegiance, his loyalty, his identification. It is his own gauge of success in life"—and even more is a woman's identity defined by her family. Because the expectations and structures of their families are so different, Americans and Indians are fundamentally differ-ent selves. According to Alan Roland, Westerners are individualistic "I-selves." They create their own identities by adolescence, draw clear lines between themselves and others, assert their autonomy in a society that ap-plauds and demands it, and exhibit rationality, efficiency, mobility, adapt-ability, and, naturally, self-consciousness. Indians, by contrast, are familial selves, or "we-selves." Ego boundaries are permeable; the we-self derives from "strong identification with the reputation and honor of the family and other groups." Autonomy is alien to such a personality, whose orien-tation is relational and whose values are therefore relative. Indians are thus many things to many people, depending on the relative positions, of-ten familial or perhaps subcaste (*jati*), of those with whom they interact. I borrow from Roland two examples of we-selfhood. The first concerns an Indian artist who confessed to being perplexed that American women felt they had to choose between career and family—that is, between two selves. The artist couldn't understand the conflict: "I feel very comfort-able slipping back and forth from being a professor to being a painter to being a mother and wife . . . I don't have to be one self or have a single identity." The second example of we-selfhood may strike a chord with Americans and Indians who have asked directions in each others' coun-tries. Americans think about space in terms of numbers, preferring to be told how many blocks or miles they must go before turning, how many houses they will pass before they reach their destination, and what the house number is. This way of mapping can confuse Indians. As Roland points out, Indians give directions by indicating where things are in relation to other things. Space is not objective but relational. A friend's flat is "adjacent to the burned-out house." The Shiva temple is past the bus stand and across from the tea stall. And so forth.[4]

The statement that personalities are the products of family types is possibly uncontroversial. But let us now move in another direction, from the domain of family and self to the realm of the nation-state. And let me put directly the premise of this chapter: The patterns of governance in a nation are modeled on those of its families, and, more profoundly, national ideology—the principles by which a state is governed and its world view—is in some measure predicated on family relations and on the type of personalities—I-selves or we-selves—families produce. The metaphors of family relationships, which figure prominently in the language of governance, are indicators of a close correspondence between ideas about family and ideas about politics. Because family structure shapes political culture, it also influences, in a way that is indirect but meaningful, the foreign policy a nation pursues. Cultural discourses of caste and class, of race, gender, and religion, are elements of the political culture that condition a nation's diplomacy. Of these discourses, those of family are first among equals, the single most powerful set of influences on how a society chooses its form of government and thus the basis for the way it relates to other people.

Though the connection between family structure and foreign policy-making has not been made elsewhere, as far as I know, the core of this argument is not new. It has been expressed most forcefully by the French scholar Emmanuel Todd in his 1985 book, *The Explanation of Ideology: Family Structures and Social Systems.* As his use of the definite article in the title indicates, Todd is not modest in his claims. "A universal hypothesis is possible," he writes. "The ideological system is everywhere the intellectual embodiment of family structure, a transposition into social relations of the fundamental values which govern elementary human relations." Todd argues that relations between family members condition ideas about authority and thus serve as a model for political institutions. Other influences may exist, but they matter less than family patterns, for "it is more difficult to absorb ideas about the republic, communism, racism, anti-Semitism, the existence of God or of castes . . . than to assimilate by instinct or imitation the stereotyped norms which govern relations between individuals belonging to the same elementary unit, the reproductive family." Family values are thus national values. One can predict the governing ideology of a nation based on whether its family structure is exogamous or endogamous, community or nuclear, authoritarian or anomic, and so on.[5]

There are some problems with an analysis so starkly drawn. Assuming, first, that family structure is tenacious, it is difficult for Todd to explain how political systems change, often quite rapidly. Moreover, the creation of a nation, and a national ideology, is never simple. A nation requires for its realization a host of things; it is what Benedict Anderson calls an "imagined community" based not just on family but on territory, language, and religion, and, as Geoff Eley and Ronald Grigor Suny have written, it needs a catalyst, an act of "political intervention . . . responsible for combining the materials into a larger collectivity." National ideology is broadly, not narrowly, determined. The efforts of political elites to create a national identity can at least tentatively overcome the contradictory pull of several family systems within a nation's borders. India, for example, has no less than three such systems, but its leaders have managed over the last fifty years to hold the nation together, in part by fabricating a common history and an incorporative mythology designed to transcend the differences— and not just family differences—within the country.[6]

Yet surely Todd is right to insist on a prominent place for the family as a determinant of national ideology. The creation of the United States government during the last thirty years of the eighteenth century and the evolution of the governments of India and Pakistan from nationalism to independence in the twentieth century involved political acts conditioned by familial relationships. Family and nation were intersecting, and sometimes competing, fields of authority. What each nation became was determined in part by what went on within the walls of its homes.

Families, Individualism, and the Formation of the United States

The English colonists who came to Plymouth and Massachusetts Bay in the seventeenth century believed that families were "little commonwealths," and that government was like a big family. This assumption was crafted into political theory by Sir Robert Filmer, who asserted that kings were fathers, holding absolute power over their children-subjects: "All the duties of a King are summed up in an universal fatherly care of his people. . . . The father of a family governs by no other law than by his own will, not by the laws or wills of his sons or servants." This would not do for John Locke. In his *Two Treatises on Government* (1689–90), Locke attacked Filmer in two ways. First, he said, the authority of a father was never as absolute as Filmer had claimed, and even if ceded such power, fathers did not always wield it. Second, whatever someone thought about the allocation of authority in families or states, one really had nothing to do with the other. It was foolish to think that authoritarian families led to authoritarian states.

These arguments were not fully accepted by Locke's contemporaries. While increasingly willing, by dint of their own experience, to reject Filmer's view that fathers should rule their families unchallenged, American colonists could not fully jettison the domestic analogy of government. This was perhaps attributable to their perception that both domestic and political life were disintegrating in much the same way. By the early eighteenth century, patriarchal attitudes were being challenged in the colonies, at least in the northern ones. Because the colonies were reasonably healthy places, and because they continued to attract immigrants, their populations grew. This put pressure on land in established communities, which in turn prompted many young men to leave family homes in search of opportunity in growing cities or on the frontier, beyond the grasp of paternal authority. Two historians have summarized these demographic changes: "By mid-century, when the Revolutionary generation was coming to maturity, the traditional pattern of prolonged filial subordination and dependency would appear to have been broken: children married at a younger age than their parents . . . , obtained their economic independence earlier, and put greater distance between themselves and their places of birth." At the same time, colonists came to believe that the political relationship between them and England had become badly unbalanced, owing to the treachery of King George III. They were not, *pace* John Locke, able to drum themselves out of England's family, but neither were they—thanks to Locke—willing to put up with the king's "abuses and usurpations." One can chart the Americans' disaffection from their imperial father (and their mother country) over time.

- In 1741 (from an unnamed colonist): "The Colonies are yet but Babes that cannot subsist but on the Breasts, and thro' the Protection of their Mother Country."
- In 1765 (John Adams): "But admitting we are children, have not children a right to complain when their parents are attempting to break their limbs, to administer poison, or sell them to enemies for slaves?"
- In May 1775 (from the *New York Journal*): "The kind intentions of our good mother—our tender, indulgent mother—are at last revealed to the world. . . . [She has revealed herself as a] vile imposter—an old abandoned prostitute—crimsoned o'er with every abominable crime, shocking to humanity."

The break came with *Common Sense* (1776), when Tom Paine called George "the Royal Brute of Great Britain," a "wretch . . . with the pretended title of FATHER OF HIS PEOPLE," and scoffed at the idea that Americans should remain dependent on a small island that relied on the colonies for many of life's necessities.

It was nevertheless frightening to rise in armed revolt against symbolic parents. Revolutionary Americans charged that George and his advisers had broken the compact that existed implicitly between family members, but they could not fully escape the Filmerian theory that family and government commingled. The revolutionary drama was written in the language of the family, and while the plot shifted the actors' roles did not. King George remained the father, but now he was a bad father, not just authoritarian but treacherous in his willingness to bring outsiders (the Hessians) into a family quarrel. The male revolutionary colonists remained children—the Liberty Boys, the Sons of Freedom, the Sons of Liberty—but now they were grown children, deeply angered by the behavior of their royal father and their mother country. Petition having failed, protest having been ignored, the children of America had no other recourse than to commit symbolic patricide. As Winthrop Jordan has written, "in 1776 George III was killed in his American provinces vicariously but very effectively." This was the climax of the American Revolution, though not its final act. For when the king was "dead," the Crown, wrote Tom Paine, should be "demolished, and scattered among the People whose right it is" to claim political power. The king's power had been shattered, and must now be distributed among his former subjects: his sons, the brothers of one another. The governing family was thus transformed from a patriarchy to a fraternity.[7]

But the drama was not yet over. For at this moment, many revolutionaries were at last disillusioned with the idea that the polity ought to be a family and accepted Locke's second objection to Filmer. A band of brothers, inherently competitive, jealous of one another, and maybe touched by guilt at having killed their father, was not much of a family. They were likely to fight over the land itself, their common mother. Melvin Yazawa has argued that "the familial paradigm" of government, eroded as patriarchal authority declined simultaneously in natal and imperial families, was destroyed by the Revolution. "Independent republicans were no longer held together or in place by affective prescriptions," Yazawa writes. Instead, family metaphors of government were replaced by scientific ones. Societies were not families but solar systems, and individuals were not family members but "republican machines," men and women who responded with mechanical logic to new situations. Even George Washington, the "father of his country," was less paterfamilias than impersonal symbol of the republic, "more an institution than a man."[8]

Yazawa pushes the argument too far. In the absence of a strong central authority following the Revolution, the states went their own ways, with the result that the new nation was exploited by other countries and derided by its own citizens. The brothers continued, in other words, to squabble. By late 1786, when Daniel Shays and his farmers refused to allow the Massachusetts legislature to raise their taxes, an American elite had resolved to strengthen the federal government. The U.S. constitution recreated a father figure (the president), and set to watch over him several groups of less exalted but still powerful relations (Congress and the Supreme Court). Yazawa's claim notwithstanding, there seems little question that Americans viewed George Washington as a reassuring, grandfatherly figure whose presence restored some order and dignity to the country. Americans continue to take comfort from paternalistic presidents. In the twentieth century, they elected Theodore Roosevelt (a vigorous, playful father, particularly good with boys), Franklin D. Roosevelt (a comforting, nurturing father in the nation's hour of crisis), Dwight Eisenhower (conservative but wise), and Ronald Reagan (dotty, but warm and amusing). The familial metaphor persists as well in the image of Uncle Sam, the clear-eyed and muscular suitor of Latin American nations, senoritas in distress, who is nevertheless made sexually unthreatening by his stars and stripes outfit and his benign, humorous face.[9]

But it will not do to discard completely Yazawa's insight. Despite the willingness of Americans to embrace Washington and some subsequent presidents as fathers, the family metaphor comes and goes, reflecting unease with authority and insistence on individual freedom that is at odds with a patriarchal family. Americans grant their political leaders parental status only during times of crisis and then reluctantly, with a sense of shame at having failed on their own. Some Americans—Jacksonian Democrats, Reagan Republicans—prescribe more individual freedom during difficult times, not less. Even twentieth-century liberals resist absolute reliance on a paternalistic state. Government social programs are for those who cannot help themselves, those who are discriminated against, and the dispossessed, like orphans or single-parent children. Welfare state liberals are not socialists. In the end, they, too, choose freedom from authority, autonomy not dependency, the private sector over the public. Government can be nurturing, like a caring parent, but it can just as easily be meddling or smothering.[10]

It is possible for Americans to support public ownership of the means or production, in the United States (the Tennessee Valley Authority) or abroad. At the same time, Americans want to know that the private sector, representing free enterprise and individual freedom, remains dominant over the public. The suspicion that attends government involvement in the economy is the result of the distance most Americans seek to put between themselves and their government, their profound unease with the familial paradigm, the suspicion that a nurturing government is likely to be a repressive one. Why, to repeat Werner Sombart's famous question, is there no socialism in the United States? Because Americans symbolically killed King George III in 1776. They have been resistant to a patriarchal federal government ever since.

Families, Communitarianism, and the Formation of Independent India

Having already asserted that Indian families produce "we-selves," are "a constant" in a changing world, and several other seemingly reductionist ideas, I offer here a few disclaimers. As in the West, no two families in India are exactly alike. While the extended family is still the norm in India, young people now frequently live in nuclear families, away from their parents and other relatives; this is especially true in cities. There are important differences between the marriage patterns of northerners and southerners, Muslims and Hindus, rich and poor, high and low castes. The Nayars of the Malabar Coast once practiced polyandry—the marriage of one woman to more than one man—and maintain a matrifocal and matrilinear system, in which property is passed from mothers to daughters. The increasing frequency of divorce, remarriage by widows, use of contraception, and visits to marriage counselors in India indicates that the belief in the static Indian family is one more Western myth.[11]

Still, it is not essentializing to claim that, despite all these differences, there remains what Stephen Tyler calls an "ideal model of family organization in India," at least for Hindus. It is the extended type, in which reside husband and wife, aged parents, their unmarried children, and often married sons with their wives and children. (When daughters marry, they live with their husbands' families.) Joint families manage estates together, pay taxes as a unit, and grow or buy and consume food together. Lines of authority are clearly established: men rule women and the old rule the young. The oldest male is thus the head of household, and only when he is incapacitated or dies does his eldest son takes charge. The wife of the head of household gives orders to younger women. Family relationships are thus hierarchical, designed to inspire obedience, security, and harmony. Older brothers may call younger brothers by name, but younger brothers must use relational terms to address older brothers. Boys submit to their fathers. Rudeness, smoking, and lying down in the presence of one's father are forbidden. Children respect their mothers but are almost always indulged by them. Mothers have near-absolute control of their children until age five, when boys are expected to join the world of men. Even then, mothers exert emotional control over their sons, pampering them with a "suffocating indulgence," encouraging their continued dependence, and even warning them against excessive sexual intercourse with their wives. Grandparents in the household subvert nuclear family discipline, plying children with sweets and sympathizing with them when they have been punished.[12]

In many ways, the Indian family serves its members well. Hierarchy brings security, consisting, observes G. Morris Carstairs, "in an acceptance of one's limited role with the knowledge that all one's kin will participate in every crisis of one's life." The father's authority in the joint family is unquestioned; there seems to be no Oedipus complex in Hindu mythology. The quest for harmony lends Indian social discourse an agreeable quality, a desire to prevent conflict by divining the hierarchies latent in a situation and accepting the positions of all participants within them. "Every man has got five fathers, and it is his duty to obey them without question, whatever they ask him to do," Hari Lal told Carstairs. "They are, his father, his elder brother, his king, his guru, and his friend."[13]

Notice here the absence of boundaries between a man's authority figures; he owes the leader of his spiritual life *and* his political life the same deference he owes the heads of his family. The family is a model, creating a hierarchy of authority that "extends . . . to every other institution in Indian life," according to Sudhir Kakar. The hierarchy that brings stability and harmony to Indian families provides these benefits to all segments of Indian society, especially politics. Before independence, Mohandas Gandhi appealed to the great landholders (*zamindars*) not to abandon their system of land tenure but to make it more humane. More than merely collect rent from their tenants, the *zamindars* should become their "trustees and trusted friends . . . [and] take a lively interest in their welfare." "Whatever the law may be," Gandhi cautioned, "the Zamindari system, to be defensible, must approach the conditions of the joint family." Saleem Sinai, Salman Rushdie's nasally gifted protagonist in *Midnight's Children*, discovered as a boy that all Indian children born at the moment of his nation's independence could communicate telepathically with each other through him. Given Saleem's powers, argued another of the children, he should be their "chief." "No," said Saleem, "never mind *chief*, just think of me as a . . . a big brother, maybe. Yes; we're a family, of a kind."

Saleem understood what Indians knew: political networks were family net-works, political parties followed the authority patterns of extended fami-lies—or if they did not, they were doomed. S. K. Dey, the government's minister for community development in 1961, worried that national poli-tics had become undisciplined. "The affairs of State conducted in a de-mocracy should move like the marriage in a joint family," he wrote. "If or-der and not chaos is to be the rule," the political universe must be "a balanced organism in which all components are related to one another by clearly defined laws which are understood, accepted, and honoured."[14]

One political system that failed either to replicate or challenge the au-thority of the joint family was the British raj. There is a powerful episode in Paul Scott's novel *The Day of the Scorpion* in which Teddie Bingham, an officer in the British army in India during World War II, is called upon to interrogate a captured Indian soldier who has evidently deserted to the advancing Japanese. Bingham and the soldier discover that they belonged to the same outfit, the Muzzafarabad Guides. The soldier grovels at Bing-ham's feet, asking forgiveness and claiming that he remains loyal to the raj, having been coerced into joining the Japanese. Bingham believes him because the Guides all knew, really knew, that their British officers were *man-bap* (or *ma-bap*), a compound contraction of the Hindi words for fa-ther and mother. "I am your father and your mother," the British told their men, and after switching the pronouns the men dutifully repeated the phrase back. But Bingham is wrong. Persuaded by the soldier that there are two more Muzzy Guides in the area looking to return home, Bingham goes in search of them, only to be lured into an ambush and killed. The Indians mouthed the words, but they had their own parents, and they never truly believed that British officers could supplant them. There was a tradition of Western presumptuousness about Indian acqui-escence in this regard. The American traveler Bayard Taylor was called "father" by his servant "son" in 1853, and Katherine Mayo declared of the Indian male in 1927 that "it is the British Deputy Commissioner, none other, who is 'his father and his mother.' " A tea plantation manager named Kenneth Warren recalled: "It was customary for a member of the labour force who had a request to make to come to you and first of all ad-dress you as *Hazar*—Your Honour, and then *ma-bap*, you are my father and my mother, I have this, that, and the other request to make." Unlike the others, Warren at least seems to have glimpsed the possibility that In-dians called officials *ma-bap* because they knew that was what the British wished to hear.[15]

This is not to say that the raj left India politically untouched. Many sons of the Indian elite were educated in England and returned to India as members of the Indian Civil Service. Gandhi, Jawaharlal Nehru, and M. A. Jinnah, along with hundreds of others, were called to the bar in London, which came ironically to be regarded as the cradle of Indian nationalism. India's top educators, scientists, diplomats, lawyers, and politicians were often British-trained, and not infrequently Anglophiles. Nor did all Indian soldiers abandon their British officers as readily as Teddie Bingham's. It is not surprising that, in a poor country with limited opportunity, some of the population came to identify with those most others regarded as oppressors. Political scientists sometimes posit a difference between state building, which involves "the problem of penetration and integration," and nation building, concerning "the problem of loyalty and commitment." In this sense, perhaps it can be said that the British built a state in India but failed to build a nation.[16]

They failed because they never managed to convince the overwhelming majority of Indians that they deserved either loyalty or commitment. The British in India were politically illegitimate. If they managed to seduce some of the bright young men of Bombay and Calcutta, if in a few cases they persuaded Indians of their energy and good will, they never shook the ties of political fealty that bound Indians to their local and regional governments, to the clans and kin that ruled them more surely than outsiders ever could. The raj was limited, as Anand Yang has put it; "government institutions simply did not extend into local society, nor was its machinery especially geared to economic or social problem solving." Families were "geared" for that. What British officials saw as Indian inscrutability, what E. M. Forster's English characters found impenetrable about their Indian counterparts, was not only cultural difference but a calculated unwillingness by Indians to make themselves known to their rulers. A British officer wrote of this with candor:

> It is generally the fashion to describe the feelings of the people as good and loyal; I believe myself that it would be much more correct to describe it as simply acquiescent. I do not think there is any actual discontent with our rule . . . but I cannot say that anything like the active feeling of loyalty exists in the minds of either Hindoos or Mohammedans. . . . At best we are an alien and, worse than that, an unbending and unsympathetic race, and the race we are called upon to rule is essentially a feeling and impulsive one. The consequence is, that as we never thaw to them, they never open to us; and we must all . . . feel that as we come to the land strangers, so we leave it, and that scarcely any of us penetrate beyond the outward shell of native feeling.

The British were rulers, not servants of the people, and they were ignored more than resisted, at least until Gandhi's *satyagraha* campaign began in earnest in 1919. Even then, the emphasis was at first on "noncooperation" with the British, withdrawal rather than confrontation, the latter of which, Gandhi thought, was the British tactic of choice. Cynical about the raj, Indians focused their political attention on localities, taking satisfaction (writes Ashis Nandy) "in face-to-face situations, in families and small systems."[17]

In retrospect, getting rid of the British looks to have been relatively easy. Because they never saw themselves as part of an imperial family, the Indians, unlike the American colonists, had no need to assure their independence by committing virtual patricide. Most Indians believed that the British managed their departure with dignity, with the obvious exception of the decision for partition. Nehru remained close to the Mountbattens, and India stayed in the Commonwealth. But the new nation needed an identity of its own, and its government required popular acceptance. Clifford Geertz has written: "Once the political revolution is accomplished, and a state, if hardly consolidated, is at least established, the question: who are we, who have done all this? re-emerges from the easy populism of the last years of decolonization and the first of independence." A week after India gained its independence, S. R. Deo, the general secretary of the All India Congress Committee, admitted "that while [the] Congress [Party] had achieved freedom, unity had slipped out of its hands; and that unless this unity could be regained the task of the Congress could not be regarded as complete."[18]

How could the men and women who had made the British quit India gain for themselves the kind of loyalty that Indians had previously given only to their families? Charles Tilly has reminded us that the strengthening of nation-states does not necessarily bring with it the expansion of political rights: "A large part of the process [of nation building has] consisted of the state's abridging, destroying or absorbing rights previously lodged in other political units: manors, communities, provinces, estates." Tilly was describing Europe; in India, "families" must be added to the list. The principal means by which families maintained their political power in localities was nepotism, the corruption that places kin before party or merit in determining who should get jobs. Westerners claim to despise nepotism because it elevates accident (birth) over accomplishment (merit), thus the irrational over the rational, the emotional over the logical. Some have understood the appeal of nepotism, without altogether appreciating its charms. Rushbrook Williams observed in 1938 that "to many Hindus the duty owed to other members of the joint family appears something far stronger then any duty owed to the State; what Westerners call nepotism is in India a positive virtue." A willingness to help family members was a litmus test of loyalty. In a society of family and caste hierarchy, where so much depends on the relationship of people to each other, it makes some sense to hire on the basis of personal knowledge of someone's character—and one is most likely to know a family member well. Nepotism assured that the joint family would remain India's "social security system," as Chester Bowles phrased it, and in a country where the state had not, prior to 1947, filled that role, there was some justification for the practice.[19]

That did not stop Nehru from attacking it vigorously, however. The part of Nehru shaped by a British education seems to have been repelled by corruption. But Nehru also understood that as long as Indians remained tied by nepotism to their families, their political loyalty to the new central government would never be assured. Loyalty to family, the result of long tradition and the perceived illegitimacy of the raj, prevented the development of faith in national political institutions. Faced with this dangerous circumstance, Nehru first reacted by attacking corruption, particularly nepotism, in the hope of breaking the bonds that held people politically to their clans. These bonds could then be reattached to the national government. Even before taking office as head of the interim government in September 1946, Nehru lashed out at what he called "the colossal corruption and nepotism that are rampant everywhere." "Corrupt people have to be swept away by a broomstick," he cried while campaigning for his Congress Party in late 1945. The attack on corruption began in earnest after Nehru became interim prime minister. He asked his home minister, Vallabhbhai Patel, to investigate state and city governments, following up allegations of "extreme corruption and deterioration of the whole administration" in Ajmer, Rajasthan.[20]

Nehru's assault on nepotism was an effort to destroy India's localized political system. His weapons were threat and exhortation, no more, and he recognized that they were inadequate to the task. Recalling Tilly's observation that new states might absorb as well as destroy rights once held by political units at other levels, we should note the government's efforts not only to eradicate but to appropriate some of the functions associated with local, family regimes. One of the ways in which the Congress Party undertook to do this was by appropriating the language of the family to define its relationship with the people. Perhaps "appropriating" is too strong a word. Rather, the language of the family came easily to the tongues of those who had long used it to describe governing, and who now moved into grander versions of roles they had played for many years under the British. The acceptance of this vocabulary came quickly and evidently by mutual agreement between governing and governed. The land or nation was "Mother India" (*Bharat mata*). Gandhi was the father of the country and of all its citizens. When he was assassinated in January 1948, it was "as if a member of [our] immediate family had died," leaving all Indians "orphaned." Nehru was a son of India, an uncle to Indian children, older brother (*bhai* or *baboo*) to adults, given the authority that comes to Indian men when their fathers die. These were roles Nehru recognized. They sometimes made him uncomfortable, but frequently he reveled in them, as he did during a speech to a hundred thousand noisy supporters in January 1954. Part way along, Nehru announced that he was putting the crowd to a test of discipline: they were to open a four-foot-wide path from the front of the dais to their last row, then let him walk back and forth along the path unimpeded and untouched. The prime minister took his stroll, returned to the platform, and announced that the crowd had won "95 out of 100 marks," having lost five because several people had tried to touch his feet. No big brother has ever led or loved or teased his siblings better.[21]

More than anything else, the government of independent India tried to usurp the welfare function traditionally held by families, creating a vast social safety apparatus designed to supplant effective but infinitesimal local caretaking networks. If citizens saw that government representatives would look after them from cradle to grave more capably than even their best-intentioned relatives, they would presumably grant their political loyalties to the national state. This is how Nehru's commitment to socialism must be understood. Nehru said a great many things about political economy, and some of them seem contradictory, as if he was unsure of his ideas or, forgivably, willing to change his mind. Most American policymakers, ignoring the mixed evidence, labeled the prime minister a socialist, or worse. Chester Bowles recalled that when he was a newly appointed ambassador about to leave for India, President Truman told him: " 'The first thing you've got to do is find out whether Nehru is a Communist. He sat right there in that chair'—he pointed to a chair in a corner of his office—'and he talked just like a Communist.' " Once, when pressed by a reporter, Nehru criticized the "free world" for its emphasis on individual freedom to the exclusion of "mass welfare," a mistake, he said, that the Soviet Union did not make. More than once, publicly, Nehru declared himself a socialist, or said that "he believed in socialism," or said that India required "socialistic planning." But Nehru also denied that he endorsed "pure Socialism," insisted that one must not approach the nationalization of industry "from a doctrinaire standpoint," and stayed aloof from a permanent political alliance with the Indian Socialist Party, whose members, he charged, "shut their mind[s] to realities of the time." "I do not see," he complained, "why I should have to define socialism in precise, rigid, terms."[22]

Nehru was in truth a pragmatist. His ideology was contained within the perimeter of the modern welfare state—he harbored dark suspicions of free market capitalists, who roamed beyond the picket—but inside this circle he felt considerable room to maneuver. Nehru wanted India to industrialize; in this way he was no Gandhian. Resentful of foreign investors and certain that the supply of investment capital at home was limited, Nehru believed that only the state had the motivation, the vision, and the financial wherewithal to underwrite backbone enterprises like steel, transportation, power, and mineral extraction. Beyond that, and even within these sectors, there was room for private capital, subject to the need for coordinated economic planning. Nehru, according to Sarvepalli Gopal, "was averse to doctrinaire and rigid thinking" about the economy, and thought that "to define socialism would be futile and even harmful," entangling planners in endless disputes over philosophical minutiae while the country staggered. Nehru was deliberately fuzzy about political economy. Socialism was always part of his thinking, but the word seldom went unmodified. He talked of a "socialistic tendency in any programme" and noted "a great and growing feeling in India in favor of some kind of a vague socialist order of society." "Socialism is a good thing," Nehru told a gathering of textile workers in early 1949. "But socialism is not a consummation." What the prime minister really wanted could be summarized without reference to ideology: "We are ultimately aiming at feeding, clothing, housing, educating, and providing better sanitary and health conditions for four hundred millions." The means for achieving this would be a welfare state that would make lives better and win the loyalty and affection of the people. One could call it whatever one wished.[23]

It was, however, impossible to place such responsibilities on a government that was structurally weak. Power, historically, had rested with local, usually family regimes; South India especially was a "segmentary state," in which local lords and clan leaders gave the orders and the influence of kings was attenuated outside dynastic capitals. Those who wrote the constitution for independent India thus hoped to claim as much power as they could for the center. Adopted in January 1950, the Indian constitution gave the national government a number of powers previously held by localities, provinces, or states. The government now took control of taxation and the nation's waterways, and got the right to name the states' governors (though not their more important chief ministers, who were to be elected). Most significantly, the president of the republic was given broad emergency powers, including the right to suspend the states' powers of legislation. The result was a federalism not unlike that of the United States, but weighted more heavily in favor of the national government in times of apparent crisis, and with little room for negotiation over the definition of states' rights.[24]

The authors of the constitution nevertheless understood that local governments would not be easily displaced. National primacy in times of emergency might be justified, but on an everyday basis the tradition of local power, reinforced by Gandhi's emphasis on village democracy and self-reliance, was unlikely to be effaced. "But is there nothing you want from the government?," John Muehl asked Gujaratis he met in 1949. The reply was always the same: "All we ask of the government is to be left alone!" Nehru found that he had no choice but to rule through established, local political institutions. He admitted that the village, while not viable as a "self-contained economic unit," might work as "a governmental or electoral unit . . . functioning as a self-governing community within the larger political framework and looking after the essential needs of the village." Unable to beat local officials at the political game, the Congress Party attempted to absorb them. It tried to organize rural dwellers through what Francine Frankel has called "pyramiding alliances," with Party leaders at the apex and the "personal followings of local leaders" at the base. In 1961, the government convened in New Delhi a National Integration Conference for representatives of local party organizations. Nehru called the delegates members of "one family" and urged that differences of religion and caste "be subordinated to the national interest." The vice president, Sarvepalli Radhakrishnan, inveighed against nepotism. Delegates resolved that school textbooks be national rather than provincial in scope, recommended the universal use of English in higher education, and endorsed the singing of the national anthem by school-children before the day's work began. In these ways did the state attempt to grasp the many levers of power already affixed to localities and long manipulated by their elites.[25]

There were so many ways in which the fragile new state could fracture: casteism, provincialism, linguistic chauvinism, "parochial" or "selfish" loyalties. Most dangerous of what Indians call "fissiparous tendencies" was "communalism," meaning religious hatred. Nehru tried especially hard to overcome this problem. He argued that India would never accept a religious basis for statehood, as Pakistan had. He spoke out sharply against Hindu fundamentalist groups that sought a theological state, and rejected efforts to invent a common tradition for independent India based on Hindu symbols and myths. Religion gripped too powerfully to be discarded altogether as a nationalist organizing principle, so the Congress Party leadership used Buddhism as a reservoir of lore; Buddhism had originated in India but there were few Buddhists left there, and they were no threat to anyone. Thus the Indian flag displayed the Buddhist Wheel of Law, and the lions of the Buddhist ruler Asoka were used for the national seal. Nehru refused to approve the song *Bandre Mataram* as the nation's anthem because it mentioned the Hindu mother goddess, settling instead for *Jana Gana Mana*, a poem by Rabindranath Tagore that lists the regions and peoples of India.[26]

In one very important sense, Nehru's exertions worked: vast numbers of Indians came to associate the postindependence government with the family, and either transferred their political loyalties to the nation-state or demonstrated, at minimum, a willingness to divide their loyalties between local and national institutions. For Krishnalal Shridharani, whose devotion to the nationalist cause led to his alienation from his family, the process of transference began even before independence. "I had come to believe," he wrote, "that to serve Mother India one must remain free and avoid all entanglements." He drifted away from "the old ways," staying aloof from caste and family rituals and "protest[ing] against the early marriage of any member of the family simply by not attending." This was not an unusual sentiment. Rebellion often demands a choice between ties to family and allegiance to revolutionary leaders whose requirements for loyalty are no less exacting. The choice is less painful if the revolutionaries can promote themselves as surrogate parents, as much concerned for the welfare of their followers as parents are for their children. "When my people [family] sent me to the University of Madras my father singled out that I was not to participate in politics to the detriment of my studies," wrote an anguished young man named Ramachandran in 1944. He agreed, but at the beginning of his second year he could no longer resist: he plunged into anti-British organizing, and thus "broke the contract with my father." When Nehru became head of the interim government in 1946, hundreds of Indians wrote to offer congratulations—and to ask for the help of their influential big brother. Young men, who might previously have requested a patronage job from a relative, now implored Nehru for assistance of various kinds. One writer complained that his rent was too high; would Nehru speak to his *zamindar*? Korath Varkej wanted "pecuniary assistance," I. S. Kapil a medical position, and N. Sharma a job in the (nonexistent) "department of detection." Krishnan wanted Nehru to send him to a foreign university for scientific training. "My elder brother," he wrote. "Your little help will change my life, and I will consider my way clear." And then, a dart, dipped in emotional poison: "Do as you like, but care so that you may not hurt anybody's soul, heart, and aim."[27]

Here was a pointed reminder of the perils of family government. The requirements of intimacy in a family far exceeded those of a political relationship. One could expect politicians to disappoint their constituents. Expectations for a family member were greater. In return for sibling loyalty, it was the obligation of a big brother not to hurt the "soul, heart, and aim" of his younger siblings. From the first, the political atmosphere of independent India was more emotionally charged than that of the United States, or most nations. While India's founders succeeded in winning the loyalty of some ordinary Indians by appropriating and extending the social functions of the family, the consequences of even this degree of success were quite serious.

In the first place, the attack on nepotism at the local level was morally subverted by its agents. Congress Party members were not out to destroy political loyalty but to acquire it for themselves, so rather than attack nepotism as a fundamental wrong they sought to absorb it into the political practices of the state. Those young men who wrote Nehru to ask for money or jobs were not abandoning nepotism but relocating it by appealing to the strongest patron in the country. Predictably, accusations of government corruption began almost immediately following independence. Sons and nephews of leading officials got jobs "with fat salaries" for which they were plainly unqualified. There emerged a class of government bureaucrats whose job it was to "fix things up" for prescribed rates: so much for a building permit, so much for a road contract, so much for an official to look the other way when goods were smuggled through Bombay. Hafiz Mohammed Ibrahim, a Congress Party official in Uttar Pradesh, apparently used state money to build a road and remodel a private airport so that guests could more conveniently attend his son's wedding. In other words, rather than eradicating nepotism, the government was absorbing it into its own precincts, feeling that there was little choice if it wished to gain legitimacy.[28]

A second great failing of the appropriative Indian state has to do with the kind of loyalty it fostered. The association of family and state was thorough, not total, and to some extent political institutions, including, for example, the foreign ministry, remained abstract bureaucracies. Citizens were in the end less loyal to the government than to the people who ran it, those leaders whose physiognomies were known. There developed around the Congress Party, and more specifically around the Nehru family members who commanded it, what Max Weber called "clan charisma," in which "extraordinary qualities" adhere not just to a person but to his family. Once political leadership is identified as family responsibility, the relationship becomes literal, and the result is dynastic government. Head of household is not an elective office. Even as Nehru's faculties dimmed, few could imagine who would replace him. When Nehru died in May 1964, the party spurned his anointed successor, daughter Indira Gandhi, but only for eighteen months. Mrs. Gandhi was prime minister for fifteen of the years between 1966 and her assassination in October 1984; she was succeeded by her recently politicized younger son, Rajiv.[29]

In adopting the corruption of local clans and in creating a dynastic democracy, the family model of governance failed because it succeeded too well. As the nation moved toward independence it became clear that religious differences could not be fully reconciled within the house of Gandhi and Nehru. Accommodating as the patriarch and his chosen son declared themselves to be—the Congress Party sought a national, not a communal state, Nehru told Great Britain's Lord Ismay in October 1947—they could not convince Hindu fundamentalists, secessionist Sikhs, and particularly most Muslims that the family of India would include them. These religious groups ultimately rejected the idea that India was a family, or at least their family, and, as heads of families are loath to permit subordinate members to depart without a struggle, with each group there was a struggle, and a violent one.[30]

The most portentous rejection of the family model of governance was that of the members of the Muslim League who supported the creation of Pakistan. There were moments when prominent Pakistanis could not prevent themselves from thinking of partition as a family division. Prime Minister Mohammed Ali told his people in a New Year's Day 1954 broadcast that "India and Pakistan were like twin sisters," a departure from the more common fraternal metaphor. And there is this suggestive passage early in the memoir of Mohammed Ayub Khan, prime minister from 1958 to 1969: "I remember the birth of my youngest brother. I was then about two and a half years old. I saw this child lying by the side of my mother. I seized a stick and wanted to beat him. I was taken away. It was great torture seeing another child sleeping by the side of my mother and it took me a long time to get over that feeling. I remember it vividly to this day." Ayub's recollection of this event possibly expressed an unconscious hatred for brother India, a rival for the motherland from which both had sprung.[31]

On the whole, though, Indians were more inclined than Pakistanis to represent South Asian political relationships in familial terms. Even in the spring of 1950, as Great Britain's high commissioner in Pakistan, L. B. Grafftey-Smith, traveled in India's high country and to New Delhi, he found an "apparently universal sentiment of regret that Pakistan ('the younger brother') should have decided to leave the family home, and the hope that sooner or later this lost sheep would return to the fold." Most Pakistanis felt differently. What mattered most to Pakistan's leaders was that the country gain standing at home and in the world as a polity separate from India, as something more than the necessary but unfortunate offspring of religious struggle in South Asia. Pakistani Islam was not an extended family to which Hindus, Sikhs, and Christians belonged. Although Liaquat Ali Khan (prime minister from 1947 to 1951) and Ayub Khan were not themselves orthodox Muslims, they understood, as Ayub put it, that Pakistan had "to establish a distinct national identity of her own," and that the only obvious source of Pakistani distinctiveness was Shariat—Islamic law. Pakistan was not a joint family but a theological expression. "For us there is only one 'ism'—Islamic Socialism," said Liaquat. "In adopting any reform, the whole matter will be carefully considered in light of the Shariat." Ayub saw statecraft as a function of the "Islamic code," which made of life a "complete cultural whole," indivisible into fraudulent categories like religion, politics, and economics. Partition was neither a Biblical nor a Freudian drama of sibling separation, but simply a recognition of religious reality.[32]

As long as he lived, Jawaharlal Nehru never accepted the religious basis for nationhood. To believe that frictions between nationalist leaders of the Congress Party (like him) and Muslim separatists were religious in nature was to trivialize them. A family made up of all religions had cast the British out. Families must stick together. Departures were not partings of business partners at odds or even incompatible lovers: they were acts of treachery by members of the same joint family.

The Contested Offspring: Kashmir

The comparative analysis of governance in the United States and India has taken us far off the path of diplomatic history—farther than we were in preceding chapters, or will be (let the reader be assured) in forthcoming ones. Because the argument is a controversial one, it seemed necessary to develop it in some detail. Now it is possible to examine the impact of this argument on United States–India relations. To what extent did the differences in American and Indian understandings of what governance should mean influence interactions between the two countries? Let me describe two episodes in Indo-U.S. affairs that illustrate the salience of the themes I have discussed.

The first episode is the rancorous and seemingly endless conflict between India and Pakistan over the state of Kashmir. No issue has troubled Indo-Pakistani relations more, and none has drawn more concern from outside powers, including the United States. At the time of partition in 1947, Kashmir, which was made up of three provinces (Ladakh, Jammu, and Kashmir itself), had a Muslim majority of 78 percent. The state was ruled, however, by a Hindu maharajah named Hari Singh, who fantasized that, whatever else happened in the subcontinent, he could maintain his hold on an independent state, beholden to neither side. The maharajah's most persistent and effective opponent was Sheikh Mohammed Abdullah. The scion of one of Kashmir's two most famous families—the Nehrus were the other—Sheikh Abdullah was head of the National Conference, a party closely associated with India's Congress (despite the Sheikh's Islamic faith). The pro-Pakistan Muslim League was also represented in the state. Its leader, along with Sheikh Abdullah, was in prison in 1947.

Hari Singh, the head of Kashmir state, wanted autonomy. Sheikh Abdullah, virtually all Hindus and Sikhs, and some of Kashmir's Muslims, sought association with India. (The sheikh liked to say that while he had a religion in common with Jinnah, he had a dream in common with Nehru.) The leaders of Pakistan, along with the Kashmiri Muslim League, assumed that Kashmir would accede to the Islamic state. Kashmir was so obviously a ticking bomb that Viceroy Mountbatten stayed clear of it, saying merely that the state, like other independent dominions in South Asia, would have to decide for itself which way to turn. Anticipating trouble, groups within and outside of Kashmir maneuvered for position during the early fall of 1947. Muslims in western Jammu revolted against the maharajah, expelled state forces with considerable loss of life among the non-Muslim civilian population, and declared the existence of a free "Azad Kashmir" government, loyal to Pakistan. In eastern Jammu, meanwhile, an influx of Hindu and Sikh refugees from Pakistan led officials to try to secure a non-Muslim majority there. Thousands of Muslims were killed, thousands more were driven off. At Nehru's urging, an overwhelmed Hari Singh released Sheikh Abdullah from prison on September 29. Nehru cultivated the sheikh, warning that should Pakistan gain control of Kashmir it was likely to exploit the state economically. Of this possibility Abdullah hardly needed convincing.

Then, on the night of October 22, thousands of armed Muslim tribals, most of them Pathans from Pakistan's Northwest Frontier Province, came across the Jhelum River near the Kashmir border town of Muzaffarabad. They traveled in trucks, and their ranks bristled with modern weapons. Claiming to have come to rescue fellow Muslims under siege in the state, they struck west toward Kashmir's summer capital of Srinagar, 140 miles away. Nehru, furious at what he saw as Pakistani government policy to win by force what it could not by other means, demanded that Mountbatten, now India's governor-general, stop the invaders with Indian forces. Mountbatten was well aware that both Indian and Pakistani armies retained British officers, complicating the situation terribly, but he sympathized with Nehru's position and agreed that Indian troops could be sent to Kashmir if the state legally acceded to India. Either on the night of October 25–26 or the morning of the 27th—the record is in dispute—V. P. Menon, India's secretary in the Ministry of States, got the panicky maharajah to sign an "Instrument of Accession" to India, subject to the will of the Kashmiri people "only . . . when law and order have been fully established." The Maharajah invited Abdullah to form an interim government. On the 27th, Indian troops were airlifted to Srinagar, where they secured the capital and blunted the attack. Fighting continued throughout the state, however, allowing Nehru to claim that "law and order" had not yet been established. An effort by Jinnah to send Pakistan army units into Kashmir was rebuffed by his British commanders, who argued that the move would mean war between the dominions and pointed out that the Pakistani military was poorly equipped for such a conflict.[33]

The parties to the dispute, and concerned observers, had dramatically different views of what had happened. Sheikh Abdullah was delighted with India's forcefulness on his behalf. In fact, he urged Nehru to issue an ultimatum to Pakistan—get out and stay out—and, if this demand was rejected, to declare war. When Nehru refused to go this far, the sheikh grew more militant, calling for an independent Kashmir. That position was hardly useful to Nehru, who had the Lion of Kashmir placed under house arrest in August 1953. (The sheikh was freed for a hundred days in early 1958, rearrested, then released for good a month before Nehru's death in 1964.) The Indians were willing to discuss a plebiscite for Kashmir, but not until foreign troops were withdrawn; and because the state's government had legally (if hastily) acceded to India, the Pakistanis were required to withdraw first, abandoning Azad Kashmir in the bargain. The Pakistanis found this proposition outrageous. The Muslim tribals who had entered Kashmir in October 1947 claimed to have done so to protect their co-religionists from Sikh and Hindu atrocities. While the government of Pakistan admitted sympathy with the tribals' goals, it denied that it had given them any assistance. It contended that the equipment they carried with them, or that carried them, into Kashmir was of their own manufacture, was Afghani, or was provided by nervous local officials anxious to get the militants off their soil. When a British diplomat visited the border town of Abbottabad in early December, he found scores of well-armed Mahsud tribes-men, "looking thoroughly piratical," in a transit camp that the provincial government had given them at a former stud farm.[34]

The location of Kashmir, its claim on the headwaters of rivers vital to ir-rigation in Pakistan and Northwest India, the contested terms of its acces-sion, and its tumultuous politics—above all its symbolic value to Indians and Pakistanis—guaranteed that the dispute over it would be long and bitter. On New Year's Day, 1948, India brought the Kashmir problem to the UN Security Council, claiming that a peaceful resolution had been thwarted by Pakistani aggression. Pakistan responded in kind, then sent troops into western Kashmir without informing the Council. The UN cre-ated a commission to handle the dispute—this was the United Nations Commission for India and Pakistan (UNCIP)—which obtained a cease-fire, effective January 1, 1949, urged the withdrawal first of Pakistani then of Indian forces from Kashmir, and recommended a plebiscite for the ter-ritory. The cease-fire for the most part held, but the two countries failed to agree on a timetable for withdrawing troops and thereby demilitarizing Kashmir. The Security Council went ahead and selected the American ad-miral Chester W. Nimitz to serve as plebiscite administrator. This step proved unavailing. Nehru refused to consider a plebiscite unless the Pak-istanis first withdrew their regular forces and tribal allies and then dis-banded the Azad government. And he insisted that the Security Council, for its part, abandon its unfairly balanced assessment of the conflict and acknowledge that India had the superior moral claim. UNCIP suggested that Nimitz arbitrate the military withdrawal issue, but Nehru turned the idea down. The Security Council president, the Canadian general A. G. L. McNaughton, proposed a phased demilitarization overseen by a UN rep-resentative. Nehru said no. The Commission dissolved itself in March 1950 and was replaced by a single mediator: Sir Owen Dixon, an Aus-tralian jurist with diplomatic experience. Dixon arrived in South Asia in late May, spent two months assessing the situation and talking with the principals involved, then arranged a meeting between Nehru and Liaquat Ali Khan in New Delhi. The result was no improvement on previous ef-forts, whereupon Dixon proposed the partition of Kashmir, with a plebiscite confined to the coveted Vale. This suggestion was hedged about by Nehru with conditions so numerous that Dixon gave up in exaspera-tion, saying he was "irritated and indeed disgusted by what he regarded as the short-sightedness of the Pakistani representatives and the tortuous chicanery of Pandit Nehru." Frank Graham, a former congressman from North Carolina, took up where Dixon had left off in the spring of 1951. Two frustrating years later, he too abandoned the quest.

Kashmir is even now a synonym for a festering and unyielding local conflict. Despite occasional thaws in India-Pakistan relations, renewed efforts by the powers to gain a settlement, and eruptions of violence so intense as to compel sobriety at least on both sides, the state has remained divided and inflamed. Unto his death, Nehru insisted that a plebiscite could take place in Kashmir, but conditions there were somehow never suitable. In 1965, Nehru's longtime confidant Krishna Menon explained that there had never been a plebiscite because "Kashmir would vote to join Pakistan and we would lose it." The Pakistanis never acknowledged their role in compromising Kashmir's fragile state of detachment in 1947.[35]

As the years passed, British and U.S. policymakers viewed the struggle over Kashmir with a sense of mounting frustration. Of all the South Asian disputes that threatened U.S. policy objectives in the region, Robert J. McMahon has written, "Kashmir proved by far the most emotional—and intractable." The Americans tried to push the British forward as negotiators, arguing that they knew the adversaries better and understood the issues involved. Reversing that logic, the British urged the Americans to intercede: the relative historical detachment of the United States from South Asia would enable American mediators to approach the situation objectively. The British won a victory when the United States reluctantly accepted membership on UNCIP, but this proved a passage to Wonderland. "So far as I know," recalled J. Wesley Adams, the adviser to the American representative on the commission, "the American delegate was completely uninstructed, because there was nothing to instruct. This was virgin ground—there was no knowledge on the part of the American Government as to what would be possible." The Americans found their early sympathy for the Indian position diminishing. In March 1948 the United States suspended shipments of military materiel to India and Pakistan; Nehru objected loudly. (The suspension ended in March 1949.) When Nehru resisted the conciliation efforts of Nimitz and McNaughton, Acheson and the UN representative Warren Austin gave Indian diplomats a thorough dressing down, and Britain's high commissioner in New Delhi, Sir Archibald Nye, spoke to Nehru about Kashmir using "language so strong that he [Nye] had not ventured to make any record of it." At various times thereafter, the Americans tried to restore good relations with India and end the conflict in Kashmir. In May 1958, President Eisenhower offered his "friendly assistance" to help solve the dispute, but Nehru's cool response left Ambassador Ellsworth Bunker "frankly disappointed." Bunker's successor, John Kenneth Galbraith, found to his surprise in September 1961 that Nehru seemed eager to discuss Kashmir, which he did "in a relaxed and, indeed, rather amusing fashion." Encouraged thus to think that the prime minister might be softening, the Kennedy administration pressed for a settlement. But Nehru scotched that effort with a stinging attack on mediation in India's Parliament in August 1963. Kennedy himself was prompted to write the prime minister that the statement would "certainly complicate our own efforts to help India."[36]

On its surface, the Kashmir conflict seemed an instance of geopolitical disagreement with strategic consequences. This was how the Americans, the British, and the Pakistanis regarded it. Two nations claimed the same piece of land that bordered both of them. If they could not resolve the dispute, the Soviet Union would exploit their differences for its own purposes, and Kashmir itself might become a target of communist expansionism. The State Department worried that American involvement in the dispute could act as a "magnet" to attract Soviet interest, and by demanding U.S. mediation the South Asians might "run the risk of calling down Soviet wrath upon their heads." The Indians especially, fumed P. F. Grey of the British Foreign Office, "must somehow be brought to see that they are fiddling while Rome is burning; in other words, that, while the shadow of Bolshevism is falling more and more over South East Asia, they are fighting with a sister Dominion without whose co-operation they are both likely to be overwhelmed." Western diplomats warned the Indians again and again that the Russians would "meddle" unless the Kashmir problem was solved, and if it came to war between the dominions the communists might seize power in India, or even ignite World War III. Perplexed by Nehru's unwillingness to be flexible, the State Department consultant William Pawley hypothesized that Kashmir's vast trove of mineral wealth was its chief attraction for India. This speculation, which had a basis in the Western myth of India as a treasure house, was in addition a projection of American values onto South Asians: anything worth clinging to so stubbornly, at the risk of international condemnation and communist intervention, must have material value.[37]

Such a scheme might have suited Pakistan, whose leaders also regarded Kashmir as a strategic matter. In fact, most Western and United Nations initiatives on the issue were agreeable to Pakistanis because they were predicated on the same assumption. On September 7, 1949, Prime Minister Liaquat wrote President Truman that his country had accepted the UN plan for arbitration by Admiral Nimitz. Liaquat took the opportunity to make his nation's case: "The geographical and strategic position of Kashmir in relation to Pakistan, the flow of its rivers, the direction of its roads, the channels of its trade, the historical, economic and cultural ties which bind its people to Pakistan, link Kashmir indissolubly with Pakistan.

Nature has so to speak fashioned the two together." (Liaquat would later tell David Lilienthal, "The strategic position of Kashmir is such that without it Pakistan cannot defend herself against an unscrupulous government that might come in India.") The finance minister, Ghulam Mohammed, made a similar case to the *New York Times* correspondent C. L. Sulzberger several months later. Kashmir's value to Pakistan could be enumerated: Pakistan's rivers had their headwaters in Kashmir. Without Kashmir, Pakistan's communications with its Northwest Frontier Province would be exposed. Pakistan relied on Kashmiri timber. And so forth.[38]

This was not India's view, or not that of Nehru, who consulted no one in his government before making decisions on Kashmir. Nehru occasionally mentioned the strategic value of Kashmir in his discussions with Western diplomats early in the crisis. But the real issue had little to do with the logic that commanded Western and Pakistani perspectives on Kashmir. For Nehru, the real issue was the family romance and tragedy of partition, the division of *Bharat Mata* along religious lines. Under duress the Indian family had split; most of its Muslim members had gone with Pakistan, leaving mostly Hindus behind. Some children—or, to condense the metaphor, a child—had not at first claimed allegiance to either parent or sided with either brother. As the child Kashmir had agonized over which brother to join, the Muslim brother began to pressure the child to side with him. When the child decided for the Hindu brother, it became imperative for India to intervene, to protect the child against Pakistani intimidation. A plebiscite was unnecessary, for the child had already chosen sides. Partition of Kashmir, a possibility raised by Owen Dixon, threatened vivisection as surely as Solomon had. What was for the Western powers and Pakistan a dispute over territory was for Nehru a threat to the idea of family, the guiding principle of independent India.

And Kashmir bore even more emotional weight because it was the birthplace of Nehrus, and of Jawaharlal himself. "You can well imagine," he wrote his fellow Kashmiri Brahmin Sir Tej Bahadur Sapru in November 1947, "that it would have been unbearable agony for me to remain a silent witness to the sack and ruin of Kashmir." To the National Assembly he confessed that he would have been "heartbroken" had the state fallen: "I was intensely interested, apart from the larger reasons which the Government have, for emotional and personal reasons." American diplomats found Nehru practically unapproachable on the issue. Secretary of State George Marshall reported in October 1948 that Nehru was "most sensitive" on Kashmir, charging that Pakistan was "backward and theocratic," its leaders "bigoted" and "unreasonable extremists." "So far as Kashmir was concerned, he would not give an inch," Ambassador Loy Henderson wrote nine months later. When Dean Acheson broached the matter with Nehru in Washington in October 1949, the prime minister "went through the roof," later calming down just enough to lecture the secretary in detail about the origins and meaning of the problem: Pakistan, a theocracy, thought it had the right to annex Kashmir because a majority of its inhabitants were Muslims—a view that "struck at the very basis of stability in the Indian sub-continent." India, a secular state, allowed all its citizens, Hindu or Muslim, to participate fully in political life. Thus, "to establish now a religious basis for adherence of provinces would have a profoundly unsettling effect upon all the Moslems in India, and upon the Hindus in Pakistan. A plebiscite campaign based on the these principles would be inflammatory and disastrous" for everyone.[39]

On some level, the Americans seemed to grasp Nehru's view. The State Department noted in April 1950 that "to Nehru, personally, Kashmir is associated with his early life and it appears to be . . . a spiritual symbol which stirs him deeply." ("To Pakistan," this memo continued, "it involves several essentially practical considerations.") The embassy in Pakistan summarized India's position in June 1956: "This is nobody's business but India's and Pakistan's. It is purely a family quarrel. (The Indians undoubtedly think that the big brother could take good care of the little brother if people outside did not interfere.)" All this was perceptively recorded. Yet, on some deeper level, the Americans did not grasp Nehru's view at all. It was impossible to escape the judgment that geography and Cold War strategy should determine who got Kashmir, or what part of it each got, and impossible to understand how meaningful the metaphors of family were to Nehru. Guided by a different set of fundamental principles of governance, Americans failed to appreciate those that shaped India—and the reverse, it must be said, was also true. For Nehru, Kashmir was a family matter. To Americans, the language with which Nehru expressed that view sounded like rhetoric. Thus did Indians and Americans talk past each other, using on the one hand the vocabulary of loyalty and betrayal, and on the other that of strategy and geopolitics.[40]

The Individuated State, the Familial State: The Bokaro Steel Mill Controversy

A much less dangerous dispute, though one bearing equally volatile symbolic meanings, emerged between the United States and India during the late 1950s and early 1960s over possible U.S. government investment in a proposed steel mill at Bokaro, in the northeastern state of Bihar. Americans had been involved in Indian iron and steel manufacturing from its inception. In 1902, J. N. Tata, the "Merchant Prince of Bombay," had come to the United States to study modern production techniques. He brought back with him two American mining engineers, who confirmed the feasibility of using Indian iron ore and coal to establish a steelmaking plant in eastern India. Soon thereafter Tata died, but his sons carried on, and in 1912 they opened a factory in Jamshedpur, 150 miles west of Calcutta. It became a remarkable success story. Through 1954, the firm had reported profits in every year but one. Wages were low, so were the costs of obtaining raw materials, and the firm was thoroughly integrated from mine to market. The Tata family made a fortune.[41]

Before independence the Tatas had competed in steel only with another prominent family, the Birlas. Nehru's government, however, convinced that steel was the backbone of economic development, moved quickly to expand production. Nehru was not about to nationalize Jamshedpur. Still, his instincts told him that steel could not be left to the private sector alone; a 50-50 split between public and private ownership would combine profitability with national security. The government invited foreign investors to underwrite public sector plants with loans. The British and West Germans responded, at Durgapur and Rourkela respectively. The Soviet Union agreed, in February 1955, to help finance a one-million-ton-capacity mill at Bhilai, in Madhya Pradesh. The Soviets provided a $112 million loan for the plant, amortized over twelve years at a bargain interest rate of 2.5 percent. Construction at Bhilai began in mid-1957, and while American visitors to the site commented archly on its lack of technical sophistication—the plant featured an air compressor that emitted a deafening "24-hour, day-in-day-out screech"—there was an undeniable sense of excitement about the place. David Burgess, labor attaché at the U.S. embassy in New Delhi, visited Bhilai in October 1959, and found "the atmosphere . . . much like that of a Texas boom town—noisy, confident, and proud." The Russian engineers on the site were hardworking and friendly, and despite their cultural differences with Indian colleagues they had won the Indians' admiration. Unlike the "secretive" British and Germans at Durgapur and Rourkela, the Russians seemed willing to "share all of their engineering secrets" and "deferred to the authority of their Indian counterparts even in cases where the Russian in question was far superior in ability." The Soviets had not interfered when the mill's Indian managers had fired 187 employees for suspected "communist leanings."[42]

The Eisenhower administration was unhappy with the Soviet presence at Bhilai. Almost immediately an opportunity arose for it to respond in kind. Late in 1954, B. M. Birla asked the U.S. Export Import (ExIm) Bank for a loan of $100 million to finance the construction of a privately held steel plant with the same capacity then proposed for Bhilai. Not to be outdone, the Tatas quickly put in a request for $62.5 million for expansion at Jamshedpur. There was a good deal of support at the ExIm Bank and in the State Department, for either request or both (though the Birla initiative soon fizzled). But the loan foundered when the Indian government, ever watchful for the specter of economic imperialism, insisted that any loan from the ExIm Bank come with an interest rate lower than the Bank's usual 5 percent, in order to cover the purchase of relatively expensive American equipment to which it would be tied. The Americans would not make this deal, arguing that it would set a bad precedent. So the Tatas turned instead to the World Bank, which offered $75 million at 4.75 percent, available for equipment purchases anywhere in the world. The Indian government preferred this arrangement, since it would itself guarantee the World Bank loan and thus retain oversight that it would lose in the event of ExIm involvement. For that reason, it was the Tatas' second choice, but they accepted it anyway in June 1956. The United States had missed its opportunity.[43]

The Indians' determination to produce more steel gave the Eisenhower administration another chance. In June 1959 the Indian government notified Ambassador Ellsworth Bunker that a fourth public-sector steel mill was in the offing, to be built at Bokaro. Would the Americans be interested in financing it? Bunker and his staff urged serious consideration of the offer as a way to compete directly with the Soviets, and endorsed a " 'rolling with [the] punch' approach" to the ideological blow of supporting the public sector. Others were not so sure. Clarence Randall, head of the Council on Foreign Economic Policy, probably spoke for Eisenhower when he advised: "We must not be doctrinaire to the point of refusing to help the public sector in industry any further, but our sympathy should be toward the private sector." Tata and Birla also muddied the waters by suggesting that the matter of public versus private ownership of the new plant was not yet settled. Confused by the initiative and at odds with itself, the administration left the scene in early 1961 without having set a course.[44]

With the advent of the Kennedy administration the Indian government sought to inject new life into the Bokaro project, requesting, in early 1961, some $900 million in U.S. financing. John Kenneth Galbraith, the economist who had just been named Kennedy's ambassador to India, took up the cause with vigor. At his first Indian press conference in April 1961, Galbraith claimed that Bokaro was "within the range of American aid," adding in his diary: "I had no instructions but one should use what freedom he has, for it is evidently a rare blessing." Frequently thereafter, with enemies of public-sector investment in staunch opposition and with the president's attention turned elsewhere, the project seemed in jeopardy. Each time Galbraith revived it. He argued that the Soviets had gotten "the jump on us" through their support of high-visibility industrial projects, while American funds were diffused into rural development efforts that for all their usefulness were hardly noticed by most Indians. Past U.S. assistance to the private sector had provoked Indians to say: " 'The Americans help the Tatas and Birlas who are already rich. By contrast, the Soviets or British build plants that belong to the people.' " Galbraith pointed out that Indian capitalists endorsed Bokaro since, as Tata had said, a mill of this size was "simply beyond the financial resources" of private enterprise in India. And he noted that the Indian government had agreed that U.S. Steel or another private American builder might be accorded "a large measure of autonomy" during construction and the plant's "running in." "In some ways," he concluded, "what would be a public operation from the Indian viewpoint would be a private operation from ours." In other words, Americans should support the project because it really wasn't in the public sector at all. No one, not even the Canadian-born Galbraith, was asking U.S. officials to endorse socialism, which so clearly ran against the grain of American ideology.[45]

Galbraith's case was not entirely persuasive. The men he sneeringly called "the bureaucrats" in the State Department and at the Agency for International Development (AID) were no less cautious about public-sector investment than their predecessors had been. President Kennedy was Galbraith's good friend, but his approval for Bokaro was in the end insufficient to carry the project; he signaled his acceptance in the spring of 1961, allowed it to be rescinded in August, then, on May 8, 1963, offered a tepid endorsement: "The Congress may have other views, but I think it would be a great mistake not to build it. India needs the steel." As Arthur Schlesinger, Jr., later wrote dourly, "Congress did have other views." Republicans seized on the March 1963 report of the Clay Committee, appointed by the president to study U.S. foreign aid programs, and quoted again and again the Committee's declaration that "the U.S. should not aid a foreign government in projects establishing government-owned industrial and commercial enterprises which compete with existing private endeavors." The Committee had Bokaro in mind. David Bell, the administrator of AID, was summoned before the House Foreign Affairs Committee during its consideration of the Foreign Assistance Act in April and May 1963. For a time Bell pleaded that he lacked sufficient information to make a sound judgment on aid for Bokaro. He did argue eventually, like Galbraith, that Bokaro was as much a private as a public enterprise. The plant's board of directors would include not just public officials but private businessmen. It would pay the same taxes as a private firm. Perhaps stock would be sold to private citizens. "Mr. Bell," interjected Representative H. R. Gross of Iowa, "can the record show that you are still betwixt and between?" "I will come to my own conclusion," Bell retorted, but Gross's characterization wasn't far wrong. No more than any other U.S. official would Bell endorse socialism.[46]

In the end, no amount of qualification would soothe conservative fears that Bokaro would crowd out Indian free enterprise, compromising freedom of the marketplace and threatening the welfare of men like Birla and Tata. Wielding the Clay report, members of Congress lashed the administration for its investment plans. "The U.S. Government cannot preserve human freedom and the importance of the individual by subsidizing socialism," said Representative Bruce Alger of Texas. "Here we see the hardearned money of U.S. citizens . . . in a capitalistic society being given by the President to that system which is in mortal combat with us, and whose leaders intend to bury us." Senator Milward Simpson of Wyoming insisted: "This steel mill at Bokaro will be working against the two privately owned steel mills in India." It would put both governments "into business in direct contravention of the fiscal policies which have placed this nation and some of those reconstructed after World War II far ahead of other economic and industrial powers." Through the spring and summer of 1963, lawmakers entered into the *Congressional Record* critical articles from such stalwartly conservative publications as *Reader's Digest, U.S. News and World Report,* and the Chicago *Sun-Times.* ("Broadly speaking," opined the *Sun-Times,* "the opposite of private enterprise and individual capitalism is state ownership, state production, and state distribution. Or, if you will, Marxism. This is precisely the status of the proposed steel mill in India.")[47]

Bokaro was ultimately delayed to death. On August 22, 1963, the House passed an amendment to the Foreign Assistance Act that would postpone for a year the funding of any overseas enterprise in excess of $100 million. Bokaro was the only such project pending. The amendment's author, William S. Broomfield of Michigan, claimed that too little was known of Bokaro's prospects to permit financial commitment to it, and called for further study. Ideological opponents of public-sector funding might have preferred that the project be terminated, but the solid majority favoring delay told the administration all it needed to know. Nehru saw the signs, too. On August 28 he sent T. T. Krishnamachari, his minister of supply, to the office of Chester Bowles, who had succeeded Galbraith as ambassador the previous month. Krishnamachari wondered whether Nehru should write to the president thanking him for his help with the project, "noting the ugly mood of Congress, and asking that Bokaro be withdrawn from consideration since he did not wish India to become a subject of contention in the United States." Bowles unhappily consented, and Nehru's letter was duly sent. Kennedy replied September 4, thanking Nehru for his sensitivity, expressing again his own support for Bokaro, and assuring India of continuing U.S. economic and military aid. Bowles feared the Soviets would step in, and they did: in January 1965, the Soviet Union offered a low-interest loan to underwrite the Bokaro mill. The first blast furnace at the site was commissioned in October 1972.[48]

While Galbraith and Bowles were anguished over the failure of their efforts, most members of Congress, and probably most Americans, shrugged the matter off. The United States, dedicated from its origins to individualism and free enterprise, was not about the business of supporting socialism. The liberals, recognizing this, had tried to portray Bokaro as a private concern, worthy of American support because of its potential impact on the Cold War contest for India's allegiance. But strategy, thus defined, could not trump ideology. Americans had rejected the paternal state as part of their birthright. They were not about to countenance strengthening India's version of it at the expense of hardy Indian entrepreneurs.

The concerns of the Indian government were different. The very legitimacy of the state rested on its ability to embody the wishes of most Indians; its power depended on the totality with which it appropriated the welfare functions of private employers. B. M. Birla and J. R. D. Tata were not heroic entrepreneurs but patriarchs of wealthy and powerful extended families. The extent to which they retained unchallenged economic power determined the strength (or weakness) of the national government. The alternative to the public sector was not private enterprise but a myriad of closed, paternal enterprises, lubricated by nepotism and resistant to democratization. In May 1963, as the Bokaro debate in Congress rang increasingly shrill, the journalist Selig Harrison observed: "The symbolic importance of Bokaro resides precisely in the fact that it is to be publicly controlled. The expanding power of a few family-held monopolies in India is a powerful political factor and the so-called 'public sector' is a rallying-cry connoting shared national values comparable in effectiveness to 'state socialism' as a political war whoop in the United States." But these were rallying cries and war whoops with a purpose, and their content reflected the difference between a people who regarded state intervention as political metastasis and another for whom it was a sine qua non of a stable and legitimate government.[49]

4

Race: Americans and Indians, at Home and in Africa

> On landing in Calcutta I was at once surrounded by a crowd of
> nearly naked "niggers." . . . These gentlemen crowded me so
> much with their black, oily bodies, that I found a vigorous beat-
> ing with my umbrella necessary to keep them at a respectful dis-
> tance.
> —Robert B. Minturn, Jr., *From New York to Delhi*

> A colonial situation is created, so to speak, the very instant a
> white man, even if he is alone, appears in the midst of a tribe,
> even if it is independent, so long as he is thought to be rich or
> powerful or merely immune to the local forces of magic, and so
> long as he derives from his position, even though only in his
> most secret self, a feeling of his own superiority.
> —O. Mannoni, *Prospero and Caliban*

Katherine Mayo's *Mother India* had a profound effect on American perceptions of India after 1927. But the first exposure to India for most Americans born between 1900 and 1965, whether they knew it or not, came from Helen Bannerman's book *Little Black Sambo*. The story concerns a boy who is given a beautiful set of new clothes by his parents, Black Mumbo and Black Jumbo, then walks off proudly into the jungle. There he is accosted by four tigers, one after the other, each of whom agrees not to eat him in exchange for an article of clothing. Sambo is left with only his *dhoti*, a skirtlike garment worn by South Indian males. As he stands there crying, Sambo overhears the tigers meet and begin to argue over which of them is "the grandest." Sambo watches as the tigers remove their clothes, circle each other warily, then seize each other by the tail and chase around so fast that they are reduced to a pool of clarified butter, called by its Indian name *ghi* (often *ghee*). Sambo's clothes are restored to him, and Black Jumbo retrieves the butter and brings it home to Black Mumbo, who uses it to make pancakes. And Little Black Sambo eats 169.

Little Black Sambo, first published in England in 1899, was enormously popular in its time, going through more than thirty editions and selling like, well, hotcakes in Great Britain and the United States. But today it is not easy to find. Many readers found its story and especially its illustrations racist, caricatures not so much of Indians but of Africans or African Americans, so it was banished from libraries and bookstores. Informal polls reveal that for every person who remembers that *Little Black Sambo* is set in India there are several who believe that it took place in Africa or the antebellum American South, never mind the tigers. One reason for this confusion was that many American editions of the book abandoned Helen Bannerman's illustrations and depicted Sambo and his parents as lurid versions of Africans or black Americans. A 1908 edition, for instance, put Black Mumbo in a kerchief and a apron and gave her a maniacally thick-lipped grin. Later editions represented Sambo as a Westerner's African, with pitch-black skin and in one case a grass skirt. Only in 1950 did a Whitman Publishing Company edition restore Sambo to India; in 1972, Black Mumbo was renamed Mama Sari.[1]

But it was not simply that Helen Bannerman's work had been corrupted, for her edition conflated Western stereotypes of Indians, Africans, and African Americans. Bannerman wrote the book in India, *ghi* is a Sanskrit word, and there are no tigers in Africa. The use of the name Sambo suggests an African or American source. The term "Mumbo Jumbo" was used by British travelers in Africa to mean "a grotesque idol . . . worshipped by certain tribes or associations of Negroes." (Emerson used it to describe railroads, mesmerism, and California.) According to Bannerman's illustrations, Sambo and his parents were indeed very black, the clothes worn by Mumbo and Jumbo were certainly not Indian, and the expressions Bannerman gave her characters are crude caricatures of African or African-American physiognomies. Above all, *Little Black Sambo* offered its readers a depiction of India as a land of racial Others, who could be classified together with dark-skinned people from exotic places and who could not be readily distinguished from them.[2]

There was no single, comparable source of Indian impressions of the United States. We do know, however, what Indians most often said to Americans when the subject of life in the United States came up. "Almost invariably," wrote the two-time American ambassador Chester Bowles, "the number one question was, 'what about America's treatment of the

Helen Bannerman's original illustration of Little Black Sambo, racially and ethnically ambiguous. Helen Bannerman, Little Black Sambo, *1986 edition.*

Negro?' " Throughout the period of Jawaharlal Nehru's prime ministry, Indians remained convinced that racial inequality, more than anything else, typified American society. It also shaped U.S. foreign relations. The contempt white Americans felt for black Americans applied as well to nonwhites in other nations, to the undifferentiated "colored populations"

Black Sambo and Black Mumbo, drawn by John B. Gruell for a 1917 American edition of the book. Elizabeth Hay, Sambo Sahib, *1981.*

of the world, as they were known from the 1940s to the 1960s. J. Saunders Redding, a black scholar who went to India in the early 1950s under State Department auspices, heard from every Indian "the implication and/or the declaration that American color prejudice is reflected in official American international policy, that our international relations reflect our domestic order." Redding, Pearl Buck, and other American visitors and officials in India were peppered with questions about racial discrimination: Do Negroes have educational or job opportunities equal to those of whites? Are the Negroes barred from hotels where whites stay? Why is Paul Robeson being persecuted? How many Negroes were lynched in the United States last year? Indians "cannot understand a functioning democracy which contains such inequality," Buck wrote. "Nor," she added, "can I explain it to them." In March 1953, as he ended what would be his first tour of duty in New Delhi, Bowles wrote Secretary of State John Foster Dulles "that in forming individual and national attitudes toward world affairs the color question is the most basic of all."[3]

Race is one of the principal threads in the webs of American and Indian political culture. Precisely what it means is difficult to say; like "culture," "race" is a complicated and refractory word. Let us begin with a definition that a Western anthropologist might have accepted during the 1950s: "a subdivision of the human species, characterized by a more or less distinctive combination of physical traits that are transmitted in descent." The "physical traits" that most often signified race during the nineteenth and twentieth centuries were skull shape, physiognomy, hair quality, and skin color. While it is difficult to disaggregate these traits in a way that will tell us which mattered most to an observer at a particular time, it is fair to say that people considered skin color the most salient racial feature. In the West, at least, skin color did not just distinguish people from one another—it ranked them. Studies of color symbolism in the West have shown that Caucasians associate the color white with innocence, joy, happiness, purity, peace, chastity, and truth. With black comes woe, gloom, dread, horror, wickedness, defilement, and death. Sixteenth-century Europeans found color the most "arresting characteristic" of newly "discovered" Africans. Certainly by the middle of the twentieth century, when phrenology was a science forgotten or dismissed, most people made racial judgments on the basis of skin color.[4]

Race played a subtle but important role in United States–India relations. White American policymakers—and virtually all policymakers during the period 1947–64 were white—inherited the racial assumptions of their British and American predecessors. They saw Indians and other dark-skinned people as racial Others, in fundamental ways different from and inferior to whites. Because racial differences were felt so deeply by whites, race thinking conditioned foreign policy decisions. American policymakers after 1947 seldom said they were making policy for racial reasons. It would not have been fashionable to do so. Race thinking had a bad odor following the racist crimes of Germany and Japan during World War II, and any assertion that racial considerations had a place in policymaking invited serious criticism. Thus, the documentary record is largely innocent of the specific vocabulary of race. And yet, there is indirect but compelling evidence that American officials were thinking in racial terms when they made policy toward Latin America, Asia, and Africa. When they talked of democracy and freedom and liberation, they had in mind Eastern Europe or other areas under communist control. Liberation did not mean what dark-skinned people took it to mean: the end of European colonialism. American policymakers were not colonialists, and not all were crude racists. In the end, however, they were unwilling to support for people of color what they, as whites, claimed as their birthright. This unthinking decision was most pronounced in U.S. policy toward southern Africa, and that is where the conflict was joined with India.

Race was also a factor in Indian foreign policy. Although they were originally classified as Caucasians, Indians regarded themselves as people of color and identified with other people of color in Asia, America, and Africa. The maintenance of Third World colonies by European nations was evidence of their racism; indeed, to Indians colonialism *was* racism. Americans refused to admit that their policies were shaped by race thinking, but Indians were convinced otherwise. United States support for the French in Indochina and Algeria, the British in Kenya, the Portuguese in Angola, Mozambique, and Goa, and the white government of South Africa meant, Indians said, that Americans favored the interests of whites over the human rights of browns and blacks. It was no surprise, really, that the Americans behaved this way, for American foreign policy reflected the brutal realities of racial discrimination in the United States. Because India was the self-proclaimed champion of people of color everywhere, it was inevitable that its foreign policy would clash with that of the United States.

The subtleties and ambiguities of race thinking were even more pronounced on the Indian side. Though Nehru and others who spoke for India emphasized their solidarity with the people of color who hoped to follow the Indian path to independence, Indian leaders were subconsciously uncertain of their racial identities. They were dark skinned, but not as dark as the Africans whose rights they vociferously proclaimed, and in plain truth Indians were treated better than blacks were in white countries. Black Africans regarded the Indians among them as economic exploiters, privileged in their relationships with colonial masters. Many Indians expressed an aesthetic preference for light skin, and there was at least a tenuous connection between race and the Indian caste system. Finally, independent India turned its back on the localist, agrarian economic vision of Mohandas Gandhi and embraced instead a version of modernization that bore a strong resemblance to Western models of development. This imitation of the colonialists caused Indian leaders great discomfort, and ultimately increased the stridency with which Indians accused whites of racism. The struggle to define the postindependence Indian self caused Indians to represent white Americans as racial Others.

Here recall the discussion of selves and Others by Sander Gilman. As noted earlier, Gilman argues that Others are the projections of selves and are constituted particularly from the categories of illness, sexuality, and race (the introduction discussed the first two). According to Gilman, it is easiest to represent Others if we can find in them "anatomical signs of difference," including "physiognomy and skin color." Race is profoundly related to perceptions of difference based on illness and sexuality. The connection of race to pathology is indicated by some of the word associations cited earlier: with white comes "purity," for example, while black connotes defilement and death. Whites regarded Indians, like blacks, as racially pathological. During epidemics in the nineteenth and early twentieth centuries, no Indians were allowed onboard European and American ships docked in Indian harbors, though Westerners were. Since the illnesses common to India did not discriminate by race, this policy was biologically indefensible. The obsession of whites with the size of black men's genitalia and the alleged hypersexuality of black women reveals just how powerful is the perceived link between race and sexuality.[5]

Recall, too, that Westerners were fascinated and disgusted by the odors of India. By the eighteenth century, according to Alain Corbin, the European bourgeoisie had come to associate bad smells not with natural phenomena but with people, especially class and racial Others. Peasants and beggars smelled bad—an 1831 report by a Paris sanitary commission described some beggars as "veritable walking dunghills"—and so did people of color. It was no longer the undifferentiated crowd that stank but certain people in it. Blacks had "such an evil-smelling odor that it is hard to stay next to them for a few minutes." Asians were also notoriously malodorous. In European lazarettos, mail from Asia was decontaminated in *parfumoirs*, wooden boxes with built-in chafing dishes for burning disinfection pellets. Selves believe that they, and their group, have no odor. They ascribe to Others disagreeable smells that are "somehow intrinsic to the group, a characteristic trait as inalterable as skin color." "I just don't like Pakis," said a white youth in England. "They stink. Pakis really reek." Kenneth J. Gergen has suggested that distaste for dark skin can be traced to the rituals of cleanliness associated with toilet training. *Defilement* is thus a term with both hygienic and racial meanings: the West's anxious loathing of excrement surely contributed to the Western perception that India, a land of racial Others and public defecation, was an impure and disorderly place.[6]

Western Racial Views of India before 1947

Long before India and Pakistan gained their independence, Westerners believed that the peoples of South Asia were racially different from whites. Westerners were not always sure where Indians belonged in the Great Chain of Being, so they often left them out altogether, relegating less complicated races like Negroes, American Indians, and Eskimos to its lower stations. When whites did classify Asian Indians, they gave them a racial status inferior to their own. British literature on India emphasized stark differences between Anglo-Saxon and Indian races. The novels of

George Alfred Henty, for the most part unknown in the United States, were highly influential in Great Britain, especially with a generation of schoolboys. According to Robin Jared Lewis, Henty "was a firm believer in the doctrine of Anglo-Saxon superiority" who "never hesitated to give his readers quick summary judgments of Indians: 'there are no better or more pleasant waiters in the world than the natives of Hindostan.' " Rudyard Kipling's stories and poems about India were as influential in the United States as books by Helen Bannerman and Katherine Mayo. Kipling himself loved India. He was less sure about its people, especially Hindus, whom he generally found despicable—though it ought to be said that he could be devastating in his depictions of the British as well. His stories emphasize the vast gulf separating the white and Indian "races," a lesson bitterly learned by a Kipling character named Trejago, who stumbles one day into a dead-end alley overlooked by a single, grated window. From the window comes "a pretty little laugh" that belongs to a fifteen-year-old widow named Bisesa. The two share a song, then Bisesa pursues Trejago, sending him messages via her handmaiden. He steals into her room, and they begin an affair that is casual for neither. Eventually, however, because he is an Englishman, Trejago is forced to escort a white *memsahib*, and though he feels nothing for the woman he is confronted by Bisesa in a jealous rage. For three weeks following the incident Trejago hears nothing from his lover, so he goes to the alley to talk to her. He climbs the wall, and as he reaches the window the grating is pulled inside: "From the black dark Bisesa held out her arms into the moonlight. Both hands had been cut off at the wrists, and the stumps were nearly healed." The moral of story, wrote Kipling, was that "a man should, whatever happens, keep to his own caste, race, and breed. Let the White go to the White and the Black go to the Black." The story's title is "Beyond the Pale," where Trejago had foolishly gone.[7]

Like the British, white Americans made racial distinctions between themselves and Indians. With Helen Bannerman, white Americans often conflated Indians with Africans and African Americans. Thomas Tingey, who sailed to Calcutta in 1795, identified Indians as "black" in his journal, and subsequent American visitors to the subcontinent followed the British practice of referring to Indians as "niggers." Anna Leonowens, later to gain fame at the court of the king of Siam, noted that the "native portion" of Calcutta was called by Westerners "Black Town." The Bombay consul William Fee lamented in 1899 that "there are two black mouths always open for every grain of rice that grows," and subsequently received a complaint from an American businessman who had borne the humiliation of having a handgun confiscated by "these muddyblooded 'Jhonnies,' which is worse than a jolt in the face." In 1900 an American engineer named George Wilson was accused in Bombay of misappropriating U.S. government funds. In his defense, Wilson argued that he had been betrayed by his clerks, all of them "natives," and pointed out that the chief prosecution witness was Indian. He was acquitted by an English judge.[8]

Whites also associated Indians in the United States with blacks. In Pennsylvania some Indian slaves became indentured servants following emancipation in 1780. Six Indian men living in Salem, Massachusetts, during the mid-nineteenth century married black women and apparently became part of the town's African-American population. In California during the 1920s, hotels and boarding houses refused to take in Indians, and the restaurants at the University of California would not serve them. Some Indians obtained U.S. citizenship in the second decade of the twentieth century, but in the *Thind* decision of 1923 the U.S. Supreme Court ruled that in common parlance Caucasian did not mean white, and thus Indians might be denied citizenship. Indians who had earlier been made citizens now found themselves fending off attempts by the Justice Department to denaturalize them and efforts by their neighbors to confiscate their land.[9]

Americans and Racialized India after 1947

By 1947 few American visitors to India and even fewer U.S. foreign policymakers expressed themselves in the vocabulary of race. Their timing was no accident. World War II had been fought against two racist nations, Germany and Japan, a fact emphasized by Allied propaganda. But the United States itself had a poor record in race relations. People of color, most notably African Americans, were denied basic rights. Southern blacks were not allowed to vote, sit on juries, or attend state universities. Segregation confined them to inferior housing, schools, jobs, accommodations, and cemeteries. Several blacks were lynched each year, and countless others were beaten or abused. Blacks who had the temerity to speak out against racism were widely criticized and in some cases hounded by the FBI. Every day, even northern blacks suffered the ritual insults of racism. Black customers in stores were ignored or followed about; white realtors "redlined" neighborhoods to prevent blacks from buying houses in them; the great major league baseball player Jackie Robinson, who desegregated the game in 1947, endured racial slurs and discrimination as he toured the country with the Brooklyn Dodgers.

This evidence of American racism was inconvenient for foreign policymakers, whose labors relied on the premise that cooperation with the United States would not require other nations to give up their freedoms, as the Soviet satellites patently had. Why should Indians and other people of color have faith in those who permitted blacks in their own country to be lynched by white mobs? If racism seemed to sophisticated American officials an embarrassing sideshow, it was to equally sophisticated leaders in the Third World the central flaw in American society. Americans found that charges of racism stood in the way of their efforts to contain communism and shore up the economies and governments of the noncommunist nations. Some were willing to criticize American racism. More often, officials hoped to trivialize or conceal it, claiming that it was confined to pockets of the South or that it was under attack by the authorities. They tried to eliminate race words from their vocabularies. Indians, American officials pointed out, ought to be reassured by Congress's decision, in 1946, to permit one hundred Indians a year to immigrate to the United States—a hundred more, that is, than had been previously permitted to enter.[10]

Still, race words occasionally crept into the private discourse of U.S. policymakers, often enough to suggest that race retained a presence in the political culture of the Cold War. Race helped demonize America's enemies—the language of the Cold War stressed the ominous Asian background of the Soviets—and helped to explain the contrary behavior of people, like Indians, who ought to have been friends. When Truman and Nehru met for the first time in the fall of 1949, they did not get along. Truman, the grandson of slaveholders whose vocabulary included the terms "Jap" and "nigger," later remarked that he thought Nehru "didn't like white folks." George Kennan, who beginning in 1947 directed long-term planning for the State Department, thought that the governments of "states with colored populations" were "the neurotic products of exotic backgrounds and tentative Western educational experiences." In June 1950 the assistant secretary of state for Near Eastern and South Asian Affairs, George McGhee, told Devadas Gandhi (the son of the Mahatma) that the American "attitude toward the color problem" did not apply to India. In any case, McGhee thought that segregation "was no real problem as the races just naturally do not wish to mix," that "intermarriage would [n]ever be accepted" by Americans, and that racial "differences really did exist . . . [as] illustrated by the fact that Africa had always been retarded in its development." Chester Bowles noted instances in which the racial attitudes of U.S. representatives in India had "caused great offense," and attributed to Dean Acheson and John Foster Dulles the question, " 'How could all these ignorant colored people run their own lives?' "

During 1953, officials in the Eisenhower administration got into a dispute over whom to support for president of the UN General Assembly: Prince Wan of Thailand or Vijayalakshmi Pandit of India. Eisenhower could not understand why the issue should be so hotly debated, since (as he put it) both candidates were Asian. In July 1961, Harris Wofford reported to President Kennedy a conversation at a cocktail party: "One of the Department's most respected Africa hands told me that the problem with Bowles and [assistant secretary of state G. Mennen] Williams was that when they saw a band of black baboons beating tom-toms they saw George Washingtons. Another said that Bowles wanted our diplomats to put on sarongs and make love to the natives."[11]

The relative scarcity of race words in the vocabulary of Americans who made policy suggests that these words were unfashionable, not that the reasons for using them originally had disappeared. One must translate apparently more benign usage in order to recover the persistent white assumption that dark-skinned people were inferior to light-skinned ones. Michael Hunt has argued that the language of racial hierarchy, once common to American foreign policy discourse, was replaced beginning in the 1940s by a language of development, which ranked nations according to their progress along a continuum of modernity established by white Westerners. The language changed, but attitudes did not; like racial theory, Hunt writes, development theory was "condescending and paternalistic." Those who would disguise their opinions about the backwardness of people of color might nevertheless claim that a hierarchy of modernity existed, in which the positions of peoples and nations were more or less fixed. "Not surprisingly," writes Hunt, "the resulting rankings were strikingly similar to the ones assigned two centuries earlier by race-conscious ancestors." Anglo-Americans came first, Europeans followed, and the nonwhite people of the Third World continued to occupy the bottom rungs of the ladder.[12]

To some extent, racial attitudes were manifest in the U.S. policy of "Europe First." Most in the State Department believed that Europe had first claim on American attention and resources. While it was possible to argue that favoring Europe was strategically sensible, only with reference to race can one explain the hypocrisy of advocating freedom for Europeans— and basing a policy on such a contention—while at the same time judging premature the quest for majority rule by black Africans. Were the people of Angola less prepared to govern themselves than the people of Bulgaria? Then too, as we have seen, strategy itself is far from a self-evident concept. Why should the freedom from communism for Europeans, to be purchased in part through cooperation with authoritarian governments, be strategically more meaningful than the liberation of Africans from colonialism and white minority rule? The American effort to keep (for example) Portugal and the white government of South Africa in the Western camp cost the United States the friendship of millions of blacks, who found themselves drawn to communism and its promises of liberation. This result was so strategically self-defeating that it is hard to escape the conclusion that other factors, among them race, must have been involved in American thinking.

In any ranking of U.S. global interests done before the late 1950s, Africa would have appeared at or near the bottom. Unlike Europe and even Asia, Africa seemed peripheral to American concerns. It was not vital for the defense of the United States; outside the southern part of the continent it held little of value to American corporations; the policymaking elite in the United States was not connected to Africa by ties of history or culture. Most Americans, Thomas J. Noer has written, got their ideas about Africa "from Tarzan movies, missionary slide shows in church basements, and Ernest Hemmingway short stories." The continent came into greater prominence in the United States in the late 1950s, with the full flowering of the campaign for African independence. The struggles for freedom bore fruit: in 1960 alone, seventeen black African nations became independent.[13]

The Truman and Eisenhower administrations witnessed these events with mixture of dismay and resignation. The problem with what policymakers called "premature independence" for black Africans was that it threatened international stability and U.S. Cold War designs. The colonialists whom the Africans challenged were British, French, Belgian, and Portuguese, all of them allies of the Americans, the first two among the most important. If African liberation weakened Western European countries, it would undermine the economy of the noncommunist world and shake the foundations of the containment strategy, by which the United States hoped to frustrate perceived Soviet expansionism. Communism itself seemed an ideological threat to emergent nations. The Americans held that communism fed on misery and instability, and "premature independence" portended both.

The Truman administration mostly sided with the Europeans, and the Democrats left office before the liberation movements at home and abroad fully crested. The Eisenhower administration, less fortunate, was swept up in the tide of events. Ghana won its freedom in 1957, Algeria and Kenya exploded into violence, and the Congo became independent in 1960 and quickly disintegrated. In South Africa, where the system of racial segregation known as apartheid had been in force since 1948, police in

Sharpeville opened fire on a group of peaceful black demonstrators in 1960, killing 69 and wounding three times that many. The administration tried to salvage some semblance of a policy in Africa. It moved to accommodate those governments that were already established, offering aid to the neutralist Kwame Nkrumah in Ghana, backing UN efforts to hold the Congo together, and supporting a UN resolution condemning the South African government. Once the 1960 presidential election was over and the Republicans had lost, however, Eisenhower reverted to a "Europe-first" policy that was more in harmony with his ideological tendencies.[14]

John F. Kennedy took office in early 1961, carrying liberal hopes that he would align the United States fully with the emerging nations. Kennedy had strongly criticized French policy in Algeria in 1957, and during the 1960 campaign he had scored points with liberals and Africans when he pledged $100,000 from a family foundation to fly a group of East African students to the United States for university training—money the State Department had twice declined to provide. Unlike Eisenhower, who compared the arrival of nationalism in Africa to a "destructive hurricane," Kennedy seemed eager to embrace the challenge offered by the new regimes. The president claimed to sympathize with the nonalignment espoused by many of the African states and India. He appointed well-known liberals to key positions in the administration: G. Mennen Williams, a staunch supporter of civil rights as governor of Minnesota, became assistant secretary of state for Africa; Chester Bowles was made undersecretary of state; Adlai Stevenson, still much admired by liberals, got the job of ambassador to the United Nations. Kennedy also chose progressive young ambassadors to the African countries. African leaders were initially well pleased with the new American president. Algeria's first premier, Ben Bella, remembered listening to 1960 election returns in his guerrilla camp: there was cheering when Kennedy led, and cursing when Nixon pulled ahead. Nkrumah professed "complete kinship" with JFK.[15]

Kennedy was genuinely interested in the progress of African nationalism, but several factors worked against the development of a bracingly new policy toward the continent. There remained the imperatives of the Cold War to consider. During the summer of 1960, the Congolese premier Patrice Lumumba had accepted extensive military aid from the Soviet Union, prompting the CIA to warn that the Congo seemed to be "another Cuba" in the making. Early the following year, the Soviet premier Nikita Khrushchev endorsed "wars of national liberation" throughout the Third World, and thereafter the Soviets fished in troubled waters in Ghana, Angola, and, to hear the South African government tell it, South-

West Africa (Namibia) as well. Related to the Soviet problem was the persistent Eurocentrism of the U.S. foreign policy establishment. For every Williams or Bowles appointed by Kennedy, there was at least one Europe-firster in a more prominent position, or acting as a powerful gray eminence behind the scenes. George Ball, Roger Hilsman, John McCone, Dean Rusk, Robert Lovett, Paul Nitze, Dean Acheson, and others argued that Western Europe remained far more important to the United States than Africa, so it did no good to antagonize the Europeans over the pace of decolonization. When European and African interests were not in conflict it was easy enough to endorse the latter. If the two sets of interests clashed, Kennedy was usually persuaded to favor the European.[16]

Overhanging the Africa policies of Truman, Eisenhower, and Kennedy was the matter of race. The foreign policymakers in all three of these administrations came to intellectual maturity at a time when black people, in the United States and elsewhere, were relegated to positions of subordination to whites. If they had known blacks at all, they had regarded them "almost exclusively as social and economic inferiors," notes Thomas Borstelmann. Because of this, U.S. officials had difficulty justifying self-government for African blacks. Truman himself, his three appointed secretaries of state, and the influential George Kennan held racial prejudices that ranged from the genteel to the overt. Eisenhower and Dulles paid little attention to Africa. Both men sedulously ignored African leaders except in times of acute crisis. The president inveighed against inviting "those niggers" to diplomatic receptions, and when Africans could not be kept away from these functions they noticed the wives of American diplomats "trying surreptitiously to slip on their white gloves" before greeting their dark-skinned guests. While Kennedy had a record of interest in African nationalism that impressed even the nationalists, his policy toward Africa did no better than hew a middle path between the positions of the Africanists and the Europeanists in his administration, an approach that reflected Kennedy's reluctance to move too quickly against racial discrimination in the American South. Throughout the period 1945–63, policymakers continued to identify with Europeans in their approach to Africa, and to see the continent through European eyes.[17]

At the same time, the black civil rights movement emerged in the United States, with dramatic effect on U.S. foreign relations. Whether U.S. policymakers liked it or not, involvement with nonwhite people abroad was linked to race issues at home. Black opponents of discrimination in the United States and nonwhite nationalists abroad worked together against the twin evils of racism and colonialism. James Baldwin observed that "the rise of Africa in world affairs [had] everything to do" with the growth of the American civil rights movement in the 1950s, and the civil rights movement served in turn to inspire Africans in their pursuit of independence. In 1947 the National Association for the Advancement of Colored People (NAACP) linked domestic to international racial discrimination by petitioning the UN in protest against American racism: "It is not Russia that threatens the United States so much as Mississippi; not Stalin and Molotov but [racist senators] Bilbo and Rankin; internal injustice done to one's brothers is far more dangerous than the aggression of strangers from abroad." The Truman administration tried to deflect some of the criticism by filing amicus curiae briefs in civil rights cases before the Supreme Court. In one of these, Dean Acheson explained that "the existence of discrimination against minority groups in this country has an adverse effect upon our relations with other countries. We are reminded over and over . . . that our treatment of various minorities leaves much to be desired. . . . Frequently we find it next to impossible to formulate a satisfactory answer to our critics in other countries."[18]

Most Africans and Asians, particularly Indians, remained skeptical of white America's intentions. The Soviet Union sought to exploit the race issue in order to gain the confidence of Third World leaders, frequently with success. When the Supreme Court decided, in the *Brown* decision of 1954, that racially segregated schools were unconstitutional, the Eisenhower administration vigorously publicized the verdict abroad—even though Eisenhower and many of his advisers were not fully in agreement with it. *Brown* improved the U.S. image in nonwhite countries, but southern resistance to the implementation of the decision and the administration's manifest lack of enthusiasm for enforcing it made many abroad suspicious of the American commitment to civil rights. Kennedy's secretary of state, Dean Rusk, admitted that racial discrimination was "the biggest single burden that we carry on our backs in our foreign relations in the 1960s."[19]

Issues of race emerged most clearly when U.S. policymakers confronted apartheid in South Africa. In May 1948 the ruling United Party of Jan Smuts was defeated at the polls by the Nationalist Party, led by Daniel Malan. Representing in large part the white, Afrikaner population, the Nationalists freed from prison those convicted during the war of sympathizing with the Nazis, announced their intention to resist communism wherever it reared its head, and, most significantly, proposed to toughen existing laws enforcing the separation of the country's white and nonwhite populations—the practice of apartheid. The Nationalists banned marriage between whites and nonwhites, placed opponents under house arrest, rigged the political process to assure their own longevity, and met protest against their actions with repression and violence. Malan and his cohorts were unapologetic racists who spoke of the importance of maintaining "white civilization" against the dual threat of communism and black political power. Apartheid was implemented with special enthusiasm by the minister of native affairs, Hendrik F. Verwoerd, who became prime minister in 1958 and soon made Malan look like a moderate. Verwoerd presided over the Sharpeville massacre, the withdrawal of South Africa from the British Commonwealth, and the jailing of the black leader Nelson Mandela. Conditions for blacks in South Africa worsened steadily during this period.

Neither Truman nor his successors welcomed the entrenchment of apartheid. Despite their assumptions about racial hierarchy, most American policymakers were distressed at the extremism of Malan and Verwoerd, and at times they criticized the South African government for the shortsightedness of its domestic policies. Still, no matter how dismayed the Americans became with apartheid, they remained unwilling to take steps to undermine it, much less break relations with the white government. The Truman administration was attached to South Africa because of its unqualified anticommunism and its vast supplies of strategically useful raw materials. The Nationalist regime promised to keep the materials flowing to the United States and lined up squarely with the West in the Cold War. The Americans resisted efforts in the UN to condemn South Africa, clinging to the logic that apartheid was a domestic matter, unsuited for discussion in international meetings. The Afrikaners were less appetizing than Smuts and his well-polished, English-speaking constituency, but they were nevertheless more like white Americans than the blacks whom they deprived of rights. "Let us remember," wrote the outgoing U.S. ambassador to South Africa in 1954, "that Western civilization was brought to the tip of Africa by the forebears of these friendly people," the Afrikaners. "The men of the Truman administration," writes Borstelmann, "found themselves sharing a deep sense of cultural and racial identity with their counterparts in Pretoria." This attitude persisted through the 1950s and early 1960s. Eisenhower considered including South Africa in the developing Middle East Defense Organization. "At heart they are our kind of folk," wrote an Eisenhower appointee of Nationalist Party leaders. "In the end they will do right." While Kennedy embargoed American arms shipments to South Africa in 1963, the president nevertheless refused to terminate International Monetary Fund loans to South Africa, would not obstruct U.S. investment there, and resisted suggestions to extend the arms embargo to other items.[20]

To what extent did race influence U.S. policy toward South Africa? Certainly the United States had strategic interests there. In 1946 American imports from South Africa totaled $230 million and included such critical materials as industrial diamonds, manganese, chromite, and uranium, a potentially fissionable material. But try a simple test: reverse the races of the parties in South Africa. A black minority now rules the country. Those in the white majority are not allowed to vote, to marry whomever they please, to travel without a pass, or to live outside white neighborhoods that are dangerous and squalid. Whites who protest against this system are beaten, jailed (having been convicted by an all-black jury), and sometimes killed. The black South Africa government, however, declares its willingness to fight communism, and permits the United States to buy as much manganese, chromite, and uranium as it likes. Would the United States conclude that black apartheid was a domestic matter and carry on economic intercourse with little fuss? One strongly suspects not.[21]

American policymakers preferred not to consider the possibility that their decision making, on South Africa and elsewhere, was tainted by race thinking, despite the accusations of African-American, African, and Indian critics. Indian barbs were particularly galling, since whatever one might say about white treatment of blacks (the Americans claimed), Indians did not face racial discrimination in the United States or elsewhere. For white Americans, not all Others were the same. Indians, despite the strangeness of their country and their dark skins, were not perceived to be as different from whites as Africans or African Americans were. A racial hierarchy continued to exist in the Cold War United States, but there was a kind of sliding scale of racism, according to which whites treated brown people somewhat better than they treated blacks. From the days when a turban could deter the harshest kind of racism in the South and actually be a "passport to high society" in the Northeast, white Americans inherited a view of the Indians' race that can best be described as ambivalent.[22]

Indians in the United States were not immune to racist treatment, and they told many stories of their humiliating experiences. The eminent physician and nationalist B. C. Roy was refused service at a restaurant in Decatur, Illinois. Chester Bowles collected many anecdotes: from once-eager Indian students in the United States grown bitter through their experience of American racism; from those who had been "thrown out of hotel lobbies, refused accommodations, and discriminated against on trains and in other public facilities" in the South; and from two women from Pakistan who were arrested in a New York department store on suspicion of being gypsies. Indian ambassador G. L. Mehta was racially abused at the Houston airport in August 1955. Six years later, a company of Indian dancers, touring the United States under the auspices of the

Asia Society, fled a Charlotte, North Carolina, restaurant when customers objected to their presence. R. L. Sharma, who came to Los Angeles as a student in 1949, took a job as a mathematician with a local company and decided to stay on. In his memoir, he reported that he was stopped by police as he took walks in the bedroom community of West Los Angeles, turned away from a Kansas City restaurant, and blocked again and again in his efforts to buy a home in Orange County.[23]

Other Indians, however, had different experiences. They often evoked white puzzlement and they were not quite treated as whites, but neither did they face the out-and-out discrimination endured by African Americans. "The Hindu resembles us except that he is black—and we are shocked to see a black white man," wrote a perplexed Californian. The remark implied that features other than skin color may have influenced whites' thinking about racial difference. Or perhaps the generally lighter skin of Indians made them less objectionable to whites than African Americans were. P. E. Dustoor, a light-skinned Bombay Parsi who visited the United States in the late 1940s, observed Jim Crow in the South but found it did not apply to him. Despite the painful acts of racial discrimination noted above, this rather mixed reception was the experience of most Indians in America by the 1950s. The writer Ved Mehta described his father about to board a train for Richmond at Union Station in Washington. The train contained cars marked Whites Only and Blacks Only. Mehta's father asked the conductor which he should take:

> The conductor stared at him. "Straight hair, straight nose, brown skin—a half-breed?"
> "Indian from India, sir."
> "Hindu? You're white."

And recall that in a 1950 edition of the story, Little Black Sambo and his family were restored to India.[24]

Because U.S. policymakers could not countenance claims that race mattered to them, or that issues involving India had anything to do with race, they proposed alternate explanations for Indian actions that were ascribed by Nehru to race. The Americans were deeply suspicious of Nehru's presumption that there was a natural solidarity between the nonwhite people of Asia and Africa. Policymakers charged that Nehru used race as a way of contriving an alliance of the "oppressed" that he sought to lead. In an October 1949 report, the State Department Office of Intelligence Research postulated that "the major objective of India's foreign policy is to obtain recognition of India's leadership among the countries

of South and Southeast Asia. To promote this objective India is unremit-
ting in its advocacy of racial equality and in its opposition to European imperialist control of these nations. . . . The concept primarily expresses India's conviction of her 'manifest destiny' as the leader of Asia." This was at
best a half-truth, but it gained currency among Americans responsible for
making India policy. Loy Henderson, who preceded Bowles as U.S. ambassador in New Delhi, was sure that Indians who complained about
racial discrimination by Western nations were bluffing. Nehru liked to
pose as the hero of the "downtrodden masses of Asia," pretending to be a
"David who regretfully faces [the] materialistic and clumsy Goliath of militarism and imperialism." Nehru, Henderson wrote Acheson in early
1951, was "constitutionally unhappy when he [was] not leading some
cause of downtrodden peoples[,] particularly of Asian or colored peoples[,] against real or imagined oppression." Even the sympathetic Bowles
referred to the Indians' "almost psychopathic suspicion of Western intentions, and to [their] deep resentment of our prejudices towards the colored races."[25]

Indian Policy and Race after 1947

If white Americans were confused or ambivalent about the place of Indians in their racial hierarchy, Indians tended only to credit evidence of
white prejudice against people of color, including them. Indians believed
that there was a basic difference between their foreign policy and that of
the West, and that the difference had much to do with race. The callous
or condescending treatment of people of color by whites was evidence
that racial attitudes had not changed much despite the experience of
World War II. The Americans were the worst in this regard because they
were hypocrites. While they represented themselves as people who had always abhorred colonialism and championed nationalism and who were
now struggling to throw off a racist past, white Americans still subscribed
to the racial hierarchy erected by their forbears to control and humiliate
those with dark skins.

These attitudes should not have been surprising. By the mid-twentieth
century, Indian sensitivities on race matters had been sharpened by years
of discrimination at the hands of the British. Newly independent Indians
in 1947 had recent memories of living under a British-style apartheid, in
which Indians were the South Asian equivalent of black Africans and
mixed Anglo-Indians stood in for South African "Coloreds." During the
raj there were benches marked Europeans Only and railway waiting

rooms and car compartments similarly separated by race. Indians carrying open umbrellas were expected to close them in the presence of whites. It seemed to Indians that the Americans, in their high-handedness, had inherited British racial attitudes. What Americans regarded as small oversights were to Indians confirmations of a pattern of Western racism.[26]

The first Americans encountered by Indians, especially in Bengal, were the soldiers who came, beginning in 1942, to build and protect the Burma Road into southwest China. Indians found the soldiers arrogant, sexually aggressive, and racially prejudiced. A Bengali reported that during a boat trip on a river he saw an American serviceman leaning dangerously over the rail. The Indian offered a friendly warning that the river was full of alligators; the soldier turned on him and snapped, "Damn you, nigger, I'll look out for myself." (The Indian was the former premier of Bengal.) When anti-British protests erupted in India in 1945, American soldiers and reporters were shocked to find themselves targets of the nationalists' wrath. "I know you are Americans," one protester explained, "but you are white." The U.S. consul in Bombay wrote in August 1948 that Indians could not understand why their country did not qualify for Marshall Plan economic aid—unless it was because Indians were not white. Indians even construed the Western response to the dispute between India and Pakistan over Kashmir as racially motivated: white governments were uninterested in brokering a fair settlement in Kashmir because "just 400,000,000 colored people make no difference," the Indians complained. Speaking to Henry Ramsey, the American consul in Madras in 1955, Krishna Menon, the Nehru confidant, future defense minister, and American bête noir, complained about the activities of "white anthropologists" in India. They were, he said, "generally in bad odor" because "they brought up color and other latent complexes." Menon asked Ramsey "how we would like numbers of Indian anthropologists wandering about America measuring heads and gathering personal statistics." (Ramsey did not reply.) When a *Newsweek* editor titled a column "Why Nehru's Face Is Red," Indians protested that the title was a racial pun, intended to associate them with American "Red" Indians.[27]

Indians identified with other Asians on the basis of racial solidarity. Indians thought, for example, that race explained the otherwise incomprehensible support the United States gave France in Indochina. The Korean War especially revealed the importance of race as a source of tension between the United States and India. While the Americans claimed that they were intervening to stop communism, Indians saw the war as a fight between whites and nonwhites. Bowles noted that "many Indians . . . admit to a certain, twisted, secret, pleasurable reaction when they hear that their fellow Asians, the Chinese, are successfully holding off the Americans in Korea." Indians were angered when General MacArthur allegedly said that "he relished the sight of some dead North Koreans," and objected when GIs described Koreans as "gooks," which they frequently did. Most alarming to India was the possibility that the United States might use atomic bombs against North Korean or Chinese targets. It would be just like Hiroshima and Nagasaki: the Americans, unwilling to drop the bomb on "white Germans," would not hesitate to blast more dark-skinned Asians—or so the argument ran. From there, it was a short step to the conclusion that some future American bomb might be used against India. The servant of an American scholar working near Madras was told by several of his friends that "despite our [the Americans'] apparently innocent appearance we were really looking for strategic atomic bombing sights [sic] for the next war." As one Indian put it, if "Bomb No. 3 [was] dropped on the 'gooks' of Korea . . . what guarantee is there that Bomb No. 13 . . . might not be dropped on Bombay or Delhi?"[28]

Indians believed that colonialism was a racial system, and that colonialists and their supporters were racists by definition. Given the pattern of racial discrimination in the United States, it was no surprise to Indians that Americans endorsed white domination, both political and racial, over the dark-skinned world. In his first speech on foreign affairs after becoming head of the Indian interim government in 1946, Nehru named opposition to colonialism and "racialism" a cornerstone of his policy, and thereafter he always mentioned the two evils together. Again and again, the Indians returned to the issues—at the United Nations, at the Asian-African Conference in Bandung, Indonesia, in 1955, and at the founding of the Organization of African Unity in 1963. The elimination of colonialism, the Indians claimed, would lead to the elimination of racial discrimination. American officials and visitors to India duly reported on Indian sentiments. After touring India for three months, J. Saunders Redding observed that Indians "believe that American policy is opposed to the 'liberation and rise' of the colored peoples of the world, and that the treatment of Negroes in America is a home demonstration of this." And, Redding added, "the color question is linked with imperialism." "Nehru would like to see us take a much more vigorous attitude on the question of Africa," Chester Bowles informed John Foster Dulles. "He believes that we would be on a much firmer ground in placing our political bets on the rising tide of colored peoples throughout the world," rather than bolstering the lingering colonialism of the Europeans. Nor could the Indians be persuaded that the Soviets were engaged in colonialism. "By reason of its own experience," wrote Ambassador John Sherman

Cooper from New Delhi in late 1956, "[India] thinks of colonialism as the rule of an Asian country or a colored people by a Western nation, with the subjugated country having no government or international entity." That let Eastern Europe out of the definition.[29]

Indian identification with people of color throughout the world began, logically enough, with Indians overseas. Indians were most concerned about their kin living in South Africa. While still under British rule, India proposed the addition of a racial equality clause to the United Nations charter. That overseas Indians in South Africa were the intended beneficiaries of this amendment soon became apparent from Indian attacks on South African treatment of people of Indian descent. Even in the years prior to Daniel Malan's electoral victory, the South African government worked to shore up the walls separating blacks, whites, and "coloreds," a category that included Indians. In early June 1946, the government, in an effort to stop Indians from buying property in previously all-white areas in the port city of Durban, approved the Asiatic Land Tenure and Indian Representation Bill, which resegregated the province of Natal. India responded angrily. Mohandas Gandhi, with his son, Manilal, who lived in Natal, called for *satyagraha*—"passive resistance," or "truth force," as Gandhi preferred—against the resegregation bill, nicknamed the South African "Ghetto Act." India recalled its high commissioner to Pretoria, announced a boycott of trade with South Africa, and banished white South Africans from Indian hotels, restaurants, and clubs. The government also protested formally to the United Nations. The immediate issue, Vijayalakshmi Pandit told the General Assembly delegates in October, was the Ghetto Act, but more important was the malign principle of racial discrimination that it represented. The communist nations and most nonwhite ones rallied to India's side. The United States, along with Great Britain and the white Commonwealth nations, the Low Countries, and a number of Latin American nations, took the side of South Africa, insisting that apartheid was an internal matter. The resolution that emerged from India's complaint required only that South Africa and India discuss their difficulties and report back to the General Assembly. It passed by a bare two-thirds majority, the United States voting against, with the result that Indians were more convinced than ever that the Americans supported colonialism and racism, their professions of solidarity to the contrary notwithstanding.[30]

The Indian identification with black Africans, though neither as consistent nor enduring as the bond with émigrés or other Asians, nevertheless strengthened steadily during the Nehru years, ultimately to a point where Nehru was willing to risk sharp Western criticism for its sake. Concern for the condition of Indians in South Africa gave way to opposition to the treatment of South African blacks, which finally superseded the natural defense of kin. Manilal Gandhi reported that all nonwhites were "treated like beasts" in South African prisons, and Nehru likened conditions for blacks in South Africa to those in (ironically) the black hole of Calcutta. The prime minister charged that apartheid was a "monstrous evil" that threatened to "uproot almost everything the modern world stands for and considers worthwhile." "What we see in South Africa," he told the Lower House of Parliament in March 1959, "is a survival . . . of all kinds of atavistic activities. Such emotions and feelings have no place in the world today." In late 1961 the *Hindu* reported a story about white Rhodesians bathing in the crocodile-infested Zambesi River rather than going to a racially integrated municipal pool. "Multi-racialism at the . . . pool has driven us to the river," said one white swimmer. "We would rather take a chance on the crocs."[31]

Finally, and of special importance for Indo-U.S. relations, Indians identified with African Americans and backed their efforts to battle discrimination at home. The treatment of African Americans was "the number one question" asked of U.S. representatives in India because it went directly to the matter of white perceptions of Indians. Segregation and oppression of African Americans, especially in the South, were well documented in India. To the first Indian ambassador in Washington, Nehru wrote: "In the U.S.A. there is the Negro problem. Our sympathies are entirely with the Negroes." An Indian traveler catching her first glimpse of the Statue of Liberty thought of a story she had read about a black man from North Carolina being denied the right to claim a Cadillac he had won in a contest, then recalled a notorious lynching. Visiting the United States with his boss in 1949, Nehru's private secretary, M. O. Mathai, planned to leave the official tour, put on American clothes, and travel throughout the southern states, assuming all the rights of a white man and watching carefully to see that they were respected. (Mathai was talked out of it.) Subsequently Nehru met, in a hastily arranged session, with African-American leaders, and in 1950 he championed Ralph Bunche for appointment as the UN representative in Kashmir.[32]

That Indians identified with African Americans was clear from the treatment white and black representatives of the United States received in India. Whites, like Bowles and Pearl Buck, were asked embarrassing questions: "How can Americans claim to believe in democracy and still insist on lynching the negroes and even refuse them the right to go to church?" Blacks, among them James Robinson, J. Saunders Redding, Carl Rowan, and Edith Sampson, would get some of the same questions but always sympathetically, and they personally were greeted with enthusiasm. Redding wrote that "dozens of Indians told me that I was 'one of them'; that (obviously because of my color) I looked like a 'Madrassi,' or a 'Bengali,' that they felt 'immediately at home' with me, and more than one Indian chairman of the meetings I addressed introduced me to audiences as in effect a 'misplaced Indian.' "[33]

Indians saw themselves as people of color, oppressed, like other Asians, Africans, and African Americans, by a legacy of white racism and colonialism. For Indians to claim solidarity with other dark-skinned people, however, was not to demonstrate it to the satisfaction of whites, blacks, or even Indians themselves. The racial identities of Indians were complicated by history and culture. In many ways, it would have been easier for Indians if they could have looked into mirrors and seen black people in the reflections. But they could not. They were not quite black, as most whites had already concluded. Had they been—had the image in the mirror been as dark as that of the African with whom the Indian claimed to identify—the effect of race on India–United States relations would have been a relatively straightforward matter. The reality was otherwise.

To understand the difference between Indians' claims about their racial identities and what Indians may have felt privately or subconsciously, it is appropriate to begin with the relationship between race and caste. The Nehru government took as one of its earliest tasks the destruction of the Hindu caste system. Untouchability and caste discrimination were proscribed by India's constitution, and previously disadvantaged groups were granted privileges through a rigorous program of affirmative action. The political confrontation with caste brought the Nehru government face to face with India's version of racial segregation. Now, caste and race are not coterminous. The darkest Indians are not automatically assigned to the lowest caste, and a light skin alone is not a ticket for upward mobility. Still, as Nehru pointed out, the Sanskrit word for caste is *varna*, or "color." There is some correlation between caste rank and the skin color of the caste's members: one isn't surprised to see a dark Brahmin in Madras, but on the whole the crowd eating lunch at a middle- class restaurant has fairer skin than the workers building a house next door. In the state of Kerala, untouchables were called *karumpan* or *karumpi*—black fellows or black girls. When Indians criticized racial discrimination in the United States, American officials often responded by comparing segregation to the Indian upper castes' mistreatment of the lower orders. The Indian reaction to this comparison—often violent, occasionally circumspect—suggests that it may have hit home. Indeed, in October 1957 the Indian finance minister, T. T. Krishnamachari, told Eisenhower that India "could well understand [segregationist obstructionism in] Little Rock since India itself had an extremely difficult problem in 'human relations.' "[34]

Despite efforts to end caste discrimination, Indians remained (and remain today) acutely color conscious. The old Indian proverb "Beware of a black Brahmin or a fair pariah!" may no longer be quoted, but the sentiment still exists. Some northern Indians look down upon darker South Indians. There are jokes about the paternity of dark-skinned upper-caste children, pointed equivalents of American gibes about offspring resembling the mailman. The heroes and heroines of Indian movies are almost pale. Advertisements in Indian newspapers indicate a strong preference for light skin: fair women peddle cigarettes, toothpaste, and Pond's Vanishing Cream, with its "fluffy powder base" that promises to "keep you looking fair and lovely all day." Papers are also famous for their "matrimonial pages," in which well-heeled young women and men search for spouses with good families, steady jobs, and light complexions. An African-American man who visited India in 1948 praised the beauty of Indian women to a South Indian acquaintance. In that case, the Indian responded, "you ought to go up north . . . we have some women there you can't tell from white!"[35]

The entanglement of caste with race and the aesthetic appreciation for light skin challenged the authenticity of India's attachment to people of color. So did the treatment Indians received in the white world. Recall that while some Indians faced discrimination in the United States, by 1947 their more common experience was unlike that of American blacks. Indians were "black white men," or Hindus were simply white, as the Washington train conductor had decided. Indians may have felt white prejudice, but candor required acknowledgment that they were brown, not black, and that on the whole they got better treatment than did those with very dark skins. Nehru's personal history may be a case in point. The descendant of Kashmiri Brahmins, Nehru had skin the color of milky coffee. Educated at Harrow and Cambridge, Nehru lived in England from 1905 to 1912, during which time he seems to have had access to elite British society. The day after he arrived in London, Nehru took in the Epsom Derby. At Harrow, Nehru was lonely and felt he was "never an exact fit," but he apparently experienced no open racism there or at Cambridge. He moved in the rarefied world of English academia, participating in rowing, taking up smoking and learning to prefer European to Indian food, and even dabbling in the anti-Semitism then in season among some British intellectuals. He summered on the Continent, sometimes with English friends. By the time he returned to India in 1912, Nehru was, by his own admission, "a

Ed Fisher © 1956 The New Yorker Magazine Inc.

"*More controversy in Alabama! You'd think those people were being asked to send their children to school with Untouchables!*"

Snide Brahmins on American racial problems; cartoonist Ed Fisher on Brahmin hypocrisy. Isaacs, Scratches on Our Minds. *Reprinted with permission from M. E. Sharpe, Inc. Publisher, Armonk, N.Y. 10504.*

bit of a prig." Thereafter Nehru went often to Europe, where he met many of the rich and famous, all without apparent racial tension. Other prominent Indians had similar experiences. Even the relatively dark-skinned Gandhi—his friend Sarojini Naidu referred to him as "that chocolate-covered Mickey Mouse"—apparently escaped racial incident in the white world until he arrived in South Africa in 1893.[36]

The Clash over Colonialism: Africa

The fairly benign treatment by white Europeans, coupled with Indians' own racial attitudes, made it unlikely that Indians would instinctively seek common cause with black Africans, and for a time they did not. Gandhi went to South Africa in 1893 to work for the rights of overseas Indians, not blacks. Before World War II, the Indian National Congress fixedly pursued better treatment for African Indians. When forced to choose between Indian and black African interests in the years immediately following independence, the Nehru government favored blood ties: India's UN resolutions on South Africa aimed at securing rights for South Africa's Indians, not its blacks, and in 1949 India objected to East African legislation, supported by most blacks, that restricted the immigration of Asians into the area.[37]

This policy infuriated African blacks, who regarded Indians in eastern and southern Africa as exploiters, not comrades in arms. Many Indians had done well in Africa. Among them were wealthy landowners, industrialists, and especially merchants, whose complaints about British rule in Kenya, for example, had not prevented them from amassing small fortunes. As one African politician put it, the black's image of the East African Indian was "that of a shopkeeper who has just robbed an ignorant African woman of her last ten cents." Africans alleged that Indians' exploitative practices were not simply functions of normal economic relationships but the result of racism. African resentment boiled over into anti-Indian riots, the worst of which occurred at Durban, South Africa, in January 1949. The Durban riot, sparked by an incident between a black African and an Indian shop owner, lasted three days. Its toll included 142 dead and nearly 2000 injured—most of them blacks—and 20,000 were left homeless by the destruction. The Malan government took advantage of black-Indian tensions by sending agents into the fray to provoke black anger against nonwhite targets, the better to keep pressure off itself and to exact revenge on India for dragging apartheid before the United Nations. Malan's strategy worked. Bad feelings lingered between the black and Indian communities, while the government was for the most part spared serious criticism.[38]

A bloodless incident in New Delhi in February 1955 proved nearly as traumatic to Indians in India as the Durban riot had. Asked to speak before the New Delhi Rotary Club, five African students who were attending Indian universities accused Indians of prejudice against blacks that was "almost as bad as that of South African Europeans." Startled and embarrassed, Indian officials issued a series of denials, clarifications, and mea culpas. A letter writer to the *Times of India* hoped that the Africans' charges would become "an eye-opener to every Indian. To show any colour discrimination," he wrote, "will mar our international reputation and will defeat our policy of universal brotherhood."[39]

The charges were jarring because the Indian government had always proclaimed its solidarity with other dark-skinned, politically oppressed people. India aspired to moral leadership of people of color who resisted alignment with either of the great power blocs. In order to assume this role, Indians had to consider themselves exemplars of those who had struggled to overcome racism and colonialism. If they were not always stigmatized by race, and if moreover they were associated by the dark people they were trying to help with the very forces of racism and colonialism they sought to destroy, they could hardly be the saviors of the so-called Third World. It was not just embarrassing, nor just a blow to one of the cherished principles of Indian foreign policy, though it was these things and therefore bad enough. The revelation that Indians might not be viewed by Africans as allies in struggle forced Indians to confront their own racial identities. If the Africans would not have them as racial partners, perhaps other people of color would not either, and if that happened Indians would have to wonder deeply who they were.

In the wake of the Durban riot and the charges at the Rotary Club, and in an effort to clarify their racial identities, Indians increasingly embraced the movements for black liberation in Africa. Where this required a choice between the interests of Indians living in Africa and those of Africans, Nehru increasingly chose the latter. The prime minister declared in 1950 that "we do not want Indian vested interests to grow in Africa at the expense of the African people." India quietly dropped its support of unlimited Asian immigration to East Africa and looked away when African governments passed laws that granted economic privileges to blacks, generally to the detriment of Asians. The Nehru government backed the Kenyan nationalist Jomo Kenyatta, and despite its distaste for the violence of the Mau Mau liberation movement, New Delhi sent a lawyer to help Kenyatta with his legal battles and gave him an official welcome in India. Out of the wreckage of the Durban riot came the Defiance Campaign, which in 1952 inaugurated cooperation between South African blacks and Indians and directed their efforts against the government in Pretoria. The Indian government assisted the protesters by once more getting a discussion of apartheid onto the UN's agenda. Nehru became a thoroughgoing critic of discrimination against black Africans. He deplored the way in which Africans were treated "almost as wild animals" and promised to oppose racial discrimination by all means short of war. He criticized nations that tiptoed around the "monstrous evil" of apartheid because of some "legal quibble" over jurisdiction. At the Asian-African Conference at Bandung in 1955, many of the delegates connected colonialism and racism. But Nehru's condemnations of the neglect of Africans' rights sounded very much like the declarations of a man hoping to atone for some terrible thing he had done. "All of us," he told the delegates, "have to bear the burden of . . . the Infinite Tragedy" of Africa. The final communiqué of the conference "deplored the policies and practices of racial segregation and discrimination" in Africa and elsewhere and pledged participants to fight against "every trace of racialism that might exist in their own countries"—possibly a reference to the caste system.[40]

Indira Gandhi, Nehru's daughter, toured East Africa in the late summer of 1961. She spent much of her time reassuring black Africans of India's support and admonishing groups of Indians to "sink their racial differences and live together with the African." "It was their duty," Gandhi said, "to contribute their share to the economic and social prosperity of the countries which made many of them prosperous." Nehru followed up his daughter's advice by telling Parliament that African Indians "should identify themselves with the movement for African freedom"; it was the "right thing to do" as well as "a desirable thing from the point of view of their own interests." Perhaps because, as a columnist put it soon afterward, "the Indian generally considers the African backward and primitive," Africans remained suspicious of Indian loyalties.[41]

Indians were surely sincere in their sympathy for African nationalism. But it was not easy for the Indian government to make policy conform to its professions of solidarity with black Africans. One of the issues that revealed the gap between profession and policy was India's decision to support the UN intervention in the Congo in 1960. The Congo became independent of Belgium on the last day of June 1960 and soon degenerated into chaos. Belgian officers and Congolese were atrociously attacked, prompting the Belgian government to send in troops. Led by the pro-Belgian Moise Tshombe, the wealthy province of Katanga seceded and declared its independence; Tshombe was rewarded with several tons of Belgian arms. The Congo's president, Joseph Kasavubu, and its premier, Patrice Lumumba, quarreled incessantly. The Eisenhower administration decided that Lumumba was a communist and a drug addict and sent the CIA to assassinate him. In September, Colonel Joseph Mobutu, with Kasavubu's cooperation, placed Lumumba under house arrest. Tshombe held on in Katanga, helped by Belgium and Great Britain and unopposed by the United States.

Meanwhile, the secretary-general of the United Nations, Dag Hammarskjöld, had concluded that only UN military intervention could unify the Congo and prevent it from becoming a cockpit of great power dispute. In July 1960 the Security Council created of a multinational force—the United Nations Operations in the Congo, or UNOC—that was to allow the withdrawal of Belgian troops and bring an end to the Katanga secession. At first, most of the UN troops were African nationals, and because of this UNOC seemed an ideal instrument for the pursuit of India's foreign policy. By supporting UNOC, India could back an African solution to an African problem, show its displeasure with the persistence of colonialism (since it regarded Katanga as a Western subsidiary), bolster the UN, and diminish the possibility of Cold War confrontation in central Africa. When President Kennedy took office in early 1961, he brought U.S. policy largely into line with that of India.

New Delhi's vigorous endorsement of Hammarskjöld's plan left India exposed when the plan's other backers became disenchanted with the UN operation. In early 1961 most of the African contributors to UNOC withdrew their forces, charging that the UN had abandoned the popular Lumumba. With a shortfall of ten thousand troops, Hammarskjöld asked India to make a contribution over and above the several hundred technical workers it then provided. With some reluctance and several conditions, the Indians agreed. Indian officers and soldiers now took the lead in efforts to unify the Congo. Still opposed by the West Europeans but joined increasingly by the United States, the Indian government demanded that its troops be permitted to take the field against Tshombe and his mercenaries. There were maddening delays. Hammarskjöld died in an air crash in the Congo in September 1961; the Belgians, British, and now the French resisted UN efforts to bring Katanga to heel; and Tshombe superficially accepted the authority of the central government, only to continue to stall during the negotiated endgame while at the same time building up his air force. Finally unleashed in December 1962, Indian and UN forces put an end to the secession.

Observers in the United Nations and the United States praised India for its role in the Congo crisis. But India's involvement came at the cost of its credibility in the more radical African states. Several African leaders, notably Ghana's Nkrumah, believed that UNOC was more interested in negotiating an end to the Katanga secession and in preventing Lumumba from becoming Congo's leader than in bringing democracy to the place. Whatever the merits of Nkrumah's argument, India's willingness to fill the gap in UN forces left by the Africans' departure and its apparent complicity with the United States made it a target of suspicion in Africa, a possible collaborator with the neocolonialists. It could be construed, moreover, as evidence that Indians did not feel a genuine solidarity with African blacks, but persisted in a moderate course that befitted its collaboration with its own nationals in Africa—the exploiters, not the friends, of black Africans.[42]

The Clash over Colonialism: Goa

It is in the context of this frustrating loss of credibility in black Africa, and in the context more generally of Indians' unsettled racial identities, that we come to Nehru's decision, made in late 1961, to seize the territory of Goa from Portugal. Like other territories held by foreign nations or Indian princes at the time of independence, Goa lay entirely within the borders of India. Goa was the largest of four territories held by Portugal—the others were Daman and the small islands of Anjadiv and Diu—and consisted of 1300 square miles and with a population of 548,000 in 1954. Goa had been conquered by the Portuguese in 1510, and although there was something unmistakably Mediterranean about Goa's culture the colony maintained its closest attachments with India. Over 60 percent of its people were Hindus, over 95 percent spoke the Indian language Konkani (although Portuguese was the official language of the colony), and virtually all of Goa's inhabitants were of Indian stock. Only 0.5 percent of Goa's exports went to Portugal and less than 10 percent of Goa's imports were Portuguese; the comparable figures for trade with India were 40 percent and 20 percent. The Indian rupee was the currency of choice, and when the Portuguese tried to ban it the Goan economy fell into a prolonged slump.[43]

One way or another, Nehru believed, the Portuguese would leave Goa. The British example, of course, was soundest: they had set a date, then left. The princely states had acceded to Indian control or had been brought into the union by force. The French had taken more time, but they too had gone, agreeing after the 1954 Geneva Conference to turn over to India the colony of Pondicherry and three other small places, and doing so in 1956. Portugal proved more stubborn. The country's dictator, Oliveira Salazar, proclaimed that Portugal had no colonies, only overseas provinces that were an integral part of the nation. In neither Goa nor in Portugal's African possessions—Guinea, Angola, and Mozambique—did the majority enjoy political or civil rights. Fewer than 1 percent of the Africans in them had ever been to school. They remained, Thomas Noer has written, "impoverished, ignorant, and exploited by white masters."[44]

Nehru tried a variety of peaceful methods to dislodge the Portuguese from Goa. Negotiations between 1950 and 1953 were fruitless; a *satyagraha* campaign in the colony in 1954 and 1955 failed to gain Nehru's blessing. On August 15, 1955, Portuguese police killed twenty Indian demonstrators. Nehru was horrified by the bloodshed and resolved to try negotiations once more. In this effort he got little help. The Soviets and Chinese supported the Indian claim to Goa, and while Nehru appreciated this he nevertheless found it unnerving to hear the support parroted by the Indian Communist Party, his nemesis. Great Britain and other NATO countries were dismayed by Salazar's intransigence but unwilling to back India's claim.[45]

Most troubling to Nehru was the position of the United States. The Truman and for a time the Eisenhower administration tried not to take sides on the issue, noting privately that any sympathy they felt for India's position was offset by Portugal's presence in NATO and especially its possession of the strategically vital Azores. On December 2, 1955, Secretary of State Dulles issued, with Portugal's foreign minister Paulo Cunha, a communiqué that referred indirectly to Goa as one of Portugal's "provinces," thus implying that colonialism was not really an issue. The Indian government, reported Ambassador John Sherman Cooper, had "mixed" feelings about the Dulles-Cunha statement, which was a delicate way of saying that the Indians were shocked, angry, and "concerned" that " 'deplorable' relations [with the] United States could result." While Cooper was shaken, Dulles was determined not to change course. In his reply to the ambassador, the secretary linked Goa to the Cold War, reminding Cooper about the importance of the Azores and observing that the Soviets had taken India's side in the dispute in order to "stir up old wounds by emotion-inciting speeches." There was nothing in the communiqué with which "the Indians could properly take offense," and the United States could not have its "foreign relations in effect dictated by the Government of India." Nehru responded by criticizing the United States for its fraudulent "neutrality" on Goa and asked pointedly whether the Americans believed it was legitimate for Portugal to hold a colony six thousand miles from Lisbon. U.S. policy had not changed by the time Nehru arrived in Washington for a visit in December 1956. The United States "is not taking sides on the merits of the Goa dispute," declared a State Department position paper. Goa was "a subject of conflicting national claims." Eisenhower subsequently told Nehru that if the Goa matter was really "as urgent as he [Nehru] thinks it is," he "would have to do something"—a cryptic comment made, the president admitted, "off the top of his head."[46]

Nehru was frustrated by Goa and American policy toward it, and the frustration seemed to paralyze him. For years, he had preached the need for peaceful settlement of international disputes, so to some extent his own rhetoric constrained him from using force. The election of Kennedy gave the prime minister hope that the United States would shift its position on the issue. As it turned out, however, Kennedy was no more willing than Eisenhower to jeopardize American access to the Azores. There was sympathy for India from the usual sources—Bowles and Galbraith, principally—but Secretary of State Dean Rusk refused to pressure the Portuguese. Nehru's biographer has written: "Not even a hint was given to Portugal that President Kennedy believed that India had a legitimate case on Goa and that the United States Government were opposed to colonialism." By the fall of 1961, Nehru was convinced that the end of Portuguese control of Goa could be achieved only through India's efforts.[47]

Ultimately, the timing of Nehru's decision to use force in Goa had little to do with the Americans' views, which remained relatively constant, and a great deal to do with India's credibility in Africa. By the late summer of 1961, Angolans had revolted against Portuguese rule, and Nehru was increasingly criticized by African leaders who thought that his policy toward Goa was too passive. He did say in Parliament, in mid-August, that "a time may come when we may even decide to send our armies" to Goa, and he declared: "I have no intention of passing away before Goa is liberated"; Nehru was then nearly seventy-two and not in perfect health. This new militancy won Nehru praise in India, but it was insufficient for many of the new African states and liberation movements. At a conference of nonaligned nations in Belgrade in early September, Nehru was put on the defensive by delegates from Ghana and several other nations, who demanded that he prove his anticolonialism and demonstrate his loyalty to the African liberation struggle by committing himself to the invasion of Goa. This Nehru flatly refused to do. He continued to talk of a peaceful resolution of the problem, and he insisted that the Belgrade delegates discuss issues other than colonialism. The Africans assailed him for having "lost his anti-colonial fire."[48]

Even more than the Belgrade conference, a seminar on the Portuguese

Nehru and Kenya's Tom Mboya at Bhavnagar, India, January 1961. They have switched hats, symbolically playing with their national and racial identities. Sarvepalli Gopal, Jawaharlal Nehru: A Biography, vol. 3, 1956–1964 (New Delhi: Oxford University Press, 1984). Reprinted with permission from S. Gopal.

colonies, held the following month in Delhi and Bombay, trained attention on Nehru's Goa policy by calling into question the prime minister's racial loyalties. African leaders made no attempt to disguise their impatience with Nehru's caution, and all of them linked the liberation of Portuguese Africa to the end of Portugal's control of Goa. Kenneth Kaunda of Rhodesia wanted India "to give a lead" in the struggle against Portuguese colonialism and argued that "mere pious resolutions" would not achieve liberation. Mozambique's Marcelino Dos Santos thought it pointless to talk of peace with colonialists. India could best contribute to the liberation of his country by liberating Goa. When Indian finance minister Moraji Desai stated his commitment to peaceful resistance, he was rebuked by the Africans. "What is needed now is action," said a Tanganyikan delegate. "Let us all address ourselves to the task of trying to find ways, concrete and positive, to end Portuguese colonialism."[49]

Whose side was India on? Did Nehru believe that the dark-skinned victims of colonialism had the right to use arms to defeat their oppressors, or did he not? Nehru opened the seminar on October 20 with some of his old ambivalence. It would not be hard, he said, for India to evict the Portuguese from Goa. But "the idea of using force was repugnant to Indian philosophy." Then Nehru publicly argued with himself: on the other hand, India "could not tolerate foreign military bases on her western coast." Should it become necessary to take "other steps" to guarantee the nation's security, he "would not hesitate to take them." Three days later, Nehru told a cheering crowd that "recent events" in Goa and elsewhere compelled India "to do some fresh thinking" about Portuguese colonialism. He would not rule out military action in Goa, for the policy of peaceful negotiation had failed. Today, in the spirit of "Afro-Asian unity," of "solidarity in the cause of freedom," he was willing to make a pledge: "Goa will soon be free." The communiqué issued at the close of the seminar on October 24 stated that "no efforts should be spared to bring about an end to Portuguese colonialism." The liberation of Goa would give heart to those fighting the hydra's other heads in Africa.[50]

If Nehru had been bluffing about the racial solidarity of Indians and black Africans, the Africans had called his bluff. Nehru went to the United States in November for talks with Kennedy. The prime minister gave a listless performance, disappointing the president and his advisers. Probably by Nehru's design the two leaders did not discuss Goa; Nehru would not have wished to mislead the president about his intentions, nor would he have wanted to be frank about them. He signaled his views on Goa and offered an oblique warning, however, by condemning Portuguese policy in Angola: "what is happening in Angola is frightening, because it is almost a supreme example of the worst aspect of colonialism." From the United States Nehru went to Mexico, where he was more blunt. India would continue to try to solve the Goa problem peacefully, Nehru told a press conference, but its patience was nearly exhausted. For twelve years the Portuguese had dragged their feet, but now reports of the torture of prisoners in Goa had excited public opinion in India. "Goa," said

Nehru, "can be taken in three days." Meanwhile, Krishna Menon, the defense minister and head of India's UN delegation, warned that India had not "abjured the use of force" in Goa. Menon linked Goa to Angola and condemned Portugal's policy in both.[51]

By the time Nehru returned to India, the press, surely orchestrated, had begun to mount a campaign designed to expose Portuguese outrages in Goa. Twice, shots fired from Anjadiv, just south of Goa, struck Indian vessels, allegedly killing an Indian fisherman. The Portuguese were reinforcing their colony; the *Hindu* reported that roads into Goa were mined, and that "thousands" of Portuguese troops, "white and Negro," had entered Goa. There were anti-Portuguese demonstrations in the colony, and on November 30 three Portuguese soldiers were killed when they reportedly tried to molest a Goanese girl. Nehru responded to these provocations, exaggerated though they may have been, by sending the Indian army to the border area. The press speculated about the world's reaction to an Indian use of force, and recalled the recent charge by Africans that India was "too soft" on Portugal and was thus "dampening the enthusiasm of freedom fighters in other countries." An increasingly alarmed Salazar called for mediation by Great Britain, protested through Brazil, and complained to the Security Council about India's threats. Kennedy and Galbraith tried to intercede. The president argued that Indian action in Goa, coupled with India's military involvement in the Congo, would make the nation of Gandhi look belligerent. After listening to Galbraith Nehru postponed the invasion twice, but in the end he would not be dissuaded from driving the Portuguese out. "Continuance of Goa under Portuguese rule is an impossibility," Nehru said on December 10.[52]

The attack came at midnight, December 17–18. Thirty thousand Indian troops entered the colony and put a quick end to it. The soldiers were greeted as liberators, and within twenty-six hours there was only mopping up left to do. Anjadiv, Diu, and Daman were liberated as well, all with minimal casualties on both sides. Some thirty-five hundred prisoners were taken, while many Portuguese fled into Pakistan. African nations were delighted with the operation. Radio Ghana hailed "the liberation of Goa" and said that the people of Ghana "long for the day when our downtrodden brethren in Angola and other Portuguese territories in Africa are also liberated." Adelino Gwambe, head of the Mozambique National Democratic Union, declared: "We fully support the use of force against Portuguese butchers." The Soviet Union helpfully vetoed an attempt by the Security Council to return Goa to the Portuguese.[53]

The Americans were less delighted with the intervention. India's friends in the United States kept an embarrassed silence, while critics insisted that the use of force in Goa demonstrated the hypocrisy of India's claim to nonviolence and its fondness for mediating Cold War disputes. To the dismay of many Indians, UN representative Adlai Stevenson, a long time supporter, bitterly denounced the action. "Tonight," he said, "we are witnessing the first act in a drama which could end with [the UN's] death." He urged India to withdraw. Krishna Menon, hardly the object of American approbation during the best of times, got into a shouting match with reporters, which ended when Menon forced one of the newsmen to apologize into a microphone.[54]

Kennedy's reaction was more circumspect. On December 29, Nehru wrote the president an eight-page letter explaining his reasons for seizing Goa and responding to criticism of the action. In his reply, Kennedy claimed to understand India's loathing for colonialism. He admitted that Americans perhaps "talk a little too unctuously about the colonial origins of the United States, now nearly two centuries in the past." But that was not the analogy Kennedy had in mind, and not why he sympathized with Nehru's position. Kennedy's people were Irish. He had grown up "in a community where the people were barely a generation away from colonial rule. And I can claim [the president added] the company of most historians in saying that the colonialism to which my immediate ancestors were subject was more sterile, oppressive, and even cruel than that of India. The legacy of Clive was on the whole more tolerable than that of Cromwell."[55]

Kennedy's argument was no doubt heartfelt, yet there was something crucial missing from it: the factor of race. As contemptible as the English found the Irish to be, they were not—in essential, racial terms—Others. Goa was for Indians so powerful an issue because it divided blacks and whites, and in this way Goa stood for many issues over which the United States and India disagreed. Nehru did not mention race in his December 29 letter to Kennedy, but he did say this: "An aspect of this question which has troubled me greatly is the vast difference between the reaction in India, in Africa and generally in Asia on the one side, and the contrary reaction chiefly in the United States and the United Kingdom. Why is it," he asked, "that something that thrills our people should be condemned in the strongest language in the United States and some other places?" Nehru answered his own question: "politics has a different face looked at from different points of view"; points of view were shaped by "geography and past conditioning." Privately Nehru was more direct: issues like the Congo and Goa were especially troubling because they divided world opinion, "to put it crudely, between white and black." For Nehru, as ever, race clung to colonialism and could not be separated from it. What Kennedy had described as his own colonial history was, quite literally, oppression of a different color.[56]

Racial Selves and Others

There is one final thing to say about the influence of race on Indian foreign policy, and it brings us back to the matter of how selves make Others
in their own projected images. If Indians felt guilty about the treatment of
black Africans by Indians in Africa, they also felt a twinge of guilt because
of the path they chose toward development. With the notable exception of
Gandhi, all Indian leaders accepted Western ideas of political and economic modernity. It may be, as the psychoanalyst Sudhir Kakar has argued, that Western-educated Indians "must to this day make a decisive
choice between being Indian in identity or western." It seems at least
equally likely that such Indians feel the need to embrace one self or the
other but cannot actually do so, and vacillate, conflicted, throughout their
adult lives. The latter description fits Nehru. The inability to shake off
Westernism, and in this case the realization that capitalists, socialists, and
even communists all shared Western ideas about political economy, made
Indian policymakers feel vaguely guilty, as if they were forsaking their own,
uniquely spiritual Indian past. These leaders may have sought self- excul-
pation by divesting themselves of the shameful "whiteness" they associated
with their eagerness for Western-style modernity. They projected this
"whiteness" onto white Westerners, and they emphasized their own special
"darkness" by wearing traditional Indian clothes, for example, and by
championing the rights of people of color in Asia and Africa even while
they harbored private doubts about the authenticity of their racial solidarity. In criticizing white Americans, their white alter egos, for their racial
practices and other bad behavior, Indians were criticizing at some remove
their own concessions to "whiteness." Divested of guilt, Indians were free
to pursue development as Westerners had defined it. The observation of
Salman Rushdie's psychic traveler Saleem Sinai is irresistible here:

> I discovered something rather odd during the first nine years after Inde-
> pendence, a . . . pigmentation disorder . . . afflicted large numbers of
> the nation's business community. All over India, I stumbled across good
> Indian businessmen, their fortunes thriving thanks to the first Five Year
> Plan, which had concentrated on building up commerce . . . business-
> men who had become or were becoming very, very pale indeed! It seems
> that the gargantuan . . . efforts involved in taking over from the British
> and becoming masters of their own destinies had drained the color from
> their cheeks. . . . The businessmen of India were turning white.

Projection, it seems, was not enough to prevent the exposure of the businessmen's true colors.[57]

5

Gender: The Upright and the Passive

> Their [Hindus] want of courage almost amounts to deliberate cowardice. Neither have they that strength of character which resists temptation and leaves men unshaken by threats or seductive promises, content to pursue the course that reason dictates. Flatter them adroitly and take them on their weak side, and there is nothing you cannot get out of them.
> —Abbé J. A. Dubois, *Hindu Manners, Customs, and Ceremonies*

> [We resent the] implication in so much said or read that U.S. was a kind of loathsome Uncle Sam, seeking to seduce the lovely virgin India. —Chester Bowles to Indira Gandhi, 1963

One of the hits of the 1824 New York theater season was *The Cataract of the Ganges,* by William T. Moncrieff. Subtitled "A Grand Romantic Melodrama," the play was set in India some time in the vague past. The action opens in the aftermath of a battle between Muslims and Hindus. The former are led by the Emperor Akbar; the latter by an honorable rajah (king) named Jam Saheb, who is advised by the courageous British officer Mordaunt. During the battle the rajah has placed his son, Prince Zamine, under the protection of another Englishman, Jack Robinson, a roguish but loyal adventurer who emulates Robinson Crusoe.

The Hindus are successful in battle, and Jam Saheb pursues his retreating foe. While he is away on this campaign he leaves the affairs of state in the hands of a Brahmin—a member of the highest Hindu caste, and in this case a priest—named Mokarra. This, it turns out, is a bad choice. Seizing the opportunity provided by Jam Saheb's absence, Mokarra secretly agrees to hand the province over to Akbar, on two conditions: first, Zamine is to marry Akbar's daughter, thus cementing the alliance between Muslims and Hindus; and, second, Mokarra himself is to be named viceroy of the province. Akbar consents. Fortunately, Jack Robinson finds a way to alert Jam Saheb, who returns from the field just in time to prevent the marriage and void the deal. To do so, however, Jam Saheb must reveal the truth: Zamine is not a prince, but a princess. Jam Saheb, whose wife died giving birth to Zamine, had concealed the identity of his daughter all these years because under the law all girl babies born in the province were to be killed. The rajah could not bear to dispatch his daughter, who, he claims, looks just like his deceased wife.

Mokarra quickly declares the rajah an outcaste for defying the infanticide law and threatens to carry out the law retroactively, then and there, unless Jam Saheb agrees to allow Zamine to spend the rest of her life as a servant of the god Brahma. In reality, as the rajah and his entourage suspect, this means that Zamine will become the love slave of the lustful Brahmin. Faced with the agonizing choice of condemning his daughter to death or degradation Jam Saheb takes the second, and Mokarra and his soldiers carry Zamine off.

The forces of good, especially the British, now rally. Jack Robinson tries to rescue Zamine. He fails, but the attempt persuades Mokarra that his efforts to ravish the princess will perpetually be interrupted. So the Brahmin seizes his prize and heads for the great cataract of the Ganges, a sacred spot where he intends to sacrifice Zamine to his god. Alerted once more by Robinson, the rajah's forces hurry toward the cataract, only to be intercepted by troops loyal to Mokarra. At this critical moment the adviser Mordaunt steps forward, and delivers a speech to the enemy in which he appeals to their virtues as men, causing them to renounce female infanticide and reject Brahminical tyranny. The Brahmin's troops open their ranks and Jam Saheb's men rush through, reaching the cataract at the last minute. Jack Robinson kills Mokarra; Zamine is rescued and betrothed to her father's Indian lieutenant as the curtain falls.

Cataract of the Ganges is filled with stereotypes about India that were largely accepted by nineteenth-century Americans. A hardly subtle message of the drama, for example, is that even good Indians are incapable of taking control during critical situations. It is the Englishman Mordaunt who makes the climatic speech that convinces Mokarra's forces to lay down their arms, and it is Jack Robinson who frees Zamine by killing Mokarra. American audiences no doubt regarded hostility between Muslims and Hindus as an essential feature of Indian life, one that made necessary the benign intercession of British imperialism.

I would like, however, to focus on what is perhaps a less obvious aspect of the play, and that is Moncrieff's analysis of Indian society in terms of gender. Consider first that Zamine is a transvestite. It is true that transvestitism was a convention in the theater—Shakespeare used it, and so did the authors of French farce and Japanese kabuki. But in Moncrieff's representation of India, cross-dressing is no charming illusion: it is a matter of life and death, for if revealed as a girl Zamine would have been killed instantly. As a boy, Zamine is weak. He blushes easily—"changes colour like a girl!" says the unwitting Jack Robinson—and he nearly faints at the sight of blood. "Pardon this weakness," Zamine apologizes early in the play. "I shall grow more manly soon." Once Zamine is exposed as a girl, she is stronger, less helpless, and more resolute. When Mokarra threatens her with immolation she sneers, "I'll welcome any fate!"

There is more. In the speech with which he convinces the Brahmin's troops to give way, Mordaunt does not criticize the immorality of female infanticide but its cowardliness. He taunts Mokarra's men, evidently hoping to shame them: "Murderers of children, you have not hearts to combat with true men!" When they accede to the rajah's authority, Mordaunt exults, "They still are men—on to the wood!" Real men don't kill babies. The way to end the ugly practice of female infanticide in India is to appeal to the supposed sense of gallantry and masculinity of Indian men.[1]

As *Cataract of the Ganges* suggests, gender is one of the vital filaments in the web of significance deployed by Americans and used to explain India. Gender analysis illuminates important aspects of relations between nations, in this case the United States, India, and, tangentially, Pakistan. Mrinalini Sinha has written, "empires and nations are gendered ideological constructs," to which I would add that nations also construct one another. For my purposes, gender, or "gendering," is not a static idea but a transnational process: it is the assignment of certain characteristics based on prevailing ideas of masculinity and femininity to a people and nation by another people and nation. Masculinity and femininity are not, in this view, biologically determined categories but culturally and socially conditioned ideas. Nations and the people who constitute them become "gendered," and this affects the policies that other nations pursue toward them.[2]

The history of U.S. foreign relations has not, until quite recently, been held to be susceptible to gender analysis. The makers of American foreign policy, almost all of them men, do not talk explicitly about gender issues or intentionally use a vocabulary of gender when they discuss their policies toward other countries. They talk about strategy and geopolitics, economics and access to raw materials, and systems, ours versus theirs. Because of this, as Joan Scott has written, most historians believe that gender "refers only to those areas . . . involving relations between the sexes. Because, on the face of it, war, diplomacy, and high politics have not been explicitly about those relationships, gender seems not to apply and so continues to be irrelevant to the thinking of historians concerned with issues of politics and power."[3]

Scott herself has argued that "high politics itself is a gendered concept," and since she wrote these words a number of diplomatic historians have pursued her insight. This chapter will show that gender was part of the political culture in Washington and New Delhi during the period 1947–64. Americans held gendered stereotypes of Hindu men and women: Men, like the unrevealed Zamine, were weak. They were also cowardly, treacherous, emotional, flighty, and given to talk rather than action. They refused to stand up to evil, preferring to compromise with it, mediating disputes instead of taking the one right side in them, failing utterly to behave like Mordaunt's "true men." Hindu men, Americans concluded, were effeminate. Not so Hindu women, who had admirable backbone, but with it the less admirable quality of ruthlessness and a regrettable penchant for emasculating men. On the other side, Indians saw American men as cowboys, gangsters, or soldiers, aggressive without cause, often violent in their treatment of their enemies, whom they recklessly defined as anyone who disagreed with them. American women, thought Indians, were aggressive too, though they were not so much physically assertive as they were socially confident, familiar in ways that made many Indians uncomfortable. These mutual perceptions shaped relations between the United States and India during the Nehru period and after.

Americans and Gendered India

To understand the significance of gendered images in the Indo-American relationship we must begin earlier, with the peculiar and persistent Western idea that India is a female country. It was not by accident that Katherine Mayo titled her exposé of Hinduism *Mother India*: she wrote in the Western tradition of representing India, the place, as female. The early twentieth-century American traveler Sydney Greenbie noted that on a map India "looked like the ponderous milk-bags of a cow holding the very living essence of Asia." Writers contrasted the West and India in ways that evoked gender. The West was grasping, materialistic, scientific, and calculating; India was spiritual, impulsive, even irrational. "The masculine science of the West," wrote Greenbie, "has found out and wooed and loved or scourged this sleepy maiden of mysticism." In the discourse of India's relations with the West, concludes Richard Cronin, "one metaphor emerges as dominant. The West is a man, the East is a woman."[4]

The Western representation of India as female conferred effeminacy on most Indian men. Caught in the enervating web of Hinduism, the majority of Indian men had been deprived of their manliness and their virility. In the context of gender, it is possible to discern three features that Westerners historically assigned to most Indian men. The first of these was passivity and its more exaggerated forms; the second was emotionalism; the third was a lack of heterosexual energy. All were associated with femininity, which Westerners regarded as effeminacy if exhibited by a man, and all imposed on India Western constructions of the feminine and the masculine.

Westerners claimed that Hindu men were passive, servile, and cowardly. Nothing, it seemed, could stir Indian men out of their torpor. They could endure anything, evidently without suffering from a sense of shame because of their inaction. They did not resist oppressors but rather regarded them with stupefying indifference. Katherine Mayo wrote: "India was . . . the flaccid subject of a foreign rule. . . . Again and again conquering forces came sweeping through the mountain passes down out of Central Asia, and the ancient Hindu stock, softly absorbing each recurrent blow, quivered—and lay still." During the 1920s and 1930s, there was a "Hindu craze" in the United States, and thousands of Americans became familiar with the "three levels of conduct" of Vedanta, the type of Hinduism most often brought to the United States by Indian spiritual leaders, or swamis. Level one was "obedient activity," level two "desireless activity," and the third and highest level "pure passivity." The terms could have been borrowed from a primer on behavior written for proper American women.[5]

The exaggerated form of passivity was servility. This, Westerners declared, Hindu men had in abundance. Many implicitly subscribed to John Stuart Mill's observation that "in truth, the Hindu, like the eunuch, excels in the qualities of the slave." Watching a German hotel manager in Bombay discipline a servant by clouting him in the jaw, and seeing the servant taking it without protest, Mark Twain was reminded of his childhood and the "forgotten fact that this was the *usual* way of explaining one's desires to a slave." The American traveler Henry M. Field was astonished and delighted with the seeming servility of Indian men. He was "surrounded and waited upon by soft-footed Hindoos, who glided about noiselessly like cats, watching every look, eager to anticipate every wish before they heard the word of command. I was never the object of such reverence before." Everyone called him "sahib," a title of respect, and the servants automatically rose in his presence. "I never knew before how great a being I was,"

Field wrote. "There is nothing like going far away from home, to the other side of the world, among Hindoos or Hottentots, to be fully appreciated."[6]

Beyond servility was cowardice. Westerners asserted that Hindu men were unwilling to stand and fight, and that this explained the apparent ease with which they were conquered. First the Muslims, then the British, had found the Hindu population unresisting, especially in Bengal. To make this argument, particularly after Bengalis were heavily involved in the Sepoy Rebellion of 1857, required tortuous reasoning. Westerners insisted that acts of Bengali—and finally all Hindu—resistance were cowardly because they relied on treachery, not confrontation. J. Henry Jones asserted that Brahmins (like Mokarra) used cunning and deceit against their opponents, attacking their victims when they were in "unguarded security." "If only he need not face his enemy," Katherine Mayo wrote of the Bengali male. "If only he may creep up behind and take his enemy in the back, he can risk almost certain capture and forfeiture of life. In other words, having in him the makings of a man, his manhood has been twisted out of shape."[7]

The idea that Indian men were passive, servile, and cowardly persisted into the Cold War period. British and American policymakers condemned Indian foreign policymakers for their unwillingness to take a stand in the conflict between the United States and the Soviet Union. A British official characterized Indian policy toward Indochina in 1950 as "non- interference i.e. doing nothing." Sir Archibald Nye, the perceptive British high commissioner in India during the late 1940s and early 1950s, blamed "Gandhian ethics" for what he called India's "quietist policy of non-resistance to aggression," and he noted that India leaders were inclined to make "pronouncements which, when trouble appears on the horizon, are not acted upon." The Americans agreed with this view. Officials in the Eisenhower administration reported that the Indians were "fearful" of U.S. arms sales to Pakistan because "physically they are weak and fear aggression," which U.S. policymakers thought alarmist. The Americans believed that Indian neutralism got its comeuppance in the fall of 1962, when Communist Chinese troops overwhelmed Indian outposts on the northeast border and pushed deep into territory claimed by India. Roger Hilsman, an assistant secretary of state who came to New Delhi with a high-level delegation to offer India help, could not refrain from a sharp observation: "We were ushered into the Prime Ministerial residence through the reception hall lined with photographs of all the neutral and unaligned Chiefs of States who have so notably failed to come to India's support during the present crisis. The irony was more than funny—it was oppressive."[8]

A second trait that according to Americans and Westerners revealed the effeminacy of Hindu men was emotionalism, usually associated with hypersensitivity. Rather than deal with issues logically and coolly, Hindu men flew off the handle—just as American women were allegedly apt to do. Americans claimed constantly to find verification for the cliché that the West was rational and tough, the East emotional and sensitive. In a 1948 profile, the Central Intelligence Agency (CIA) described the Indian prime minister: "Nehru is a man of broad vision and of integrity, but his character is weakened by a tendency toward emotionalism which at times destroys his sense of values. He is gracious as well as brilliant, but volatile and quick-tempered." A sense of pride came naturally with independence, but the Indians were an especially prickly people. In 1954 the law partner of Secretary of State John Foster Dulles wrote that Indians had "an almost feminine hypersensitiveness with respect to the prestige of their country." President Eisenhower agreed. Reading of Indian objections to the administration's plan to provide arms for Pakistan, Eisenhower wrote Dulles: "This is one area of the world where, even more than most cases, emotion rather than reason seems to dictate policy."[9]

Americans also believed that Hindu men failed to show a healthy sexual interest in women. This failure was, of course, not a characteristic of American women but of unmanly American men. Hindu men seemed inclined to homosexuality or, like Mahatma Gandhi, sexual renunciation. Visitors to India noticed Indian men holding hands, as they do still. Sculptures of beings that were bifurcated into male and female halves added to the apparent confusion of gender roles in India. In the mid-1950s, Harold Isaacs surveyed 181 prominent Americans, including several foreign policymakers, about their attitudes toward India. Respondents offered a host of gendered, and censorious, descriptors: Indian men were servile, cringing, submissive, effete, weak, and effeminate. They were characterized by passivity, inertia, and docility, and they lacked vigor, industry, stamina, virility, and muscles. One scholar unleashed the following: "Indians? I think of fakiry, spelled both ways. It's the same thing. It means deception. . . . Somehow I am almost tempted to use the word feminine. I feel a certain effeminateness about Indians that bothers me, although I am not bothered in general by homosexuals. . . . Effete is a word I think of."[10]

Where did these American representations of India come from? Who constructed India, and why? One answer, perhaps the simplest, is that these stereotypes came from the British, and were deployed to serve the purposes of empire. Americans often saw India through British eyes, and the British made a distinction between tough, masculine Indian men from the north and west, who were usually Muslims, and the weak, effeminate Hindus from the south and especially Bengal. The stories of Rudyard Kipling made archetypes of the loyally militant Muslim and the craven, underhanded Bengali. Kipling's verse "East is East and West is West, and never the twain shall meet" is well known, but few remember the next two lines: "But there is neither East nor West, Border nor Breed nor Birth/When two strong men stand face to face, though they come from the ends of the earth." Kipling was referring to the camaraderie between British soldiers and the Muslim Pathans of the Northwest Frontier. The British in India regarded the Bengali, on the other hand, as "litigious" and "effeminate," a "trouble-maker" who "doesn't appeal to many British people in the same way as the very much more manly, direct type from upper India." Bishop Reginald Heber, author of hymns that made their singers feel sorry for South Asians, observed that the Bengalis were "the greatest cowards in India." John Strachey's book *India* led the syllabus for British candidates training for the Indian Civil Service in the late nineteenth century. It included this quotation from Thomas Babington Macaulay:

> The physical organization of the Bengali is feeble even to effeminacy. He lives in a constant vapor bath. His pursuits are sedentary, his limbs delicate, his movements languid. During many ages he has been trampled on by men of bolder and more hardy breeds . . . his mind bears a singular analogy to his body. It is weak even to helplessness for purposes of manly resistance; but its suppleness and tact move the children of sterner climates to admiration not unmingled with contempt. . . . Englishmen who know Bengal, and the extraordinary effeminacy of its people, find it difficult to treat seriously many of the political declamations in which English-speaking Bengalis are often fond of indulging.[11]

The Macauley comment gives it away: gendered British thinking about India emerged simultaneously with the rise of British imperialism. Gender inspired imperialism, allowed it to grow, and justified its tortuous evolution. Ashis Nandy has argued that premodern Europe, with its agrarian economy and "peasant cosmology," valued the attributes of "femininity, childhood, and . . . 'primitivism.' " The emergence of capitalism and its concomitants "achievement and productivity" resulted in the rejection of feminine, agrarian values, and their projection onto the so-called low cultures of Europe and America, Africa, and Asia. By this process, Nandy writes, West Europeans came to see "uncivilized" Others as innocent children, on the one hand, and as people "devious, effeminate, and passive-aggressive" on the other. Gender helped explain to the British why India needed their help. The innocent children of India required the protection of the strong men of the West. Other nations, especially Russia, threatened India. The British also saw themselves as guardians of the weakest elements of Indian society. They argued that despite their effeminate cowardliness—or because of it—Hindu men frequently brutalized the lower castes. Like Mokarra, Brahmins mistreated women. They promoted child marriage, abused brides who married with insufficient dowries, and encouraged *sati*, the self-immolation of widows. The imperialists insisted that interposing their power between the male upper castes and the helpless masses was their only humane course.[12]

Protection, yes, but the gendered view of Indians as "devious, effeminate, and passive-aggressive" ultimately engaged the British in a different enterprise: the control of their flighty and mischievous wards. The language of Bengali effeminacy, invented with the eighteenth-century establishment of the East India Company raj, emerged with particular force after the Sepoy Rebellion of 1857. Now came a new imperialism; on August 2, 1858, the British Parliament transferred the company's rights in India to the crown. The crown soon made clear its indifference to the need to protect the weak in Indian society, and instead turned its attention to the rehabilitation of the shaken Indian army. With the purposes of control firmly in mind, the government reduced the ratio of Indian troops to British troops overall. More important, because the British blamed upper-caste Bengalis for masterminding the uprising, they thereafter refused to admit high-born Bengalis to the armed forces. Instead, the British relied increasingly on Sikhs and Muslims, whom they proclaimed the "martial races of India." Imperialism was also necessary if the "political declamations" of effeminate Bengali men were not worth taking seriously. The irrationality of feminine India required a firm hand, "a stern man," as one observer has written, "who will impose on her the discipline she is too feckless to impose on herself."[13]

The Americans learned a great deal about empire from the British. The United States became an imperialist nation in its own right, with its own causes and slogans and justifications, but like the British raj the American empire was undergirded by gendered perceptions. Gendered imagery, linked to ideas about race, figured prominently in the white subjugation of Native Americans. The image of the noble savage, childlike and innocent and in communion with Mother Earth, gave way to the image of the bloodthirsty savage who threatened white womanhood and therefore had to be controlled. When American policymakers looked abroad in the late nineteenth century, they beheld nations whose populations seemed to cry out for the protection and discipline that only white men could provide. As Emily Rosenberg notes, "women, nonwhite races, and tropical countries often received the same kinds of symbolic characterizations from white male policymakers: emotional, irrational, irresponsible, unbusinesslike, unstable, and childlike." Concerned, perhaps, that their own masculinity was at risk—a concern of American men as far back as the Revolution, when Tom Paine had charged them to awaken from "fatal and unmanly slumbers"—policymakers developed patriarchal designs on the weaker members of the family of nations. There were figurative children out there who needed help, and there were figurative women who were too soft or emotional to take care of themselves. U.S. policymakers depicted the countries of Latin America, especially Cuba and Puerto Rico, as women in distress, victims of Spanish villainy. Delicate Chinese mandarins required protection against the brutalities of men from Europe, Russia, and Japan. Theodore Roosevelt's emphasis on the strenuous life and manly virtues of combat gave rhetorical substance to images of Others based on gender.[14]

The Americans also learned much of what they knew about India from the British. During the nineteenth and early twentieth centuries, they watched with interest as the British played the Great Game against Russia. They competed with the British for markets in the region. And they adopted the gendered British view of the peoples of India. *Cataract of the Ganges* was not the first American play about India: in 1800 a Boston theater presented David Humphrey's *Widow of Malabar*, featuring the burning of a Hindu widow. The American traveler Robert Minturn thought that Indian soldiers lacked only one thing—"manly courage." India itself was a "rich and fertile country," but it was "inhabited by a cowardly and effeminate race." Nearly a century later, John K. Fairbank, stationed in British India during the Second World War, found Indians "timorous cowering creatures, too delicate to fight like the Chinese." The United States did not become an imperialist nation in India, but it replaced Great Britain as the principal Western power in South Asia, and Americans brought with them many British assumptions about gender.[15]

Another reason why Americans saw Hindu men, and India itself, as feminine was the sharp line traditionally drawn between the genders in the United States. As Susan Jeffords has argued, while the American definition of masculinity may change over time, "it remains consistently opposed to the 'feminine,' those characteristics that must be discarded in order to actualize masculinity." Hindu men subscribe to codes of masculinity that are not the same as Western ones. In ancient Hindu myth, pride of place is reserved for feminine principles. The cosmos was the creation of Shakti, or energy, which has a feminine gender in Sanskrit. The first mortal couple were the twins Yama and Yami. The woman, Yami, was not derived from Yama as Eve was derived from Adam, but had her own, powerful identity. A twenty-year old princess, the Rani of Jansi, was the Indian hero of the 1857 Rebellion.[16]

Hindu ideas of how men should look and what they should be involve what most Westerners would regard as a female aesthetic. In India, a boy or a man can be called beautiful without embarrassment. The ideal man, wrote Krishnalal Shridharani, has "regular features, eyes that move languidly, lashes that fringe, hair that resembles velvet." In contrast, American "girls favor men with jutting chins, hair that stands on end [this was the early 1940s], bulging nostrils, hands that can break down doors, and one-way eyes that express Harpo-Marxian intensity." In his ethnography of a North Indian village, G. Morris Carstairs observed that when the popular drama Ram-Lila was performed, "the centre of interest was the elegant young man who played the part of the heroine Sita. Everyone spoke with admiration of his good looks, and he received many encores." In general, the line drawn in the West between masculine and feminine behavior is drawn in a different place in India. Readers of the epics *Ramayana* and *Mahabharata* know that there is a place in Hindu mythology for what Westerners would view as acts of masculine prowess. At the same time, Hindu men are not uncomfortable to appear nurturing, and they do not believe that their potency is at risk should they seem to lack aggressiveness. By incorporating so-called female attributes into their personalities, Hindu men fulfill themselves, round themselves off. Androgyny is not a pathology but a virtue; bisexuality is "an indicator of saintliness and yogic accomplishments." As for homosexuality, herewith an excerpt from a song called "The Wounded Heart," sung by the hearty, Pushtu-speaking Muslim men of the far northwest: "There's a boy across the river with a bottom like a peach/But, alas, I cannot swim."[17]

Hindu males' perceptions of their masculinity seemed distressingly consistent with the British derogation of their physical courage. Moreover, if one accepted the British idea that Muslims were manly and Hindus pusillanimous, it became, on the surface at least, difficult to argue that India deserved to be independent. Left to their own devices, Hindu men could not establish authority and could not defend themselves against invaders. The result of this perception was the emergence, in the late nineteenth century, of a Bengali renaissance that attempted to prepare the ground intellectually for Indian nationalism. The leaders of the renaissance, Ashis Nandy explains, tried to prove that Hindus had mettle by rewriting some of the classic Hindu texts. Michael Madhusudan Dutt turned Rama and Lakshmana, the heroes of the *Ramayana* and both traditionally complex figures, into "weak-kneed, passive-aggressive, feminine villains," while he made the ten-headed demon Ravanna a hero. The defeat of Ravanna was in Madhusudan's revision a tragedy, for it meant the death of all that was "courageous, proud, achievement-oriented, competitive, efficient, [and] technologically superior." In the same spirit, Bankimchandra Chatterjee recast the Hindu god Krishna. Usually depicted as "soft," "androgynous," and "philosophically sensitive" (the terms are Nandy's), Bankimchandra's Krishna "was a respectable, righteous, didactic, 'hard' god, protecting the glories of Hinduism as a proper religion and presenting it as an internally consistent moral and cultural system."[18]

It is doubtful that this effort to put muscle into Hinduism could have produced a vital independence movement. By accepting Western ideas about masculinity as suitable for India, the renaissance writers in effect proposed to beat the British at their own game. Hindus, they argued, were tough enough to expel the British from India and tough enough to defend themselves against future enemies. That argument invited confrontation and repression by the British. (It also threatened Muslims, who later cited fears of Hindu militancy to argue for a separate state in South Asia.) Far more subtle were the actions of Mahatma Gandhi, whose nationalism directly challenged Western perceptions of gender. Gandhi personified the distortion of gender categories as Westerners understood them. In his own life Gandhi practiced *brahmacharya*, or self-control, which included not only a limited diet and rigorous mental discipline but abstinence from sexual relations (and refusal of self-made sexual temptation). Gandhi hoped to achieve in his sex life what Lloyd and Susanne Hoeber Rudolph call "the serenity of neutrality," a phrase that is revealing to a diplomatic historian. Gandhi turned Western gender discourse to his own purposes, deliberately challenging it in order to attack both British colonialism and the Indian caste system. As Nandy writes, Gandhi "rejected the British . . . equation between manhood and dominance, between masculinity and legitimate violence, and between femininity and passive submissiveness." Gandhi's political activism was inspired by what he called *satyagraha*, popularly translated as "passive resistance." Gandhi disliked the translation, preferring "truth force," but the sight of the nationalists walking calmly into beatings and arrests suggested to Westerners a kind of resignation. In fact, Gandhi hoped to separate bravery, which the nationalists had in abundance, from aggressiveness, a trait he associated with Western maleness. Gandhi opened the ranks of the movement to women, and *satyagraha* embodied what Gandhi held to be the peculiar strengths of women—compassion, endurance, and courage. This position, as Nandy contends, challenged patriarchy and thus negated the very basis of colonial culture.[19]

Some Westerners joined Gandhi's movement; a good number of them were women. But Gandhi's appeal perplexed many Europeans and Americans. British conservatives found the Mahatma exasperating—Churchill growled his contempt for the "little naked faqir"—and were frustrated by his unwillingness to do battle in traditional terms. While most of Harold Isaacs's respondents admired Gandhi, their admiration was qualified by a concern, as one put it, that "passivity breeds submission to totalitarianism." The New York columnist Arthur Brisbane voiced his scorn for Gandhi's methods: "In these days, you only get justice when you fight for it. Even then it is slow." On board a ship bound for the United States in 1943, Nehru's nieces, Nayantara and Lekha Sahgal, chatted with some marines about Gandhi. "Our talk of non-violence only made them laugh," Nayantara remembered. " 'This guy Gandhi must be crazy. Suppose a man came along and killed his sister; would he sit still and not do anything about it?' " The Mahatma's unwillingness to take up cudgels for his cause seemed proof that he was insufficiently manly. His opponents were made to feel guilty for using force against those who seemed to glory in their quiet courage.[20]

Members of the ruling Congress Party carried with them the conviction that courage in world affairs need not be confused with Western definitions of manliness. In fact, they cultivated the gendered view that India, despite its independent status, was a female still at risk of being seduced or brutalized by the West. Nehru had long believed this. Writing to an American friend in 1938, he declared: "India is a feminine country. . . . Anyway she has certain feminine virtues and certainly the feminine vices." The prime minister never abandoned this image. Other, less refined nations wished India harm. The United States in particular had to be watched, for it was "a blundering giant with no finer feelings or regard for Asian sentiment," the inheritor of "rapacious tendencies" previously monopolized by the British. The mistreatment of Indian women by U.S. soldiers stationed in Calcutta in 1945 seemed to confirm Indian perceptions that American men were sexually aggressive. In any case, and as it had with the British, this characterization served a useful purpose for Indian leaders: it rallied a diverse people around the defense of the motherland, and by representing the state as weak it elevated unity and self-defense to a high moral plane.[21]

The femaleness associated by Westerners with India did not have the same implications for all of India's people. As I have indicated, Westerners judged Hindu men to be effeminate, allegedly passive, cowardly, servile, emotional, and bi- or homosexual. Westerners represented Indian women differently. Indian women were alleged to be seductresses, waiting to lure unsuspecting men into danger. The practice of purdah, or the seclusion of women, supposedly functioned as a way of tempting men, driving them to distraction without the promise of sexual fulfillment. As Sydney Greenbie saw it, "forty million women live in seclusion, and all their inexperience, all their ignorance, all their suppressed desires, deny and condemn and withhold from men the fullness of life which they crave." Westerners also regarded Indian women as glorified housekeepers incapable of loving their husbands, superstitious lightweights whose heads were turned by pseudo-religions and shiny baubles, or haridans who spent their lives scolding men.[22]

The most dominant Western image represented Indian women as heartless, domineering, and emasculating. This image emerged most strongly with reference to the Hindu goddess Kali, one of the forms of the god Shiva's wife. Kali, who has appeared over the years in a variety of American media, is a frightening figure to a Western man. In the March 1950 issue of *Fate* magazine—a kind of occult *Reader's Digest* with stories such as "They Eat Dirt and Like It"—Kali is depicted as a beautiful but cruel destroyer of men. Three of her four arms hold a bloody cutlass, a man's head the cutlass has severed, and a pan into which drips blood from the head. She stands on the chest of another man, who is intact but comatose. She wears a belt made of human arms; around her neck is a wreath of heads of the giants she has slain. This image of Kali would not be unfamiliar to an Indian viewer. But the text of the article goes on: "Before her goddess each worshipper is a Kali herself, and she would recognize no male in the presence of Kali." Here is a totalizing image, in which all Indian women are conflated with the bloody-minded, emasculating deity they allegedly venerate.[23]

If she is not killing men, the Western version of Kali is making them do terrible things in her name. The sensationalist paperback *Woman of Kali*, published by Gold Medal Books in 1954, had as its title character "Sharita, high priestess of the cult of death" in "barbaric India, land of languor, intrigue, strange appetites, exotic women, cruel and scheming men!" Sharita's army of thugs carry out her murderous wishes. So do the thugs in the 1939 film *Gunga Din* and the 1984 picture *Indiana Jones and the Temple of Doom*, though these movie thugs worship Kali directly. (In the latter film Kali has hordes of male slaves, who lose their free will when they drink her blood.)[24]

In Hindu mythology, Kali plays a more complex role. She represents Shakti, the female energizing principle. The comatose man who lies at

The goddess Kali, "destroyer and murderess" of men. Fate, *March 1950.*

her feet is in fact inert potential, waiting to be stirred to life by Kali's ani-
mating touch. An Indian worshipper of Kali may find her frightening, but
she is engaged in fighting evil, not in serving it. In the West, however, Kali
has become an exaggerated prototype for powerful Indian women, the
opposites of quavering Hindu men. Like Kali, Indian women are represented as heartless. They are, after all, capable of killing their own baby
daughters. Here is an excerpt from a poem called "The Heathen
Mother," printed in a nineteenth-century American children's book:

> See that heathen mother stand
> Where the sacred current flows;
> With her own maternal hand
> Mid the waves her babe she throws.
>
> Hark! I hear the piteous scream;
> Frightful monsters seize their prey,
> Or the dark and bloody stream
> Bears the struggling child away.
>
> Fainter now, and fainter still,
> Breaks the cry upon the ear;
> But the mother's heart is steel
> She unmoved that cry can hear.
>
> Send, oh send the Bible there,
> Let its precepts reach the heart;
> She may then her children spare—
> Act the tender mother's part.

Female infanticide occurred with appalling frequency in nineteenth-century India. The complicity of mothers with the practice, however, should
be considered unlikely.[25]

Even more threatening to men was the allegation that Kali, or women
formed in her image, emasculated men, robbed them of their potency. In
one story, Shiva was able to stop his wife's destructiveness only by throwing himself at her feet, an act American men would have deemed humiliating. The nineteenth-century visitor Saleni Hopkins claimed that Hindu
men were inclined to "docility, effeminancy" [sic] and "lack of vigor" because their mothers breastfed them through the age of six. More sinister
were the allegations, made by Katherine Mayo, that Indian mothers habit-
ually masturbated their sons. The result, wrote Mayo, was devastating to
Indian manhood:

Highest medical authority in widely scattered sections attests that practically every child brought under observation, for whatever reason, bears
on its body the signs of this habit. Whatever opinion may be held as to its
physical effects during childhood, its effect upon early thought-training
cannot be overlooked. And, when constantly practiced during mature
life, its devastation of body and nerves will scarcely be questioned. . . .
Small surprise will meet the statement that from one end of the land to
the other the average male Hindu of thirty years, provided he has means
to command his pleasure, is an old man; and that from seven to eight out
of every ten such males between the ages of twenty-five and thirty are impotent.[26]

Indians and Gendered America

Indian views of Americans were gendered, too. Recall (from the introduction) that Indians regarded American men as licentious, swaggering,
and self-righteous, abusers of alcohol (like the boozy baseball team from
Calcutta), rational to the exclusion of spiritual sensitivity, and above all
lovers of violence, either in their fantasies of frontier gunplay or in the
brute realities of their treatment of black men. While Americans distinguished between Indian men (passive, hypersensitive, cowardly) and Indian women (cruel and emasculating), Indian men tended to see American women much as they saw American men: less logical and violent,
perhaps, but just as familiar, domineering, and promiscuous. These descriptors were partly projections of attitudes that Hindu men held toward
Hindu women—unsurprisingly, given the limited contact between Indian men and American women in those days. The male subjects of G. M.
Carstairs agreed that women had greater sexual appetites than men and
were thus responsible for promiscuity. Said one: "Even God himself
doesn't know a woman's hidden intentions." Once revealed, however,
these could hardly be misunderstood, especially those of American
women. Some Hindu men enjoyed the female attention they received in
the United States, the perceived flirtatiousness and frankness. Women
made up most of the audience wherever Swami Vivekananda spoke during his 1893 tour of the United States. "Oh boy!" he wrote a friend back
home. "Am I dumbfounded by my encounter with their girls! . . . They
are [like] the Goddess Lakshmi herself in their beauty and [like]
Saraswati, the goddess of Learning in their [intellectual] qualities. . . . I
am their adopted brat, and they, my boy, are indeed the Mother Goddess
incarnate." As for Indians, "your men are not worth their toe-nails and I
better say nothing about your women!" The predominant impression

among Indian men was that American women presumed too much, allowed themselves intimacies that Indians of both sexes found terribly embarrassing, and pursued men with unseemly ardor, even if the object was less sexual than material. The reporter Prakash C. Jain heard with astonishment an office colloquy in which a male boss said to a female employee: " 'Say, you look so nice and bright this morning! What did you do last night?' " The woman seemed unbothered by the question which, if asked of a woman in India, would be likely to "lead to a staff strike or a demand for an unqualified apology."[27]

For the immigrant R. L. Sharma, epiphany arrived at his first high school dance, in the form of a "buxom girl" who asked him ("still a 90-pound weakling") to dance. Ignoring Sharma's clumsiness, the girl pressed close, then asked whether he had a car. He said no, whereupon "she untwined herself from me and disappeared. I sat down on the stupid chair again, and . . . reflected upon whether the girl was looking for love or a maharaja." Krishnalal Shridharani's encounter with a confident young woman was better. Over the Christmas holiday, he went home with a graduate school friend, who introduced the Indian to his married sister ("Mrs. Joliffe"). Years later, Shridharani breathlessly recalled a sled ride with her:

> The noise brought Mrs. Joliffe out of the house, which was beautiful in the moonlight. We trailed up the hill, with the air full of shrill cries and more laughter. There was more in store for me, it seemed, because, to my surprise, Mrs. Joliffe said, "Let me take you down." I didn't know exactly what this portended, and I had a vague idea her husband wouldn't approve. . . . Rusty, his girl, and Mollie closed in on us, and without too much hesitation I found myself sitting upright on the sled, the lovely matron seated behind me with her slim, unrubbered feet on the "guides."
> (author's ellipses)

And down they went.[28]

What impact the supposed aggressiveness of American women had on the United States generally was a matter of dispute among Indians. Vivekananda implied that women warmed a nation otherwise bereft of spirituality. The Parsi visitor P. E. Dustoor went further, claiming that the prominence of women in American public life—"they run the offices, they run the shops, they run the men"—threatened to make the United States "a nation of hand-holders and cuddlers and sissies." Most Indians, though, thought the currents of influence ran the other way: with American women asserting themselves much like American men, the country was doubly in danger of losing its soul. The families that in India nurtured and protected children were in the United States flying apart, and a high divorce rate was the natural result of "the quest for happiness" pursued with equal vigor by men and women. There was no one to champion the so-called quieter arts of peacemaking, reflection, conversation, and diplomacy. The Americans, wrote Nehru in 1950, "for all their great achievements, impress me less and less, so far as their human quality is concerned." Four years later, he complained that "no one knows what it [American policy] is, except strong language and powerful emotions." Americans "seem to imagine that every problem can be solved if there is enough talking and shouting about it. My own view is that a little silence might help." Possessed of a surplus of "technical knowledge," Americans lacked the finer virtues. "The United States," Nehru concluded, "is hardly a place one would go at present in search of higher culture."[29]

Gender Relations, Foreign Relations: The United States and India during the Nehru Years

What has the discussion of gender perceptions to do with United States–South Asia relations during the Nehru period? The contention here is that ideas about gender, particularly the American belief that Indian men were effeminate, conditioned American policy toward India as the Cold War developed in South Asia from the 1940s to the 1960s, reinforcing and entwining with American strategic and economic concerns and ideas about race, religion, governance, and caste or class. We can see gender at work by looking at the language used by U.S. policymakers to describe their encounters with India. This means finding what Geoffrey S. Smith has called "gendered code phrases," words that indicate gendered thinking to a fair-minded interpreter even in the absence of direct cause-effect statements, which, it should be said, are hardly more common in studies of diplomacy that emphasize strategic or economic motives than in those using cultural analysis. Smith suggests, for example, that conservative criticism of U.S. foreign aid programs for "wasting money" targeted "an imputed female trait," though in the Indian case the sin of waste was ascribed by conservatives to the Indians, not to the Americans who provided funds. Loy Henderson, ambassador to India from 1948 to 1951, urged diplomats to use "persuasion" with the Indians, "cushioned in a velvet glove and accompanied by friendly handshakes," "flattery," and "firmness." The use of "pressure" was likely to prompt "stiffening resistance," which plainly no one wanted. John Kenneth Galbraith, who became ambassador in 1961, frequently had the task of negotiating with the difficult Krishna Menon. Following a Menon session in mid-July 1961, Galbraith

marveled: "He can take any position and argue for it ruthlessly, with a certain moral indignation and peripheral vagueness which make him invul-
nerable. Presently he reduces you, or anyhow me, to impotence." Passivity
was evidently not Menon's problem; instead, he was querulous, fuzzy, and
in the end emasculating—a male Kali.[30]

Another sort of language was spoken by popular American images of
India. Nearly every reader can summon up the most obvious caricatures
of Indians—as snake charmers, rope trick artists, riders of magic carpets,
and perhaps holy men recumbent on beds of nails. In this post-Freudian
age one hesitates slightly to point out that there is a theme common to
these images. But only slightly: the first three, anyway, seem references to
the ability of men to maintain erections. Of course, if Americans perceive
Indian men (and the images nearly always represent Hindus) as sexually
potent, it cannot be argued that Americans see Indian men as effeminate.
In each image, however, the possibility of Indian male potency is in some
way undercut, usually by ridicule or the suggestion that object tumes-
cence is an illusion. A cartoon by Gary Larson shows a cobra emerging
from a basket wearing a Groucho Marx disguise, while the snake charmer
thinks darkly: "I'll get him for this." In a 1955 episode of the CBS television show *Our Miss Brooks*, the eponymous star dreams that she has entered a maharajah's palace. When Miss Brooks complains that she has
been kept awake by the "serenading" of a palace guard, the man explains
that he has been trying to train his snake. Unfortunately, he has succeeded only in charming his necktie into curling up against his throat,
like a cobra. (At the moment of Indian independence, crowds in Calcutta
surrounded Western men and cut off their ties below the knot.) No one
could explain the rope trick, and when an American photographer tried
to take a picture of it, nothing appeared on the film. He decided this was
because witnesses were in fact "victims of a mass mesmeric hallucination."
In a 1955 *New York Times* cartoon, a vertical rope spells out "Neutrality,"
an unsubtle invitation to viewers to regard with skepticism the potency of
Nehru, who sits atop the rope.[31]

Americans also believed that Nehru, who personified India, had inherited feminine qualities from Gandhi. Partly this was a matter of Nehru's
style. He wore the traditional North Indian shirt, the kurta, that flowed
past his hips like a skirt. He loved flowers. He was rarely seen without a
small rose in his lapel, and on birthdays he exchanged bouquets with
other male government leaders. Nehru drank fruit juice, never alcohol.
Admirers and critics alike noted Nehru's supposed feminine features.
Harold Isaacs's respondents characterized the prime minister as "naive"
and "fluffheaded," among other things. "Nehru is so delicate and graceful

If charmed cobras suggest erect phalluses, the suggestion is mocked by the Groucho-Marxian version shown in this Gary Larson cartoon. THE FAR SIDE © 1985 FARWORKS, INC. Used by permission. All rights reserved.

India may have entered the jet age, but still on a magic carpet. Indian male potency? Ridiculous. Marcus, from L. Lariar, Best Cartoons of the Year, 1956 *(New York, 1957).*

that he makes one feel awkward," confessed C. L. Sulzberger of the *New York Times*. Sir Olaf Caroe, the British statesman who had served as governor of the Northwest Frontier Province and would later try his hand at negotiating an end to the Kashmir dispute, compared Nehru to *Madame* Chiang Kai-shek, and dismissed his reputed courage as "bravado, with something feminine in its composition." Christopher Isherwood likened Nehru to "a tremendous nanny," Nina Padover thought Nehru's "perhaps the most beautiful face I have ever seen," and Eleanor Roosevelt described him as "sensitive and gentle."[32]

But it was not just style that made Nehru seem effeminate. Nehru's foreign policy was designed to keep India out of the Cold War. The nation, he declared, would follow the path of nonalignment, operating in the space between the contending power blocs, committed to neither. Consistent with the independence movement's calculated rejection of Western definitions of masculinity, there was a gendered aspect to this strategy that Nehru cultivated. While Nehru rejected the application to India's policy of the term "neutralism," with its implication of indecisiveness and impotence, he endorsed what he called the "indirect approach" to diplomacy, claiming, in several speeches to American audiences in 1949, "that it was usually more successful than a direct frontal charge." An observer

THE ROPE TRICK.

New York Times, 1955

Nehru performs the rope trick of neutrality, while the puzzled world looks on. Isaacs, Scratches on Our Minds. *Reprinted with permission from M. E. Sharpe, Inc. Publisher, Armonk, N.Y. 10504.*

noted that this was likely "a gentle admonition to the United States that if they wished to woo him they should do it with a little more subtlety." Nehru appeared to valorize India's weakness as a way of preempting unwanted superpower interest in South Asia.[33]

As part of his nonalignment policy, Nehru sought a role as mediator, choosing to act as an impartial referee who would keep disputes between the powers from erupting into global war. Nehru worked to resolve conflicts outside the subcontinent—not, as Sir Archibald Nye had observed in 1951, inside it—without resort to war, or to limit wars that had already broken out. It had always been thus, insisted Vijayalakshmi Pandit, who was president of the UN General Assembly in late 1953. Conflict resolution was "inherent" in Indian history and philosophy. "She has never played an aggressive role anywhere. Her role has always been toward peace, mediation, coming together, working out solutions and so on." India was head of the five-member International Commission for Supervision and Control of the Indochina cease-fire that emerged from the 1954 Geneva conference, from which vantage point it urged the creation of coalition governments in Laos and Vietnam. At Nehru's behest, Krishna Menon attempted to mediate the Suez Canal dispute in 1956, and from 1960 practically unto his death in May 1964 the prime minister tried in various ways to encourage a U.S.-Soviet arms limitation agreement, a ban on testing nuclear weapons in the atmosphere, or, failing those, at least frequent summits to air critical issues. "Either they will blow themselves up or come to some agreement," Nehru commented dourly in late 1961.[34]

India played a prominent role in seeking an armistice in the Korean war. In the immediate aftermath of the North Korean attack on June 25, 1950, Nehru supported U.S.-sponsored resolutions in the United Nations branding North Korea an aggressor and (with some hesitation) calling for material support of South Korea. But Nehru nevertheless harbored "some hope that we might be able to play a useful role in preventing the conflict from spreading or in bringing the warring factions nearer to one another." In mid-July, India proposed immediate peace talks, predicated on the admission of the People's Republic of China, the expulsion of Taiwan, and the return of the boycotting Soviet Union to the UN. The Americans angrily rejected this plan for rewarding communist aggression. (They also noted that the proposal came in different versions depending on which Indian diplomat communicated it.) India sent field hospitals to both Koreas and continued to press for a truce.

The Indian and American positions steadily grew apart. When the military tide turned in favor of the United States in October 1950, India refused to support a U.S.-sponsored resolution calling for the unification of Korea, and when Chinese forces joined the battle and reversed U.S. fortunes later that fall India spurned an American effort to name China as the aggressor, working instead to organize Asian and Arab UN representatives into "mediation committees." The Indians lost that battle in early

1951. Still, Nehru did not give up. He urged moderation on the Chinese, and called on the UN to declare that its objective was to "limit the conflict" in Korea. Eventually these efforts were rewarded. By 1952, the two sides were snarling their way toward a settlement when they found themselves stymied by disagreement over what to do with prisoners of war (POWs): the North Koreans and Chinese wanted all POWs returned, period, while the South Koreans and Americans, anticipating a propaganda coup, insisted that repatriation be voluntary. India, whose previous infidelities might now be more usefully seen as flexibility, stepped forward to help resolve the dispute. Showing formidable patience despite opposition from China and the United States, Indian diplomats, and particularly Krishna Menon, ultimately produced an acceptable solution to the repatriation problem. India became one of five nations on the Custodial Commission for POWs, its representatives charged with deciding whether prisoner refusals to be repatriated were genuine or coerced. The soldiers required to oversee this fractious process were entirely supplied by India.[35]

The Americans thought it came out all right, but the episode failed to erase U.S. suspicions that Indian mediation efforts sprang from cowardice and fear, not a determination to make the world more peaceful. India had been lucky, not good. Public opinion in the United States rapidly soured on Nehru; an editorialist for the *New York Herald Tribune* declared that "an ineluctable condition of leadership is that one should lead. A mere wringing of the hands over all the obvious difficulties and perils of the situation is not leadership." Even more frequently, U.S. officials criticized Nehru, and Indian policy, using language evocative of gender. Like fickle women, or effeminate men, the Indians "could not be relied upon," Acheson insisted heatedly in late 1950. They were soft, determined to mediate "even though such mediation might involve appeasement," wrote Loy Henderson. Sarvepalli Radhakrishnan, the Indian ambassador in Moscow, was "vague and starry-eyed," "naive" about the communists, and apparently incapable of "paying close attention to what was being told him," reported U.S. ambassador Alan Kirk; all of these were epithets indicating a lack of rootedness in the real world. Indians avoided the call of duty: "If there is anything which disturbs an Indian, it is a situation in which responsibility is placed squarely on his shoulders," claimed a U.S. official. Indians were beguiled by the spiritual, and their minds were clouded by mystery and illusion. Kirk described Nehru's truce proposal of July 1950 as "a misty proposition," and UN ambassador Warren Austin told Acheson in December that Indian (and Chinese) positions were unfathomable because "we were dealing with Orientals who had only taken off the 6th veil." Krishna Menon's proposal on the POW issue was, according to Acheson, "fuzzy" and "soft." Even after John Foster Dulles grudgingly admitted that the Indians might be useful intermediaries between the Americans and the Chinese, they would only be "messenger boys" shuttling between the warring powers, too diminutive and trivial themselves to have opinions of consequence.[36]

Nehru did not believe that his, or India's, manhood was at stake in these matters. This was in part because masculinity in India absorbs rather than rejects the feminine, as the reader will recall; the two are complementary, not at odds. Mediation is honored in Hindu social and political relations, and mediators are generally men who resolve conflicts between other men. Peacemakers are ubiquitous in Indian villages, intervening (observed G. M. Carstairs) "between the disputants, reminding them how wrong it was to give way to anger, urging self-control and compromise." Carstairs was impressed to see that mediation nearly always worked, at least behaviorally, sublimating hostility even if it failed to eliminate it. Mediators were not just honorable but also powerful: "The role of moral adviser," he noted, "is one which compels an impulse to obey." Far from behaving timidly, an Indian mediator demands "a surrender, however temporary, of one's customary suspicions." What Americans saw as a lack of Indian resolve, an embrace of unreality, a willingness to listen to cant and to compromise with evil, was in fact an assertion of power over nations that had shamefully lost control of themselves and threatened to drag other members of the international community into their conflicts. In early 1954, as the POW repatriation issue played itself out under Indian supervision in Korea, a columnist for the *Times of India* chided the Americans: "The dynamic possibilities of non-alignment are too often underestimated in the mistaken belief that 'neutrality' is passive, supine, and indifferent. India's efforts in Korea have demonstrated otherwise." "A strong country," Nehru told an audience in Los Angeles in 1961, "would not lose its strength in gentle approaches to solving the cold war issues of the day." It took a strong nation to avoid conflicts, and a stronger one yet to demand the moral authority to resolve them.[37]

Nehru deeply resented Americans' attempts to bully him by insisting on their toughness, and on his lack of it. Before the Korean mediation effort bore fruit, the prime minister lamented that Indian initiatives failed "before the big stick of the United States." And when the United States made clear its opposition to the Geneva Agreement on Indochina in the summer of 1954, Nehru characterized U.S. policy as nothing "except strong language and powerful emotions." To American policymakers, there was something wrong with India's insistence on mediating. It smacked of naiveté, cowardice, and moral evasiveness. There was a right side and a wrong side in the Cold War, and it was dangerous for Nehru to pretend otherwise. President Truman reportedly complained in late 1950: "Nehru has sold us down the Hudson. His attitude has been responsible for our losing the war in Korea." Dwight Eisenhower, who (as we will see) respected Nehru and appreciated his policies more than Truman did, nevertheless put the prime minister off his efforts to bring the Soviets and Americans together on arms control; a summit would serve no purpose, the president wrote in October 1960, given the belligerency of Soviet policy. In Southeast Asia, India's pursuit of negotiations was tantamount to suspending moral judgment in a situation plainly demanding it. "We simply do not understand how Nehru can equate the two parties fighting in Laos," wrote an exasperated State Department official in early 1961. It was not the careful calculation of India's interest that inclined Nehru to seek a settlement. Instead, the Indians lacked resolve and clear perspective. They were irrational and emotional. U.S. policymakers believed that India, in its foreign policy, was acting just like a frightened woman.[38]

The three state visits Nehru made to the United States—in the fall of 1949, December 1956, and November 1961—gave the Truman, Eisenhower, and Kennedy administrations opportunities for close examination of the Indian leader. Each encounter illustrated the influence of gendered thinking on American explanations of what made Nehru tick. President Truman was not unsympathetic to Indian problems, and a week before Nehru arrived in the United States Loy Henderson pleaded with the State Department for a generous program of economic aid for India. But Henderson had previously expressed reservations about the president's imminent guest. "Nehru," Henderson had written, "is a vain, sensitive, emotional and complicated person." While in school in England, Nehru had adopted the attitudes of "a group of rather supercilious upper-middle-class men who fancied themselves rather precious"—here is the unconcealed vocabulary of scorn for the supposed effeminacy of the Oxbridge dandy. Truman himself had spent over four years demonstrating that he was "not afraid of the Russians" and that it was essential to "stand firm" and not "baby" the adversary. In Nehru he beheld a man with a rose in his lapel who reviewed the U.S. honor guard arrayed at the airport with evident distaste. The two men simply did not click. Truman found Nehru uncommunicative and suspicious. The reason, Nehru later confided, was that he had been put off by the president's extended discussion of the merits of Kentucky bourbon with Vice President Alben Barkley. As Sarvepalli Gopal puts it, "Truman's cocky vulgarity had grated" on the prime minister.[39]

Gender perceptions also played a role in Dwight Eisenhower's meetings with Nehru in late 1956. On the basis of ideology alone, there was no reason to suspect that Eisenhower and Nehru would get along. Secretary of State Dulles was a staunch opponent of nonalignment and an advocate of military alliances, in two of which resided Pakistan. Eisenhower had of course approved these arrangements. But the president knew of Nehru's dislike of military pacts and deliberately soft-pedaled their importance. In fact, Eisenhower seemed largely untroubled by Indian "neutralism." Though he concurred with Dulles and others that Indians were "emotional," he was neither threatened by this nor stirred to acts of paternalism. Eisenhower was a grandfatherly figure. His manhood had been established by his successful generalship during World War II. He felt no need to "stand up to the Soviets" merely for the sake of posturing. There was something "strange, even feminine" about the president that made him attractive, editorialized the *Eastern Economist* of New Delhi. Rather than try to impress Nehru with the pomp and glitter of Washington, Eisenhower took the prime minister off to his Gettysburg farm, where the two men talked intimately for hours. They disagreed on many issues, including U.S. policy toward Pakistan, the disposition of Kashmir, and the relative strength of nationalism and communism. But Eisenhower listened equably and never lectured his guest about the moral failings of nonalignment. Even before the visit, the *Chicago Tribune* found the president's policy incomprehensible. "Every Indian kick," an editorial complained, "is rewarded by us with another favor. The Administration's behavior is neither manly nor sensible." Nehru told reporters that the president was "thoroughly honest" and had "a certain moral quality." "Of the American Presidents of his time, it was, curiously, Eisenhower with whom Nehru got on best," Gopal observes. The attraction is less curious if the relationship is analyzed in terms of gender.[40]

The Nehru-Eisenhower relationship stood in contrast to the one that emerged between Nehru and John F. Kennedy. On the basis of ideology alone, there was every reason to imagine that Kennedy and Nehru would get along. Kennedy had long championed economic aid for India. For his part Nehru, urged on by Ambassador Galbraith, looked forward to meeting the president; much excitement preceded the prime minister's visit to the United States in November 1961. As with Truman and Nehru, however, something failed to work. Kennedy seemed insecure, and his determination to act with vigor in world affairs highlighted rather than concealed his anxieties. He would not promise to forbear from nuclear weapons testing or military intervention in Vietnam. Particularly after the Bay of Pigs fiasco in Cuba in April 1961, Kennedy felt the need to stand up to the Soviets, to show that he was neither callow nor cowardly—to

Nehru (October 1949) and Liaquat Ali Khan (May 1950) review the troops on arriving in Washington. Above, Nehru leaves considerable distance between himself and the soldiers, walking in front of a line of men who stand apart from the ranks. Nehru's face is tight, his body turned slightly away from the troops. Below, Liaquat, who is on Truman's left, walks so close to the soldiers that he could, if he wished, almost touch them. He walks confidently, shoulders square, and his face and Truman's show satisfaction. White House Files and U.S. Dept. of State, Courtesy Harry S. Truman Library.

prove he was a man. " 'Toughness,' Henry Fairlie has written, "was one of the most prominent words in the vocabulary of the New Frontier; perhaps no other quality was so highly regarded." Nehru found Kennedy "brash, aggressive and inexperienced." For the president, the meeting was even more disappointing. Nehru, who flinched visibly with each shot from a welcoming gun salute, was "passive and inward looking" and "simply did not respond" to the president's attempts to draw him out. Kennedy later called the encounter "the worst head of state visit I have had." Nehru seemed to confirm his reputation in policymaking circles as a man lacking vigor and resolve.[41]

In contrast, the Americans noted with approval the "manly" behavior of India's neighbor and rival, Pakistan. The Americans inherited from the British the idea that Muslims were more aggressive, decisive, and otherwise more masculine than Hindus. "From the very beginning," recalled Elbert G. Mathews, who directed the State Department's Office of South Asian Affairs from 1948 to 1951, "there was, in the U.S. Government . . . a strong view, based on the reading of Kipling, that the martial races of India were in the north, and much was now Pakistan. And therefore, the sensible thing for us to do was to cozy up to these martial races; they would be a great value to us in the fight against communism." Harold Isaacs summarized ideas about Muslims and Hindus elicited by his interviews: "Even the poor Muslim is a vigorous man, while the poor Hindu is buckling at the knees; Pakistanis seemed energetic Western types, easier to talk to; . . . I hear from people that the Pakistanis are up and coming, good people, good fighters, whereas the Hindus are said to be mystics, dreamers, hypocrites; . . . Muslim faith is more dynamic . . . more masculinity." In late 1957, James M. Langley, the U.S. ambassador in Pakistan, recalled being told that Pakistan was "the anchor of the Baghdad Pact, and of SEATO," and "that the Paks are strong, direct, friendly, and virile." This is not just the language of gender, but it is hard to resist altogether the impression that these adjectives convey long-standing concerns of American men about how they and other men are supposed to act, and supposed not to.[42]

American statesmen, always uncomfortable with Nehru, embraced a succession of Pakistani leaders. The gestures and body language of diplomacy reveal much about the American-Pakistani relationship. On visits to the United States, Pakistani officials, all of them men, wore suits and ties and drank alcohol. George McGhee, assistant secretary of state for Near Eastern, South Asian, and African affairs, was impressed with Prime Minister Liaquat Ali Khan. "He was a big, strong, confident man with considerable international stature," McGhee remembered. "I liked him, as a man you could do business with." Loy Henderson had described Nehru as "vain, sensitive, emotional and complicated"; according to a State Department profile Liaquat's characteristics included "calmness, imperturbability, industry, energy, [and] perseverance." Unlike Nehru, Liaquat seemed to relish reviewing the troops at the airport. Mohammed Ali, prime minister from 1953 to 1955, toured the United States in October 1954. The British ambassador in Washington, Sir Roger Makins, attended a dinner for the prime minister one evening and found him "rather moody and distrait," retiring to a corner after the meal to look at "coloured stereoscopic pictures of ladies." Mohammed Ali nevertheless wore well on the Americans. The prime minister delighted in drawing a "parallel between the young, new Pakistan striving to become a great virile nation and the American nineteenth century tradition." "It all goes down extremely well," Sir Roger concluded. When Prime Minister H. S. Suhrawardy came to Washington in 1957, Eisenhower hosted a stag luncheon for him.[43]

The general Mohammed Ayub Khan, who came to power in a coup in 1958, was a favorite of Eisenhower's. According to a *New York Times* profile, Ayub was "a tall, erect outdoorsman with a bristling mustache who usually carried a swagger stick at his side. He spoke in clipped British tones, always with the emphasis on 'no nonsense—let's get on with it, old boy.' He liked hunting and fishing and an occasional whisky-soda in the officer's mess." When Eisenhower learned that Ayub was planning to switch the greens on the Rawalpindi golf course from sand to grass, he sent the general enough nursery stock of a grass called Tifgreen to do the job. In the meantime, Ayub played a round of golf with generals Nathan Twining and Omar Bradley at the Burning Tree Country Club outside Washington. "During play Twining kept talking to Bradley about Pakistan and our armed forces in warm terms," Ayub noted with obvious satisfaction. On a tour of Asia in 1961, Vice President Lyndon Johnson wrote to President Kennedy that Ayub was "seasoned as a leader where others are not; confident, straightforward and I would judge dependable."[44]

It was too much for Chester Bowles. On his second tour as ambassador to India in 1963, Bowles let loose his frustrations in his diary. "For fifteen years," he wrote, "our relationship with South Asia has suffered from our habit of sending important personages to this area who have no knowledge of the forces at work here. They come convinced that all Asians are 'inscrutable' products of the 'Inscrutable East.' And then in Karachi they meet Asians they can really understand, Asians who argue the advantages of an olive over an onion in a martini and who know friends they know in London. Here at last," Bowles went on, "are Asians who make sense, who understand our problems, who face up to the realities, who understand the menace of whatever may worry us at the moment. And so we agree to more F-104s or C130s or whatever may be currently required as political therapy to ease wounded Pakistani feelings."[45]

Most of all, as Bowles pointed out, the Pakistanis respected and valued armaments and were quite willing to side with the United States in the Cold War in order to get them. Recall that, beginning in the early 1950s, the United States favored Pakistan as the most reliable and potentially useful nation in South Asia. The two countries signed an arms agreement in 1954, and the Eisenhower administration induced Pakistan to join the Southeast Asia Treaty Organization (SEATO) in 1954 and the Baghdad Pact (later CENTO) in 1955. As I indicated in chapter 1, there were historical and strategic reasons for these alliances. But it was also true that the Americans felt most comfortable standing with real men against the menace of communism. Pakistani leaders, who ate meat, drank liquor, and knew the value of a well-tuned military machine, were real men.

Indian men were not. Westerners had long represented Hindus as cowardly and morally phlegmatic. Gandhi and Nehru were effeminate, soft on communism, and too squeamish to take a forceful stand against evil. Indian women were regarded by Westerners as dangerous Kalis, intent on eclipsing the manhood of their male opponents. Ironically, this won for India's chief female leader, Nehru's daughter Indira Gandhi, a measure of Western respect. Gandhi was India's prime minister from 1966 to 1977 and again from 1980 until her assassination in 1984. Even before her father died she was admired for her toughness; as the British high commissioner in India once put it, "Indira is the best man in India." Despite policy differences with the Gandhi government, U.S. policymakers grudgingly respected the prime minister's backbone. Henry Kissinger noted that Richard Nixon disliked Indira Gandhi personally but "had an understanding for leaders who operated on an unsentimental assessment of the national interest. Once one cut through the strident, self-righteous rhetoric, Mrs. Gandhi had few peers in the cold-blooded calculation of the elements of power."[46]

6

Religion: Christians, Hindus, and Muslims

> The roots of Indo-American tension must indeed be found in
> cultural and religious dissonance. The Hindu concepts of time
> and the cosmos . . . lead to relativistic foreign policy attitudes,
> making it easier for India to accept optimal solutions in a world
> where preferred ones are rarely possible and easier to rational-
> ize what others do (e.g. Soviet behavior in Hungary or
> Afghanistan) if this suits Indian interests. Conversely, American
> "itchiness" concerning nonalignment is explained in signifi-
> cant measure by the fact that many Americans are conditioned
> by religious traditions based on revealed dogma.
> —Selig S. Harrison

> In this Season we must work in the true spirit of religion. Love
> is vain if we do not treat other human beings as brothers; it is
> empty if we do not adopt an attitude of patience, sympathy and
> understanding when dealing with problems which seem to sep-
> arate us. Love is bound to win.
> —Sarvepalli Radhakrishnan, Vice President of India, 1952–62

American scholars have usually resisted interpreting U.S. foreign
policy as a product of religious thinking. The idea makes many
Americans uncomfortable, for we are supposed to live in a country
where politics and religion do not mix. We know, of course, that they do
mix. Televangelists run for president, politicians go conspicuously to
church, opponents are demonized or tainted by association with devils,
like Willie Horton in the presidential campaign of 1988. To some extent,
religion is encoded in political practice, taking the form of what Robert
Bellah has called "civil religion," the translation of religious language and
symbols into secularisms. The administration of John F. Kennedy, notes
Garry Wills, "had its own rites and sacred symbols (touch football, PT-109,

tie clips), even its own religious order (the Peace Corps)." But religion—specifically Protestantism—has also been openly associated with U.S. foreign policy. Protestant missionaries carried American values to other countries. Westward expansionism was sanctified by a sense of mission. It liberated Cubans and Filipinos from papist overlords. Mission underlay the American decision to fight Germany in 1917 and Japan in 1941; both Woodrow Wilson and Franklin Roosevelt invoked God's name in their war messages.[1]

The sense of religious mission carried into the Cold War. The Soviet Union was not just an enemy but the Antichrist, the "devil we knew" (according to H. W. Brands), especially John Foster Dulles's devil (Townsend Hoopes). Several monographs on United States policy during the Cold War have the word "crusade" in their titles; there were U.S. crusades in China, the Philippines, Vietnam, and Korea, and on behalf of human rights and free trade. The West, warned Averell Harriman, faced a "barbarian invasion of Europe." A senator proclaimed in 1950 that "America must move forward with the atomic bomb in one hand and the cross in the other." Accepting the Republican nomination for president in 1952, Dwight Eisenhower said: "You have summoned me . . . to lead a great crusade—for freedom in America and freedom in the world."[2]

The three secretaries of state most responsible for shaping U.S. policy during the period 1947–64 had thorough Protestant upbringings. Dean Acheson (1949–53) grew up in a rectory in Middletown, Connecticut; his father, Edward, was the Episcopalian bishop of the state diocese. Acheson's biographer has written that rectory life made "a frame within which the essential drama of growing up took place." "From the moral homilies of his father Dean acquired a sharp sense of right and wrong and . . . the words of the Collect and the *Book of Common Prayer* made an enduring contribution to his thought." The frequency with which Secretary of State Acheson quoted scripture and used religious imagery indicates the truth of this statement. When asked about the perjury conviction of Alger Hiss, for instance, Acheson cited chapter and verse of the Gospel according to St. Matthew. Speaking to the National Council of Churches in the fall of 1952, Acheson contrasted the "God-loving" and "God-fearing" community of early New England with the Soviet philosophy that hate for one's enemies was a necessary prerequisite of patriotism.[3]

Dean Rusk was named secretary of state by John F. Kennedy in late 1960, and he would serve through the end of Lyndon Johnson's administration in 1969. Rusk's views on foreign policy, his son has written, derived in part from "southern Presbyterianism with its Calvinist overtones . . . reading aloud from the Bible as a boy, and earning 'pearls'

for passages memorized." Rusk's father, Robert, was ordained a Presbyterian minister, but was forced to abandon the pulpit because of a throat ail-
ment. Rusk would remember that his impoverished family owned three
books of consequence: the *Farmer's Almanac*, the Sears and Roebuck catalog (ultimately used for toilet paper), and the Bible; the family also subscribed to the *Christian Observer* magazine. At Davidson College, Rusk
"gave much thought to becoming a Presbyterian minister." As secretary of
state, Rusk was a man of prim sensibility, abjuring profanity and discouraging it in others; of dogged loyalty to the two presidents he served; of
dedication to the principles of collective security embodied in the United
Nations charter, drafted, he wrote, with a "prayer on our lips"; and of determination to stop communism in Southeast Asia, a mission Rusk never
regretted.[4]

John Foster Dulles, who was appointed secretary of state by Eisenhower
late in 1952, was the most deeply religious man of the three. Dulles's father was a Presbyterian minister, and Christianity was embedded in John
Foster's life. He came closer than Rusk to becoming a minister, and when
in 1946 a friend needled him about disappointing his mother when he rejected the pulpit, Dulles snapped, "nearly broke her heart." But Dulles
the lawyer and diplomat never strayed from the idea that Christianity prescribed a universal moral law that formed the basis for American political
institutions and foreign policy. In the period following World War II,
atavistic despotism had returned in the form of the godless and powerful
Soviet Union. For Dulles, writes Mark Toulouse, "the Cold War acted as a
revelatory event." Faced by an implacable foe, the United States needed
to rediscover its faith and rededicate itself to its mission of spreading its
God-given democratic institutions throughout the world. A strong military would help: "Christians," after all, "are not negative, supine people,"
said Dulles. But more critical to America's success was an understanding
that the practice of diplomacy must remain harnessed to spiritual commitment. The separation of the two was the principal crime of communism. The leaders of the Soviet Union nourished a "materialistic creed
which denies the existence of moral law. It denies that men are spiritual
beings. It denies that there are any such things as eternal verities." There
could be no compromise between the Americans and Soviets because
there was no common basis for understanding. There was, however, a curious parallel between communism and Christianity: both were missionary creeds. You could not talk sense to "atheistic," "Godless" communists
because "there is no nook or cranny in all the world into which Communist influence does not penetrate," wrote Dulles, echoing George Kennan. Communism was the evil mirror image of missionary Christianity,

which also sought influence without boundary. "You can no more make a 'deal' with Communism to limit itself to certain areas than you can make a 'deal' with Christianity to limit itself to certain areas," Dulles claimed. The Cold War was Armageddon, a contest between expansionist forces, one beneficent, the other malign.

People everywhere needed Christian faith if they were to win the battle against evil. Fraud that it was, communism nevertheless appealed to the "masses" across the globe: "The spider spins a beautiful web which shimmers in the sunlight, and he invites the fly into his parlor. Communist propaganda, like the spider's web, does attract." The United States did battle for the hearts of innocents seduced by the spider's work, interposing its creed between them and the bright lure of communism. So, for example, the Korean War was a crusade. "We have borne a Christian witness," said Dulles in a November 1950 radio address. "We need have no remorse. Also we need not despair. We have acted as God gave us to see the right." George V. Allen, who was ambassador to India from 1953 to 1955, recalled that Dulles, whom he respected, nevertheless "seemed to feel that he had . . . a 'pipeline on high'—that is, that he was receiving his instructions from a superior source. . . . Regardless of what his staff felt or what world opinion was, if he thought that he was doing right—and there was a certain mysticism in his feeling of right being handed down from on high—he did it."[5]

Dulles's version of the United States as a Christian republic had a qualified South Asian counterpart in Pakistan. In 1947 the founders of Pakistan were concerned about losing their identities and privileges as Muslims in an independent India. They argued that only Pakistan, a separate, Muslim state, would protect them. Pakistan need not be, in the strictest sense, a theocracy. Indeed, M. A. Jinnah, the man most responsible for the creation of Pakistan, was a worldly and secular man who disclaimed any intention to base the country's constitution on Islamic law. Pakistan's government was run by British-trained civil servants until the late 1950s, then by generals whose Islamic faith was seldom more than skin deep. But, as Omar Noman has put it, "there were obvious contradictions in the demand for a separate, but *secular*, Muslim state." The most obvious sprang from the founders' refusal to countenance the possibility that Muslims could live happily in a secular but mostly Hindu India: Pakistan was necessary because Muslim identity in South Asia would otherwise be eclipsed. Finding it difficult to write a constitution for a secular Muslim state, especially with conservative clerics looking on suspiciously, Pakistan's Constituent Assembly approved a resolution on the "Aims and Objects of the Constitution" in March 1949. It tried to split differences. Pakistanis would be guaranteed "fundamental rights," among them "freedom of thought, expression, and worship," but all of these were subject to "law and public morality." The "principles of democracy, freedom, equality, tolerance and social justice" would be observed—"as enunciated by Islam." And the resolution's preamble began: "In the name of Allah, the Beneficent, the Merciful," and acknowledged "sovereignty over the entire universe . . . to God Almighty alone," who "delegated" authority to Pakistan. The secular Muslims who led Pakistan through the early decades of the Cold War kept an eye on their fundamentalist critics, trying at all times to give their pronouncements and policies a properly Islamic cast without surrendering themselves entirely to theological statecraft.[6]

As in Pakistan, though for different reasons, leaders in India proclaimed theirs a secular state. Mohandas Gandhi hoped to erase religious boundaries by appealing to universal values of justice, freedom, and peace. Jawaharlal Nehru decried the "superstition" of Indians, who needed (he thought) to solve their problems soberly. As a young man Nehru renounced religion, India's "old man of the sea" that had "not only broken our backs but stunted and almost killed all originality of thought and mind." Nehru ate meat, and made derisive references to sadhus—Hindu holy men—in speeches. But Hinduism was not readily removed from India's political discourse. Americans and Pakistanis who are not fundamentalists spend much effort trying to demarcate the boundary dividing the sacred from the secular. Hindus do not. For them, the distinction between the two is artificial. Hindu society is imagined as an organic whole, in which religious values shape the patterns of everyday life.

Again and again, Indian political leaders were forced to acknowledge the religiosity of many Indians, and forced to make concessions to it. All castes, for example, are encouraged to see the characters in the Hindu epics *Ramayana* and *Mahabharata* as models for behavior. Indians, notes Alan Roland, "tend to be constantly on the look-out for signs and predictors, relying a great deal on the magic-cosmic to arrange and manage their practical affairs and relationships—marriage, education, career, children, health, wealth, and power—as auspiciously as possible." An Indian businessman who handles matters in the office with vigorous rationality maintains a religious home life. He is abstemious, a vegetarian, and frowns on remarriage by widows. He has a tape player primarily so that he can listen to Sanskrit chants. Astrologers advise him on domestic matters. When someone is sick, homeopaths are brought in if modern doctors fail. In May 1950 the *Times of India* carried an anecdote about an ambitious man who had been passed over for promotion because several of his colleagues had opposed it. Was he bitter? No, he told the writer placidly: it was "God's will . . . God's hour-hand has not pointed the time for my 'lift.' When that hour comes, no one can stop it." Even India's most scientific political actors, the Communists, found it impossible to resist the call to religion. Meeting in the southern temple city of Madurai in late December 1953, delegates to the Third Communist Party Congress abandoned debate over launching an agrarian revolution to join a procession of Hindu worshipers following a cart-borne image of a deity through the streets. "After all," explained one of the delegates, "we must submit to God," and another admitted, "if you go deep, you will find every party worker and every party member in the city [is] a tradition-loving, ardent devotee of the Goddess Meenakshi."[7]

One illustration of the infusion of the sacred into the secular in India involves the Hindu practice known as *darshan*. The word means "seeing," and it refers to human witness of an image of a god—Shiva, Brahma, Vishnu, and so forth—or of a saint, sadhu, or *sanyasin* (renouncer of worldly comforts). Hindus travel to temples and sacred sites in order to see the holy object or person, to "take *darśan* [darshan]" as Diana Eck has explained it. It is "the central act of Hindu worship," Eck writes, "to stand in the presence of the deity." Darshan is a reciprocal process. The human worshiper "takes *darśan*," and the deity or venerated person "gives *darśan*"; the god "presents himself to be seen by the villagers." The importance of this mutual witnessing is understood by all Hindus.[8]

Reading a variety of sources from the early years of independent India, one is struck by the presence of darshan in political life, outside a setting that Westerners would call religious. Certainly Gandhi became for Indians a *sanyasin* who had renounced material goods. Wherever Gandhi went in India he attracted thousands of admirers eager to "take his darshan," even if that meant no more than a quick glimpse of the great man in his third-class railway compartment. The case of Nehru is more complicated, given his hostility to "superstition." But it is impossible to miss the element of renunciation in Nehru's life: it was a critical part of the process by which he became, after Gandhi, the leading nationalist hero, in the epic tradition of great renouncers. Nehru, the son of Kashmiri Brahmins and by his own admission the spoiled product of a first-rate British education, abandoned what would have been a lucrative career in law to join Gandhi in the struggle for independence. From 1921 to 1945, Nehru was jailed for his political activities nine times for a total of more than ten years. He was widowed in 1936 and never remarried. Following Gandhi's assassination in early 1948, Nehru became state *sanyasin*. Once aloof, he now seemed to gather energy from the crowds who flocked to him for darshan. They could not always hear him when he spoke, and because he often gave speeches in English many in the audience could not understand him. But he was there, presenting himself for witness, allowing thousands of eyes to gaze at him, giving darshan. Michael Brecher traveled with the prime minister during the spring of 1956, and recorded this scene:

> At one village, 10,000 had gathered to greet the Prime Minister. As our caravan rounded the bend they broke into a frenzied run towards the opposite side in order to get another look at him. The race for *darshan* was like an instinctive, compelling drive, a craving for association with an exalted man, however brief. Throughout the journey there was a mumble among the crowds which was translated for my benefit. "We saw him, we saw him," they were saying in ecstasy to their families. In the evening, on the return journey, the road was again lined with people. There was not the slightest possibility of seeing Nehru, for he was in a closed car travelling at fifty miles per hour in the dark. Yet they stood patiently to see the car go by.[9]

It was not just Nehru who gave darshan. The practice was implicit in relationships between Indians and between Indians and foreigners. Just prior to independence, for example, the Calcutta-based newspaper the *Statesman* printed photographs of prominent leaders of the Muslim League, the organization instrumental in the creation of Pakistan. Days later, the paper ran eight letters from readers protesting the *Statesman*'s publication of the photos. "You think you will live in Hindustan [India] yet preach against the Hindus. You must leave Hindustan otherwise your life is in danger," warned one of the correspondents. "You must stop publication of your paper because it is anti-Hindu and anti-Sikh and shows favor to Mussalmans. I am waiting here with my loaded pistol." The letter was signed by "DEMON." The threat seems a burlesque, until one recalls subsequent events in Calcutta and throughout South Asia. What is striking is how seriously Demon and other readers took the mere publication of pictures. Only among people who regard the act of seeing and being seen as akin to benediction—and the *Statesman*'s correspondents in this instance were surely Hindu fundamentalists—could the presentation of images have carried so great a charge. The *Statesman*'s editors had had the temerity to present for darshan the very men who would divide and thus betray India.[10]

There is nothing quite comparable to darshan in the United States, and Americans could not understand the importance of seeing and being seen that Indians implicitly recognized. This difference in perception created frequent misunderstandings. One involved Krishna Menon, who was at various times India's high commissioner in London, chair of the Indian delegation to the United Nations, and the minister of defense. Other than Nehru, few people in or outside of India liked Krishna Menon. The diplomat K. P. S. Menon, who was unrelated to Krishna but often mistaken for him, called his namesake "the most insufferable human being I have yet come across." British Foreign Office officials distinguished between K. P. S. ("a good lad") and Krishna ("not so good"), regarding the latter as "an agitator" and "a rather extremist henchman of Pandit Nehru." American officials referred to him variously as "a very adroit and unscrupulous maneuverer," "untrustworthy and emotionally biased against the United States," and an "angry, embittered prophet hurling the word of God at the human race." (Nehru once said, "Krishna Menon is my answer to Dulles.")[11]

One of Menon's most exasperating characteristics was his insistence on the strictest observance of protocol. On his way to India to assume his post as U.S. ambassador in October 1948, Loy Henderson stopped off in London and during his stay paid a courtesy call on Menon, who was then the high commissioner. When Henderson was ushered into the office, Menon stood behind his desk and took Henderson's outstretched hand only reluctantly. "Well, this is interesting," Menon said. "You are the first American Ambassador who has ever darkened my threshold." The U.S. ambassador in London, it seemed, had not called on Menon, nor had Menon been invited to the U.S. embassy. Henderson and Menon's deputy tried to change the subject, but Menon would not let up. At last the discussion turned to such matters as travel in India and the housing shortage in Delhi. Still, Henderson noted, "Menon was not placated. Such friendly remarks that I made elicited only cold silence or sarcastic rejoinder." Even as Henderson took his leave, "Mr. Menon again referred to his lack of contact here with the American Embassy." And Menon repeated the complaint for Henderson when the two met in New Delhi six months later.[12]

The Americans put this behavior down to Menon's egotism and truculence, and this was accurate, as far as it went. But Menon, concerned about his status, was angry that he had not been asked by the Americans either to give or take darshan. An important man, one who had renounced a life of leisure and material comfort with his family in Kerala, deserved to be asked.

Nehru thought so too. He was less prickly than Krishna Menon, but he agreed that relationships between Indians and Americans had come out of balance. Nehru believed that he should give darshan to his fellow Indians, and that Americans were entitled to take darshan from him. Americans must also, however, provide Indian officials with the opportunity to take darshan from them. On the last day of February 1951, Frank Roberts, Great Britain's deputy high commissioner in New Delhi, spoke with G. S. Bajpai, secretary-general of the Ministry of External Affairs. Bajpai gave vent to his frustrations about American "hamhandedness," as Roberts recorded the term. The previous year, the deputy foreign minister, B. V. Keskar, had gone to Washington for what he had expected would be meetings with high-ranking officials. His appointment with Secretary of State Acheson had been canceled, however, and the only "reasonably senior person" Keskar saw was Assistant Secretary George McGhee. Keskar was insulted, and when Nehru learned of the incident he was insulted too. Nehru had always been willing to receive U.S. officials, even when they were not especially high ranking. No more. Not only had Americans presumed on Nehru's availability: a recent American visitor to New Delhi had antagonized officials by the "superior tone" he had adopted toward them. It was not the first time that an American had abused his position. "It was a pity," Bajpai concluded, that "the Americans could not see themselves as others saw them and mend their behaviour since in Asia, at least, their generous policies and admirable intentions tended to be overlooked in the general irritation against their behaviour."[13]

The United States and the Religious Construction of South Asia

American ideas about South Asian religions had deep roots. The first Americans to have sustained contact with Indians—Muslim, Hindu, and otherwise—were Protestant missionaries. Cotton Mather's *India Christiana*, published in 1721, was a how-to guide for converting Asian Indians to Christianity. The first two American missionaries to India arrived in Calcutta in June 1812. The number of missionaries rose from three hundred in the mid-nineteenth century to nearly twenty-five hundred by 1922. By them, almost half of U.S. investments in India were in religious institutions. And because the United States maintained a low diplomatic profile until the 1940s, American missionaries, along with their European counterparts and occasional lay travelers, were the country's eyes and ears in South Asia.[14]

Some of these missionaries feared or loathed or simply mistrusted Muslims. The late-twentieth-century stereotype of the Muslim as a religious fanatic originated in an earlier time. The Muslim, notes Ronald Inden, "was a potentially dangerous Alter Ego" of the Christian Westerner, his Islam "a false, fanatical cousin of Christianity." Missionary accounts and, later,

Western literature depicted Muslims as vicious, haughty, violent, authoritarian, sexually depraved, and wicked. Cruel in war as the enemies of the Crusaders, keepers of slaves, men who had harems or (like the prophet Mohammed) several wives, women who gestured seductively from beneath their veils, the Muslims could be a perverse lot. Were it not for the presence of a "strong Christian power" in India, wrote a nineteenth-century missionary, the Muslims "would have put all non-Muslims to death."[15]

But there was another and more prominent side to this image. Westerners believed that Muslims had admirable qualities, especially when they were contrasted with Hindus. Here we arrive at a point in the web of American culture where the filaments of religion and gender entwine. Descriptions of Muslims as brave and manly came in language that was both gendered and religiously inflected. Traveling in Northwest India early in the twentieth century, Price Collier noted the sheer toughness of the local Muslims: "Never have I seen, in a one hour's walk, so many lean, upstanding, fearless-looking, fine-featured, eagle-eyed men." Missionaries and Cold Warriors agreed that Muslim men, unlike Hindus, were "vigorous," "energetic," and "good fighters" because the "Muslim faith is more dynamic" than the Hindu. Above all, the Muslims of Pakistan resembled Christians in their monotheism. Hindus believed in many gods, and thus presumably in many versions of the truth. Not so Muslims. Their God was not precisely the New Testament God, and His word came to men and women through Mohammed, not Christ. But there was no confusion about the source of the Word, and no heavenly babble beguiled Muslims and Christians: righteousness spoke with a single voice. Westerners frequently touted this crucial similarity between Islam and Christianity as the reason for cooperation between the United States and the Muslim world; it was an understanding that predicted trust and made outsiders of those who did not share it.[16]

In November 1893 the American schooner *Frank S. Warren*, with a crew of nine, foundered in the South Atlantic. To the rescue came the *S. S. Iran*, crewed by lascars—Indian sailors—and skippered by a Muslim named Mahomed Nusseeb. Nusseeb coolly directed a quick and effective operation that saved the entire crew of the *Warren*. At a ceremony held at the Bombay Shipping Office, attended by over a thousand lascars arranged by rank in the great hall, the grateful American consul, H. J. Sommer, Jr., presented Nusseeb with a gold medal, authorized by President Cleveland. Nusseeb had acted with courage, said Sommer, because he had "a devout belief in an All-Seeing Eye," which "imbued" Nusseeb and his men "with the bravery necessary to perform the heroic deed." Humbly and graciously, Nusseeb accepted the medal, insisting afterward that the audience give three cheers for the British raj, three more for President Cleveland, and three for Mr. Sommer and the American shipping master—all of them fellow believers in "an All-Seeing Eye."[17]

Rudyard Kipling planted the idea that Muslims were brave and Hindus craven. Katherine Mayo brought the idea to fruit in the United States. The Muslim, she wrote in 1935, "is the purest of monotheists. . . . No matter what his station . . . he worships One God and Him only, Omniscient, Omnipresent, Omnipotent . . . and the Ten Commandments of Moses are embedded in his law." The Hindu, by contrast, "is the most elaborate of Polytheists. He worships millions of gods, some by acts that are cardinal offences against any moral code of civilized humanity." And on it went. Muslims rejected religious hierarchy; Hindus embraced it. Muslims accepted the Old and New Testaments as the Word of God, believed that Christ (like Mohammed) was God's prophet, and permitted intermarriage with Christians and Jews. Hindus regarded Christians and Jews as "outcastes," contact with whom amounted to "defilement." Above all, Muslims, believing as they did in something—a single and very important something—would fight to preserve and extend their faith. Which conclusion brought Mayo to the story of Mahmoud of Ghazni.

Mahmoud was an accomplished young prince living in what is now Afghanistan late in the tenth century. Given grand titles by the Caliph of Baghdad, Mahmoud resolved that he must earn them. "By the One God," he swore (according to Mayo), "and for the love of His Holy Prophet," he would ride against the Hindu infidels beyond the frontier passes and show them the one true way. Beginning in about 1000, and for a quarter of a century thereafter, Mahmoud led his armies south in a series of military campaigns.

This is what Mahmoud did: he destroyed thousands of Hindu temples, monuments, and sculptures. Following one foray, he carried some sixty-five tons of gold back through the mountains to Central Asia. No one knows exactly how many Hindus he killed, though clearly it was a lot; histories indicate that some fifty thousand lost their lives while defending a Shiva temple at Somnath. Mahmoud was not interested in creating an empire in India. His aims were glory, loot, and, most of all, the destruction of Hinduism. Hindus regard him today much as Europeans regard Attila the Hun or Genghis Khan. To Mayo, however, he was a latter-day Joshua, Gideon, or David, Jewish heroes who had secured the Holy Land against the pagans. These men had pulled down the foul idols of Moloch, Baal, and Ashtoreth, just as Mahmoud destroyed the dreadful lingam, the phallic representation of Shiva. And—to move ahead to Mayo's time—what if the British were to leave India, to grant it independence? The result would be the end of South Asian Islam, "the overwhelming or, worse, the spiritual debasement of a simple, devout, and brave people, a helpless and fiercely loyal people, today as ready as Mahmoud of Ghazni was ready, as Joshua, Gideon and David were ready, to throw away life itself for the honour of the One God, the Lord God of Israel, acknowledged alike and alone by them all." Refining the stereotype of the God-fearing, beleaguered Muslim, Mayo anticipated Pakistan by a dozen years.[18]

Hinduism was altogether different. Americans believed that Hinduism—and caste, its logical and odious outgrowth—gave India its identity: "more than a religion; it is a way of life," as a Congressional briefing book noted in 1961. And what a way of life! Seldom did a Western visitor to India have anything good to say about Hinduism. The nineteenth-century traveler Robert Minturn called it "the most confused, contradictory, beastly tissue of incredible fables." Henry M. Field ventured into a Hindu temple, which was "filled with hideous idols" and sacred cows, "which the people would consider it a far greater crime to kill than to kill a Christian." He observed the reverence shown nearly naked sadhus. "Filthy creatures," he wrote; "more disgusting objects I never looked upon, not even in an asylum for the insane." "Hindooism must rank as the most despotic, the most cruel, and the vilest of all that is called religion among men," Field concluded. One of Katherine Mayo's correspondents was so disgusted she forgot the rules of punctuation: Hindus were "the horrible diseased slimy corrupt foul dregs of all depravity and hideousness." On Sunday mornings, American churchgoers raised their hymnals and sang Bishop Reginald Heber's "From Greenland's Icy Mountains," which included this verse:

> What though the spicy breezes
> Blow soft o'er Ceylon's isle,
> Though every prospect pleases
> And only man is vile,
> In vain with lavish kindness
> The gifts of God are strown,
> The heathen in his blindness
> Bows down to wood and stone.

After they sang, congregants might contribute a few coins to save starving South Asians.[19]

Hinduism was also a stagnant religion, impeding progress, inspiring passivity, weakness, impracticality, and selfishness. Hindus "have always been accustomed to bow their heads beneath the yoke of a cruel and oppressive despotism," wrote the Abbé J. A. Dubois. "We do not find amongst them," the abbé wrote, "any trace of mental or moral improvement, any sign of advance in the arts and sciences." Hindus were "patient and pathetic" (wrote Sara Bard Field), submissive by nature (Bayard Taylor), and so self-absorbed as to be "blamelessly indifferent to others' welfare" (Katherine Mayo, who attributed the alleged passivity of Hindus to their vegetarian diet). In the late 1940s, the reporter John Muehl was appalled at Hindus' "blind and unquestioning" acceptance of "degenerate" holy men, who sat "in the bazaar idly scratching their testicles or searching for fleas in their pubic hair." Even those sympathetic to some Hindu practices cautioned against excessive enthusiasm for them. Hereward Carrington admitted the virtues of yoga, but advised Americans not to go overboard: "Is it suggested, then, that we should all become Yogis? By no means! . . . India—and Oriental countries generally—have hindered their progress enormously because of their lop-sided interest in and absorption in religious and spiritual ideas" of the wrong sort.[20]

Most critical was the Western view that Hindu polytheism, indicating as it did an unwillingness to settle on a single source of ultimate authority, laid India open to political temptations of every description. One of the things about India that most frustrates Americans is the apparent mutability of truth, and the inconsistency of Indians' positions on things in general. There is abundant testimony to this in Harold Isaacs's *Scratches on Our Minds.* Indians, reported Isaacs's subjects, were "unable to be completely straightforward or honest with you"; they were "double-faced, wily . . . always twisting up and embarrassing you; [they] try to trap you and confuse you and catch you up, rather than try to get at the truth." "I don't ever quite know where they stand, and I feel distrustful of them," said one of Isaacs's subjects. "I have learned not to be surprised if they give the opposite impression twenty-four hours later. They are something of a problem." A missionary accused Indians of "a lack of integrity and straightforwardness. . . . I have often felt and said that an Indian can harbor in his mind two opposite views and seem to do it with equanimity. . . . They become almost two different personalities. This is not quite everything I mean. The fact is that they lie."[21]

It would not be inaccurate to say that, in India, truth is shaped by context. How an individual views reality is conditioned by his or her position within the social hierarchy, and how one conveys the truth depends on one's position in relation to the audience. The contextual basis for Hindu ethics is emphasized by *The Laws of Manu,* written by several Brahmin authors around the first century A.D. and one of the core texts of Hinduism. A. K. Ramanujan has pointed to Manu's "extraordinary lack of universality": Manu "seems to have no clear notion of a universal *human* nature from which one can deduce ethical decrees like, 'Man shall not kill,' or 'Man shall not tell an untruth.' " Indeed, "truth-telling is not an unconditional imperative. . . . To be moral, for Manu, is to particularize—to ask who did what to whom and when. . . . Each class (*jati*) of man has his own laws, his own proper ethic not to be universalized." Seen in this way, the apparent duplicity Americans find in Hindus is not a deliberate effort to deceive but a reflection of the shifting association between the social positions of the questioner and the questioned.[22]

The idea that truth is contextual is distressing to a Christian. If truth and falsehood are relative matters—if, as a smiling holy man said to Henry Field one day on the bank of the Kumbh River, "You are God and I am God!"—there are no absolutes. "Moral distinctions are destroyed," wrote Field grimly, "and vice and virtue are together banished from the world." One could put this less apocalyptically and say that Hindus find truth difficult to reduce to a single holy text and believe it comes in many forms. Unlike Christians and Muslims, Hindus are "not at all disconcerted by the juxtaposition of opposites," as G. Morris Carstairs has written. A village official denies that he believes in ghosts, then reveals that he recently saw a ghost in the jungle. "I hate all Mussalmans, they are not to be trusted," says another man, who then adds: "that Moslem driver is my good friend." When John Muehl asked the Brahmins of Halvad separately about the history of their town, he got different answers from all of them. At the end of the interviews, he gathered his respondents, pointed out the incompatibility of their accounts, and pressed them to tell him which story was true. "Why, all of them are true!" they replied. "There is no such thing as a history of Halvad," Muehl concluded, and if he meant by that a single, internally consistent narrative, he was right. Each Hindu god gives its own meaning to the world, and Hindus implicitly embrace the likelihood that all of these meanings are simultaneously valid. I insert here a personal anecdote. One morning while we were living in Madras, our Hindu cook was late for work. When she arrived she apologized: she had gone to the "Mary temple"—the local Catholic church—to pray for her son, who was having health problems. "Mary is a very powerful god," she told us, the Hindu temple *kumkum* (holy ash) still fresh on her forehead.[23]

Religion and Cold War Diplomacy

The American Cold War unfolded as a particular sort of Christian enterprise, sustained by the conviction that the American cause was right and

that the communists were evil. In this the crusade mirrored the movement of American Protestantism. In the late 1940s and early 1950s,
Protestants worried about secularization, were suspicious—as ever—of
Catholics, and, with a few exceptions, were deeply apprehensive of a
global communist menace. As Martin Marty has written, "the world of religion did not lack people who knew how to apply various toughness
tests," and this was particularly true of American Protestantism. Evangelical Protestants, led by the charismatic preacher Billy Graham, were most
prominent in their anticommunism. "There are Communists everywhere," Graham told an audience in Charlotte in 1947. "Here, too, for
that matter." When the Soviets tested an atomic bomb in August 1949,
Graham warned that communism was "against God, against Christ,
against the Bible, and against all religion." Except that embodied by itself:
"Communism is a religion that is inspired, directed, and motivated by the
Devil himself who has declared war against Almighty God." Such rhetoric
was used mostly by evangelicals, but the thinking was widely shared. A former Methodist minister and former communist named J. B. Mathews
turned against his Stalinist past by becoming a chief investigator for the
House Committee on Un-American Activities (HUAC). The July 1953 issue of *American Mercury* carried his essay "Reds and Our Churches," in
which he charged that over the past five years "the Communist Party of
this country has placed more and more reliance upon the ranks of the
Protestant clergy to provide the party's subversive apparatus with its
agents, stooges, dupes, front men, and fellow-travelers." G. Bromley Ox-
nam, head of the World Council of Churches, demanded an audience
with HUAC and defended the clergy from Mathews's accusations by insisting on his own loathing of communism. The Protestant tradition was
the American tradition of individualism and freedom of thought, declared Clarence W. Hall, managing editor of the *Christian Herald.* Why
had so many great American thinkers been Protestant? Because "the unshackled mind is the only truly creative mind," and the Protestant-capital-
ist system that best produced unshackled minds was being "pilloried by
every pink from Moscow to Manhattan."[24]

The leading figure in postwar American Protestantism was the theolo-
gian Reinhold Niebuhr. Niebuhr's position on the communist threat, unlike that of Graham and Mathews, was not without subtlety. He believed,
for instance, that there was no "simple dichotomy between an evil Soviet
empire and a virtuous American democracy," as biographer Richard W.
Fox has put it; that war on behalf of Chinese generalissimo Chiang Kai-
shek would be pointlessly destructive; and that the U.S. monopoly on the
atomic bomb represented less the triumph of American virtue than the

ironic paradox of American development—with mastery came misery. But the period from 1945 to 1954 was generally intolerant of subtlety, and over time Niebuhr fully entered the anticommunist camp. He affirmed the presence of "slightly more than a dozen fellow travelers in the churches" (by which he meant high-ranking clerics) and initially saw no reason to spare the lives of the convicted atomic spies Ethel and Julius Rosenberg. Joe McCarthy was a problem, in Niebuhr's view, because he was ineffective, not because of his contempt for civil liberties. If capitalism had its peccadilloes, it nevertheless preserved human freedom—unlike despotic communism. Niebuhr even accused Eisenhower of "a new pacifism and a new isolationism" in his apparent willingness to accept at face value Soviet professions of good will. Niebuhr thus indicated the direction of the Protestant church in an era when temporizing seemed impossible.[25]

There were American statesmen who, like the early Niebuhr, were Christian without being Manichean, diplomats whose faith taught them tolerance and charity toward others, even bad others. But theirs was an increasingly untenable position in the wake of World War II and the Holocaust. If the Soviets had inherited from the Nazis aggressiveness and indifference to moral concerns, then accommodation was no option; righteous resistance was the only possible course. Those who could not understand that had lost their own moral compass, and thus put at risk not only international security but basic human values of right and wrong.

The Cold War crusade influenced the development of U.S. policy toward South Asia following partition in 1947, reviving and making salient many of the religious stereotypes that had emerged during earlier times. Certainly the view persisted that Muslim men, now mostly in Pakistan, were forthright, vigorous, combative in a healthy way, and monotheistic—in short, they were much like Americans. The men who governed Pakistan were straight shooters and good sports. Liaquat Ali Khan, prime minister from 1948 until his assassination in 1951, came to the United States in the spring of 1950 and, as the previous chapter indicated, clearly impressed his hosts. "The people of Pakistan believe in the supreme sovereignty of God," he said several times. Muslims were monotheists and Hindus polytheists; Muslims believed in the Old Testament prophets and Jesus Christ while Hindus did not; and the Hindu caste system "made it a sin for those at the top of the hierarchy to eat with the so-called lower human beings, whereas the Muslims believed in the equality of man." ("He feeds them with the right kind of stuff," grumbled an Indian observer.) Liaquat hosted an extravagant reception at the Pakistani embassy, during which champagne and scotch flowed freely and the prime minister danced with Bess Truman. Assistant Secretary of State George McGhee,

riding the train with Liaquat from Washington to New York, watched apprehensively as the prime minister downed two stiff drinks. But at a speaking engagement later, Liaquat "gave no evidence of having had anything
to drink at all." Overall, McGhee was "impressed" with Liaquat's "forthright positive approach" to world problems.[26]

In his novel *Midnight's Children*, Salman Rushdie imagined the scene of
Pakistani generals planning their coup in Rawalpindi, in October 1958.
One general wanted to mine the Indo-Pak border. " 'Let's get organized!'
he would exclaim. "Let's give those Hindus something to worry! We'll
blow their invaders into so many pieces, there'll be no damn thing left to
reincarnate." Allegedly watching the scene, Zafar Zulfikar, the cousin of
the narrator, wet his pants. "In cold fury my uncle hurled his son from the
room; 'Pimp! Woman!' followed Zafar out of the dining chamber, in his
father's thin sharp voice; 'Coward! Homosexual! Hindu!' " This is doubtless a colorful version of the proceedings. But Mohammed Ayub Khan,
the real-life general who led the coup, won praise from American policymakers and the press despite his authoritarianism. Or rather, because of
it: *Newsweek's* associate editor Gordon Heiner, who was captivated by
Ayub's "strongman" approach, declared that "not every young nation is
ready for democracy." He reported with admiration an incident in which
an "over-enthusiastic" man tried to board a railway car carrying Ayub and
Egyptian president Gamal Abdel Nasser. Ayub "calmly stiff-armed the
man back into the street." On a visit to the United States in the summer of
1961, Ayub played golf, drank whisky, ate barbecue, and received as a
presidential gift a double-barreled shotgun.[27]

Americans responded favorably to the Pakistani willingness to stand
with the West in the crusade against communism. Muslims were "aggressive, more upstanding figure[s], willing and able to fight." Communism
might settle among people like Hindus, confused about their deities.
Shiva? Vishnu? Brahma? What was Marx, Lenin, or even Stalin, but one
more god? The Muslims had their God. The idea that Islam rendered
Pakistan resistant to communism whereas Hinduism made India susceptible was pervasive, and there can be little doubt that it influenced U.S. policy. A 1952 study by the State Department's Office of South Asian Affairs
concluded: "Like our American forefathers, Pakistan's founders were
schooled in the democratic philosophy and were willing to labor for their
independence. Pledged to create a state in harmony with the principles of
Islam, they are opposed to the godless ideology of communism, and they
are alert to efforts by subversive elements within their country to undermine the bases of orderly government." It was not so in India, observed an
American official. India had "a relatively strong and well organized Com-

munist party." Pakistani Islam "presents a more effective deterrent to the acceptance of communist doctrines than Hinduism. . . . A deep devotion to Islam and strong control by local Mullahs and other religious leaders in Pakistan make it highly unlikely that any large percentage of the population would accept the atheistic tenets of communism." The United States could rely on Pakistan to assert itself in the struggle against the Soviet Union. No similar confidence could be vested in India.[28]

The problem with Hinduism was that it inspired in its adherents depravity and indifference to depravity, otherworldliness, cowardice, submissiveness, and moral laxity—the result of an inability to tell right from wrong or distinguish between the word of God and the bizarre mythology that surrounded Hindu deities. Westerners attributed these features to Nehru himself; he was a reluctant Hindu, perhaps, but one nevertheless marked by his Brahmin ancestry and his role as state *sanyasin*. Nehru, thought Western officials, was "a dreamer," a source of "balloon-like ideas" that required "pegging down to Earth" by Westerners and his more logical advisers. British officials told their American counterparts in April 1951 that Nehru's position on international issues "was an outward expression of something deep within the Hindu character": namely, the "negativism and passivism [*sic*] which found its roots in Hindu emotion and philosophy." Nehru aside, should the United States give economic aid, for example, to a people so inclined to accept their fate that they might even resist efforts to nudge them along the path toward development? Donald Kennedy, director of the State Department Office of South Asian Affairs in early 1953, doubted "whether enough Indian people possess within themselves the force and zeal and energy to sustain a forward looking and progressive [land reform] program. I do not see," Kennedy concluded, "how Hinduism provides the base for this." When George V. Allen, ambassador to New Delhi from 1953 to 1955, went into Indian villages, he liked to test this proposition on local officials. Why, he asked, did the village need a new well? Wasn't the old muddy hole in the ground good enough? It was good enough for previous generations: "Isn't it contrary to your religious system, your philosophy, that you want to change things? . . . But the idea of trying to change things yourselves overnight here—it's sort of shocking, I would have thought," Allen taunted. When villagers insisted that they did indeed want a new well, Allen thought it was "almost like the fairy story of Prince Charming going and kissing the girl who's been asleep for twenty years and waking her up"—a fairy-tale happy ending for a bizarre religion.[29]

The decision to accept or reject assistance was ultimately India's to make, and there was no immediate harm to the noncommunist world in the event of a negative decision. If Hindus proved passive in the face of communist invasion or subversion, however, the danger would be grave. British and American policymakers fretted about India's policy of Cold War nonalignment, which they persisted in labeling "neutrality" in the belief that Hindus simply did not care who ruled them. In the fall of 1950, officials in the British Foreign Office wrote a series of minutes—brief commentaries—on "The Hindu Attitude to Foreign Affairs." That they presumed the subject worthy of exploration was meaningful. But several officials asserted that a vast majority of Indians would "accept, as they have in the past, conquest from without, provided they are convinced that this would enable them to maintain the Hindu system intact," as C. P. Scott put it. "Hindu politicians [would] "bow to what they believe to be the inevitable," for "Hindu India is at present much less a potential third world force than an international football," he concluded. M. S. Stephenson added that "the traditional Hindu method of dealing with conquerors is absorption rather than uncompromising resistance." The analysis confirmed American fears that Hindu India would never make common cause with the West. It would be a minor miracle if Indians decided even to defend themselves.[30]

Polytheism predicted India's diplomatic inconstancy. In the fall of 1950, as war raged in Korea and the Chinese communists warned that they would intervene should United Nations forces come too close to the Yalu River, the Indian ambassador in Beijing, K. M. Pannikar, spoke of the Chinese revolution in laudatory terms and expressed hope that China and India would remain friends, united as they were in the anti-imperialism of their recent pasts. Yet, India had supported UN action in Korea to that point. Pannikar's speech, therefore, was "the most abject trimming to the Chinese People's Government," fumed S. J. Olver of the Foreign Office. How could Pannikar live with the contradiction of his sympathy for both sides in the conflict? Because, said Olver, like Nehru, Pannikar was "subject to the common Indian failing of unconsciously twisting the truth so as to make it palatable to the recipient." Indian efforts to mediate the Korean War seemed wracked by contradiction, too. Dean Acheson, who had no interest in Indian peace initiatives in any case, recalled with frustration that each Indian diplomat who approached an American "presented the scheme a little differently," the outcome being "multisplendored confusion." At the end of the war, India's position on the critical prisoner repatriation issue seemed no position at all: of the Indians who chaired the neutral nations repatriation commission, the *Times of London* wrote, "General Thimayya appears to wish both to eat his cake and have it." In early 1954, the U.S. ambassador to the UN, Arthur Dean, told an

Indian official that Americans "were considerably annoyed at the rather mystical attitude that Prime Minister Nehru took toward international Communism, and were somewhat inclined to base our policy on one of the sayings of Jesus that 'He who is not for me is against me,' and that there ought not to be any doubt in people's minds where the Indians stand." "It is India's moral neutrality that raises hackles here," declared the State Department's Elbert Mathews. "The fact that Nehru and other Indian leaders do not overtly recognize our moral superiority over the Communists is the real irritant." It was perhaps easier to deal with communists than to figure out Indians; as an American policymaker put it, "at least we know where the Russians stand, but the Indians—we can never be sure."[31]

India and the Religious Construction of America

Let us now shift the lens and stand with the Indians, who tried to make sense of American Christianity and its influence on U.S. foreign policy. Missionaries interpreted India for Americans during the nineteenth and early twentieth centuries. The single most important Indian missionary to the United States was Vivekananda, the perceptive swami from Bengal, who visited America three times between 1893 and 1900. In 1893, Vivekananda made a series of addresses at the Parliament of Religions in Chicago, in which he attempted to explain Hinduism to his audiences and to commend to them spirituality more generally. Vivekananda became something of a sensation, and he followed his Chicago appearances with a lecture tour of the Midwest and the establishment of centers for the practice of yoga in New York and California. His mission was to share with Americans the spiritual wisdom of the East. And it seemed possible that he could learn something from American Christianity, that India could "assimilate what is best in their society," as he wrote a colleague at home.

Or it seemed possible at first. Despite Vivekananda's excitement over the prospect of exchanging religious ideas with Americans, he soon found that Christianity was not nearly as open to syncretism as he had hoped. He traced this apparent inflexibility to Christianity's history of prejudice, aggression, and intolerance, traits that had distorted Christ's original purposes. "If the Christian faith still had its power in Europe," he charged, "it would have burnt alive scientists like Pasteur and Koch and impaled men like Darwin." At the Chicago Parliament, Vivekananda dismissed the idea that a nation's economic success was the result of Christian virtue. Prosperous Christian Great Britain had "her foot on the neck of 250,000,000 Asiatics. . . . Christianity wins its prosperity by cutting the throats of its fellow men. At such a price the Hindoo will not have prosperity." The swami had in mind British and French imperialism, not American. But he aimed his shafts at religious belief, not national character, and had Vivekananda lived long into the twentieth century—he died in 1902 at the age of thirty-nine—it is likely that he would have condemned American imperialism in the same way that he attacked the expansionist Christians of Europe.

For now, the Americans were different from their European cousins. Vivekananda liked them, especially the women. The youthfulness and freshness of the Americans stood in contrast to the heavy decadence of Europe, where even the furniture looked ponderous, and it appeared that Americans would not be smothered by the deadening doctrine that passed for Christianity in the Old World. The problem was not so much that Americans were overbearing Christians. Rather, they seemed largely uninterested in the spiritual life, except as an affectation or a fad. In the United States, it was clear, prosperity had become a substitute for religious practice. The Americans "are a fine people in every way," Vivekananda declared, "but the satisfaction of appetites is their true God. Hence the rivers of wealth, floods of beauty, waves of learning and surfeit of luxury." As Tapan Raychaudhuri concludes, while Vivekananda "appreciated the welcome extended to him in the USA, he had serious doubts about the depth of spiritual concern which apparently inspired it."[32]

If the Americans who dealt as diplomats with Hindu India in the 1940s, 1950s, and 1960s were the heirs of the Abbé Dubois, Rudyard Kipling, and Katherine Mayo, Indians who encountered Americans followed Swami Vivekananda's analysis of Christianity and its role in shaping American culture. To some extent, the lack of American spirituality explained the insensitivity with which Americans treated other people. Indians felt it was immoral, for example, to talk about conditions under which economic aid might be offered to India when America was suffocating in surplus food and Indians were going hungry. The demands made on India by U.S. investors and businesspeople smacked of a materialism untroubled by any Biblical admonitions against greed. Nehru even professed to see a striking similarity between the United States and the Soviet Union: in both countries people " 'worship[ped]' the machine to the possible exclusion of deeper aspects of life." In mid-1954 the Indian high commissioner to Great Britain casually noted, to two American diplomats, "the lack of spirituality of the American nation." He was "honestly surprised" when the diplomats remonstrated.[33]

Vivekananda had anticipated that U.S. foreign policy would become a crusade, and with the arrival of the Cold War most Indians believed that it had. Convinced that they had cornered God's truth, equally convinced that Soviet communism represented evil, American policymakers (said Indians) had set out to cleanse the world of sin and excise its moral rot. Traveling in India a year before independence, Pearl Buck was peppered with questions about American religious practices. Some were general: "What is the place of religion in the daily life of an American?" Others went more to the point: "Can you tell me what is the religious sentiment in America and if the average American sahib thinks it is his divine mission to convert alien peoples?" On his visit to the United States in October 1949, Nehru told journalists that he would not wish to live in a "flat, regimented world with one way of thinking, eating, and dressing," and urged understanding for countries that took alternative paths. This was probably too subtle a criticism for most Americans, who could not imagine that Nehru was criticizing them. So in late 1953, as rumors flew that the Eisenhower administration was contemplating a military alliance with Pakistan, Nehru fired again, this time in an interview with Norman Cousins. There was, Nehru said, a "lack of toleration" in the world, "a desire to force your will on the other person or the other nation." It resulted from a "narrow religious outlook on politics," a charge that left no doubt about the target of the accusation. Nehru was responding in part to the Indian visit of Vice President Richard Nixon, who had in a radio address divided the world into "those countries whose peoples are free and those whose people are under the iron heel of Communist dictatorship." It appeared, the *Times of India* remarked, that the United States was "prepared to tolerate the continued existence of [the] 'old colonialism' in its crusade against Communism." There would be no means test for allies. A crusade, the Indians recognized, needs adherents loyal to the cause of correcting error and overcoming apostasy.[34]

There was good reason why the Indians found the prospect of a Cold War crusade so obnoxious. Hinduism embodies what Krishnalal Shridharani called the "philosophical abhorrence of absolutes." At the root of Indian foreign policy was a belief in relativism, an understanding that there are "many shades between black and white." All human beings and all nations are capable of doing both good and evil. No one can be holier than thou. No one is unalterably wicked. Because life is "a series of compromises" between apparently fixed positions, the logical course for a nation is a "golden middle path"—in diplomatic terms, nonalignment. While this philosophy did not preclude Indians from taking a stand on particular issues, it did prevent India from choosing sides permanently. Hindu myth provided the proper model for Indian diplomacy. In the epic *Ma-habharata*, the Hindu world, human and divine, is engulfed in war. Balarama, older brother of the god Krishna, is horrified by the fratricide and leaves the field, unwilling to shed or draw blood, disgusted by war's glorification, and most of all convinced, as one commentator has written, that humanity is a "whole," not divided into "right and wrong parties of a warring world." War is self-destructive no matter who wins.[35]

The religious-mythic basis for Indian statecraft had direct implications for India's relations with the People's Republic of China in the 1950s and early 1960s. Recall the account, in chapter 1, of the nations' dispute over the location of the boundary between them. The Chinese prime minister, Zhou Enlai, insisted that the boundary was artifice, the legacy of imperialists who had divided the two nations arbitrarily and for their own purposes. Nehru responded that this was nonsense: India had boundaries long established by "history, geography, custom, and tradition." In 1959 India's Ministry of External Affairs issued a white paper on the issue, complete with elaborate references to Hindu texts. A quotation from the *Vishnu Purana* asserted that India was Bharat, that country north of the ocean and south of the Himalayas, and that "all born in it are called Bharatiyas or Indians." The implications of this claim were evidently clear to India. The Chinese could perhaps be forgiven for insisting that it failed to settle anything, and three years later they launched the attack that left Nehru embarrassed and the border just where the Chinese wanted it.[36]

For the fifteen years before that critical event, Western policymakers saw India acting not out of a Hindu sense of relativism or consistent with the wisdom of the great myths, but out of Hindu equivocation, moral insensibility, and cowardice. While Indians and Westerners understood the implications of Hinduism differently, there is no question that Hinduism was increasingly associated with the state. Independence had affirmed Hinduism as a touchstone of authenticity for a struggling new nation seeking its identity. Other religions prominent in Indian history, including Islam and Christianity, were set in opposition to Hinduism; despite Hinduism's storied tolerance of other religions and the acknowledged dangers of fundamentalism, Indians succumbed to the logic of defining themselves by identifying religious Others, and in this way subverted their determination to avoid theocracy. They now "depreciated" the past activities of American missionaries, claimed the U.S. charge in New Delhi in 1948. Resentful of the role played in partition by Muslim intellectuals, who were regarded in India as sponsors of the pernicious "two nation theory," Hindus criticized Islam as divisive and belligerent. Hindu fundamentalists played most treacherously with these views, but neither were they unfamiliar to mainstream Hindus.[37]

Religion and the Formation of the U.S.-Pakistan Alliance, 1953–54

When Indians slid down the slope of religious identity, they confirmed the American view that India was a state determined by Hinduism. The moral relativism of Hinduism was really moral laxity, and India's neutrality in the Cold War proved that Hindus could not tell right from wrong. A few Americans sympathized with India's position. Most did not. "At the root of India's naivete towards the dangers of Communism . . . was Hinduism," a British correspondent told American diplomats in India, and, as in many things concerning South Asia, the Americans followed the British on this point. Again and again, U.S. policymakers attacked what they called India's "complete neutrality in the present ideological conflict in the world," and Indian leaders' " 'plague on both of their houses' approach" to the United States and the Soviet Union. The Indians seemed bent on "mediation for mediation's sake (or 'peace's' sake), divorced from moral considerations." "In the long run . . . the free world cannot permit South Asia to remain neutral," concluded the authors of NSC 5409 in February 1954. "South Asia must be made to realize that its ultimate choice lies with the Kremlin or the West." Choose good or evil. If India would not make this choice, it was time to cultivate Pakistan as a Cold War ally.[38]

The Pakistanis were abundantly, almost pathetically, available. The Americans and they "seemed to talk more the same language" than the Americans and the Indians. Impatient with India's unwillingness to distinguish right from wrong, the Americans found it bracing when Pakistan's leaders were eager to take their side in the battle against communism. In Hindu India there was theistic promiscuity, and where God was not a fixture neither was foreign policy. During the Cold War, there could be no atheists, or polytheists, in foxholes. Leader after Pakistani leader gave assurances that he hated communism, that he would fight against communism, and that he admired the United States's insistence on standing against evil. The "clash between the Western and Communist-dominated world is inevitable," said finance minister Ghulam Mohammed in June 1949, and "so far only Mr. Truman . . . has taken a realistic view of the world situation" in his effort "to contain Communism as an expansive force." In the United States a year later, Prime Minister Liaquat told cadets at West Point that "we might as well be frank about it . . . the world today is divided into two camps. . . . Pakistan is with most of the nations of the world in the non-communist camp. It is almost Joe Stalin against the world." Liaquat's successor, Mohammed Ali, pronounced himself "almost as rabid on the subject [of communism] as McCarthy." (Ali and *his* successor, Mohammad Ayub Khan, confessed that they hoped to retire to the United States; Ali wanted "to run a motel in Florida or California.")[39]

Alice and Dean Acheson share a laugh with the Begum and Liaquat Ali Khan, Washington, 1950. U.S. Dept. of State, Courtesy Harry S. Truman Library.

And so, as South Asians and Americans imagined themselves and each other as religious men and women, as they shaped political cultures that included Islam, Hinduism, and Christianity, they approached other nations with religious ideas in mind. Religious thinking helps explain the American decision, guided by John Foster Dulles, to forge a military alliance with Pakistan. Recall that Dulles was an intensely religious Presbyterian, who saw the Soviet Union as dangerous for its atheism as well as its military power. Communism thus posed a particular threat to those countries in which religious faith was inconstant. Faith, that is, as Dulles understood it: Christian if possible, but if not that at least deeply held, congregational, morally consistent, and above all monotheistic. Nations in which dominant religions met these criteria could counted on, or could at minimum be reached. Hinduism left much to be desired on nearly every score. Dulles excoriated atheistic communism because under it there was "no such thing as universal and equal justice," and humans were "free of the moral restraints and compulsions which prevail in a religious society." India was not communist, but the same criticism applied. "These neutral governments do not seem to realize that the Communist intentions are so diabolical and so hostile to their freedom and independence," Dulles complained in 1956. He feared "that they would eventually succumb unless they could develop a crusading spirit against the evil forces of Communism." Dulles's reluctance to provide aid for nonaligned nations like India indicated, according to Mark Toulouse, "the way in which Dulles secularized the Biblical injunction [in Revelations], 'Because you are lukewarm, and neither cold nor hot, I will spew you out of my mouth.' " Neutralism was "immoral."[40]

The Pakistanis, in contrast, were committed by their faith to do battle against malignant communism, and Dulles was therefore happy to help them. In 1953 and 1954, Dulles spearheaded the effort to arm Pakistan and bring the nation into the U.S. alliance system. Dulles wanted to create military alliances in order to contain Soviet expansionism. South Asia was not the most vital front in this effort, but given the totalizing nature of the Cold War, no area was unimportant; in a constant-sum game every gain for the other side was loss for yours, and South Asia was close to Mideast oil fields that were crucial to the economic stability and security of the West. But the fundamental, religious affinity between the United States and Pakistan, between Dulles and Pakistani leaders in particular, led the two nations to the threshold of military cooperation independent of precise strategic thinking. In Dulles's world, the United States wished to make allies of nations like itself. The strategic calculus on which the alliance rested could be figured up later.

A visit to South Asia in May 1953 convinced Dulles that Pakistan, not India, would be a suitable ally. Nehru, he reported to the National Security Council, was "an utterly impractical statesman." In Pakistan, by contrast, he had been "immensely impressed by the martial and religious characteristics" of the people. "Pakistan was a potential strong point for us" and a "dependable bulwark against communism." Thereafter (it will be recalled), subject to an intense lobbying campaign by the Pakistanis and growing concern over Asian security by officials in the Defense Department, the Eisenhower administration moved to formalize the relationship. Overcoming the objections of the British (who feared a sharp reaction by India), of American officials with India experience (including Chester Bowles and George Allen), and of India itself (whose bitterness fully confirmed British and American fears), the administration decided that an unarmed Pakistan, eager as it was to join the containment effort, was a wasting asset. Here were the stout-hearted, monotheistic Muslims made famous by Kipling and Mayo, to say nothing of Mahmoud of Ghazni. *U.S. News and World Report*, for one, was convinced of Pakistan's reliability. "The United States is discovering that it has a powerful friend in the heart of an area made 'soft' by India's attitude," a reporter wrote in

late 1953. The leaders of "80 million Muslims" were coming to Washington to ask for arms, and who would deny the "warrior people, mainly
6–footers" and "rugged eaters of meat and wheat"? "To U.S. military planners, accustomed to European reluctance to arm and India's neutrality,
Pakistan looks the answer to a prayer."[41]

Dulles answered his own prayer in early December 1953 when he told
the British that India had no right to veto a Mideast–South Asia alliance
against the Russians. Vice President Nixon, just back from his own Asian
trip, weighed in at a meeting of the National Security Council on December
23: Nehru's "thirst for power over Southeast Asia" must not prevent the
United States from acting in its best interests. Pakistan, on the other hand,
was "a country I would like to do everything for. The people have less complexes than the Indians. . . . It will be disastrous if the Pakistan aid does not
go through." It did go through: on February 25, 1954, the administration
announced that it would give a substantial amount of military aid to Pakistan. Seven months later Pakistan joined SEATO, and the following year it
joined the Baghdad Pact, which looked to protect the Middle East.[42]

There was no turning back from this American commitment, despite India's vigorous protests. The growing militarization of Pakistan's government, ratified by the 1958 coup, did nothing to weaken U.S. loyalty to its
stalwart friend. In fact, Ayub's takeover confirmed the Pakistanis' penchant
for order, their martial spirit, and their attachment to a single source of
truth. Monocracy corresponded to monotheism. In May 1959 the State Department did a study of the previous year's military coups in Burma, the Su-
dan, and Pakistan. Citing experience with Latin American countries, the
authors of the paper found that "authoritarianism is required to lead backward societies through their socio-economic revolutions," so "it should be
our purpose that this progression repeat itself in the contest for 'management' of the developmental process in Free Asia." Long after Dulles had
left the scene, American statesmen continued to admire Ayub's strongman
regime. Vice President Lyndon Johnson went to South and Southeast Asia
during the spring of 1961. While Johnson got along reasonably well with
Nehru, he was enraptured with Ayub. The vice president told William
Rountree, the ambassador to Pakistan, that Ayub was the "most impressive
leader he had met" during his Asian tour, and that Ayub was an "outstand-
ing spokesman [for the] free world position, who potentially can be of even
far greater value to [the] free world in dealing with [the] problems of
Asia"—this praise for a general with nearly dictatorial power.[43]

India was uninterested in forging military alliances, with the United
States or anyone else. The U.S.-Pakistan agreement meant that India's
worst fears had been realized: aggressive Christianity and fanatical Islam

Ambassador Chester Bowles and family, fully garlanded in Hindu style, prepare to leave India, 1953. Chester Bowles Papers, Manuscripts and Archives, Yale University Library.

had combined in a way that threatened India's security. In late 1953 the *Times of India* condemned the emerging alliance using mixed religious images. "If Pakistan wishes to mortgage her hard-won independence for a mess of pottage that is her own affair," the editors wrote, though they were plainly whistling past the graveyard. "The spectacle of Mr. Dulles as an amiable Santa Claus doling out guns and aircraft as America's Xmas gift to Pakistan with a bland Christian assurance of peace and goodwill to all men on earth is too incongruous to be impressive." The Americans were "hysterical" over communism, and Indians feared "a holy war or crusade" that would engulf their country. "Mr. Dulles speaks in the solemn accents of Washington and the Old Testament," wrote an Indian columnist in early 1954. Even after Dulles had died, Indians discerned his influence in U.S. policy. The United States seemed to have "acquired a special mandate from heaven," the *Times* noted caustically in May 1961. "The fervently moralistic element in Mr. Dulles's policies persists[,] as also the tendency to interpret political situations in terms of good and evil."[44]

Analyzing the U.S. relationship with South Asia from 1947 to 1964 from the standpoint of religion yields the conclusion that U.S.-India—Christian-Hindu—relations were uneasy, while U.S.-Pakistan—Christian-

Muslim—relations were friendly. Americans loathed the alleged depravity of Hinduism, mistrusted India's polytheists, and suspected Hindus generally of bizarre spiritual practices that left them passive and besotted in the face of a serious threat from international communism. On the other hand, Americans regarded Pakistan's Muslims as fellow monotheists who rejected relativism and neutrality in favor of a single received truth and an ardent commitment to defend it. The Pakistanis reciprocated this view. Hindus believed Christians and Muslims inclined toward fanaticism, because neither religion allowed its adherents the flexibility to deal with a complex world in which new situations must be confronted each day, in which right and wrong were mutable. When it came time to choose sides, as U.S. policymakers like John Foster Dulles felt they must, the choice was clear: inconstant India was left out.

But even during the Dulles years, the United States did not abandon India, nor did it give the Pakistanis all they wanted. Recall that Nehru got along well with President Eisenhower, and that U.S. aid for India increased through the 1950s. Pakistanis who hoped that military cooperation with the Americans would bring them every weapon they wanted and unqualified support for their position in Kashmir were disappointed. In part this happened because perceptions and needs other than religious ones influenced U.S.–South Asia relations. And the religious perceptions themselves—other than the Hindu ones, anyway—took shape as binary oppositions, which pivoted exactly 180 degrees around a central axis. Religions that see human behavior as good or evil cannot allow for categories to emerge between or beyond good and evil; a person can be good or evil, not both simultaneously or partially either one. To Christians, Muslims who may once be stalwart and fierce defenders of right may suddenly become treacherous (that is, stalwart for the other, wrong side) and fanatical. One side's crusader is the other side's zealous enemy. At the same time, Hindus whose spirituality seems promiscuous at one juncture may hold the key to the world's problems at another. There are crises that call for a balanced perspective, for an ability to find merit in the positions of both sides. I know of no U.S. policymakers who during the 1960s practiced yoga or transcendental meditation, or took up the sitar. Still, the possibility of transcending the violence of the Vietnam War, or negotiating its end, occurred to some of them. And perhaps one or two recalled that when Robert Oppenheimer watched the successful test of the atomic bomb at Alamogordo in July 1945, he quoted, with a sense of awe and shame, from the Bhagavad Gita section of the *Mahabharata*: "I am become Death, destroyer of worlds."

7

Class, Caste, and Status: The Gestures of Diplomacy

> Aristocracy had made a chain of all the members of the community: . . . democracy breaks that chain and severs every link of it. . . . Thus, not only does democracy make every man forget his ancestors, but it hides his descendants, and separates his contemporaries from him; it throws him back for ever upon himself alone, and threatens in the end to confine him entirely within the solitude of his own heart.
>
> —Alexis de Tocqueville, *Democracy in America*

> You give us a great deal of aid. It makes us feel like beggars. How does it make you feel?
>
> —Nirmal Kumar Bose to Nathan Glazer

I begin this, the final substantive chapter of the book, by reprising the lead argument from the earlier chapter on strategy: how a nation defines its strategic interests is partly determined by its history and identity, by the way in which its people imagine themselves as members of a society of individuals and their nation as a member of a society of nations. American men look outward, to horizons that inspire their curiosity. Frontiers for them are not limits but opportunities, sites where dreams are realized and destinies transacted; space itself exists to be explored and taken up. Indians look inward from their borders. Horizons—beyond the Himalayas or the Bay of Bengal, or merely beyond the rice paddies or tree lines that adjoin rural villages—are threatening, not inviting. Most Indians feel nervous about crossing boundaries, and evidently few fantasize about traveling in space.

Chapter 1 emphasized the historical and geographical sources of American and Indian attitudes toward space. This chapter probes a bit deeper, or moves in a different direction, by linking these attitudes to ideas about social position and social mobility, to matters of class, caste, and status. It contends that these ideas affected the way Americans and Indians saw their places in the world, and by extension the places of their nations. Ideas about class and caste thus shaped the relationship between the United States and India. Where one stood in the social system influenced how one thought about and acted toward others. Like perceptions based on race and gender, the apprehension of others through the prisms of class and caste led to misunderstandings that are excruciating to contemplate even now. And yet these apprehensions were not always damaging: they help us understand not only the failures of the Indo-American relationship but also some of its successes.

There were no more pervasive or profound American images of India than those involving the caste system. It was as if India in totality could be explained with reference to caste, or as if the supposed inscrutability of the place could be explained as the result of a system that seemed to leave no room for human agency. In his classic survey of American attitudes toward China and India, Harold Isaacs noted that the typical American in India was "horrified by the rigidities of Indian caste," which established "an immediate barrier of incomprehensibility, a first and powerful impulse of rejection." Any Indian criticism of American society met with a rejoinder about caste. Even racial discrimination in the United States in the 1940s and 1950s might be explained away by whites as an unfortunate vestige of slavery, long dead, not a hierarchical caste system that seemed to be accepted by nearly every citizen following centuries of practice.[1]

While Indians who met Americans rarely defended caste, some pointed out that the American social system was so fluid that it destabilized human relationships and washed away all sense of community. Or, said Indians, the gap between rich and poor in the United States was a good deal wider than the defenders of the American class system cared to admit, and the American boast that anyone could make it to the top was empty. In the end, Indians claimed, there wasn't much difference between the two social systems. In October 1961, the Madras *Hindu* ran an ad for the Hollywood film "Tammy Tell Me True," in which a college professor (played by John Gavin) is seduced by Tammy (Sandra Dee), a Mississippi river boat girl turned student. "A Hilarious Delight!" burbled the ad. "It's just like a fisherman's daughter from Adyar Beach attending a Madras college!"[2]

It was not quite the same. The *Hindu's* analogy called forth any caste prejudices held by the paper's readers, for as much as they were poor people the fisherfolk of Adyar were more securely members of a subcaste, or *jati*, that was unlikely to be represented at a Madras college in 1961. The comparison would have been more apt had Tammy been black, and her seduction of the professor thus a violation of a fundamental social taboo, not merely the transgression of class boundaries. This distinction bids us grapple with definitions of caste, class, and status. *Caste* is a system of social classification based on what Gerald D. Berreman has called "institutionalized inequality." The system is made up of largely fixed social stations in which membership is conferred by birth, and in which rank in relationship to other castes is hierarchical and reinforced by proscriptions against commensality (sharing food) and intermarriage. The Hindu caste system in India is best known to Americans; other modern examples of caste include the American south before the erosion of Jim Crow segregation in the 1960s, and South Africa prior to the elimination of state-mandated segregation in the early 1990s. *Class*, too, is a system of social classification, a way of ranking people by some combination of education, social aptitude, and especially wealth. Berreman has summarized the essential difference between caste and class: "In a caste system an individual displays the attributes of his caste because he is a member of it. In a class system, an individual is a member of his class because he displays its attributes." There is in theory no social mobility within a caste system, while mobility is theoretically possible in a class system. Finally, the word *status* means standing, the regard with which one is held by others. The relationship between status and caste is direct: caste confers status. The relationship between status and class is more complicated. While in some societies wealth brings social regard, it does not always, and modest means do not always confer low status. Max Weber pointed out that status and class were not coterminous, and examples from our time—an unemployed woman who wins the lottery, or a poorly paid campaigner for social justice—indicate the truth of Weber's insight.[3]

To Americans, the most fascinating, perplexing, essential, and abhorrent feature of India has always been the caste system. This is true in large part, one suspects, because the rigidity of caste stands in sharp contrast to the marvelous flexibility Americans claim for their own social system. Americans have frequently boasted that the United States is free of class. The willingness with which Americans classify themselves as "middle class," however, suggests that they really mean the American class system is fluid, allowing for nearly universal social mobility. Historically, the key to social mobility in America has been the perception of physical mobility, the belief that difficult economic circumstances need not be overcome as long as they can be escaped. As noted in chapter 1, Frederick Jackson

Turner postulated that the western frontier served as a "safety valve" for eighteenth- and nineteenth-century Americans, providing a refuge for those who felt that the class system had hardened against them, that there was nowhere to go but out. While a new generation of historians has demonstrated that the West was not really so free and open as Turner claimed, especially not for Indians, women, blacks, and Asians, the frontier myth had a powerful effect on the consciousness of white American men. Because they still had space, American men thought of themselves as free individuals, bound neither by class nor caste. Contrast this, said Americans, with India, where people were stuck in a particular social station because of an accident of birth. The caste system created inefficiency, stifled ambition, degraded labor, and fostered such cruelties as infanticide and widow burning. Caste in India, Harold Isaacs concluded, was for Americans "the symbol of ultra stratification and . . . a symbol for all the elements in Hindu society which retard the country's advance."[4]

Western misunderstandings of caste have taken several forms. First, Westerners have tended to focus on the four great Hindu castes: the Brahmins (teachers and religious leaders), Kshatriyas (warriors), Vaisyas (merchants), and Sudras (cultivators, artisans, and servants), with the outcastes (so-called untouchables, called by Gandhi "Harijans") arrayed below. This system of classification is far less meaningful than one based on *jati*, the smaller subcastes with which Indians themselves are more likely to identify. Indians may, for example, be Brahmins, but they are more significantly Lohars, Ahirs, Nairs, or Mahishyas, to name just a few Brahmin *jati*. Reference to only the four major castes oversimplifies the complex reality of Hindu social distinctions.[5]

Second, the contrast between the supposed social rigidity of Hindu caste and the apparent fluidity of the American class system is less compelling than it seems at first glance. Safety valve or no, the American system does not permit perfect mobility. The Hindu caste system does not absolutely prevent it. Historically, what was forbidden in theory could nonetheless occur: subcastes could move up the social ladder if they could appropriate the rituals of more exalted groups. M. N. Srinivas called this process "Sanskritization," noting that a low subcaste could rise in the hierarchy "by adopting vegetarianism and teetotalism, and by Sanskritizing its ritual and pantheon"—by imitating, in other words, the high-caste Brahmins. Westerners have also explained the alleged passivity of Hindus with reference to caste. If an individual is fated at birth for a certain social and economic destiny, such as caste would seem to confer, there is no reason to struggle against the situation, or even to resent it;

one is what one is. But there is caste resentment in India. Consider these words sung by a betel nut vendor in Maharashtra during the mid-1940s:

> The Brahmins, they say, are the chosen of God.
> Chosen to own and to rule the land.
> And I, lucky fellow, am the chosen of the Brahmin.
> Chosen to support him in luxury and idleness.[6]

Finally, Westerners have allowed their fascination with caste to delude them into thinking that caste *is* India, or that caste determines all that happens there. As Arjun Appadurai has put it, Western discourse has "essentialized" and "totalized" caste, making it the fundamental institution of India and expecting that it represented the whole of Indian society. Caste offered a quick explanation of India to Westerners who would otherwise have been baffled by the real complexity of the place, and Americans found this explanation satisfying. Indians, reflected Chester Bowles, twice ambassador to India, were not very good at "selling" themselves or being decisive; "I think," said Bowles, "that you can make a theory on that." The caste system "has always protected them against decisionmaking," since all "decisions have been made within the caste structure." As a result, Indians had become "great adaptors, very skillful at adjusting to decisions made by others." An essential and total institution, caste, Westerners thought, gave India its national character.[7]

Let us acknowledge that caste was most meaningful to Indians when it was actually subcaste, when it was understood to exist alongside and in relation to other loci of identity, particularly family and village, and when it was known not to be the sole determinant of an Indian's personality, the essence of India, or a metonym for Indian society. Let us also acknowledge that, despite the efforts of the independent Indian government to expunge caste from national life and the abolition of caste by the Indian constitution in 1950, subcaste remained important to the identity of Indians. Even a casual observer of India from independence to the present knows this is true. For many Hindus, caste persists as "fortification against the frightening ocean of anonymity," a way more specifically of classifying human beings along a scale of purity and pollution. Westernized Hindus would in most cases deny that they care about these things; for them, the psychologist Sudhir Kakar has written, "*jati* has become a dirty word to be mentioned only in a covert whisper." But Kakar notes that even modern Indians cannot help identifying themselves with a subcaste. A respected civil servant confessed to Kakar that he "took pride in stories" that members of his subcaste, the Khatris, "did not intermarry or interdine with the Aroras. . . . I used to take pride that Khatris are, by and large, good-looking and have a fair complexion, without bothering about the fact that I possessed neither. I know I do not possess any attributes of the warrior class, yet I cling to the dogma of being a warrior type of yore, of being a ruling type with all the obligations of conduct that go with it."[8]

Jawaharlal Nehru led the fight against caste injustices and a host of inegalitarian practices he dismissed as "superstitions." But Nehru was descended from Kashmiri Brahmins, a caste association he never fully jettisoned. One of Nehru's biographers concluded that Nehru "remain[ed] a Brahmin with everything that this status connotes." Nehru himself admitted as much. "India clings to me as she does to all her children, in innumerable ways," he wrote, "and behind me lie, somewhere in the subconscious, racial memories of a hundred, or whatever the number may be, generations of Brahmins. I cannot get rid of . . . that past inheritance."[9]

Recall here the argument, made in chapter 3, that Indian political institutions are modeled on the extended family. To this argument we can now add a corollary: the organizational structure of government institutions also corresponds to the hierarchy of *jati*. An Indian is loyal in the first place to his or her family and in the second place to the larger circle of *jati*. Government institutions are an extension of this same system of concentric circles; they are not shaped in isolation from family and *jati* but are instead sustained by the same personal connections. The Indian government that was made to transcend loyalties to family and caste rather came to reflect these institutions. If, as Kakar explains, a government clerk accepts bribes to put an orphaned niece through school, that is not corruption but an expression of the clerk's most important responsibility, his "lifelong obligation to his kith and kin." He must subordinate any abstract sense of propriety "to the welfare of the extended family and *jati* communities."[10]

Proper Place, and the Importance of Behavior

The previous chapter suggested that Westerners are frequently distressed by what they see as the elusive nature of truth in India, at least among Hindus. Truth for Hindus, as A. K. Ramanujan has argued, is contextual, and context is shaped by religious belief (where there is more than one god there is more than one truth), and by the *jati* system. Ramanujan remarks: "Each class (*jati*) of man has his own laws, his own proper ethic not to be universalized." What is true for one subcaste may be untrue for another, and tellers of truths shape their tales according to the caste position of their listeners. Along with that, the position one holds within a *jati* entails certain social expectations to which one must conform. One must, in other words, play a role. One's role changes depending on context. With a social equal one is friendly, though not effusive. Members of the same *jati* (and sex) may converse openly, share food, and touch. With a social superior one is deferential, presuming nothing; Westerners often find lower-caste or outcaste Indians obsequious in their behavior toward the higher castes. With a social inferior one may be peremptory, even dismissive. During the 1930s, a debate emerged among the high-caste Nairs of Travancore concerning the right of access to roads near an important Hindu temple. Worried about pollution by proximity, Nairs decided that members of lower *jati* wishing to use these public thoroughfares must stay a prescribed number of steps away from them. Outcastes had literally to run off the road when they saw a Nair coming.[11]

While what you say in India matters very much, how you say it, and how you behave generally, matter more. Behavior is an act of self-presentation, critical as a reflection and affirmation of proper place in the hierarchy. How you act toward others indicates your position in relation to theirs; in situating yourself and others in the social hierarchy, you are showing respect for it and contributing to its long-term stability. One must show (toward an equal) politeness, grace, and tact, or (toward an inferior) strength and firmness, or (toward a superior) humility and respect. In his study of a North Indian village, G. Morris Carstairs noticed that "formality of demeanour was highly esteemed. The exchange of courtesies of speech and gesture appropriate to each other's age and caste was a habitual and enjoyable activity. At such times, people spoke with confidence and dignity as if good manners had power to neutralize all that was uncertain and inimical in a shifting world"—and by affirming the integrity of the hierarchy, "good manners" in fact did have such power. The requirement that behavior indicate proper place created acute sensitivity among *jati* and laid the basis for social injury should behavior fail to conform to *jati* position. The psychologist Alan Roland noted in his Indian patients "tremendous need and expectations on one hand, and on the other, vulnerability to the other's approval or rejection, no matter which end of the hierarchy one is on. Slights are quickly registered, and anger easily evoked even if infrequently expressed."[12]

That behavior was a reflection of proper place was indicated as well in India's relations with foreign nations. *How* Americans and others acted toward Indians and India had an enormous effect on India's policy. In October 1953, G. S. Bajpai, governor of Bombay state and former secretary-general at the Ministry of External Affairs, told the U.S. consul in Bombay that "tact must characterize all of America's work in India. . . . No matter how imaginative Americans are in seeing *what* is to be done and *how* things should be done, they must bear in mind that they are dealing with someone else's country when they operate abroad. Hence, along with their consummate imagination and ability, Americans must have consummate tact."[13]

British policymakers were better attuned than Americans to the importance of tact when dealing with Indians, and British representatives in India often found themselves mediating disputes between Americans and Indians, much as a marriage counselor might attempt to reconcile a quarreling couple. The mutual goodwill that followed Indian independence was due in part to Great Britain's experience in India, and in good part to Nehru's decision to keep India in the Commonwealth despite past friction. But the ability of Britons and Indians to talk to each other had a deeper source: both Great Britain and India were hierarchical societies, in which a sense of proper place, as reflected in contextually correct behavior, was fully realized. "Wherever there is caste, and its half-brother, aristocracy, as in India and England, formula dominates social life," wrote a perceptive American visitor to India in the 1920s. Deepak Lal has used this argument to contrast the relative harmony of British-Indian relations after independence with the difficult Indian relationship with the United States. Lal contends that Americans have tried to eradicate hierarchy in their society. Post-Enlightenment Great Britain, on the other hand, maintained "a social system dominated by pre-modern 'aristocratic' manners," leaving the classes committed to the kind of hierarchy that Americans refused to accept. But it was a system familiar to Indians, unlike the society of rootless individuals that existed in the United States. Lal writes:

> This uncertainty in placing people correctly in the social hierarchy through visible signs, such as manners and life styles, is profoundly disturbing to Indians (and I suspect the British) with their infinitely developed social antennae which can determine a man's place in the world through various overt behavioral indicators, such as forms of speech and personal manners. For an Indian brought up with complicated notions of purity and impurity covering most aspects of life . . . the easy intermingling of different social strata, and the lack of any permanent personal behavioral signposts to status apart from material wealth, can appear to be that dreaded "confusion of castes," which of course every good Hindu knows can only lead to social disorder.[14]

In a conversation with the *New York Times* reporter Robert Trumbull and the New Delhi embassy official Sheldon Mills, P. S. Lokanathan, the director of the UN's Economic Commission on Asia and the Far East, explained that "the trouble with Americans is usually not what they do but how they do it." Indians often felt "hustled" by Americans. At a recent conference, Lokanathan said, "the stands taken by the British were almost all wrong but they accompanied them with pleasant words and no one took offense. On the other hand the steps taken by the Americans were mostly right but antagonism was built up by the hustling and 'straight talk' methods of seeking support." For the Indians, attitude, as expressed in "pleasant words," mattered a great deal.[15]

Again and again, Indian officials objected to the way their American counterparts said and did things, rather than to what they said and did. Discussing U.S.-India relations in general with Assistant Secretary of State for African, Near Eastern and South Asian Affairs George McGhee in November 1950, India's ambassador in Washington, Vijayalakshmi Pandit, complained that her brother, Prime Minister Nehru, was "disturbed by the 'pressure' which the U.S. seemed to apply to India in efforts to win India over to U.S. views." McGhee asked Pandit to cite an example of such "pressure." Had it something to do with relations with the Soviet Union? United Nations' military strategy in Korea? Possible U.S. arbitration of the Kashmir problem? None of these specifically, replied the ambassador; it was rather "the urgency which seemed to characterize our approaches to the Indian Government." Indians, she said, "liked to think things out and did not like to feel they were being rushed into making decisions." Nehru resented the presumptuousness of Americans in India—"We have had quite enough of American superiority," he snapped in mid-1953—and the rise of American power since 1945 "made [the Americans] look down on almost every country, friend or foe, and they have developed a habit of irritating others by their overbearing attitudes." At the Madras consulate in July 1961, Ambassador John Kenneth Galbraith discovered a letter from the consulate's Indian staff, "asking that the Americans be less arrogant to them." ("The letter was typed but not signed," Galbraith added, "so I think I may safely ignore it.") Then there was an incident that occurred during Nehru's first visit to the United States, in the fall of 1949. At a dinner given for Nehru by Secretary of State Dean Acheson, Elbert Mathews, head of the State Department's South Asia Division, was seated across the table from Indira Gandhi, Nehru's daughter and official hostess. Mathews described what happened next:

Well, unfortunately, a little late and obviously having stopped somewhere for more than one or two bourbons and branchwater, [Treasury
Secretary] John Snyder rolls in and sits down about three seats from Indira. I'm not sure whether he realized that Indira was there. Well, he
sure as hell didn't know who Indira was and at that point didn't care, and
he started talking about these foreigners who come over here and take
our money from us.

Mathews and Acheson's daughter tried to silence Snyder and eventually
succeeded, but Gandhi "was sitting there just seething." Snyder's drunken
boorishness was "obviously reported to her father in spades and with em-
bellishment."[16]

Let it be said that the Indians and British are not the only people sensitive to social slights or plain obnoxious behavior. Erving Goffman has
noted that "we tend to blind ourselves to the fact that everyday secular
performances in our own Anglo-American society must often pass a strict
test of aptness, fitness, propriety, and decorum." Certainly U.S. consuls in
nineteenth-century India worried about keeping up appearances for the
"natives." And yet, to use behavior as an emblem of social standing runs
against the grain in the United States. The canon of civility is supposed to
be universal: people are to treat each other courteously because everyone
is theoretically equal. Since the class system is supposed to be fluid, it
should be impossible to assign certain behavior deterministically to a class
or a group. Standards of behavior do not change according to social context because in a real sense there is no context, just the democratic universe to which all Americans are supposed to belong. The solvent of democracy dissolves barriers that would permanently divide groups from
each other.[17]

Americans thus believe that what one says is more important than how
one says it. With the onset of the Cold War in 1947, one was supposed to
say, according to U.S. policymakers: "We're on your side, with the forces
of good against the forces of evil." How one made this declaration—that
is, how a government sympathetic to the U.S. position behaved toward its
own people—was relatively unimportant. The American-led anticommunist coalition consisted of Latin American dictators, Greek colonels,
South African segregationists, and ersatz Vietnamese democrats. American policymakers refused to ask hard questions about how these leaders
treated their constituents. It was enough that the leaders agreed to stand
with them against communism.

That is one reason why the Americans quickly grew impatient with India's seeming equivocations during the early Cold War, and why Ameri-

cans were annoyed with Indian sensitivity in matters involving status and their emphasis on behavior and style. Rather than focus on what was to U.S. policymakers the central issue of the Cold War, Indians harped on issues that were peripheral to the struggle against evil. "You're hurting our feelings," or "you're treating us with arrogance," the Indians complained. In exasperation, the Americans responded that these charges, even if true, really did not matter very much in a world of terrible danger. Feelings were trivial; facts were facts. In early 1956, Benjamin Fleck, the American vice consul in Madras, sent to the State Department some observations on the "debating style" of C. Rajagopalachari ("CR"), the former Indian home minister and then chief minister of Madras state. It was Fleck's impression "that C.R. was more interested in trying to antagonize the other participants . . . than in listening with an open mind to their arguments or in trying to reach a meeting of the minds. . . . The subject discussed is much less important than the technique employed by the two sides. The participant most skilled in debating techniques wins the argument, in his opinion, regardless of facts, logic, or other such extraneous matters. . . . All too often," Fleck concluded, "the result of the conversation is that the American goes away with increased irritation at Indian self-righteousness and refusal to accept facts, while C. R. goes away with his opinions undisturbed and his ego bolstered by what he considers to be another victory." The Indians, decided an American professor in India, gave little thought to substance and obsessed over style because they could not hope to compete with Americans economically; their apparent pettiness was the result of "egotism and jealousy." He was wrong about the reasons for Indians' behavior, but right about the behavior itself.[18]

Right Conduct and Reciprocal Obligations

Humility and Respect: The Gestures of Diplomacy

What types of behavior led to misunderstandings in Indo-U.S. relations? We start small, looking at what might be called the gestures of diplomacy. The word "gesture" has two meanings. First, it is a nonverbal cue, a part of body language: a gesture is an expressive wave of the hand, a crossing of the legs, a raised eyebrow. Second, a gesture in a more general sense is a small but symbolically weighted act, intended (according to a dictionary) "for effect or formality." A gesture of this sort is a little act of kindness (say) that one does for someone as an indication of support or sympathy.

Americans have seldom concerned themselves with the subtleties of body language. Studies of the phenomenon are generally treated with scorn, the property of counterculture faddists who cannot be convinced that body movements are usually random and that people say what they wish to say with words. Gesture in its second definition is also a suspect concept in the United States. A synonym for it might be "token," and Americans hold it to be a substitute for a more effective action. To make a gesture is to lack full commitment to the person at whom the gesture is aimed, and thus to lack sincerity. As a type of behavior, gesture does not indicate anything about place or standing in a supposedly fluid society. The dismissal of gesture as a meaningful act extends to diplomacy. During a low point in U.S.-India relations in mid-1950, Secretary of State Acheson had a talk with Ambassador Pandit. As Acheson recorded the conversation, Pandit said that she was "pretty sure" of America's friendship for India, but added that the Indian people were "disappointed" in the "lack [of] any concrete evidence thereof." The ambassador "urged repeatedly some IMMED gesture demonstrating [the] substantive meaning [of] our many expressions [of] good will for India." Acheson explained that the U.S. government was "not adapted [for a] gesture type approach [to] serious problems," and said that he could not believe that "longterm Indo-AMER relations [were] dependent on small *ad hoc* gestures."[19]

He was wrong. For Indians, gestures in both physical and symbolic senses were important as indications of proper place and manifestations of correct behavior. Body language reflects one's regard for another; whether one feels affection, amusement, contempt, or distaste can be read in movements and postures. As Alan Roland has observed, "closeness need not necessarily be verbalized, but can often be conveyed simply by a glance or smile—reflecting the strong non-verbal communication of emotion in Indian relationships." Indians are attuned to read the messages of the body, including those broadcast by American statesmen: by John Foster Dulles, who sat stiffly cross-legged and did not smile, or by Chester Bowles, who abandoned pretension, and a jacket and tie, to help a fisherman haul in a net.[20]

Indians believe not only that human society is hierarchical but that the international system is too. On a scale of power and prestige, some nations rank higher than others. Nations should conduct themselves according to their place in the hierarchy. India, Nehru acknowledged, was "not a Power that counts" in 1947. As a newly independent nation, India must address the world appropriately. We will be humble, Nehru implied, as befits a new and weak nation. We will behave as a subordinate of the United States. Thus, the face we Indians present to the world, the gestures we make toward others, must be respectful, for subordinates respect their superiors. It was, for example, essential that Indian diplomats, especially those posted to other countries, perform their jobs with dignity and humility. Even before the government of independent India was established, Nehru admonished India's representatives abroad to avoid pompous imitation of the British, and to develop "restraint" and "discipline" in interactions with others. "Our first appointments," Nehru told a confidant, "must be above reproach." Nehru also spoke out against the "flaunting of wealth and the feasting that goes on in Delhi," both officially and unofficially, and pronounced himself "disgusted" at the cocktail parties and the "ostentatious display of wealth" in the capital, all of which he considered "bad form."[21]

The diplomat who most seriously transgressed the standards of proper place behavior was Asaf Ali, whom Nehru appointed ambassador to Washington in late 1946. Ali, a Muslim who had served in Nehru's interim cabinet, immediately demanded from Delhi those things he deemed the necessary accouterments of his newly elevated status. The furniture in the embassy, Ali complained, was "shoddy." Nehru found this hard to believe. Similarly, the ambassador's insistence on having silver salt cellars seemed excessive. "I do hope that you will not try to compete with others in pomp," Nehru wrote irritably. "We can neither afford it, nor is it suitable." In June 1947 Nehru responded sharply to Ali's request for a higher salary. "I view with great disfavor," he wrote, "anything in the nature of unnecessary expenditure. I am not interested at the present moment in personal questions of salaries and allowances and everyone should realise that more important things are being done in India." As for Ali's request for an air conditioner to help him through Washington's stifling summers, Nehru pointed out that the American capital could "hardly be worse than Delhi," and noted that he himself managed to do without a cooler. Nehru was particularly annoyed to hear that the ambassador "had been drinking excessively in Washington." A source of embarrassment, Ali was recalled in April 1948.[22]

If Indians felt obliged to behave respectfully toward representatives of more powerful countries, they also believed that those representatives had obligations to them. Like superiors, subordinates had the right to be treated with respect. Superiors must never flaunt their status: indeed, *because* Indians were willing to accept inferior status—their proper place— their superiors must allow them to save face. Do not sell us short, the Indians told the world, for we have "made a tryst with destiny," as Nehru said on the eve of independence. And never forget, Nehru said, that while the United States and the Soviet Union were stronger than India, in Asia India was already a nation that led by example. Nehru's India was a "mother country" to its neighbors, "the centre of things," a "connecting link" between the parts of a "renascent" Asia. While India's diplomacy must have "its full complement of good manners and courtesy"—these were India's obligations—India was "in no mood to be patronised" by the powers, "much less to suffer threats" or be "bullied." India, as Nehru put it in a speech to the Indian Council on World Affairs in March 1949, "cannot be ignored."[23]

In fact, the United States frequently did ignore India, undermining India's status and sense of place. Resentment over their neglect led Indian officials to demand (or plead for) due consideration on a variety of issues:

1. Don't patronize us—we are entitled to high status in the United Nations. From the founding of the UN in 1945, Indians saw the organization as a forum in which they could compete equally with the great powers. The Indian delegation quickly asserted itself when it raised for discussion the matter of apartheid in South Africa and played a leading role in the struggle against colonialism and racism, thereby damaging relations with the United States. Prior to the UN session in the fall of 1946, Nehru wrote to M. C. Chagla, a newly appointed delegate: "We want to make a splash at this General Assembly meeting." This India did. Its representatives were elected to all six of the UNO Commissions, and India's delegation promoted its views with asperity. The probability that Indian behavior might put others off did not deter Nehru from advocating for causes unpopular with powerful nations. "I am more anxious to make the world feel that we have got a will of our own than to gain a seat in any committee or council," he wrote the delegation. "I do not want to function on the sufferance of anybody. If any nation or group of nations wants to be tough with us, we can be tough with them also. . . . I have no doubt this has displeased many people, but it is about time they knew that they have to deal with a new India which will not tolerate the old practices."[24]

2. Don't insult us—our representatives deserve respectful treatment when they visit the United States on official business. Racism could be a serious problem for Indian visitors to the United States, as chapter 4 demonstrated. The Indians perceived smaller but nonetheless stinging insults as well. On Nehru's first visit in the fall of 1949 came John Snyder's obnoxious commentary on nations that bilked the United States for aid, and the notorious remark by a businessman that Nehru was lunching with men worth $20 billion. State Department officials unthinkingly addressed Ambassador Pandit as "Madam Pandit," a holdover from the heyday of Madam Chiang Kai-shek. ("Why do you call me Madam?" the ambassador, who despised Madam Chiang, snapped at Elbert Mathews one day. "I'm

Mrs. Pandit.") In the mid-1950s, U.S. policymakers fielded complaints from official Indian visitors that the twelve dollars per diem paid by the U.S. government was inadequate to cover the Indians' expenses, and it was much lower than the sums granted to Indians in the Soviet Union and China. Was this not further evidence of American scorn for Indians as supplicants in the land of the wealthy?[25]

3. Don't behave with arrogance when you come to our country. Despite the insults Indians thought they faced in the United States, many Indians found the freedom of American life liberating. Americans could be refreshingly unconscious of class and caste boundaries; the backslapping familiarity that so offended Nehru and other Brahminical types delighted Indians who chafed under a system in which social position was formalized and frequently fixed. One of these was M. K. Mehta, who was in 1959 the chief instruments engineer at India's Bhilai steel mill. Mehta had lived in the United States between 1938 and 1946, attending college in New York and then working for General Motors. He returned to India, worked for GM in Bombay for a year, then ultimately settled in at Bhilai, the Soviet-built plant whose staff included many Russian advisers. Mehta recounted with fondness his eight years in America, where he was "always treated as an equal" by his associates at college and work. But things changed when he returned to India after the war. He received a lower salary than American engineers doing exactly the same work at the Bombay GM plant, and "he was not allowed to buy at a discount certain prized American items," including major appliances, though his American counterparts were. The Americans in India had "an air of superiority," and "looked down on him as an Indian." The Americans drew astronomically high salaries, which they spent "rather recklessly," and they shuttered themselves away in air-conditioned homes, to which they seldom invited Indians. The wives of the American engineers were just as bad: "A woman who had to dump out her own garbage in the States became a lady of high society in India and an administrator of many household servants." Mehta contrasted this with the behavior of the Russians at Bhilai. Their salaries were modest, they lived humbly, they treated their Indian counterparts as equals, and any who made trouble were promptly sent home. "In my opinion," concluded Mehta, "the Russians are the most effective engineers in India. If I had my way, I would commission them to help us build other steel plants and other factories." The Americans, Mehta declared, "would not change their habits."[26]

4. Above all, the Indians pleaded with the Americans, let us know, in some small way, that we can expect your favor and count on your help. Don't ignore us. Give us, at least, a gesture to indicate your good will.

Again and again, American officials, who were (like Dean Acheson) skeptical that gestures had any lasting significance, were urged by Indians to signal that they cared about India, that they wanted to help, and that they liked Indians as people. Americans generally seemed little interested in India. In June 1950, C. R. Srinivasan, the president of the All-India Newspaper Editors Conference, told Elbert Mathews "that what was necessary to reverse the [anti-American] trend of Indian opinion was some act or gesture by the United States which would have dramatic impact on the emotional people of India"—some economic aid, perhaps. C. R. Mandy, editor of the *Illustrated Weekly of India*, toured the United States in 1951. The Americans, he later told an Indian newspaper, were utterly self-absorbed. He had checked a big city American paper one day and found only two items that mentioned India: one told of how a woman in Chicago had sent a chutney recipe to Vijayalakshmi Pandit, and the other recounted a suggestion, allegedly made by the head of a tribe of Nagas, that President Truman and Premier Stalin meet in the nude "so they would have nothing to hide from each other." In a fashion consistent with British efforts to instruct the Americans in how to treat the Indians, the British high commissioner in Delhi, Sir Alexander Clutterbuck, told Donald Kennedy, the U.S. chargé d'affaires, in September 1954 that Nehru "would not be pushed around" by the Americans, and that Indian officials resented that Americans "sounded off" while they were in India. "There was also the question of 'saving face,' " Kennedy noted, "and Sir Alexander was of the opinion that this was of more importance than we gave it." But in his summary of the conversation, Kennedy omitted reference to Clutterbuck's comments, in all likelihood dismissing the Indian need for "saving face" as a matter unworthy of serious concern.[27]

Gratitude, *Dana*, and the Wheat Loan of 1951

Gratitude has a critical function in behavior. Americans regard gratitude as a natural response to an act of kindness or generosity. If one appreciates what another has done, one expresses gratitude. The exchange between donor and recipient is now even: the donor has given something of value, and the recipient returns thanks for the gift. Gratitude confers status on the donor for giving. I have sacrificed, the donor implies. You, the recipient, must repay your debt with the coin of gratitude.

The Indian view of gratitude is different. It is shaped by a tradition of *dana*, which means, roughly, "magnanimous giving." *Dana* is based on a mutual understanding of proper place and the set of obligations that are predicated on the social positions of the parties involved. The king, prince, or any powerful and wealthy superior, should feel obliged to give to those less powerful and wealthy. He or she is by definition a donor, expected by all parties to be generous. No recipient should have to ask the donor to give, but if asked the donor should give without hesitation and unstintingly. A superior who refuses to give, who gives only grudgingly, who gives only because it benefits him or her, or who attaches conditions to the gift, has violated the obligations of the donor and may be spurned by the recipient.

The obligations of the subordinate in a relationship based on *dana* are of a negative sort. If a subordinate is forced to ask a superior for help, the subordinate is embarrassed and loses status. The relationship is, after all, already rigged against the subordinate, since the individual who is asked for help is presumably of higher status than the person doing the asking. But the negative obligation incurred most forcefully by the *dana* subordinate is that he or she *not* express gratitude for a gift. To do so would so skew the relationship in favor of the donor that it would humiliate the recipient. Donors must not expect thanks for doing what *dana* requires them to do.

Westerners perpetually found Indians for whom they did favors incapable of gratitude. In his eighteenth-century study of Hindu manners, the Abbé J. A. Dubois attributed "the ingratitude with which [Indians] are so often and so justly accused" to the "phlegmatic disposition" of Hindus. "Gratitude—which is a feeling that springs up spontaneously in all true hearts, which is a duty that bare justice prescribes, and which is a natural result of benefactions received—is a virtue to which the Hindu shuts his heart entirely," the abbé concluded. The Reverend A. D. Rowe, a nineteenth-century American traveler in India, argued that "the worst qualities in the character of the [Indian] people lay in their ingratitude and deceit, their motto being . . . 'get, get, get, but never give.' " More recently, and more cogently, the psychologist Alan Roland has recounted his experience with an Indian patient of the pseudonym Ashis. The relationship that developed between the two men was dominated, Roland soon realized, by his patient, whose expectations of his therapist were governed by the Indian belief in hierarchy. Ashis told Roland flatly what his "dependency needs" were, and just as flatly told him that he was not sure when he could pay for Roland's services. In doing this, as Roland noted, Ashis "subtly accorded me a superior position in the relationship, where my gratification and esteem would derive from helping him." That was all the thanks—and possibly all the remuneration—Roland would get.[28]

The failure of Indians to show gratitude for kindnesses done for them is, it should be said, only partly the result of a tradition peculiar to India.

O. Mannoni noted a similar phenomenon in the Malagasies, among whom he lived for many years. "The sequence of events," wrote Mannoni, "is something like this. A Malagasy receives from a European some favour which he badly needs but would never have dreamed of asking for. Afterwards he comes of his own accord and asks for favours he could very well do without; he appears to feel he has some sort of claim upon the European who did him a kindness"—a Malagasy version of *dana*! "Furthermore," Mannoni went on, "he shows no gratitude—in our sense of the word—for the favours he has received." Mannoni recalled that children in Europe had to be taught gratitude, and that this was an artificial process, for "a certain independence" was a necessary prerequisite for a genuine expression of gratitude. Western travelers who encountered "the natives' lack of gratitude, not specially in Madagascar but in all countries that used to be called 'primitive,' " should remember that "dependence excludes gratitude." Westerners who complained about "primitive" ingratitude tended to "project upon the native their own desire for reward," which blinded them to the difficulty natives themselves had in offering thanks to a perceived superior. "Gratitude cannot be demanded," Mannoni decided. "It can exist only where persons are equal. Dependence proper . . . is incompatible with equality." Europeans and Americans came from societies where equality was presumed to exist. Malagasies and Indians confronted Westerners as subordinates meeting superiors, as those who could not surrender what status remained to them in the unequal relationship by showing gratitude.[29]

And so, when the government of independent India found itself needing assistance from the United States, it was faced with the unhappy prospect of having to ask for help, and then having the Americans expect thanks for the help that it was their obligation to provide. Having to ask was excruciating; being told to ask by well-meaning but naive American officials was humiliating in the extreme. Americans must have found it puzzling to see Nehru go to extraordinary lengths, during his visit to the United States in 1949, to deny that he had come as a supplicant. Almost immediately on arriving in New York, Nehru told members of the city's Indian community that he had not come to the United States "to ask for or expect any gift from America. We are too proud and cultured a people," he said, "to seek favours from others." His audience surely understood what Nehru was saying: what was for Americans a peculiarly defensive declaration was for Indians a painful but vital statement about proper place. Following Nehru's visit, Ambassador Loy Henderson queried G. S. Bajpai about the parlous state of Indo-American relations—which Henderson found strange, given the attention the United States had lavished on India. Bajpai replied that Indians had the impression that Americans helped others only when there was something to be gained, and that, for example, while India had had to grovel before American authorities when requesting food aid, nations that professed a commitment to the U.S. side in the Cold War had found the Americans far more accommodating. "Indians," Bajpai told Henderson, "were accustomed [to] regard expressions of friendship as empty unless they were accompanied by acts of generosity." Eleven years later, Vice President Lyndon Johnson came to India and barnstormed through a number of villages. At one stop, he asked an elderly peasant what he would like President Kennedy to do for him. Nothing, the old man replied. Who knew what kinds of obligations he would incur, and how much status he stood to lose, by accepting a gift from a remote and apparently powerful man?[30]

When Americans expected Indians, like Johnson's peasant, to ask them for boons, when they publicized their help or expected Indians to be grateful for it, they were taking advantage of their already superior position in the relationship and abusing the protocols of *dana*. Americans expected gratitude when they bestowed favors on India and were affronted when it was not forthcoming. Henry Grady, the first U.S. ambassador to independent India, told some State Department colleagues that Indians "never express their thanks or show their gratitude for the things which are done to help India." Grady thought ingratitude "was sort of a natural attribute of Indians generally." In October 1950, George McGhee told Ambassador Pandit that "if India both needed and really wanted our assistance, the apparent indifference of Nehru and other Indian government officials would make it difficult for us"—difficult for the administration, that is, faced with Congressional opposition to aid for nonaligned India. When Secretary of State Dulles visited India in 1953, he reportedly told the New Delhi embassy staff and other American representatives that the way to handle Indians was to "make them come to you." "Why, if we just tell them to get on our side for foreign economic assistance," Dulles said (according to Chester Bowles), "they will come crawling on their hands and knees."[31]

Was it possible for Indians to change? Writing in the *Times of India* in December 1953, B. R. Naik defined gratitude and urged fellow Indians to learn to express it. Naik thought it appropriate to return a favor with a word of thanks: "Sometimes it may be embarrassing, but it is certainly not difficult if one wishes it." There is little evidence, however, that Indians were able or willing to shed the mutual obligations of *dana*. Time and again, Indians asked for things bluntly, failed to accept things graciously, or simply refused to ask outright for that which both sides knew they wanted. An association of Indian farmers, for example, addressing the World Bank in 1949, insisted that it was the "duty" of the "U.S.A. and other richer nations" to provide aid for Indian agriculture. In December 1950 the *Times of India* editorialized that India would be grateful for American help. "But any attempt to give negotiations [for U.S. aid] the appearance of a bargain for concessions and alliances will be resented and resisted in this country," the paper cautioned. "Esteem is lost when asked and bargained for." Sarvepalli Radhakrishnan, the philosopher who served as India's vice president from 1952 to 1962, told a U.S. official in June 1952:

> We resent your continuous publicizing of your own achievements. You are a strong country, and should be able to make concessions to our current psychology. It is we who need building up. . . . You don't need this building up. Keep yourselves in the background and help us to grow, by helping us to feel a sense of pride in our progress. By publicizing yourselves, you deprive us of the psychological help which is so vital to us at this stage of our development.[32]

This was a psychological condition the Americans did not understand, though Radhakrishnan perhaps overestimated American feelings of self-confidence during the early 1950s; probably Americans did need some "building up." In either case, they could not help pushing themselves awkwardly into situations that called for tact. Lyndon Johnson, in India in 1961, thought he had found a way to help a people who were reluctant to ask for favors: he would take a physically handicapped child back to the United States for medical treatment. The symbolism of this act—the advanced United States would help a victim of backwardness whose afflictions were beyond the abilities of his fellow Indians to cure—was appalling to members of the Indian government, who objected to John Kenneth Galbraith. The ambassador put a stop to Johnson's plan, though of the Indians he remarked in his diary, "I think they are too sensitive."[33]

They were "too sensitive" because Johnson's was an act of generosity, and like all Americans he had the purest intentions, even if his methods were clumsy. The Americans often wondered why their efforts to help Indians were treated with such hostility. In April 1950, Dean Acheson expressed to Loy Henderson his puzzlement over the attitude of Indian officials toward U.S. aid. On the one hand, Indians criticized the United States for failing to provide them with enough assistance. On the other, when the United States showed its willingness to help, Indians intimated that their country either "did not need assistance" or "that U.S. aid [was an] instrument of 'dollar imperialism.' "[34]

The Americans failed to understand Indian resistance to losing status by asking or showing gratitude for help. Far too often for it to have been a casual concern, Nehru decried what he saw as the Western determination to turn India into a nation of beggars, with himself as chief supplicant. In caste terms this was intolerable, for beggars were outcastes, and they had, thought Nehru, forsaken their pride, the very emotion that was essential to a truly independent India. In late 1946, Nehru wrote to the prodigal Asaf Ali of his hopes that India would remain friendly with the United States. "Nevertheless," the prime minister added, "I should like it to be made clear that we do not propose to be subservient to anybody and we do not welcome any kind of patronage. . . . There is no need whatever to appear as suppliants before any country." "We shall be glad if on the economic plane we get help from America," Nehru wrote his chief ministers on the eve of his 1949 visit to the United States. "That does not mean that we are going as beggars to the U.S. or to any other country. It is better to starve than to beg and become dependent on others." At Bhopal in June 1954, Nehru told his audience that the country would develop only if people worked hard: "They [were] not going [to] beg for assistance from other countries because he did not want [the] people of this great land [to] become beggars." Speaking to a British reporter in the early 1960s, the prime minister stressed the importance of a country's approach to foreign assistance. "The ways and means of giving aid are far more important than the amount of aid given," he said. "Some countries think that they can buy up a country by giving aid, and even when they do not think that, like the Americans, they want to tear every shred of self-respect away from the countries before they give aid. You either have to crawl before them, toe their line at the United Nations, or beg them to save you from starvation or political chaos." India would refuse aid given as "charity or blackmail."[35]

Sympathetic Americans had an inkling that the Indians wished to avoid groveling, but in general the two sides failed to appreciate each other's sensitivities in these matters. The American decision to provide a loan of wheat to famine-stricken India, made in the spring of 1951, was profoundly affected by issues of class, caste, and status. Under threat of widespread famine, the government of India, through Ambassador Pandit, requested on December 16, 1950, that the United States supply it with two million tons of wheat. Secretary Acheson, who received the request, promised to "explore the situation urgently and thoroughly," though he noted that the magnitude of the request meant that Congressional action would be required. After a month of study, the State Department concluded that the request should be honored. Acheson wrote Truman on

February 2, 1951, that "to refuse assistance to India in its time of critical need would run counter to American traditions," and recommended that aid be offered as a grant, not a loan. By this time, the White House had collected a bulging file of letters from churches, organizations, and individuals, entreating the president to send food to India. Truman met with key members of Congress on the 6th. In this group too there was sympathy for India's request, and although one representative suggested that "ways be found to increase shipments of manganese and chrome from India to this country," the discussants decided that cooperation along these lines "should not be made a condition" for providing the wheat. The president formally requested the aid, $190 million worth, on February 12, and a few days later supporters of the proposal in the House and Senate introduced bills that would give the Indians food.

While the House Foreign Affairs Committee approved its bill, opposition to it developed in the House itself, and the legislation ultimately got stuck in the Rules Committee for two months. The Senate aid bill failed to clear the Foreign Relations Committee. Members of Congress opposed the proposal for several reasons. Some argued that India should be required to trade strategic materials, among them manganese, beryl, mica, and monazite, to the United States in return for the wheat. Others claimed that the Indian government had squandered opportunities to alleviate the suffering of its people when it refused to reconcile with Pakistan, which had offered India food. And why, a few House members asked, should the United States help a country that was led by a communist (Nehru), that consorted with the Soviets and Chinese communists, and that refused to back the United Nations in its battle against aggression in Korea? Finally, even some of those willing to provide food for India felt that the aid should be given as a loan, not a grant. India, they said, could afford to pay for its food, and if it had to do so it would behave more responsibly in the future.

The administration tried to rally the pro-aid forces. At a March 29 press conference, Truman urged Congress to pass the legislation. Friends of India in the House watered down a Senate amendment that required India to repay a portion of its debt to the United States with manganese and monazite, so that the final version of the food bill called for repayment in part by "materials required by the United States," without mentioning what the materials might be. Nehru cooperated too, though with gritted teeth. He sent word that he would prefer a loan to a grant of food, anticipating that the terms of the former would be less onerous to India than the concessions the Americans would expect following a gift. And the prime minister yielded somewhat on the strategic materials issue, telling his Parliament on May 10 that, while India would not sell potential atomic materials abroad, he would not object to using other resources to help pay off the loan. The food loan bill, as rewritten by a House-Senate conference committee, passed the House on June 6 and the Senate on June 11; Truman signed it on the 15th.[36]

It had been an unexpectedly hard fight, but the Truman administration had won. American food would be sent to feed hungry Indians. It would be sent as a loan, part of which might be paid off in strategic materials in scarce supply in the United States. Administration officials, especially Ambassador Loy Henderson, had hoped that the generosity of American aid would create sympathy among Indians for U.S. foreign policy positions. Since Congressional action was favorable, since the *outcome* of the process was good, they dared believe that a grateful Nehru would reevaluate his suspicions of the materialistic Americans.

That is not what happened. Instead, as Robert McMahon has written, "the long delay, the intemperate statements of certain legislators, and the crude efforts to use the specter of imminent starvation had left deep scars" on the Indo-U.S. relationship. While Americans focused on the outcome of the wheat loan debate, Nehru could not forgive Americans for the humiliations they heaped on India during the debate itself, during the process, that is, of making what turned out to be a positive decision. Despite the insistence of the State Department that it was attaching no "political strings" to the food bill, Indian officials were never convinced of this. There was the discussion of tying the loan to sales by India of strategic materials. Nor did the Americans confine themselves to strategic materials: they also sought changes in Indian foreign policy generally as payment for their largesse. In late December 1950, less than two weeks after Ambassador Pandit had approached Acheson about India's need for wheat, the ambassador and the secretary, along with George McGhee and T. Eliot Weil of the South Asia Office, had a discussion of foreign policy differences between their countries. They talked about China, and especially the military situation in Korea. But the conversation kept circling back to the aid request. Between their expressions of dismay over Nehru's policy, Acheson and McGhee professed full support for the wheat proposal. The administration merely sought India's help in persuading Congress to fund the proposal. Why not resolve problems with Pakistan, including the dispute over Kashmir? "If this were done," said Acheson, "the people on the Hill would be favorably impressed." In the early months of 1951, while Congress considered, then refused to consider, the Wheat Bill, members of the administration returned to these issues. They bristled at Nehru's implied criticisms of U.S. policy. McGhee advised Acheson "that if Madame Pandit queries you regarding the food grains request you [should] inform her that it is under active study and is viewed sympathetically on humanitarian grounds, but that in the light of Mr. Nehru's apparent attitude toward the US, prospects of obtaining action . . . are not improving." Members of the House chastised Nehru for refusing to support the U.S. position in Korea. "India has proved to us that it is not our friend in the Korean struggle," said the Wisconsin Republican Alvin O'Konski. "We are going to look like a bunch of stupid jackasses if we pick that nation and give them a gift of $190,000,000." From India's point of view, even to suggest these conditions for aid was to violate the mutual obligations of *dana*, according to which the superior party was to give without reservation.[37]

In the end, of course, Congress chose not to make a gift of American grain, deciding instead that it would some day have to be paid for. The decision to switch from grant to loan was inspired by the belief of some members of Congress that India was not doing enough to help itself or to support the United States, and the administration acceded to it reluctantly. Ironically, despite the good intentions behind the original grant proposal, the Indians would have preferred a loan from the start. A grant imposed obligations on the Indians that were deeper than financial. It would have required the demonstration of gratitude, even though a gift by its nature would undercut India's status. Gifts from the United States always came wrapped in contingencies. During the discussion of the Wheat Bill, Michigan Senator Homer Ferguson recalled a roundtable discussion with a group of Asian students. "It was very difficult for them to understand how America could offer gifts to another nation," Ferguson recounted. "They asked, 'Well, what do you really want? What do you want in return?' They said they would rather know in advance what would be expected in return, rather than be told at some later time." This was Nehru's feeling too, and it was why he stated his preference for a loan over a grant in May 1951. As he explained in a radio address to the nation, such help that India received from other countries "must not have political strings attached. . . . We would be unworthy of the high responsibilities with which we have been charged if we bartered away in the slightest degree out country's self-respect or freedom of action, even for something which we need so badly."[38]

Throughout the lugubrious debate over the food grains legislation, American policymakers were struck, and clearly perturbed, by Nehru's refusal to thank them for their exertions. Loy Henderson wrote from New Delhi that when the food aid issue came up, Nehru "did not . . . express any hopes on the subject or any appreciation of the efforts on India's behalf of the United States Government," and that in several conversations Nehru failed to mention the subject at all, despite its obvious importance. An American writer named Edgar Mowrer met with Nehru in March 1951. "Nehru appeared bent forward and glum," Mowrer reported. "Expression: underlip protruding, chewing on something like gum and obviously expecting to accomplish an unpleasant duty. I countered by giving him greetings from his sister in Washington and telling him of a slight effort which I made to help them get their wheat by personal telegram to Congressman [John] Vorys. He remained glum." Later in the conversation, Mowrer noted that the United States had received very little help at the United Nations from several countries, including India. At this, "Nehru flew into a temper." He excoriated General Douglas MacArthur, then turned to the Wheat Bill: "The way in which you are handling our request for grain is insulting and outrageous. I can tell you that if we go through centuries of poverty and if millions of our people die of hunger we shall never submit to outside pressure." A week later, an Indian newspaper ran a cartoon depicting a buxom blonde identified as "United States" curled around a pie labeled "Food for India." The woman is telling a starving Indian man at the far end of the table, "First tell me you love me, honey." When Nehru announced that he would rather have a loan than a grant, he justified his preference with the argument that the grant bill led "practically to converting India into some kind of semi-colonial country." "I realize completely," he added, "the consequences of our refusal of this gift. Nevertheless, I cannot bring myself to agree to this final humiliation." Members of the U.S. Congress could not understand why the Indian prime minister was so touchy, but they put it down to churlishness and ingratitude and voted for a loan instead. Over two decades later, Loy Henderson had sour memories of Nehru's behavior. Nehru would "at times consent to accept American aid," said Henderson, "but when he did so it was usually with reluctance and without grace or gratitude."[39]

Finally, just as Nehru had feared, American friends and foes alike represented India as a beggar, or as a country full of beggars. India was so hungry, claimed supporters of aid, that it desperately needed America's wheat. How could Americans turn their backs on starving millions? As the Truman administration began its campaign for the Wheat Bill in January 1951, Acheson requested from the embassy in New Delhi materials that would reveal to Congress the extent of India's distress, even "graphic material . . . including revealing photographs" of the afflicted. In April and early May, with the Wheat Bill mired in committee, the Washington *Post* cartoonist Herblock scathingly depicted Congressional opponents of aid as overfed plutocrats who taunted Indians by demanding that conditions be met before they would provide food. Herblock sympathized with India, but in each cartoon he represented India as a famished suppliant, grim faced and seemingly defeated. Opponents of aiding India used the beggar image less sympathetically. The Georgia Congressman Edward E. Cox, the House's most outspoken critic of the Wheat Bill, insisted that any food sent to India was likely to be wasted. India, said Cox, had 180 million sacred cows, 136 million sacred monkeys, and "10,000,000 sacred or professional beggars—and all these sacred things will have a first claim on any wheat that may be procured by money lent to India."[40]

There were beggars in India, of course, and their ranks had been swelled by the millions of victims of the famine. To use graphic pictures of starving Indians seemed logical to Americans who sought to help, and anyone could see that Herblock's ire was directed at supercilious members of Congress, not poor Indians. Nevertheless, there the image was: India as beggar, an outcaste, powerless and humiliated. The representation of India as a beggar, even for a magnanimous purpose, dismayed Indians because of what it seemed to say about the status of their country. Following his receipt of Acheson's request for illustrations of India's distress, Ambassador Henderson, along with the embassy's agricultural counselor Clifford Taylor, met with K. M. Munshi, the food minister, and Vishnu Sahay, the food and agriculture secretary. Taylor asked Munshi to estimate the number of deaths that would result from the anticipated grain shortfall. Munshi refused to do so. Publicizing India's famine, even in the United States, would undermine his efforts to prevent starvation in India. Photos of the starved would provide "evidence [of] his failure," and would "create panic" that would greatly complicate his work. So Taylor answered his own question—he thought India might have an "extra 1 million or 2 million deaths"—to which Sahay responded that "this was as good a reply as could be made." Left unmentioned was the Indians' discomfort over the subject itself, the rendering of Indians as beggars, dependent on others for help. In May, an editorial in the pro-U.S. paper *Amrita Bazar Patrika* spoke of the loan as "India's sacrifice of self-respect in exchange for food," and another column admonished: "To say hungry people can have food only at the price of their self-respect and sovereignty is not the best way to reach the heart."[41]

Status, Behavior, and Cooperation

The Wheat Bill affair marked a low point in Indo-U.S. relations, one of many during the Nehru period. One last time, however, it is necessary to reiterate that there were good moments, too. Some of these resulted from a coincidence of Indian and American views on world events. More often, Indo-U.S. relations improved incrementally because of a warm meeting be-

Congressmen pontificate and withhold food while Indians starve in this April 1951 Herblock cartoon. While Herblock meant to sympathize with Indians, his depiction of India as a beggar humiliated them. Herbert Block, The Herblock Book *(Beacon Press, 1952).*

tween Nehru and some U.S. official, because of a kindness shown, a sensitivity respected—in other words, because an American behaved toward Nehru in a manner that paid deference to India's status and conformed to the rules of *dana*. An American's recognition of proper place went a long way toward making United States–India relations better overall.

It is easy enough to compile a list of U.S. policymakers with whom Nehru failed to get along: Loy Henderson, Dean Acheson, Harry Truman, John Foster Dulles (Nehru thought him "nasty"), and John F. Kennedy. But the list of Americans whom Nehru liked is equally long. It included Chester Bowles, ambassador from 1951 to 1953 and again from 1963 to 1969; Dwight Eisenhower; Ambassador John Sherman Cooper (1955–1958); and Ambassador John Kenneth Galbraith (1961–1963).

The difference between the men in these two groups has to do with how they acted toward Nehru and toward India in general. Nehru frequently made clear that an individual's behavior, revealing as it did the quality of the person with whom he dealt, mattered very much to him. He wished to be treated with dignity, even by representatives of a great power. In November 1949 he told an audience in California that if the United States hoped to have influence in India and Asia, it must use "the human touch." "Crudeness and directness," he said, would serve to "alienate Asia from the West." Face to face contact was useful because it gave Nehru and his colleagues an opportunity to assess the human qualities of American officials. There was an instance of this in the mid-1950s, when the Indian government, through the Ford Foundation, invited Paul Appleby, head of Syracuse University's Maxwell School of Public Administration, to study Indian administrative practices. Prior to Appleby's arrival, Douglas Ensminger, the director of the Ford Foundation in India, asked Finance Minister C. D. Deshmukh how he planned to use Appleby. Deshmukh replied, "I can't tell you . . . until [he] gets here." First, Deshmukh would have at least a couple of two-hour visits with Appleby. He would "explore Appleby's mind," get to know "how Appleby thought," and learn "something about his philosophy of life." Only then would the two experts get down to business. It was a way of doing things utterly alien to Westerners—one can almost picture Appleby at these marathon sessions, growing ever more perplexed about their purpose—but it was something Indians did (and do) in order to place the other, and to assess his or her fitness for the task to be undertaken.[42]

The Americans with whom Nehru felt he could not work failed this test because they behaved with arrogance. They put on airs; they acted superior to their Indian counterparts; they set conditions for their help; they lacked tact and humility and good manners; and they showed a stupendous ignorance of Indian culture, about which they manifestly cared little. Although Nehru regarded Dulles as the worst example of this sort of diplomat, let him stand for the others. On his visit to India in 1953, Dulles spoke to the U.S. embassy staff of his personal interest in India, the result of his family's long involvement in the country. Dulles's grandfather had been a missionary in India, one of his uncles had been born there, and his brother Allen, who was head of the Central Intelligence Agency, had spent a year at an agricultural institute in Allahabad after his graduation from college. And besides, Dulles could not forbear from adding, he had a fondness for rice. It was an offhand comment, meant harmlessly to amuse, and it probably got a laugh from the Americans in the group. It is unlikely that Indians, who read the comment in the *Times of India* the next day, laughed very much. Dulles, like the other men on Nehru's undesirable list, offended against the protocols of class, caste, and status that Indians felt strongly about. These Americans were patricians who presumed to insert themselves into India's social hierarchy at its highest level. Without benefit of birth or of having earned their position through merit, these American policymakers had arrogated to themselves the privileges of behavior reserved for members of the leading *jati*. Theirs was an outrageous breach of propriety.[43]

By contrast, those Westerners with whom Nehru found he could work kept themselves humbly removed from the Indian caste system. They acted respectfully toward Indians, and they adopted an informal style of life that conformed to no prescribed pattern of behavior. That was precisely what recommended them to Nehru. As outsiders—non-Hindus and foreigners—Westerners were not to presume that they had a place anywhere inside the social hierarchy. They had to behave as if there were no social expectations of them, as indeed there were not. To act patrician, like Henderson, Dulles, and the others, was to usurp the prerogatives of Brahmins. To act as members of any of the subordinate *jati* was unlikely, but if an American had (for example) substituted obsequiousness for respect, he or she would have been scorned for behaving as a representative of a lower caste. Informality marked Westerners as those without a place in the hierarchy. Remaining outside the caste system was the only legitimate course for those who were genuinely not of it.

Each of the men on Nehru's "favored" list demonstrated respect for the Indian social system by behaving with informality, graciousness, and sincerity toward Indian officials. John Sherman Cooper, by being friendly and forthright during his term as ambassador, "captured the confidence and admiration" of Indians, according to an editor. Dwight Eisenhower was Nehru's favorite American president. Eisenhower seemed unthreatening from the standpoint of gender, but unlike other American statesmen the president also understood the value of respectful behavior. He once wrote Dulles, "I am struck by the amount of evidence we have that Nehru seems to be often more swayed by personality than by logical argument." When Nehru came to the United States in late 1956, Eisenhower took the prime minister off to his Gettysburg farm in order to get to know him personally, outside the formal setting of Washington. In India, an invitation to one's home is a gesture of intimacy, and undoubtedly Nehru saw it that way. Eisenhower came to India in December 1959, and his visit was "one of the personal triumphs of his career," as H. W. Brands has put it. The president told the Delhi embassy staff that it must show courtesy to every Indian visitor, "no matter how poorly he was dressed or whatever his status was." Ambassador Ellsworth Bunker was struck by the warmth of the "common man's" reaction to Eisenhower: "For the head of such a powerful and envied country to appear as [a] good, friendly, sincere man who was approachable, considerate enough to apologize for arriving late, and who placed his trust in God . . . created [a] tremendous sympathetic response." Ambassador Galbraith seemed to speak to Indians "from the depths of his being," eschewing "lofty" pronouncements (Indians were charmed by the "ehhs" and "uhs" that sprinkled his speech) and putting on a party for four hundred workers building a new U.S. embassy in New Delhi, during which the ambassador and his wife, Kitty, joined in an energetic Punjabi dance.[44]

The most successful American diplomat in India during the Nehru period was Chester Bowles. Even as he arrived in India in October 1951, the ambassador tasked himself with demystifying the embassy and improving relations between Americans in India and their hosts. He wrote to newly arrived embassy staff, urging them to treat Indian staff members considerately, to examine themselves for hints of racial prejudice, and to drive carefully through the crowded streets of the capital. He included a cautionary anecdote about an American woman who worried aloud at a dinner party that her pedigreed dog would be petted by "dirty Indian children" and thereby get an infection. The Bowleses resisted such imperious behavior. They sent their children to Indian schools and frequently invited Indians into their home. Dorothy Bowles took Hindi lessons. Chester rode a bicycle. Bowles still may not have understood how important these gestures were. "We were astonished," he wrote, "at the repeated emphasis on my wearing of the Italian Ambassador's dress clothes, the children's enrollment in an Indian school, our preference for . . . informality . . . and my willingness to answer questions put to me by Indian newspapermen." "It is frequently said," wrote one of these correspondents in retrospect, "that Mr. Bowles did a marvellous job of public relations in India—which is true enough. What he really did was to make

The unaffected Chester Bowles rides his bicycle in New Delhi, endearing himself to his Indian hosts. Chester Bowles Papers, Manuscripts and Archives, Yale University Library.

American informality, American friendliness and American generosity come to life." What Bowles really did, in other words, was to take his proper place outside the Indian social system. He thus approached Indians without any presumptions based on status.[45]

Let it be said, finally, that the United States was not the only country affected by Indian perceptions of caste and status. In late 1955 the Soviet premier Nikita Khrushchev and several other Russian officials toured India. They drew large crowds, said what seemed to be many of the right things about the prospects for foreign aid and the need for India to maintain its independent policies, and appeared to have the approval of the Nehru government throughout their visit. Privately, however, the Indian perspective was different. On December 4, Vice President Sarvepalli Radhakrishnan told the U.S. embassy's deputy chief of public affairs, Clifford Manshardt, that Khrushchev and the other Soviets were "goondas, hooligans, and beggars," all highly derogatory terms in the context of caste. Every Indian official "from the Prime Minister down" would be delighted to see them go, "as they were abusing all courtesies." And what had the Russians done? They had masqueraded as Indians, inserting themselves into the caste system by "embracing their barber and presenting him with a munificent gift." No one should do something like that—barbers have very low status in India—least of all an outsider, whose very presence within the caste system was an affront to Indians. The barber himself would have felt patronized.[46]

Nor was India the only country affected by the American belief that gratitude was a reasonable return on a favor or a gift. Policymakers contrasted Nehru's behavior with that of the Pakistani leaders with whom they dealt. In early 1953 Pakistan faced a food shortage comparable to the one faced by India two years before. The Pakistanis asked the Americans for help, and at a meeting on January 28, State Department officials told the Pakistanis that they would provide food. The finance minister, Sir Zafrulla Khan, "indicated surprised gratification" at the decision. The United States, he said, "had no obligation to assist them or the rest of the world in the manner in which it had," and "the United States had not received sufficient gratitude from the world" for its previous acts of generosity. Indeed: when Sir Zafrulla returned to ask for more help eighteen months later, he expressed regret that while he always "seemed to have a request to make of the United States . . . it was Pakistan's belief that the 'beggar's bowl' should never be concealed." There is no need to wonder at whom Sir Zafrulla's remarks were aimed. The Indians spat in America's eye. The Pakistanis said thank you. It followed that the latter were more like Americans, and much more pleasant to work with.[47]

Epilogue

The Persistence of Culture: Indo-U.S. Relations after Nehru

> I have an idea that many of our present problems—international troubles—are due to the fact that the emotional and cultural backgrounds of people differ so much. It is not easy for a person from one country to enter into the background of another country.
>
> —Jawaharlal Nehru, 1949

Early in the morning of May 27, 1964, Jawaharlal Nehru, having just put in a full day of work, suffered a ruptured aorta and died. The people of India grieved deeply for the man who had helped lead them through the independence struggle, endured with them the shocks of partition, comforted them after Gandhi's murder, and guided them during their first years as citizens of a new India. He was the only prime minister they knew. And the vast majority also loved him, as a man who spoke from the heart of their fondest dreams for the country. Hundreds of thousands thronged the capital in the hope of seeing their big brother one last time, taking darshan, participating by their presence in the Hindu rituals of death. *"Panditji amar rahe!"* they cried mournfully. "Panditji has become immortal!" Around the world people mourned too. The American president, Lyndon Johnson, said solemnly: "There could be no more fitting memorial to him than a world without war." U.S. military intervention in Vietnam was then less than ten months away.[1]

In the years following Nehru's death, the United States and India continued not to be preoccupied with each other. The Americans remained most concerned with the Cold War and increasingly with its Vietnamese front. President Johnson sent the first combat troops to South Vietnam in March 1965, and matters spiraled out of control after that, with steady troop escalations for almost three years, the intensification of bombing, the maddening paradox of apparent victory on the battlefield accompanied by the deterioration of the overall position in Vietnam (along with the erosion of military morale and public support), and Richard Nixon's eventual decision to withdraw U.S. troops, which led to the unification of Vietnam under communist control in 1975. Some Americans were relieved that the war was over and philosophical (or chastened) about their nation's failure to work its will in Southeast Asia. Others were outraged, and warned that the United States had suffered a defeat that would damage its international position, weakening the faith of its allies, emboldening its enemies, and earning it the scorn of everyone else. The Cassandras were wrong. Ten years after the fall of Saigon Mikhail Gorbachev came to power in the Soviet Union, and before the end of the decade the Soviet empire lay shattered. Once recovered from the shock, Americans indulged in a frenzy of triumphalism, undergirded by the faith that they had won the Cold War. Associated good things happened, among them the end of racist apartheid in South Africa, a peace agreement in Northern Ireland, and first steps toward a settlement between Israelis and Palestinians. But much of the celebrating was premature. The United States faced serious economic challenges: from the nations formerly under Soviet control and the former Soviet Union itself, now desperately in need of economic aid; from East Asian nations, led by Japan, that first threatened to rival the United States economically and then in 1997 experienced tremors that threatened to destroy the world financial system; from debt-ridden Latin American neighbors; and from Western Europe, which had established a common currency by the end of the twentieth century and was emerging as an economic giant of resource and determination. Nor did the end of superpower confrontation bring peace to the world. Authoritarianism in the Soviet Union and Eastern Europe was reinvented, or succeeded by bloody ethnic conflict, particularly in Yugoslavia. The Middle East remained tense, and Americans came to associate the region with extremists: Jews who would not compromise with Palestinians, Islamic terrorists backed by Libya and Iran, and the bellicose Iraq of Saddam Hussein. There was brutal fighting in Rwanda, Liberia, and the Horn of Africa.

In India, where Nehru had kept the Cold War at arm's length—or maybe arm's width—old conflicts persisted. Dynastic government continued for a time, with Nehru's daughter Indira Gandhi (prime minister 1966–77 and 1980–84) and grandson Rajiv Gandhi (1984–89). Politics have since come unstuck. The Congress Party can no longer count on winning elections, and the ruling party at this writing is the fundamentalist Hindu Bharatiya Janata Party (BJP). India's population has grown close to one billion and its middle class has swelled, but the nation still struggles with wretched poverty and illiteracy and serious health care problems. The scope of the nation's power is hardly more commensurate with the size of its population than it was in 1964, though as nearly everyone knows India exploded a small nuclear device in 1974 and several larger ones in 1998. Its most significant foreign relations problems continue to involve its neighbors. India has fought two victorious wars with Pakistan, in 1965 and 1971; the cause of the first was Kashmir, while the latter assured the secession of the former East Pakistan and the creation from it of independent Bangladesh. Rebellious Tamils in Sri Lanka enjoyed support from India for a time. When Rajiv Gandhi terminated that support in 1987 he signed his death warrant: he was assassinated by a Sri Lankan Tamil suicide bomber in 1991. India has kept a wary eye on China. Several government ministers could not help boasting in May 1998 that India's nuclear tests had sent a message to the Chinese, and though they were hastily repudiated by other officials, the Chinese were not amused; "China went hyper," observed the magazine *India Today*.[2]

Indo-U.S. relations from Nehru's death forward have remained heavily influenced by culture. Perceptions of the other persisted, and they were based on stereotypes and symbolic representations durable enough to survive the changes wrought by nearly four decades. India remains for Americans an exotic place. It is still threatening because it harbors illness. As the U.S. ambassador Daniel Patrick Moynihan once sneered, "India has nothing to export except communicable diseases." Moynihan's outburst aside, Westerners have increasingly expressed the threat of illness, physical and mental, from India in metaphors. For example, the emergence in the United States of Hindu cults during the 1980s, led by allegedly conspiratorial gurus and yogis, became part of Hinduism's "World Plan" to infect the West. Of the Maharishi Mahesh Yogi, one cult-buster wrote: "It would be naive to believe that this Hindu mystic has dedicated his life to a world crusade to help people relax! Behind such innocently devised trappings is a disciplined, esoteric organization in which spiritual pride, moral pragmatism, power and rigid mind control are all brought to bear upon the final goal of initiating and 'enlightening' the whole human race." India is still odd. In the fall of 1997, Northwest and KLM airlines introduced daily flights to India from New York. The ad for the service featured a lovely and soulful *bharat natyam* dancer, and pointed out that "while India may be exotic, mysterious, and unpredictable, getting there isn't." Indeed: the flights would depart with "soothing regularity," would be routed through "Amsterdam's wonderfully efficient Schipol Airport," and offered "spacious comforts" in business class—all of these opposites of the uncertainty, inefficiency, and crowding travelers could expect once they arrived in Bombay.[3]

And India still carries for Americans the cachet of spirituality, other-worldly to be sure, but a godsend for Westerners needing relief from their stressful careers in the real world. By the summer of 1998, India had become a fashionable destination for American celebrities in search of inner tranquillity. The supermodels Kate Moss and Naomi Campbell recharged in Rajasthan prior to the start of the fashion show season in March, while Marie-Anne Oudejans, founder of the fashion house Tocca, resigned suddenly and left no forwarding address; she turned up in the city of Udaipur. Hindu religious centers (ashrams) are especially popular with Americans in India. Anne Cushman, coauthor of *From Here to Nirvana: The Yoga Journal Guide to Spiritual India*, explained: "Boomers are getting older. They've achieved a lot of the material goals they thought were going to make them so happy. They've discovered that they're not as blissful as they should be with that house, that car and that second marriage." "We've been lucky this year," said a grateful Ronjon Lahiri, assistant director of the India Tourist Office. "We've cornered the cultural market."[4]

So, too, did Indian perceptions of Americans persist. The Americans still tried to humiliate Indians, lording over them their excessive power and ill-gotten wealth. Soon after she became prime minister in January 1966, Indira Gandhi faced the prospect of famine in the country. She prepared to go to the United States seeking help, though she would not admit publicly how vital it was: "If we get help, it is welcome. But if we don't get help, we shall manage. . . . A lot of people, even quite poor people, come to me and say: 'We don't like this attitude of begging.' " Whatever she did, or didn't do, Gandhi won from Washington a promise to supply 3.5 million tons of foodgrain. The Americans, however, were slow to deliver the grain, evidently waiting for India to line up behind U.S. policy in Vietnam. The halting deliveries gave Gandhi "a bitter lesson in the disadvantages of living on foreign charity," and one of her advisers reported her determination never to be in the position of supplicant again. The Americans continued to treat India with contempt, acting as though Indians should be honored to take the U.S. side in international disputes, bullying and swaggering and resorting to violence in situations (Libya, Panama, Iraq) that demanded tact and diplomacy. "We are too big to be camp followers, and too proud to be clients," said a former Indian government minister, and the Americans could not accept that. Nor did

Cartoonist David Horsey warns American advocates of school prayer that they might get more than they bargained for. Reprinted with permission, Seattle Post-Intelligencer.

American men lose their licentiousness after 1964. They were constantly leering at nations, or the people who represented them, trying to seduce them. Sometimes this was merely annoying, as when President Johnson insisted on asking Mrs. Gandhi to dance at a White House banquet in 1966. ("My countrymen would not approve if they heard I had been dancing," she demurred.) It was worse when the United States heard and heeded the call of siren Pakistan for more arms. "You shouldn't help them," an India defense official protested. "Pakistan is like a prostitute that gives herself to everyone. It is easy to be unchaste, but difficult to be chaste, like India, which has no plans to invade Pakistan." It did no good to lecture; the Americans, it seemed, could not keep themselves away from the brothel, bearing gifts of military hardware.[5]

The strategic conceptions of both nations, rooted as they were in history and culture, outlasted the Cold War. Americans still see space as an opportunity. Despite the demise of the Soviet Union as a military threat, U.S. interests remain global, and space travel and a space-based missile defense system remain alive in federal budgets and the popular imagination, suggesting that Americans continue to disdain the presence of boundaries. Indian strategy is still constrained not only by the limits of power but by the Hindu apprehension of space as terra incognita or worse. The nation has limited influence abroad. Policymakers continue to operate from a kind of inside-out perspective. When, for example, Iraq invaded Kuwait in August 1990, the almost exclusive concern of the government was for the fate of Indian nationals caught in the fighting. Within its own sphere, India remained as assertive as ever. India's government was incensed when the United States opened a naval base on the Indian Ocean island of Diego Garcia in the mid-1970s, outraged with the American decision to assist Afghani mujahideen in their battle against the Soviet Union in 1980, and apoplectic when it learned of the Reagan administration's determination to provide Pakistan with advanced F-16 jet fighters. "We are against the collection of highly sophisticated arms in the region," said prime minister Indira Gandhi, echoing her father. As in 1954, the United States had raised the stakes of the Cold War in South Asia, within India's most intimate circle of interest.[6]

So, too, have ideas about economics persisted, and so have they continued to influence the Indo-U.S. relationship. That cultural stereotypes are flexible, capable of migrating as circumstances demand, is revealed in the language of Western policymakers who have become fed up with Iraq's refusal to open its weapons' facilities to outside inspection. The "Oriental bargaining" once ascribed to Indians, it turns out, exists with equally maddening results in predominantly Muslim countries. In June 1995, after hearing of Iraqi attempts to avoid disclosing the extent of their biological weapons program, Great Britain's UN representative fumed that "they're trying to do deals all the time. But," he warned, "we're not talking about buying carpets, we're talking about compliance with Security Council resolutions." Madeleine Albright, then the U.S. representative, added: "The Iraqis are acting as if they are in a position to bargain, as if they were in a bazaar, about what they will comply with and not comply with." There were nevertheless plenty of economic stereotypes left for Americans and Indians to apply to each other. Several emerged into the light of day when, in May 1989, the George Bush administration, using the Super 301 provision of the Omnibus Trade Act, placed India on a list of unfair traders, alongside notoriously protectionist Japan and Brazil. The administration took the step because, it said, India's tariffs were too high, its interest in foreign investment was too low, and it failed to allow American insurance companies to compete for customers within its borders. India was still hoarding, in this case its markets; having thrown Coca Cola out in 1977 (in part, ironically, because company officials refused to divulge to Indian managers the soft drink's secret formula) and IBM the following year, the Indians were behaving as selfishly as their ancestors and their

Nehruvian forbears, who refused to open their treasure house to all com-
ers. The Indian bureaucracy, sclerotic as ever, remained an obstacle to
trade and foreign investment. An American reporter acknowledged that
Indira and Rajiv Gandhi had started to dismantle Nehru's "inefficient"
domestic industries and his "virtually impenetrable tariff walls," but added
that India remained "a relative newcomer in the big leagues of world
trade" and thus lagged "far behind much of the rest the world." India was,
in other words, still peculiarly stunted in being simultaneously too young
and too old to develop properly.[7]

Rajiv hit back irritably. "We will not be dictated to by anybody as to how
to run the country and make our laws," he said. It seemed particularly unfair that the Americans accuse his ministry of protectionism, since he
more than anyone else had worked to liberalize the economy. The public
sector, Rajiv declared, must not become "an albatross round the people's
neck." Yet he would not abandon government- owned enterprise, claiming a "vibrant, dynamic public sector that works for the people" as the
cause of "true socialists." Americans have rejected socialism even more
completely than their Cold War predecessors, to the point where a Democratic president (and not, one suspects, a father figure) can propose
investing Social Security savings in the stock market. But Rajiv Gandhi,
like his mother and grandfather before him, sensed that the legitimacy of
India's national government depended on its ability to provide for the
people the goods and services once offered mainly by families. If the government backs away too quickly from its responsibility for the economy—
if it abandons the public sector—it will cede its authority to other institutions that can provide for the citizenry and undermine national unity.
This has, in fact, to some extent started to happen. In Bombay, India's financial capital, there is good money to be made these days if one has an
enterprising spirit, good connections, and if possible some muscle and a
willingness to use it. Arun Gawali is a well-heeled man who has offered to
pay the widow of any Bombay policeman killed in the line of duty the
equivalent of $2400 from his own healthy bank account. Outraged au-
thorities charge that Gawali has made his fortune through extortion, and
that he is a gangland boss who routinely orders the murder of those
whom he deems a threat to his affairs. But Gawali, who spends his days sitting placidly beneath a photograph of Mahatma Gandhi and Nehru while
receiving admirers who call him "Daddy," denies the charges, almost. "I
was a rebel," he says. "And if you are a rebel, one way leads to politics and
the other to jail. In jail they call you a goonda. In politics they call you a
minister."[8]

India has recently reentered America's consciousness because of its nu-

clear tests in May 1998. In the physical remnants and diplomatic fallout of
these five blasts one can discern a cluster of messages having to do with
race, gender, religion, and status. India had long spurned as neocolonialist and therefore racist the superpower logic that only those nations that already had nuclear weapons should be allowed to have nuclear weapons.
For this reason neither India nor Pakistan signed the 1996 Comprehen-
sive Test Ban Treaty. It rankled with Indians that Westerners regarded India's nuclear industry as a derivative of the West's and thus presumed it
subject to Western control. The Indians "don't want outside help" with
their program, lamented an American arms control expert. "They think
it's too much like colonialism." More to the point, as Pratap Bhanu Mehta
has noted, Indians regard the five nuclear powers "as discriminatory for
not allowing India to act on the kind of strategic considerations that they
have acted on themselves in continuing to possess nuclear arsenals." At the
root of the West's dismay over India's tests lie "unstated cultural assumptions: that the subcontinent is full of unstable people with deep historical
resentments, incapable of acting rationally or managing a technologically
sophisticated arsenal." Some Western officials seemed incredulous at India's success; their impulse was to disparage Indian reports of the power of
the devices. It was evidently hard for them to accept that supposedly backward Indians had been competent enough to pull the tests off.[9]

The tests reflected gender issues too. The Western stereotype that
Hindu men are effeminate, cowardly, and passive (and Indian women
cruel and emasculating) had been reinforced during Indira Gandhi's
"Emergency" of 1975, when Gandhi's son Sanjay orchestrated mass steril-
izations of impoverished young men. To some extent, the nuclear blasts
confirmed the image. Why did American intelligence fail to detect the
tests in advance? "They fooled the entire U.S. Government," confessed a
Clinton administration official. "We made the mistake of assuming they
would act rationally"—but women, or the womanish, seldom do. Or when
(surprisingly) they do, Westerners are appalled, among them the journalist Mary McGrory. Likening the BJP leadership to "nuclear boys behaving
badly," McGrory scolded Prime Minister Atal Bihari Vajpayee, "who
wished to establish his machismo" through the tests, and nostalgically recalled "a time when India was given to lecturing the West from position of
moral superiority. . . . But now lofty India wants to be one of the nuclear
boys. People who can't read, write, or feed their children are forgetting
these lamentable circumstances in the ghastly glory of being able to burn
the planet or their enemies to a crisp." Men of the BJP, heirs to the
counter-Gandhian tradition of masculinized Hinduism, had proclaimed
their intention to make India a nuclear power. Following the tests, they

hardly attempted to conceal their swagger. The subtler, nonnuclear policy of the BJP's predecessor government "was a lot of toothless waffle,"
scoffed an aide to Vajpayee. The powerful Hindu nationalist and Bombay
power broker Bal Thackeray said: "We have to prove we are not eunuchs."
Hindu men had swallowed their nuclear Viagra. It does not seem coinci-
dental that, following nuclear tests by Pakistan on May 28 and 30, India's
defense minister disparaged the test weapons as "Ping-Pong balls"—hard,
hollow, and impotent.[10]

More than ever, religion pervades political discourse in the United
States and India. In 1968, 53 percent of Americans polled said churches
should keep out of politics; by 1996 54 percent thought it reasonable that
churches get involved. In India, P. V. Narasimha Rao, prime minister
from 1991 to 1996, had a colorful spiritual adviser named Chandraswamy
(the *Indian Express* called him the "controversial godman"), and during
his unsuccessful campaign in 1996 Rao visited Hindu holy sites ten times.
The nuclear tests were signatures of the BJP's Hindu assertiveness—here,
once again, the cultural filaments of gender and religion cannot be fully
untangled. The BJP saw itself "as bathed in triumph and glory," and *India
Today* asserted that the "tests and their aftermath have radically redefined
India's image of being a yogi in today's world of realpolitik." Even by BJP
standards, some Hindus got carried away. A few announced that they
would gather "sacred soil" from the test area and carry it in holy vessels
throughout the country, the idea being, a BJP leader explained, "to
spread the feeling of national self-confidence," never mind radioactivity.
Cooler heads prevailed, and the plan was dropped. Other Hindu fundamentalists hoped to build a temple at the blast site.[11]

The tests were also about status, India's attainment of proper place in
the world. Nehru had never brooked insults, to himself or his nation, but
he had always acknowledged that "India is not a power that counts," as he
put it in 1947. The nuclear explosions of 1974 and especially 1998 were
designed to make India count. Many Indians, noted Selig Harrison after
the most recent tests, have "a post-dated self-image. Since India is one of
the world's oldest and largest civilizations, its people take its great-power
status for granted and expect others to do the same." Years of patronizing
behavior by the United States had convinced Indians "that only nuclear
muscle-flexing would get American attention." BJP rhetoric in the days
following the blasts emphasized status concerns. The party declared May
16 a "day of prestige" to celebrate the nation's technological prowess.
One official spoke of the "transformation" of India's foreign policy "from
the moralistic to the realistic. It is one-sixth of humanity seeking its right-
ful place under the sun in the calculus of great powers." Seventy-two year-

old Chunni Lal steadied himself on a cane and blinked back tears. "It's a moment of great pride for me today," he told a reporter. "Today my country is safe, my city is safe and my house is safe." The Pakistani explosion was less than two weeks away.[12]

Despite some brave words about mutual deterrence bringing peace, the India-Pakistan relationship has grown worse since the tests. The flash point remains Kashmir. In early 1999, Islamic fighters took up positions in the rugged Kargil heights, on the Indian side of the line of control. Indian forces mounted an operation to dislodge them, and at considerable sacrifice managed in good part to do so. At the worst moment in the crisis—July 4, of all days—the Pakistani prime minister Nawaz Sharif met at the White House with President Clinton, after which Sharif disavowed responsibility for the infiltrators and promised to withdraw them. The Indians claimed victory, and subsequently shot down a Pakistani training aircraft they said had strayed into India's airspace (though the wreckage of the plane was recovered in Pakistani territory). The two nations teetered once more on the brink of war while Americans watched, concerned but perplexed as ever at the odd and reckless behavior of South Asians.

Notes

Preface

1. H. W. Brands, *India and the United States: The Cold Peace* (Boston, 1990); G. W. Choudhury, *India, Pakistan, Bangladesh, and the Major Powers* (New York, 1975); Robert J. McMahon, *The Cold War on the Periphery: The United States, India, and Pakistan* (New York, 1994); Dennis Merrill, *Bread and the Ballot: The United States and India's Economic Development* (Chapel Hill, 1990). See also W. Norman Brown, *The United States and India, Pakistan, Bangladesh,* 3d ed. (Cambridge, Mass., 1972); M. S. Venkataramani, *The American Role in Pakistan, 1947–1958* (New Delhi, 1982); Selig S. Harrison, *India: The Most Dangerous Decades* (Princeton, 1960); A. P. Rana, ed., *Four Decades of Indo-U.S. Relations: A Commemorative Retrospective* (New Delhi, 1994); and M. Srinivas Chary, *The Eagle and the Peacock: U.S. Foreign Policy toward India since Independence* (Westport, Conn., 1995).

2. Raymond Williams, *Keywords: A Vocabulary of Culture and Society* (New York, 1983), 87; Clifford Geertz, *The Interpretation of Cultures* (New York, 1973), 5.

3. Geertz, *Interpretation of Cultures,* 14; Robert H. Winthrop, *Dictionary of Concepts in Cultural Anthropology* (New York, 1991), 50–59; Alan Barnard and Jonathan Spencer, "Culture," in Barnard and Spencer, eds., *Encyclopedia of Social and Cultural Anthropology* (London, 1996), 136–42.

4. Barnard and Spencer, "Culture," 140–41; Winthrop, *Dictionary of Concepts,* 56–57; Melvyn Leffler, "New Approaches, Old Interpretations, and Prospective Reconfigurations," *Diplomatic History* 19, 2 (1995): 173–96.

5. Bernard S. Cohn, "History and Anthropology: The State of Play," in *An Anthropologist among the Historians and Other Essays* (New Delhi, 1987), 26. See also John Dower, *War without Mercy* (New York, 1986), 118–46.

6. Akira Iriye, "Culture and Power: International Relations as Intercultural Relations," *Diplomatic History* 3, 2 (1979): 115–28; idem, *Power and Culture: The Japanese-American War 1941–1945* (Cambridge, Mass., 1981); idem, "Culture," *Journal of American History* 77, 1 (1990): 99–107.

7. Michael H. Hunt, *Ideology and U.S. Foreign Policy* (New Haven, 1987); idem, "Ideology," *Journal of American History* 77, 1 (1990): 108–15.

8. Bruce Cumings, " 'Revising Postrevisionism,' or, The Poverty of Theory in Diplomatic History, *Diplomatic History* 17, 4 (1993): 439–69; Frank Ninkovich, "Interests and Discourse in Diplomatic History," *Diplomatic History* 13, 2 (1989): 135–61; idem, *Modernity and Power: A History of the Domino Theory in the Twentieth Century* (Chicago, 1994); Anders Stephanson, *Kennan and the Art of Foreign Policy* (Cambridge, Mass., 1989).

9. Alastair Iain Johnston, *Cultural Realism: Strategic Culture and Grand Strategy in Chinese History* (Princeton, 1995).

10. Emily S. Rosenberg, "Gender," *Journal of American History* 77, 2 (1990): 116–24; idem, "Walking the Borders," *Diplomatic History* 14, 4 (1990): 565–73; idem, " 'Foreign Affairs' after World War II: Connecting Sexual and International Politics," *Diplomatic History* 18, 1 (1994): 59–70; idem, "Revisiting Dollar Diplomacy," *Diplomatic History* 22, 2 (1998): 155–76; Geoffrey Smith, "National Security and Personal Isolation: Sex, Gender, and Disease in the Cold War United States," *International History Review* 14, 2 (1992): 307–37; Laura McEnaney, "He-Men and Christian Mothers: The America First Movement and the Gendered Meanings of Patriotism and Isolationism," *Diplomatic History* 18, 1 (1994): 47–57; Michelle Mart, "Tough Guys and American Cold War Policy: Images of Israel, 1948–1960," *Diplomatic History* 20, 3 (1996): 357–80; Frank Costigliola, " 'Unceasing Pressure for Penetration': Gender, Pathology, and Emotion in George Kennan's Formation of the Cold War," *Journal of American History* 83, 4 (1997): 1309–39; idem, "The Nuclear Family: Tropes of Gender and Pathology in the Western Alliance, *Diplomatic History* 21, 2 (1997): 163–83; Robert D. Dean, "Masculinity as Ideology: John F. Kennedy and the Domestic Politics of Foreign Policy," *Diplomatic History* 22, 1 (1998): 21–62; Kristin L. Hoganson, *Fighting for American Manhood: How Gender Politics Provoked the Spanish-American and Philippine-American Wars* (New Haven, 1998).

11. Gerald Horne, *Black and Red: W. E. B. Du Bois and the Afro-American Response to the Cold War, 1944–1963* (Albany, 1986); Dower, *War without Mercy*; Mary Dudziak, "Desegregation as a Cold War Imperative," *Stanford Law Review* 41 (November 1988): 61–120; Paul Gordon Lauren, *Power and Prejudice: The Politics and Diplomacy of Racial Discrimination* (Boulder, 1988); Alexander DeConde, *Ethnicity, Race, and American Foreign Policy: A History* (Boston, 1992); Thomas Borstelmann, "From Montgomery to the Congo: Dwight Eisenhower and the Rise of People of Color in the United States and Abroad," unpublished paper, 1996, in author's possession; Penny M. Von Eschen, *Race against Empire: Black Americans and Anticolonialism, 1937–1957* (Ithaca, 1996); Brenda Gayle Plummer, *Rising Wind: Black Americans and U.S. Foreign Affairs, 1935–1960* (Chapel Hill, 1996).

12. Nathan Glazer, "Introduction," in Sulochana Raghavan Glazer and Nathan Glazer, eds., *Conflicting Images: India and the United States* (Glenn Dale, Md., 1990), 3.

13. Sidney Verba, "Comparative Political Culture," in Lucian Pye and Sidney Verba, eds., *Political Culture and Political Development* (Princeton, 1965), 513. See also Gabriel Almond and Sidney Verba, *The Civic Culture* (Princeton, 1963); Gabriel Almond and James S. Coleman, eds., *The Politics of Developing Areas* (Princeton, 1960); and Lucian Pye, *The Mandarin and the Cadre* (Ann Arbor, 1988), 1–35.

14. Lucian Pye, "Introduction: Political Culture and Political Development," in Pye and Verba, *Political Culture*, 7–8.

15. Costigliola, "Tropes of Gender and Pathology," 163–64; Loy Henderson to Dean Acheson, June 18, 1949, Loy Henderson Papers, box 8, Manuscript Division, Library of Congress, Washington, D.C.

16. Richard H. Immerman, "Psychology," *Journal of American History* 77, 1 (1990): 169–80; Alexander L. George and Juliette L. George, *Woodrow Wilson and Colonel House: A Personality Study* (New York, 1964); Robert Jervis, *Perception and Misperception in International Politics* (Princeton, 1976); Alan Roland, *In Search of Self in India and Japan* (Princeton, 1988), 4.

17. Edward Said, "Criticism/Self Criticism," *Lingua Franca*, February–March 1992, 39–40.

18. John Lewis Gaddis, *Strategies of Containment* (New York, 1982), vii.

19. Bruce Kuklick, "Commentary: Confessions of an Intransigent Revisionist about Cultural Studies," *Diplomatic History* 18, 1 (1994): 122.

Introduction

1. Harold Isaacs, *Scratches on Our Minds: American Views of China and India* (New York, 1958), 269–71.

2. Harry H. Field, *After Mother India* (New York, 1929), 275–86; Mrinalini Sinha, "Reading *Mother India*: Empire, Nation and the Female Voice," *Journal of Women's History* 6, 2 (1994): 6–44; "India Diary" of Katherine Mayo [kept by M. Moyca Newell], Katherine Mayo Papers, box 14, folder 113, Yale University Library, New Haven, Conn.

3. Katherine Mayo, *Mother India* (New York, 1927); Mayo, notes on interviews with Miss [Muriel] Simon, n.d. [January 26, 1926], Mayo Papers, box 34, folder 180.

4. Katherine Mayo to David Boyle, December 17, 1926, Mayo Papers, box 5, folder 36; Boyle to Mayo, January 6, 1927, ibid.; signature illegible [H. Chamard?] to Katherine Mayo, November 18, 1927, Mayo Papers, box 5, folder 40; Bernice Blackwell to Mayo, September 25, 1927, Mayo Papers, box 5, folder 38; Field, *After Mother India*, 195; Sinha, "Reading *Mother India*," 6. Mayo's other books on India were *Slaves of the Gods* (New York, 1929), *Volume Two* (New York, 1931), and *The Face of Mother India* (New York, 1935).

5. Field, *After Mother India*, 3–14, 36–37, 245; Vidya Nath Kohli to Katherine Mayo, September 30, 1927, Mayo Papers, box 5, folder 38; Sheikh Abdul Karim to Mayo, October 29, 1927, Mayo Papers, box 5, folder 39; R. K. Gupta, *The Great Encounter* (New Delhi, 1986), 142; A. M. Rosenthal, " 'Mother India' Thirty Years After," *Foreign Affairs* 35, 4 (1957): 620–30.

6. Dorothy B. Jones, *The Portrayal of China and India on the American Screen, 1896–1955* (Cambridge, Mass., 1955), 65.

7. Roselle Mercier Montgomery to Katherine Mayo, October 1, 1927, Mayo Papers, box 5, folder 39; Mayo, *Mother India*, 28, 411; Veena Das, "The Imaging of Indian Women: Missionaries and Journalists," in Sulochana Raghavan Glazer and Nathan Glazer, eds., *Conflicting Images: India and the United States* (Glenn Dale, Md., 1990), 217; L. Louise Haas to Mayo, January 11, 1928, Mayo Papers, box 6, folder 42.

8. Kirin Narayan, "Refractions of the Field at Home: American Representations of Hindu Holy Men in Nineteenth and Twentieth Centuries," *Cultural Anthropology* 8, 4 (1993): 480–81. The post-Nehru generation of Americans could learn about India from Walt Disney. The movie *The Jungle Book* (1967), based loosely on the Kipling stories, featured a landscape of stereotypes, and ended when a seductive young girl lured the hero, Mowgli, out of the jungle and into her rude but neat village. The 1992 film *Aladdin* cheerfully mixed images of the Arab "Middle East" and South Asia. It was set in the city of "Agrabah" where, according to one of movie's songs, "They'll cut off your ear if they don't like your face / It's barbaric—but hey! it's home." There was also a book called *The Little Lost Elephant*. Sold with an audio tape of its text, it recounted a visit to India by Mickey Mouse and Goofy. The Disney characters encounter "strange birds and animals"—mostly refugees from *The Jungle Book*—vast riches (the elephant of the title wears a ruby on her forehead), and hordes of purple-skinned mouse-folk. "I knew India had lots of people," says Goofy, "but I didn't think they'd all be at the airport."

9. Sander L. Gilman, *Difference and Pathology: Stereotypes of Sexuality, Race, and Madness* (Ithaca, 1985), 12, 19–25.

10. Ronald Inden, *Imagining India* (New York, 1990), 2–3, 51; Lloyd I. Rudolph and Susanne Hoeber Rudolph, *The Modernity of Tradition: Political Development in India* (Chicago, 1967), 9; Edward Said, *Orientalism* (New York, 1978), 2–3; Arjun Appadurai, "Putting Hierarchy in its Place," *Cultural Anthropology* 3, 1 (1988): 36–49.

11. For Indian-English words generally, see Henry Yule and A. C. Burnell, *Hobson-Jobson: A Glossary of Colloquial Anglo-Indian Words and Phrases* (London, 1986 [1886]).

12. Gupta, *Great Encounter*, 127; Harry S. Truman to Dean Acheson, September 15, 1952, Harry S. Truman Papers, President's Secretary's Files (PSF), box 180, Harry S. Truman Library (HSTL), Independence, Mo.; C. L. Sulzberger, *A Long Row of Candles: Memoirs and Diaries* [1934–54] (Toronto, 1969), 526; Ariel Dorfman and Armand Mattelart, *How To Read Donald Duck: Imperialist Ideology in the Disney Comic* (New York, 1975), 44.

13. Gilman, *Difference and Pathology*, 18.

14. Reischauer quoted in Nathan Glazer, "Introduction," in Sulochana Raghavan Glazer and Nathan Glazer, eds., *Conflicting Images: India and the United States* (Glenn Dale, Md., 1990), 15; Milton Singer, *When a Great Tradition Modernizes: An Anthropological Approach to Indian Civilization* (Chicago, 1972), 13; Krishnalal Shridharani, *My India, My America* (Garden City, N.Y., 1943), 92–93; Rudyard Kipling, "Yoked with an Unbeliever," *Plain Tales from the Hills* (Oxford, 1987), 30.

15. Charles Allen, ed., *Plain Tales from the Raj* (New York, 1985), 36–39, 54, 56; Edward Rice, *Sir Richard Francis Burton* (New York, 1990), 82; Sydney Greenbie, *The Romantic East* (New York, 1930), 40–41; Abbé J. A. Dubois, *Hindu Manners, Customs and Ceremonies* (Oxford, 1905 [1816]), 83–84, 325, 329.

16. Patrick Süskind, *Perfume: The Story of a Murderer* (London, 1987), 86–87; Alain Corbin, *The Foul and the Fragrant: Odor and the French Social Imagination* (Cambridge, 1986), 7; Abbé Dubois, *Hindu Manners*, 190; Donald M. Lowe, *History of Bourgeois Perception* (Chicago, 1982); Uri Almagor, "The Cycle and Stagnation of Smells: Pastoralists-Fishermen Relationships in an East African Society," *Res* 13 (spring 1987): 106–21.

17. Stephen Kern, *The Culture of Time and Space 1880–1918* (Cambridge, 1983), 222; Isaacs, *Scratches on Our Minds*, 273; Ehrlich quoted in Charles H. Heimsath, "The American Images of India as Factors in U.S. Foreign Policy Making," *Asian Thought and Society* 2, 3 (1977): 271–89.

18. William Fee to Elihu Root, May 29, 1906, Department of State, *Despatches of U.S. Consuls at Bombay*, 1838–1906 (microfilm), University of California–Berkeley Library; Price Collier, *The West in the East* (New York, 1911), 140–41; Allen, *Plain Tales*, 37.

19. Singer, *When a Great Tradition Modernizes*, 13; Thomas Cook and Son, *India, Burma, Ceylon and South Africa: Information for Travellers and Residents* (London, 1903), 90; Diary of Mrs. M. A. Roy, December 18, 1877; January 3, 1888, Mrs. M. A. Roy Papers, Bancroft Library, University of California–Berkeley; Henry M. Field, *From Egypt to Japan* (New York, 1877), 132. "I hate all snakes," says Kipling's Kim. Kipling himself adds, "No native training can quench the white man's horror of the serpent."

20. Field, *From Egypt to Japan*, 116; Greenbie, *Romantic East*, 83, 104; Collier, *The West in the East*, 96–97.

21. For a summary of Foucault's views, only slightly less abstruse than the writings of Foucault himself, see Paul Rabinow, "Introduction," in Rabinow, ed., *The Foucault Reader* (New York, 1984), 3–29.

22. Mary Douglas, *Purity and Danger: An Analysis of Concepts of Pollution and Taboo* (New York, 1966), 2, 5, 36, 40; Erving Goffman, *Relations in Public: Microstudies of the Public Order* (New York, 1971), 46–47.

23. Gertrude Williams, *Understanding India* (New York, 1928), 68; Allen, *Plain Tales*, 99; Bayard Taylor, *A Visit to India, China, and Japan in the Year 1853* (New York, 1891), 57; Abbé Dubois, *Hindu Manners*, 594–95; Mayo, *Mother India*, 225.

24. Nathaniel Jacobs to F. W. Seward, July 21, 1866, *Despatches from U.S. Consuls in Calcutta*, 1792–1906 (microfilm), University of California–Berkeley Library; A. C. Litchfield to John L. Cadwalader, September 5, 1876, ibid.; B. F. Bonham to J. D. Porter, August 12, 1886, ibid.; Bonham to George L. Rives, June 2, 1888, ibid.; William T. Fee to David J. Hill, July 27, 1900, *Despatches from Consuls in Bombay*; Fee to John Hay, March 23, 1904, ibid.

25. Nathaniel Jacobs to F. W. Seward, July 16, 1866, *Despatches from Consuls in Calcutta*;

Mayo, *Mother India*, 371; Joan M. Jensen, *Passage from India: Asian Indian Immigrants in North America* (New Haven, 1988), 44–45, 105, 112.

26. Erving Goffman, *Stigma: Notes on the Management of Spoiled Identity* (New York, 1974), 4–5; Alan M. Kraut, *Silent Travelers: Germs, Genes, and the "Immigrant Menace"* (Baltimore, 1994), 26.

27. Anna Harriet Leonowens, *Life and Travel in India* (Philadelphia, 1897), 65; George C. Foulk to his family, March 26, 1884, George C. Foulk Papers, Library of Congress; Mark Twain, *Following the Equator* (Hartford, 1897), 371–78.

28. George Trumbull Ladd, *Intimate Glimpses of Life in India* (Boston, 1919), 180–81; Twain, *Following the Equator*, 500.

29. *Jawaharlal Nehru's Speeches*, vol. 1, *1946–1949* (New Delhi, 1949), 29. Nehru had served since September 1946 as head of the Interim National Government, a transitional body between British rule and full independence.

30. Chester Bowles, interview by Neal Gold, 1963, Bowles Papers, box 396, folder 177; Dean Acheson, *Present at the Creation* (New York, 1969), 420; J. Wesley Adams, interview by Richard McKinzie, December 18, 1972, HSTL; *Times of India* (*TOI*), Bombay, December 19, 1950; Philip Jessup, "Conversation with Madame Pandit," August 17, 1950, Record Group (RG) 59, 611.91/8-1750, box 2857, National Archives (NA), Washington, D.C. As a matter of interest, Nehru did not stand on his head each morning, contrary to reports in the American press. When asked why he did not, the prime minister replied, "I have got no time." *TOI*, December 12, 1959.

31. John W. Dower, *War without Mercy: Race and Power in the Pacific War* (New York, 1986); Loy Henderson to Robert Rossow, April 4, 1950, Loy Henderson Papers, box 8, Library of Congress; "Report of Senators Green and Ferguson on their Round-the-World Trip," January 10, 1951, RG 59, Lot File 57D259, box 7, NA.

32. Chester Bowles, *Ambassador's Report* (London, 1954), 7; Bowles, interview; Richard Cronin, *Imagining India* (New York, 1989), 1–2; John Frederick Muehl, *Interview with India* (New York, 1950), 30; Arthur Koestler, *The Lotus and the Robot* (New York, 1961), 15; memorandum of conversation with the President, September 26, 1960, Dwight Eisenhower Papers, Ann Whitman File (AWF), International Series (IS), box 27, Dwight D. Eisenhower Library (DDEL), Abilene, Kans.

33. Background memoranda on visit to the United States of Pandit Jawaharlal Nehru, October 3, 1949, Truman Papers, PSF, box 180; Adams, interview; minute by L. A. C. Fry, May 13, 1950, Foreign Office (FO) 371, file 84254, doc. FL10118/89, Public Record Office (PRO), Kew, England; Jones, *Portrayal of China and India*, 54–55; George McGhee, *Envoy to the Middle World: Adventures in Diplomacy* (New York, 1983), 103; minute by P. F. Grey, November 22, 1948, FO 371, file 69724, doc. F/6541, PRO; William C. Bullitt, "The Old Ills of Modern India," *Life*, October 1, 1951, 110–26; Heimsath, "American Images," 280; Isaacs, *Scratches on Our Minds*, 245–46.

34. "India, 1957–62, A Study" (summary), November 8, 1957, in Department of State, *Foreign Relations of the United States (FRUS)*, *1955–57*, vol. 8, *South Asia* (Washington, D.C., 1987), 396–401; "India: Liberty and Death," *Time*, October 27, 1947, 34–41.

35. McGhee, *Envoy to the Middle World*, 99; John Kenneth Galbraith, *Ambassador's Journal: A Personal Account of the Kennedy Years* (Boston, 1969), 91.

36. Muehl, *Interview with India*, 47; Thomas D. Clark to Chester Bowles, January 3, 1953, Bowles Papers, box 111, folder 499; Eileen Watkins to Bowles, n.d. [March 15, 1953], ibid., box 103, folder 381; Bowles to Donald Kennedy, December 15, 1952, ibid., box 95, folder 268; Bowles to Donald Kennedy, October 13, 1952, ibid., box 95, folder 267; Fraser Wilkins, interview by William W. Moss, February 23, 1971, John F. Kennedy Library (JFKL), Boston, Mass.

37. William H. McNeill, *Plagues and People* (Garden City, N.Y., 1976), 235–91; prescription for Chester Bowles and family from Dr. Edward Nichols, September 25, 1951, Bowles Papers, box 104, folder 394; Bowles, interview; Bowles, *Ambassador's Report*, 17; "Post Report," American Embassy, October 31, 1946, Delhi, RG 84, New Delhi Embassy General

Records 1946, box 46, Washington National Records Center (WNRC), Suitland, Md.; Bowles to Allen, March 22, 1953, Bowles Papers, box 93, folder 229; "Health and Medical Information," American Embassy, New Delhi, June 27, 1951, ibid., box 107, folder 444.

38. The remaining 8 percent of those surveyed either provided too little information or "views so particularized or so balanced" that they couldn't be classified. In contrast, 70 percent of those polled expressed predominantly favorable views of the Chinese. Isaacs, *Scratches on Our Minds*, 328–29, 352, 382; Chester Bowles to Acheson, December 6, 1951, *FRUS* (1951), vol. 6, *Asia and the Pacific* (Washington, D.C., 1977), 2191–2202; D. J. C. Crawley to Sir Saville Garner, Commonwealth Relations Office, Sept. 29, 1954, FO 371, file 112212, doc. DL10345/14, PRO.

39. Jawaharlal Nehru to Motitlal Nehru, September 22, 1911, in Sarvepalli Gopal, ed., *The Selected Works of Jawaharlal Nehru*, ser. 1, vol. 1 (New Delhi, 1972), 92; Sulzberger, *Long Row of Candles*, 541; Central Intelligence Agency, "India-Pakistan," SR-21, September 16, 1948, Truman Papers, PSF; Isaacs, *Scratches on Our Minds*, 312; Bullitt, "Old Ills," 115.

40. Dean Acheson to President Truman, September 12, 1949, Truman Papers, PSF, box 180; M. O. Mathai, *Reminiscences of the Nehru Age* (New Delhi, 1978), 198; Selig S. Harrison, "Nehru's Visit in Retrospect," *New Republic*, December 31, 1956, 7–8; memo of conversation by Acheson, October 12, 1949, Dean Acheson Papers, Memoranda of Conversations, box 64, HSTL; Acheson, *Present at the Creation*, 336.

41. Sarvepalli Gopal, *Jawaharlal Nehru: A Biography*, vol. 2, *1947–1956* (New Delhi, 1979), 60; Sir Archibald Nye to Commonwealth Relations Office, December 9, 1949, FO 371, file 76097, doc. F18771, PRO; Elbert Mathews, interview by Richard McKinzie, June 13, 1975, HSTL.

42. Department of State, "The Circumstances of the Nehru Visit: Background Paper," December 12, 1956, released to author following Freedom of Information Act request; Dwight Eisenhower, Memorandum of conversations with Prime Minister Nehru, December 17–18, 1956, Eisenhower Papers, AWF, IS, box 28, DDEL; *TOI* (Bombay), December 2, 19, 20, 1956; "The Twain Have Met," *The Nation*, January 5, 1957, 1; memo by John Sherman Cooper, December 13, 1956, AWF, IS, box 28, DDEL.

43. Arthur M. Schlesinger, Jr., *A Thousand Days* (Boston, 1965), 526; Galbraith, *Ambassador's Journal*, 220–32; Harry A. Rositzke to John Kenneth Galbraith, n.d. [November 1961], President's Office Files, India Security, Briefing Book, Box 118a, JFKL; *TOI* (Bombay), November 7–10, 1961; Isaacs, *Scratches on Our Minds*, 303–4.

44. Vivekananda quoted in Tapan Raychaudhuri, *Europe Reconsidered: Perceptions of the West in Nineteenth Century Bengal* (New Delhi, 1988), 267; Isaacs, *Scratches on Our Minds*, 374–75.

45. Partha Chatterjee, *Nationalist Thought and the Colonial World: A Derivative Discourse* (Minneapolis, 1993 [1986]); Sinha, "Reading Mother India," 6–7.

46. M. S. Venkataramani, "The Evolution of Indian Images of American Political Motivations," in Glazer and Glazer, *Conflicting Images*, 27.

47. Gupta, *Great Encounter*, 212, 214; "Report on Western Films" by a British observer in India, n.d. [early 1953], Bowles Papers, box 112, folder 500; Chester Bowles, "How to Win Friends and Influence Asia," *New York Times Magazine*, January 4, 1953, 10; *TOI* (Bombay), May 12, 1961. In his novel *Midnight's Children*, Salman Rushdie creates a wonderful inversion: an Indian film called *Gai-Wallah* (Cow-Fellow), an "eastern Western" in which the portly hero rides the range (the Indo-Gangetic plain), vanquishing cattlemen in order to liberate the sacred cows. Salman Rushdie, *Midnight's Children* (New York, 1980), 51.

48. Constance Classen, David Howes, Anthony Synnott, *Aroma: The Cultural History of Smell* (London, 1994), 168; *TOI* (Bombay), January 31, 1954; Rushdie, *Midnight's Children*; David Shulman, "The Scent of Memory in Hindu South India," *Res* 13 (spring 1987): 131.

49. Stephen A. Tyler, *India: An Anthropological Perspective* (Prospect Heights, Ill., 1986), 2; P. E. Dustoor, *American Days: A Traveller's Diary* (Bombay, 1952), 17–18; *TOI* (Bombay), December 20, 1956.

50. Gita Mehta, *Karma Cola: Marketing the Mysterious East* (New York, 1979), 93; Roshan

Lal Sharma, *Holy Men and Holy Cows: The Adventures and Philosophies of an Americanized Hindu* (New York, 1968), n.p.; Shridharani, *My India, My America*, 55–56.

51. Prescott Childs to Department of State, December 7, 1951, RG 59, 611.91/12-751, box 2858, NA.

52. Shridharani, *My India, My America*, 143; Pearl S. Buck, "Questions Indians Ask Me," *Asia and the Americas*, May 1946, 203; Nayantara Sahgal, *Prison and Chocolate Cake* (New York, 1954), 160; Cynthia Bowles, *At Home in India* (New York, 1956), 28; McGhee, *Envoy to the Middle World*, 103–4; Deepak Lal, "Manners, Morals, and Materialism: Some Indian Perceptions of America and Great Britain," in Sulochana Raghavan Glazer and Nathan Glazer, eds., *Conflicting Images: India and the United States* (Glenn Dale, Md., 1990), 274.

53. Mehta, *Karma Cola*, 84–85; Tyler, *India*, 78–80; G. Morris Carstairs, *The Twice-Born: A Study of a Community of High-Caste Hindus* (Bloomington, 1961), 107; Douglas, *Purity and Danger*, 9.

54. Dustoor, *American Days*, 35; Raychaudhuri, *Europe Reconsidered*, 303, 305; Corbin, *Foul and the Fragrant*, 178; Goffman, *Relations in Public*, 53–54; Shridharani, *My India, My America*, 53, 136; David Arnold, "Touching the Body: Perspectives on the Indian Plague, 1896–1900," in Ranajit Guha, ed., *Subaltern Studies V: Writings on South Asian History and Society* (New Delhi, 1987), 55–90.

55. John J. Macdonald to Secretary of State, October 6, 1947, RG 59, 845.00/10-647, box 6071, NA; *TOI* (Bombay), November 13, 1953; Record of conversation between Sir Girja Bajpai and Frank Roberts, November 13, 1948, FO 371, file 69724, doc. F16460, PRO; J. D. Murray to B. A. B. Burrows, June 18, 1951, FO 371, file 93018, doc. FZ1023/20, PRO; document prepared in American Embassy, New Delhi, August 23, 1950, RG 59, 611.91/8-2350, box 2857, NA; Gopal, *Jawaharlal Nehru*, 2:274.

56. Chester Bowles to David Bruce, February 5, 1953, Bowles Papers, box 94, folder 236; *TOI* (Bombay), December 30, 1953; Shridharani, *My India, My America*, 54–55; Dustoor, *American Days*, 254.

57. Tyler, *India*, 3, 6; *TOI* (Bombay), January 12, 1954; December 3, 1956; Memo for the ambassador by E. A. Gilmore, July 16, 1950, RG 84, Foreign Service Posts of the Department of State: India General Records, box 56, WNRC.

58. Kusum Nair, "Galbraith in India," *Harper's*, December 1961, 46–54; memo of conversation by E. P. Maffitt, November 21, 1949, RG 59, Lot File 54D341: Records of the Office of South Asian Affairs, 1939–53, box 19, NA; Bowles, *Ambassador's Report*, 113; Frank Roberts to Sir Cecil Syers, February 9, 1950, FO 371, file 84211, doc. FL1015/110, PRO; Mathai, *Reminiscences of the Nehru Age*, 107.

59. Gopal, *Jawaharlal Nehru*, 2:226.

60. Dustoor, *American Days*, 244–45; Gupta, *Great Encounter*, 235; *TOI* (Bombay), November 28, 1956; Raychaudhuri, *Europe Reconsidered*, 310; George Merrell to Secretary of State, June 10, 1946, *FRUS* (1946), vol. 5, *The British Commonwealth; Western and Central Europe* (Washington, D.C., 1969), 88–92; Prakash C. Jain, "The Friendly Americans," *Saturday Evening Post*, July 23, 1960, 70.

61. Jain, "Friendly Americans," 24; John J. Macdonald to Secretary of State, August 1, 1947, RG 59, 711.45/8-147, box 3323, NA; *TOI* (Bombay), December 27, 1953; memo of conversation by Chester Bowles, July 15, 1952, Bowles Papers, box 98, folder 323; Charles D. Withers to Secretary of State, December 8, 1947, RG 59, 845.00/12-847, box 6071, NA.

62. Gary R. Hess, "Accommodation amid Discord: The United States, India, and the Third World," *Diplomatic History*, 16, 1 (1992), 1–22.

63. Arthur Christy, *The Orient in American Transcendentalism* (New York, 1932), 23; Singer, *When a Great Tradition Modernizes*, 11–38; T. J. Jackson Lears, *No Place of Grace: Antimodernism and the Transformation of American Culture, 1880–1920* (New York, 1981), 218–41; Harvey Cox, *Turning East: The Promise and Peril of the New Orientalism* (New York, 1977).

64. M. S. Venkataramani and B. K. Shrivastava, *Quit India: The American Response to the 1942 Struggle* (New Delhi, 1979); idem, *Roosevelt, Gandhi, Churchill: America and the Last Phase*

of India's Freedom Struggle (New Delhi, 1983); Gary R. Hess, *America Encounters India, 1941–1947* (Baltimore, 1971); Kenton J. Clymer, "Franklin D. Roosevelt, Louis Johnson, India, and Anticolonialism: Another Look," *Pacific Historical Review* 57 (August 1988): 261–84; idem, "Jawaharlal Nehru and the United States: The Preindependence Years," *Diplomatic History* 14, 2 (1990): 143–61.

65. Minute by J. E. Cable, April 1, 1954, FO 371, file 112212, doc. DL10345/5, PRO; Sir Archibald Nye to FO, October 31, 1950, FO 371, file 84499, doc. FZ10114/108, PRO; Bowles, interview; *Bombay Chronicle*, May 21, 1953; Shridharani, *My India, My America*, 113–14.

66. Paul Berman, "Introduction: The Other and the Almost the Same," in Berman, ed., *Blacks and Jews: Alliances and Arguments* (New York, 1994), 5–6.

67. O. Mannoni, *Prospero and Caliban: The Psychology of Colonization* (New York, 1956), 21; Gupta, *Great Encounter*, 38.

68. Speech by G. L. Mehta to the Academy of Political and Social Science, Philadelphia, April 3, 1954, RG 59, 611.91/4-654, box 2858, NA; Ashis Nandy, *At the Edge of Psychology: Essays in Politics and Culture* (New Delhi, 1980), 47–98.

69. Rushdie, *Midnight's Children*, 341.

1. Strategy

1. Anonymous [Sir Robert Wilson], *A Sketch of the Military and Political Power of Russia, in the Year 1817* (New York, 1817). See the discussion of Wilson's *Sketch* in Peter Hopkirk, *The Great Game: The Struggle for Empire in Central Asia* (New York, 1992).

2. Michael Edwardes, *Playing the Great Game: A Victorian Cold War* (London, 1975).

3. John Lewis Gaddis, "New Conceptual Approaches to the Study of American Foreign Relations: Interdisciplinary Perspectives," *Diplomatic History* 14, 3 (1990): 417–18; idem, *Strategies of Containment: A Critical Appraisal of Postwar American National Security Policy* (New York, 1982), viii. Gaddis's casual association of space and time is problematical, since not everyone sees them as related in the same way. Out of deference to pre-Einsteinian physics, I'll treat ideas about space in this chapter, ideas about time in the next.

4. Alastair Iain Johnston, *Cultural Realism: Strategic Culture and Grand Strategy in Chinese History* (Princeton, 1995), 16–17.

5. Ibid., 1–6.

6. Bernard S. Cohn, *An Anthropologist among the Historians and Other Essays* (New York, 1987), 51; William Appleman Williams, *America Confronts a Revolutionary World, 1776–1976* (New York, 1976), 42.

7. Drew R. McCoy, *The Elusive Republic: Political Economy in Jeffersonian America* (Chapel Hill, 1980); Thomas R. Hietala, *Manifest Design: Anxious Aggrandizement in Late Jacksonian America* (Ithaca, 1985); Walter LaFeber, *The New Empire: An Interpretation of American Expansion 1860–1898* (Ithaca, 1963); William Appleman Williams, *The Tragedy of American Diplomacy*, 2d ed. (New York, 1972), 202–75.

8. Jawaharlal Nehru, *An Autobiography* (London, 1936), 15.

9. Lattimore quoted in Ainslie Embry, *Imagining India: Essays on Indian History*, ed. Mark Juergensmeyer (New York, 1989), 131. To some Indians, the external was simply unimaginable. After talking for some days with villagers in Gujarat, the American journalist John Frederick Muehl concluded: "I had discovered . . . that it was foolish to talk about the influence of outside forces in the villages; Khan's own statement seemed almost axiomatically true: 'In India there are no outside forces.' " John Frederick Muehl, *Interview with India* (New York, 1950), 143.

10. Sudhir Kakar, *The Inner World: A Psycho-Analytic Study of Childhood and Society in India*, 2d ed. (New Delhi, 1981), 48–50.

11. R. F. Gombrich, "Ancient Indian Cosmology," in Carmen Blacker and Michael Loewe, eds., *Ancient Cosmologies* (London, 1975), 125–27; Friedhelm Hardy, *The Religious Culture of India: Power, Love, Wisdom* (Cambridge, 1994), 29.

12. Hardy, *Religious Culture of India*, 53, 62, 68–72, 133, 167, 178, 189; Herbert Stroup, *Like a Great River: An Introduction to Hinduism* (New York, 1972), 47–48, 129–30; Robert Kanigel, *The Man Who Knew Infinity: A Life of the Genius Ramanujan* (New York, 1991), 174, 185–88, 316, 329; speech by G. L. Mehta in New York, May 17, 1953, Dorothy Norman Papers, ser. 4, box 2, Syracuse University Library.

13. Alan Roland, *In Search of Self in India and Japan: Toward a Cross-Cultural Psychology* (Princeton, 1988), 245; Gita Mehta, *Karma Cola: Marketing the Mysterious East* (New York, 1979), 84–85.

14. Louis J. Halle, *The Cold War as History* (New York, 1967), 23, 152, 154; Gaddis, *Strategies of Containment*, 91, 131; Stephen E. Ambrose, *Rise to Globalism: American Foreign Policy since 1938*, 4th ed. (New York, 1985), 180.

15. Sir Archibald Nye to Secretary of State (SOS) for Commonwealth Relations, May 21, 1951, Foreign Office (FO) 371, file 92870, doc. FL1022/11/G, Public Record Office (PRO), Kew, England. See also Nye to Commonwealth Relations Office (CRO), March 2, 1950, FO 371, File 84252, doc. FL1011/5, PRO.

16. Hopkirk, *The Great Game*, 33–34, 304; Hossain Shahid Faroqui, "In the Shadow of Globalism: The United States, South Asia, and the Cold War, 1939–1953" (Ph.D. diss., Cornell University, 1986), 143–44.

17. Hopkirk, *The Great Game*, 422–25, 500.

18. Ibid., 175–87, 465–69, 483–501; Edward Rice, *Captain Sir Richard Francis Burton* (New York, 1990), 30; Algernon Durand, *The Making of a Frontier* (Karachi, 1977), 2–3, 41–43.

19. Hopkirk, *The Great Game*, 519–21; Faroqui, "In the Shadow of Globalism," 145–46; Robert H. Donaldson, *Soviet Policy toward India: Ideology and Strategy* (Cambridge, Mass., 1974), 6–7.

20. Robert C. Tucker, "The Cold War in Stalin's Time: What the New Sources Reveal," *Diplomatic History* 21, 2 (1997): 278–79; Vladislav Zubok, "Stalin's Plans and Russian Archives," ibid., 295–97; Odd Arne Westad, "Secrets of the Second World: The Russian Archives and the Reinterpretation of Cold War History," ibid., 266; Vladislav Zubok and Constantine Pleshakov, *Inside the Kremlin's Cold War: From Stalin to Khrushchev* (Cambridge, Mass., 1996), 69.

21. Zubok, "Stalin's Plans," 296–97; Donaldson, *Soviet Policy toward India*, 61–113; Nikita Khrushchev, *Khrushchev Remembers*, ed. and trans. Strobe Talbott (Boston, 1974), 306–11.

22. W. Roger Louis, *Imperialism at Bay: The United States and the Decolonization of the British Empire 1941–1945* (New York, 1978); Lord Gladwyn, *The Memoirs of Lord Gladwyn* (New York, 1972), 208; note of discussion between Archibald Nye and Raymond Hare, May 25, 1949, FO 371, file 76090, doc. F8014, PRO.

23. Joint memo by Ernest Bevin and Lord Pethick-Lawrence, August 30, 1946, L/P & S/12/4645, Collection 48, India Office Library (IOL), London; minute by illegible initialer, April 22, 1948, L/P & S/12/4646, ibid.; Jawaharlal Nehru, "India's Foreign Policy," March 8, 1948, in Sarvepalli Gopal, ed., *Selected Works of Jawaharlal Nehru* (SWJN), 2d. ser., vol. 5 (New Delhi, 1987), 495–507; Charles H. Heimsath and Surjit Mansingh, *A Diplomatic History of Modern India* (Bombay, 1971), 45–46.

24. Lord Inverchapel to FO, January 5, 1948, FO 371, file 69705, doc. F278, PRO; Sir Alexander Cadogan to FO, November 26, 1948, file 69724, doc. F16653, ibid.; P. F. Grey to FO, November 27, 1948, file 69725, doc. F16691, ibid.

25. SANACC 360/14, "Report by the SANACC Subcommittee for the Near and Middle East," April 19, 1949, U.S., Department of State, *Foreign Relations of the United States* (*FRUS*), 1949, vol. 6, *The Near East, South Asia, and Africa* (Washington, D.C., 1977), 8–31.

26. Ibid.; Minutes of 42nd Meeting of National Security Council (NSC), June 16, 1949, Harry S. Truman Papers, President's Secretary's File (PSF), National Security Council Meetings, box 206, Harry S. Truman Library (HSTL), Independence, Mo.; NSC 48/1, December 30, 1949, U.S. Congress, House of Representatives, Committee on Armed Services, *U. S.-Vietnam Relations, 1945–1967: A Study Prepared by the Department of Defense*, vol. 8 (Washington, D.C. 1971), 272.

27. Gaddis, *Strategies of Containment*, 89–126.

28. Dennis Merrill, *Bread and the Ballot: The United States and India's Economic Development* (Chapel Hill, 1990), 169–203; W. W. Rostow, *Eisenhower, Kennedy and Foreign Aid* (Austin, 1985); Elbert G. Mathews, interview by Richard McKinzie, June 13, 1975, HSTL.

29. Henry Grady to SOS, March 20, 1948, *FRUS* (1948), vol. 5, *The Near East, South Asia, and Africa* (Washington, D.C., 1975), 498–99; memo of conversation by Joseph S. Sparks, May 10, 1948, ibid., 508–10; memo of conversation by Sparks, October 19, 1949, ibid., 1752–56; memo of conversation by Sparks, September 21, 1948, RG 59, Lot File 54D341: Records of Office of South Asian Affairs, 1939–53, box 18, National Archives (NA), Washington, D.C.; Elbert Mathews to McGhee, March 2, 1949, ibid.; Dean Acheson to Louis Johnson, May 17, 1949, RG 59, FW845.20/6-749, box 6114; McGhee to John H. Ohly, August 9, 1950, RG 59, Lot 54D341, box 17; Norwood W. Watts to Richard D. Gatewood, September 28, 1950, ibid.

30. George McGhee to Philip Jessup, August 29, 1951, RG 59, Lot 54D341, box 18; Chester Bowles to Jessup, December 6, 1951, Chester Bowles Papers, box 95, folder 262, Yale University Library, New Haven; memo of conversation by John D. Hickerson, January 22, 1952, RG 59, Lot 57D259, box 6.

31. Sir L. Grafftey Smith to CRO, December 9, 1947, FO 371, file 69728, doc. F234, PRO; FO to Embassy in Washington, February 7, 1949, FO 371, file 76103, doc. F2070, PRO; memo of conversation by Sir William Strang, February 22, 1950, FO 371, file 84212, doc. FL1015/130, PRO; Franks to FO, May 19, 1950, FO 371, file 84255, doc. FL10118/101, PRO; memo of conversation by George McGhee, November 1, 1950, RG 59, Lot 54D341, box 25; record of conversation at FO with McGhee, April 3, 1951, FO 371, file 92875, doc. FL1027/1, PRO.

32. Memo by Stephen J. Spingarn, August 23, 1949, Stephen J. Spingarn Papers, box 19, HSTL; DOS, "Policy Statement: Pakistan," April 3, 1950, *FRUS* (1950), 5:1490–99; Olaf Caroe, *Wells of Power: The Oilfields of South-Western Asia* (London, 1951), 166–67.

33. Caroe, *Wells of Power*, 169, 188–92.

34. "Indian and Pakistan in Relation to Middle East Defence," CRO, n.d. [June 1951], FO 371, file 92875, doc. FL1027/2, PRO; memo by Burton Y. Berry, March 20, 1951, *FRUS* (1951), 6:1664–88; DOS Policy Statement, "Pakistan," July 1, 1951, ibid., 2208; Chester Bowles to Thomas E. Morgan, March 24, 1959, John F. Kennedy Papers, President's Office Files (POF), Special Correspondence (SC), box 28, John F. Kennedy Library (JFKL), Boston.

35. Record of conversation between P. C. Gordon-Walker and Zafrulla Khan, August 30, 1951, FO 371, file 92875, doc. FL1027/6, PRO; memo of conversation by George McGhee and memo of conversation by Thomas W. Simons, October 18, 1951, *FRUS* (1951), 6:2220–24.

36. Memo of conversation by Dean Acheson, October 22, 1951; memo of conversation by Lee E. Metcalf, November 16, 1951; memo of conversation by Acheson, November 17, 1951, *FRUS* (1951), 6:2225–28.

37. Minute by J. D. Murray, October 11, 1951, FO 371, file 92875, doc. FL1027/8/G, PRO; FO to Embassy in Washington, December 12, 1951, FO 371, file 92876, doc. FL1027/19, PRO; B. A. B. Burrows to FO, December 19, 1951, FO 371, file 92876, doc. FL1027/29, PRO.

38. Minute by H. H. Phillips, February 14, 1952, FO 371, file 101198, doc. FY1023/2/G, PRO; Burton Y. Berry to Loy Henderson, February 9, 1951, *FRUS* (1951), 6:2115–17; memo of conversation by Dean Acheson, July 18, 1952, Dean Acheson Papers, box 67, HSTL; memo of conversation by Acheson, January 13, 1953, Acheson Papers, box 67a, HSTL; Faroqui, "In the Shadow of Globalism," 364; Robert J. McMahon, *The Cold War on the Periphery: The United States, India, and Pakistan* (New York, 1994), 151.

39. Memo of discussion at special meeting of the NSC, March 31, 1953, Eisenhower Papers, Ann Whitman Files (AWF), NSC Series, box 4, Dwight D. Eisenhower Library (DDEL), Abilene, Kans.; CRO paper, "Proposed United States Military Aid for Pakistan," n.d. [Octo-

ber 1953], FO 371, file 106935, doc. FY1192/14, PRO; memo by Dulles, n.d. [January 4, 1954], John Foster Dulles Papers, Memoranda Series, box 1, DDEL; memo of conversation by Dulles, January 5, 1954, *FRUS* (1952–54), vol. 11, *Africa and South Asia* (Washington, D.C., 1983), 1838–39; Mohammad Ayub Khan, *Friends Not Masters: A Political Autobiography* (London, 1967), 130; McMahon, *Cold War on the Periphery*, 154–88.

40. John Foster Dulles to President Eisenhower, n.d. [January 4, 1954], Dulles Papers, Memoranda Series, box 1, DDEL; NIE 53–56, "Probable Developments in Afghanistan's International Position," January 10, 1956, *FRUS* (1955–57), vol. 8, *South Asia* (Washington, D.C., 1987), 217–19; discussion at the 285th Meeting of the NSC, May 17, 1956, released to author following Freedom of Information Act request; Chester Bowles to Thomas E. Morgan, March 24, 1959, Kennedy Papers, POF, SC, box 28, JFKL. On Afghanistan generally, see Anthony Arnold, *Afghanistan: The Soviet Invasion in Perspective*, rev. ed. (Stanford, 1985), 32–44; Brian Holden Reid, "The 'Northern Tier' and the Baghdad Pact," in John W. Young, ed., *The Foreign Policy of Churchill's Peacetime Administration 1951–1955* (Leicester, 1988), 159–79; Leon B. Poullada, "The Road to Crisis 1919–1980: American Failures, Afghan Errors and Soviet Successes," in Rosanne Klass, ed., *Afghanistan: The Great Game Revisited*, rev. ed. (New York, 1990), 37–69.

41. Memo by H. Struve Hensel, February 17, 1955, *FRUS* (1955–57), 8:418–20; memo of discussion at 280th meeting of the NSC, March 22, 1956, Eisenhower Papers, AWF, NSC Series, box 7; memo of discussion at 308th meeting of the NSC, January 3, 1957, *FRUS* (1955–57), 8:25–26; Neville Maxwell, *India's China War* (London, 1970), 214.

42. NIE-79, "Probable Developments in South Asia," June 30, 1953, *FRUS* (1952–54), 11:1083; James M. Langley to William Rountree, December 27, 1957, *FRUS* (1955–57), 8:488–89; Chief of U.S. Element, CENTO, to Joint Chiefs of Staff, June 4, 1962, Kennedy Papers, National Security Files (NSF), Regional Security Series (RSS), box 211, JFKL; G. W. Choudhury, *India, Pakistan, Bangladesh, and the Major Powers* (New York, 1975), 26; McMahon, *Cold War on the Periphery*, 175.

43. Column by Alastair Cooke, printed in the *Times of India* (*TOI*), Bombay, January 8, 1954.

44. Embry, *Imagining India*, 187; P. A. Clutterback to CRO, November 30, 1953, FO 371, file 106936, doc. FY1192/52, PRO; George V. Allen to SOS, December 2, 1953, RG 59, 611.91/12-353, NA; Allen to DOS, February 24, 1954, *FRUS* (1952–54), 11:1737–39; *TOI* (Bombay), November 6, 16; December 12, 16, 1953; *Hindustan Times* (*HT*), New Delhi, March 2, 11, 1954.

45. *HT* (New Delhi), March 4, 1954.

46. *TOI* (Bombay), November 17, 1953; January 4, 1954; *HT* (New Delhi), March 21, 1954; Jawaharlal Nehru, *India's Foreign Policy* (New Delhi, 1961), 271.

47. Draft letter by Loy Henderson, August 11, 1976, Loy Henderson Papers, box 9, Library of Congress, Washington, D.C.; memo of conversation by Elbert Mathews, April 2, 1948, *FRUS* (1948), 5:503; M. E. Dening to Archibald Nye, March 15, 1951, FO 371, file 92870, doc. FL1022/10/G, PRO; George V. Allen to DOS, November 25, 1954, *FRUS* (1952–54), 11:1781–83.

48. George V. Allen's presentation to the NSC, October 27, 1958, Eisenhower Papers, White House Office of Special Assistant for National Security Affairs (WHOSANSA), OCB Series, Subject Subseries, box 3, DDEL. My thanks to Thomas Borstelmann for sharing this document with me.

49. Jawaharlal Nehru, *The Discovery of India* (Calcutta, 1946), 580; Dwight D. Eisenhower to Jawaharlal Nehru, November 5, 1956, Eisenhower Papers, AWF, International Series (IS), box 26, DDEL; "Background Paper: U.S.-Indian Relations," n.d. [May 1961], Kennedy Papers, National Security Files, Trips and Conferences Series, box 242, JFKL; John Kenneth Galbraith, *Ambassador's Journal: A Personal Account of the Kennedy Years* (Boston, 1969), 89.

50. Chester Bowles, interview by Neal Gold, 1963, Bowles Papers, box 396, folder 178; Loy Henderson to SOS, December 22, 1948, *FRUS* (1948), 5:520–21; Donald Kennedy to George McGhee, December 27, 1950, RG 59, Lot File 54D341, box 18, NA.

51. K. P. S. Menon, interview, Nehru Memorial Museum and Library (NMML), New Delhi; K. M. Panikkar to Dillon Ripley, January 5, 1950 [1951], RG 59, Lot File 57D259, box 7, NA; "Indian-Tibetan Relations," n.d. [January 1951?], RG 59, Lot File 57D259, box 7, NA. As Chester Bowles observed, India's fear of the PRC "is partially compensated for by a subconscious and vicarious thrill at the spectacle of a new and strong Asian power which has thrown off the domination of white westerners and is able to deal with them on equal terms"; see memo of conversation by Bowles, July 15, 1952, Bowles Papers, box 98, folder 323.

52. This account of the Border War is based on Maxwell, *India's China War,* quotations are on 74, 314, 361, 444, 448, 489. See also Sarvepalli Gopal, *Jawaharlal Nehru: A Biography,* vol. 3, *1956–1964* (New Delhi, 1984), 204–39; B. M. Kaul, *The Untold Story* (Bombay, 1967); J. P. Dalvi, *Himalayan Blunder* (Bombay, 1969); Galbraith, *Ambassador's Journal,* 428–93; *FRUS* (1961–63), vol. 19, *South Asia* (Washington, D.C., 1996), 340–517.

53. Maxwell, *India's China War,* 125, 407.

54. Gopal, *Jawaharlal Nehru,* 223; Stanley Wolpert, *Nehru: Tryst with Destiny* (New York, 1996), 488.

55. John F. Kennedy to Jawaharlal Nehru, October 22, 1962, Kennedy Papers, POF, Countries Series (CS), box 118a, JFKL; memorandum on U.S. Policy in the Sino-Indian Conflict, November 3, 1962, Roger Hilsman Papers, CS, box 1, JFKL; Thomas L. Hughes to Kennedy, November 21, 1962, Hilsman Papers, CS, box 1, JFKL; Kennedy to Averell Harriman, November 24, 1962, Kennedy Papers, POF, CS, box 118a, JFKL; memorandum by McGeorge Bundy, May 10, 1963, Kennedy Papers, NSF, Meetings and Memoranda Series, box 314, JFKL; memo of conversation by Dean Rusk, May 17, 1963, *FRUS* (1961–63), 19:599–600; U.S. House, Hearings before the Committee on Foreign Affairs, April 30, 1963, 88th Cong., 1st session (Washington, D.C., 1963), 430.

56. Gopal, *Jawaharlal Nehru,* 251–55; Sudhir Ghosh to Nehru, December 31, 1962, and Nehru to Ghosh, January 5, 1963, Kennedy Papers, POF, CS, box 118a, JFKL; Hubert Humphrey to the President, March 26, 1963, ibid.; memo by Chester Bowles, May 4, 1963, Kennedy Papers, NSF, Meetings and Memoranda Series, box 314, JFKL.

2. Economics

1. David Dean Shulman, *Tamil Temple Myths: Sacrifice and Divine Marriage in the South Indian Saiva Tradition* (Princeton, 1980), 146–47. I am grateful to J. C. Kaimal for telling me this myth.

2. S. Nallaperumal, "Mineral Sands of Travancore," *Indian Express,* Madras, September 10, 1950; Jonathan E. Helmreich, *Gathering Rare Ores: The Diplomacy of Uranium Acquisition, 1943–1954* (Princeton, 1986), 51; Alfred E. Eckes, Jr., *The United States and the Global Struggle for Minerals* (Austin, 1979), 126.

3. See, for example, Charles Wolf, Jr., *Foreign Aid: Theory and Practice in Southern Asia* (Princeton, 1960); W. W. Rostow, *Eisenhower, Kennedy and Foreign Aid* (Austin, 1985); and Dennis Merrill, *Bread and the Ballot: The United States and India's Economic Development* (Chapel Hill, 1990).

4. Amy Kaplan, "Domesticating Foreign Policy," *Diplomatic History* 18, 1 (1994): 97–105.

5. Milton Singer, *When a Great Tradition Modernizes: An Anthropological Approach to Indian Civilization* (Chicago, 1972), 16; Harold R. Isaacs, *Scratches on Our Minds: American Views of China and India* (New York, 1958), 243–49, 280; Hans Mattson to John Davis, December 23, 1882, Department of State (DOS), *Despatches of U.S. Consuls in Calcutta, 1792–1906* (microfilm), University of California–Berkeley Library; "Regional Policy Statement: South Asia," October 9, 1950, DOS, *Foreign Relations of the United States (FRUS),* 1950, vol. 5, *The Near East, South Asia and Africa* (Washington, D.C., 1978), 246.

6. Robert B. Minturn, Jr., *From New York to Delhi* (New York, 1858), 128.

7. Katherine Mayo, *Mother India* (New York, 1927), 401.

8. Jessup's notes on meetings in New Delhi, February 23, 1950, Record Group (RG) 59, 611.91/2-1750, box 2857, National Archives (NA), Washington, D.C.; minute by F. C. Benham, October 24, 1949, Foreign Office (FO) 371, file 76097, doc. F18749, Public Record Office (PRO), Kew, England; John Kenneth Galbraith, *Ambassador's Journal: A Personal Account of the Kennedy Years* (Boston, 1969), 156.

9. S. Simpson to J. M. Clayton, April 16, 1850, DOS, *Despatches of U.S. Consuls at Bombay, 1838–1906* (microfilm), University of California–Berkeley Library; Minturn, *From New York to Delhi*, 300–303.

10. Philip Noel-Baker to FO, January 27, 1948, FO 371, file 69707, doc. F1391, PRO; Richard P. Butrick to DOS, May 4, 1953, RG 59, 611.91/5-453, DOS, NA; Eugene Braderman to John Loftus, January 6, 1953, Chester Bowles Papers, box 107, folder 435, Yale University Library, New Haven, Conn.; minute by Peter Murray September 19, 1947, FO 371, file 63569, doc. 12685, PRO.

11. Merrill, *Bread and the Ballot*, 12; Raymond Williams, *Keywords: A Vocabulary of Culture and Society*, rev. ed. (New York, 1983), 103; George Lakoff, "Metaphor and War," *East Bay Express*, February 22, 1991, 13.

12. Hans Mattson to Robert R. Hill, January 18, 1882, *Despatches from U.S. Consuls in Calcutta*; NSC 5409, n.d. [February 19, 1954], *FRUS* (1952–54), vol. 11, *Africa and South Asia* (Washington, D.C., 1983), 1107; Rostow, *Eisenhower, Kennedy, and Foreign Aid*, 45; idem, *The Stages of Economic Growth: A Non-Communist Manifesto*, 2d ed. (Cambridge, Mass., 1971).

13. *Times of India* (*TOI*), Bombay, December 14, 1959; statement by Ambassador-Designate John Kenneth Galbraith, April 8, 1961, John Kenneth Galbraith Papers, Ambassador to India File: 1961–63, box 79, John F. Kennedy Library (JFKL), Boston. Michael Hunt analyzes American cartoons that depict Asians as petulant and ungrateful children. Missing from Hunt's interpretation of these images is a recognition that the characters, while small in stature and childish in their behavior, have the faces of old people; they are simultaneously young and old. Michael H. Hunt, *Ideology and U.S. Foreign Policy* (New Haven, 1987), 76–77, 86–87.

14. Ashis Nandy, *The Intimate Enemy: Loss and Recovery of Self under Colonialism* (New Delhi, 1983), 17; A. L. Basham, *The Wonder That Was India: A Survey of the Culture of the Indian Sub-Continent before the Coming of the Muslims* (New York, 1959); Merle Curti, "My Discovery of America in India," *The American Scholar*, autumn 1947, 429; transcript of interview with Elbert Mathews and others on television show *Facts We Face*, April 9, 1951, FO 371, file 93018, doc. FZ1023/19, PRO; Marie Buck to "Friends," April 13, 1952, Dorothy Norman Papers, ser. 1, box 1, Syracuse University Library.

15. George R. Merrell to Secretary of State (SOS), March 26, 1946, RG 59, 711.45/3-2646, NA; Dean Acheson to Loy Henderson, April 21, 1950, *FRUS* (1950), 5:1466.

16. Alain Corbin, *The Foul and the Fragrant: Odor and the French Social Imagination* (Cambridge, 1986), 214. Old Indian civilization could produce childish forms. Undersecretary of State George McGhee described a Hindu temple he visited in 1949: "The buildings were all red and white with flowers and bell-shaped cupolas and whatnots piled on top, looking like something a child would make with blocks." George McGhee, *Envoy to the Middle World: Adventures in Diplomacy* (New York, 1983), 102.

17. The connection between immaturity and a disregard for time came to me at two o'clock one morning when I was trying to soothe my infant daughter, who unlike me had no interest in going to sleep. My thanks to Sophie Kaimal Rotter for this insight.

18. Mircea Eliade, *Myths, Rites, Symbols*, vol. 1 (New York, 1976), 5; T. N. Madan, "India in American Anthropology," in Nathan Glazer and Sulochana Raghavan Glazer, eds., *Conflicting Images: India and the United States* (Glenn Dale, Md., 1990), 191–94; Stephen Kern, *The Culture of Time and Space 1880–1918* (Cambridge, 1983), 1, 19; R. S. Khare, "The Concept of Time and Time-Reckoning among the Hindus: An Anthropological Viewpoint," *Eastern Anthropologist* 20, 1 (1967), 48; George Lakoff and Mark Johnson, *Metaphors We Live By* (Chicago, 1980), 7–9; Alan Roland, *In Search of Self in India and Japan: Toward a Cross-Cultural Psy-*

chology (Princeton, 1988), 11–12; G. Morris Carstairs, *The Twice-Born: A Study of a Community of High-Caste Hindus* (Bloomington, 1961), 48.

19. Lloyd I. and Susanne Hoeber Rudolph, *The Modernity of Tradition: Political Development in India* (Chicago, 1967), 222; Abbé J. A. Dubois, *Hindu Manners, Customs and Ceremonies*, 3d ed. (Oxford, 1905), 321; Bayard Taylor, *A Visit to India, China, and Japan in the Year 1853* (New York, 1891), 162; Price Collier, *The West in the East* (New York, 1911), 44, 253–54.

20. Katherine Mayo, *Mother India* (New York, 1927), 295.

21. Nandy, *Intimate Enemy*, 15–16; Rudyard Kipling, "His Chance in Life," *Plain Tales from the Hills* (Oxford, 1987), 61; Stanley Wolpert, *Jinnah of Pakistan* (New Delhi, 1984), 276; Robert W. Rydell, *All the World's a Fair* (Chicago, 1984), 178; Stuart Creighton Miller, *"Benevolent Assimilation": The American Conquest of the Philippines, 1899–1903* (New Haven, 1982), 55; Hunt, *Ideology and U.S. Foreign Policy*, 166.

22. Chester Bowles, *Ambassador's Report* (London, 1954), 61.

23. Joseph Satterthwaite to SOS, October 5, 1948, RG 59, 845.002/10-548, box 6114, NA; Loy Henderson to Joseph Sparks, July 23, 1949, RG 59, Lot File 54D341: Records of the Office of South Asian Affairs, 1939–53, box 19, NA; Henderson to DOS, February 6, 1950, RG 59, 611.91/2-650, box 2857, NA.

24. J. G. Parsons and S. K. C. Kopper to SOS, October 14, 1948, RG 59, 845.002/10-1448, box 6114, NA; DOS Policy Statement, "India," May 20, 1948, RG 59, 711.45/4-248, box 3323, NA; minute by M. Esler Dening, January 31, 1949, file 76098, doc. F2069, ibid.; minute by L. A. C. Fry, June 2, 1950, file 84219, doc. FL1015/244, ibid.; note by R. A. Burrows, December 23, 1953, file 106937, doc. FY1192/88(A), ibid.; *TOI* (Bombay), December 17, 1953; Chester Bowles to Donald Kennedy, January 22, 1953, Bowles Papers, box 95, folder 268.

25. *Hindustan Times* (*HT*), New Delhi, January 3, 1954.

26. Kusum Nair, "Galbraith in India," *Harper's*, December 1961, 46–54; Ernest Fisk to DOS, June 9, 1947, RG 59, 711.45/6-947, box 3323, NA.

27. *TOI* (Bombay), December 7, 1950.

28. Memo of conversation by E. P. Maffitt, November 21, 1949, RG 59, Lot File 54D341, box 19, NA; M. O. Mathai, *Reminiscences of the Nehru Age* (New Delhi, 1978), 107; Loy Henderson to Dean Acheson, January 8, 1949, RG 59, 711.45/1-849, box 3323, NA; Henderson to A. R. Field, June 7, 1978, Loy Henderson Papers, box 8, Library of Congress, Washington, D.C.; memo by Nehru, July 29, 1949, MEA, file 45–192/49, National Archives of India; Nehru address in New York, October 19, 1949, in Jawaharlal Nehru, *India's Foreign Policy* (New Delhi, 1961), 597; George V. Allen to DOS, November 12, 1954, *FRUS* (1952–54), 11:1778–79.

29. Krishnalal Shridharani, *My India, My America* (Garden City, 1943), 118–21, 174–75; P. E. Dustoor, *American Days: A Traveller's Diary* (Bombay, 1952), 40; *TOI* (Bombay), December 4, 1950; Deepak Lal, "Manners, Morals, and Materialism: Some Indian Perceptions of America and Great Britain," in Glazer and Glazer, *Conflicting Images*, 274.

30. P. A. Clutterbuck to Commonwealth Relations Office, December 30, 1953, FO 371, file 106937, doc. FY1192/102, PRO; Sarvepalli Gopal, *Jawaharlal Nehru: A Biography*, vol. 2, *1947–1956* (New Delhi, 1979), 44, 63, 101; Taya Zinkin, *Reporting India* (London, 1962), 211.

31. *TOI* (Bombay), May 21, 1950; January 2, 1954; Sarvepalli Gopal, ed., *The Selected Works of Jawaharlal Nehru* (*SWJN*), 1st ser., vol. 14 (New Delhi, 1982), 623, 626–27; 2d ser., vol. 2 (New Delhi, 1985), 501; Jawaharlal Nehru, *Jawaharlal Nehru's Speeches*, vol. 1 (New Delhi, 1949), 25–27; Nehru to Frances Gunther, September 5, 1945, Frances Gunther Papers, File 190, Jawaharlal Nehru Memorial Museum and Library (NMML), New Delhi; proposal by V. B. Naidu, December 9, 1948, All India Congress Committee Papers, file 8, part 2, NMML; Willard Thorp to New Delhi Embassy, March 22, 1948, RG 84, India, New Delhi Embassy, Top Secret General Records, box 1, Washington National Records Center (WNRC), Suitland, Md.; Nehru, *India's Foreign Policy*, 590–91; Joseph Sparks to Donald

Kennedy, March 16, 1950, RG 59, Lot File 54D341, box 18, NA; George V. Allen to DOS, May 21, 1953, *FRUS* (1952–54), 11:1694–95.

32. Incidental Intelligence Report, May 7, 1947, FO 371, file 63534, doc. 7288, PRO; John Kenneth Galbraith to President Kennedy, July 11, 1961, President's Office File (POF), Special Correspondence Series (SC), box 29a, JFKL; Hans Mattson to Robert R. Hill, January 18, 1882, *Despatches of Consuls in Calcutta*.

33. Tapan Raychaudhuri, *Europe Reconsidered: Perceptions of the West in Nineteenth Century Bengal* (New Delhi, 1988), 309; Shridharani, *My India, My America*, 118–21, 174–75.

34. R. K. Gupta, *The Great Encounter: A Study of Indo-American Literature and Cultural Relations* (New Delhi, 1986), 3–6; G. Bhagat, *Americans in India 1784–1860* (New York, 1970), ix, 30–31, 106–8; Hossain Shahid Faroqui, "In the Shadow of Globalism: The United States, South Asia, and the Cold War, 1939–1953" (Ph.D. diss., Cornell University, 1986), 118–19; various dispatches of U.S. Consuls at Bombay and Calcutta.

35. Charles H. Heimsath and Surjit Mansingh, *A Diplomatic History of Modern India* (Bombay, 1971), 32; Andrew J. Rotter, *The Path to Vietnam: Origins of the American Commitment to Southeast Asia* (Ithaca, 1987), 49–50; Jawaharlal Nehru interview at Allahabad, June 25, 1945, *SWJN*, 1st ser., 14:437; Nehru to Asaf Ali, October 11, 1946, *SWJN*, 2d ser., vol. 1 (New Delhi, 1984), 516–18.

36. Faroqui, "In the Shadow of Globalism," 222–24, 241; Robert J. McMahon, *The Cold War on the Periphery: The United States, India, and Pakistan* (New York, 1994), 17–19; B. R. Tomlinson, "Indo-British Relations in the Post-Colonial Era: The Sterling Balances Negotiations, 1947–1949," *Journal of Imperial and Commonwealth History* 13, 3 (1985): 151; Chester Bowles to John Allison, April 14, 1952, Bowles Papers, box 93, folder 229.

37. Eckes, *United States and Global Struggle*, 121–73; Mutual Security Program, "Strategic Materials from India Vital to the U.S. Economy and National Defense," n.d. [1951], RG 59, Lot File 57D259, box 8, NA; records of cabinet meetings of November 19 and December 17, 1954, Dwight D. Eisenhower Papers, Ann Whitman File (AWF), Cabinet Series (CS), Dwight D. Eisenhower Library (DDEL), Abilene, Kans.

38. William Fee to DOS, October 16, 1903, *Despatches from Consuls at Bombay*; M. S. Venkataramani, "Manganese as a Factor in Indo-American Relations," *India Quarterly* 14, 2 (1958), 131–54; Eckes, *United States and Global Struggle*, 171; CIA, "Review of the World Situation," December 16, 1948, Truman Papers, National Security Council (NSC) Meetings, President's Secretary's File (PSF), box 205, Harry S. Truman Library (HSTL), Independence, Mo.; "United States and World Reserves and Potential Sources of Selected Minerals and Metals," Papers of the President's Materials Policy Commission (PMPC), June 1951, box 10, HSTL; "Manganese (Preliminary Outline)," n.d. [September 1951], PMPC Papers, box 12, HSTL; DOS, "Policy Statement: India," December 1, 1950, *FRUS* (1950), 5:1479–80; Special Estimate 32, "Consequences of Communist Control over South Asia," October 3, 1952, *FRUS* (1952–54), 11:1062–67; Faroqui, "In the Shadow of Globalism," 260.

39. Burton Berry to SOS, April 3, 1952, RG 59, 411.919/4-352, box 1857, NA; "Manganese: Summary," PMPC Papers, September 25, 1951, box 12; "Commodity Studies," vol. 2, "Manganese," March 24, 1952, ibid., box 28.

40. V. P. Chopra, *India's Industrialization and Mineral Exports* (New Delhi, 1965), 30–31; memo of conversation, December 17, 1948, RG 59, Lot File 54D341, box 18, NA; "India—Manganese," n.d. [September 1951], PMPC Papers, box 12; memo of Interagency Meeting on Indian Steel Problems, January 12, 1960, released to author following Freedom of Information Act (FOIA) request.

41. "India—Manganese"; Interagency Meeting, January 6, 1960; Loyd Steere to DOS, January 28, 1952, RG 59, 891.2546/1-2852, box 5601, NA.

42. Harold Linder to William Pawley, June 1, 1951, RG 59, 891.2546/6-151, box 5601, NA.

43. Helmreich, *Gathering Rare Ores*, 50–51; Henry L. Deimel to DOS, April 3, 1950, RG 59, 891.2546/4-350, box 5601, NA.

44. Memo of conversation, March 13, 1951, RG 59, Lot File 54D341, box 16, NA; Jack K. McFall to Jacob Javits, April 4, 1951, RG 59, 891.2546/4-451, box 5601, NA.

45. Helmreich, *Gathering Rare Ores*, 166–68; Jack McFall to Charles J. Kersten, March 8, 1951, RG 59, Lot File 54D341, box 16, NA; Howard Donovan to DOS, January 2, 1950, RG 59, 891.2546/1-250, box 5600, NA; Loy Henderson to SOS, March 24, 1951, RG 59, 891.2546/3-2451, box 5601, NA; Andrew V. Corry to DOS, March 5, 1953, 891.2546/3-553, ibid.; R. Gordon Arneson to George V. Allen, April 2, 1953, 891.2546, ibid.

A parallel situation developed in uranium. Refining Travancore monazite produced a small amount of uranium, and in July 1951 the Indians found a rich uranium deposit in Bihar. In October 1952, Bhatnagar told William Pawley that India was prepared to trade two tons of uranium for ten tons of American heavy water, in which hydrogen atoms have been replaced by deuterium; heavy water is used to moderate the reaction in a nuclear pile. Gordon Dean, director of the U.S. AEC, replied on January 15, 1953, that while the United States was interested in the offer, its supply of heavy water was insufficient to make the trade "for at least three years." When the Indians made the deal instead with France, the Americans suddenly became more helpful. An American firm, the Vittro Corporation, designed a heavy water plant in Punjab, and the United States later provided an $80 million loan to help India build a nuclear power plant at Tarapur, near Bombay. Documentation on these issues can be found in RG 59, file 891.2546, Box 5601, NA.

46. Howard Donovan to SOS, May 6, 1948, RG 84, India, New Delhi Embassy, Top Secret General Records, box 1, WNRC; Dean Acheson to New Delhi Embassy, September 29, 1950, RG 59, 891.2546/9-2950, box 5601, NA; Loy Henderson to DOS, December 22, 1950, 891.2546/12-2250, ibid.

47. Merrill, *Bread and the Ballot*, 60–71; Jack McFall to Charles J. Kersten, March 8, 1951, RG 59, Lot File 54D341, box 16, NA; Dean Acheson to New Delhi Embassy, April 4, 1951, RG 59, 891.2546/3-2751, box 5601, NA.

48. McFall to Kersten; memo of conversation, March 13, 1951; Acheson (Arneson) to Loy Henderson, March 16, 1951, RG 59, 891.2546/3-1651, box 5601, NA; Acheson (Arneson) to Henderson, March 23, 1951, 891.2546/3-2351, ibid.

49. Merrill, *Bread and the Ballot*, 71–73; Henderson to Acheson, March 24, 1951; Henry L. Deimel to DOS, April 3, 1951, RG 59, 891.2546/4-351, box 5601, NA; memo of conversation by Elbert G. Mathews, May 8, 1951, *FRUS* (1951), vol. 6, *Asia and the Pacific* (Washington, D.C.), 2159–60; Acheson to Henderson, May 24, 1951, RG 59, 891.2546/5-2451, box 5601, NA.

50. William Pawley to Dean Acheson and Gordon Arneson, June 29, 1951, RG 59, 891.2546/6-2951, box 5601, NA; Pawley to George McGhee and Arneson, July 6, 1951, 891.2546/7651, ibid.; report of William Pawley, October 23, 1952, 891.2546/10-2352, ibid.; Corry to DOS; Arneson to Allen.

51. Helmreich, *Gathering Rare Ores*, 231–32; Sheldon Mills to SOS, April 16, 1953, RG 59, 493.919/4-1653, box 2216, NA; George V. Allen to SOS, July 25, 1953, 493.919/7-2553, ibid.; John Foster Dulles to New Delhi Embassy, July 26, 1953, 493.919/7-2553, ibid.; Allen to DOS, July 28, 1953, *FRUS* (1952–54), 11:1700–1702.

52. Helmreich, *Gathering Rare Ores*, 233; George V. Allen to John Foster Dulles, July 29, 1953, *FRUS* (1952–54), 11:1702–5; memo by Henry Byroade and Samuel Waugh, July 31, 1953, ibid., 1710–11; Allen to DOS, August 14, 1953, ibid., 1714; Allen to DOS, August 25, 1953, ibid., 1715; memo of conversation with Mr. Stassen, October 5, 1953, released to author following FOIA request; New Delhi Embassy to DOS, November 27, 1953, RG 59, 891.2546/11-2753, box 5601, NA.

53. Helmreich, *Gathering Rare Ores*, 234–35; Allen to DOS, November 27, 1953; Allen to SOS, December 30, 1953, RG 59, 891.2546/12-3053, box 5607, NA; Allen to DOS, July 29, 1953, *FRUS* (1952–54), 11:1702–3; Harold Stassen to SOS, July 2, 1954, ibid., 1763–64; Office of South Asian Affairs, "India—Some Current Economic Problems," January 19, 1955, *FRUS* (1955–57), vol. 8, *South Asia* (Washington, D.C., 1987), 276; Office of South Asian Af-

fairs, "US-India Relations in Field of Atomic Energy," December 10, 1956, released to author following FOIA request.

54. Montgomery M. Green, "The Monazite Mystery," *American Mercury* 74, 342 (June 1952), 33–39; memo of conversation, March 13, 1951; U.S. Congress, House, *Congressional Record*, 82/1, vol. 97, pt. 4 (Washington, D.C., 1951), 5813.

55. Helmreich, *Gathering Rare Ores*, 234–35; Allen to SOS, December 30, 1953; Henderson to DOS, December 22, 1950.

56. Henry L. Deimel to DOS, September 9, 1950, RG 59, 891.2546/9-950, box 5601, NA; Stanley A. McGeary to DOS, February 26, 1951, RG 59, 891.2546/2-2651, box 5601, NA; Acheson (Arneson) to Henderson, March 23, 1951; Henderson to SOS, March 24, 1951.

57. Helmreich, *Gathering Rare Ores*, 168–71; Arneson to Allen, April 2, 1953; John Jernegan to the Acting SOS, September 29, 1954, *FRUS* (1952–54), 11:1767–70.

58. Memo by Andrew Corry, February 25, 1948, released to author following FOIA request; Loy Henderson to SOS, June 16, 1949, RG 59, Lot File 54D341, box 17, NA.

59. Loy Henderson to SOS, May 31, 1950, RG 59, 891.2546/5-3150, box 5601, NA; Henderson to SOS, October 19, 1950, RG 59, 891.2546/10-1950, box 5601, NA.

60. Memo by Corry, February 25, 1948; J. Robert Fluker to DOS, February 14, 1957, RG 59, 891.2546/2-1457, box 5047, NA.

61. Rostow, *Eisenhower, Kennedy and Foreign Aid*; Wolf, *Foreign Aid*; Merrill, *Bread and the Ballot*; G. W. Choudhury, *India, Pakistan, Bangladesh, and the Major Powers* (New York, 1975), 77–78; position paper for Prime Minister Nehru's Visit, November 6–10, 1961, POF, CS, Box 118a, JFKL.

62. Chester Bowles to President Truman, with attachment to Harriman, September 11, 1952, Truman Papers, Official File (OF), box 1278, HSTL; memo of discussion at NSC Meeting, February 3, 1955, Eisenhower Papers, AWF, NSC Series, Box 6, DDEL; memo of discussion at NSC Meeting, January 31, 1957, AWF, NSC Series, Box 8; Symington quoted in McMahon, *Cold War on the Periphery*, 285.

63. Mutual Security Program, Foreign Aid Presentation, n.d., Lot File 57D259, RG 59, NA; Gopal, *Jawaharlal Nehru*, 63.

64. Garrett H. Soulen to DOS, December 4, 1953, RG 59, 611.91/12-453, box 2858, NA; Bowles, *Ambassador's Report*, 167.

65. Loy Henderson to SOS, February 6, 1950, RG 59, 611.91/2-650, box 2859, NA; Edward Mason to Philip Tresize, n.d. [July 1950], Gordon Gray Papers, Box 4, HSTL; Dean Acheson to Averell Harriman, February 8, 1952, released to author following FOIA request; Merrill, *Bread and the Ballot*, 154–55, 198.

66. William Fee to DOS, January 30, 1906, *Despatches of U.S. Consuls at Bombay*; Faroqui, "In the Shadow of Globalism," 251–53; memo of conversation, October 8, 1957, AWF, IS, Box 26; memo of conversation, May 13, 1957, CFEP, Office of the Chairman Files (OCF), Randall Series (RS), box 6, DDEL; Elliott K. Baker to Paul H. Cullen, December 5, 1959, ibid.

67. Memo of a conference with the President by A. J. Goodpaster, November 12, 1957, *FRUS* (1955–57), 8:404–6; Galbraith, *Ambassador's Journal*, 302–3.

68. *New York Times*, April 17, 1947; Jawaharlal Nehru to Westmore Willcox, April 29, 1947, *SWJN*, 2d ser., 2:589; Merrill, *Bread and the Ballot*, 22; Dean Acheson to Loy Henderson, December 30, 1950, *FRUS* (1950), 5:1481–82; *TOI* (Bombay), December 31, 1953; George C. Lodge, "Informal Report on Indian Trip," December 10, 1958, CFEP, OCF, RS, box 6.

69. Henderson to DOS, February 6, 1950.

70. Quoted in Gupta, *Great Encounter*, 99.

71. *HT* (New Delhi), March 4, 1954; *TOI* (Bombay), January 1, 1954.

72. "SdC.," in *TOI* (Bombay), October 23, 1961.

73. National Council of Applied Economic Research, *Saving in India: A Monograph* (New Delhi, 1961), vii, 11.

74. Jawaharlal Nehru, speech at reception for President Eisenhower, December 13, 1959, in Nehru, *India's Foreign Policy*, 602; Vivekananda quoted in Singer, *When a Great Tradition Modernizes*, 29.

3. Governance

1. Alan Roland, *In Search of Self in India and Japan: Toward a Cross-Cultural Psychology* (Princeton, 1988), 209–10, 226.

2. Roland, *In Search of Self*, 210; Stephen Tyler, *India: An Anthropological Perspective* (Prospect Heights, Ill., 1986), 2–3, 129.

3. Chester Bowles, *Ambassador's Report* (London, 1954), 216–17.

4. David G. Mandelbaum, "Family, *Jati*, Village," in Milton Singer and Bernard S. Cohn, eds., *Structure and Change in Indian Society* (Chicago, 1968), 36–37; Roland, *In Search of Self*, 7–9, 205–6, 225, 272–73.

5. Emmanuel Todd, *The Explanation of Ideology: Family Structures and Social Systems* (Oxford, 1985), 6, 12, 17.

6. Benedict Anderson, *Imagined Communities: Reflections on the Origin and Spread of Nationalism* (London, 1983), 15–16; Geoff Eley and Ronald Grigor Suny, eds., *Becoming National: A Reader* (New York, 1996), 7–9; Milton Singer, *When a Great Tradition Modernizes: An Anthropological Approach to Indian Civilization* (Chicago, 1972), 269–70.

7. Edwin G. Burrows and Michael Wallace, "The American Revolution: The Ideology and Psychology of National Liberation," *Perspectives in American History* 6 (1972): 167–267; Winthrop Jordan, "Familial Politics: Thomas Paine and the Killing of the King, 1776," *Journal of American History* 61, 2 (1973): 294–308; Mary Beth Norton, *Founding Mothers and Fathers: Gendered Power and the Forming of American Society* (New York, 1996), 13–15; Lynn Hunt, *The Family Romance of the French Revolution* (Berkeley, 1992), xiii–xv, 3, 71–73.

8. Melvin Yazawa, *From Colonies to Commonwealth: Familial Ideology and the Beginnings of the American Republic* (Baltimore, 1985), 3–4, 87, 111–35, 195–98.

9. Hunt, *Family Romance*, 72.

10. George Lakoff, *Moral Politics: What Conservatives Know that Liberals Don't* (Chicago, 1996), 12–13, 35, 153–58.

11. Todd, *Explanation of Ideology*, 133, 155; Joseph W. Elder, "Religious Beliefs and Political Attitudes," in Donald E. Smith, ed., *South Asian Politics and Religion* (Princeton, 1966), 260–65; Thomas Trautman, *Dravidian Kinship* (New York, 1981); Irawati Karmarkar Karve, *Kinship Organization in India*, 2d. ed. (Bombay, 1965).

12. Tyler, *India*, 129–38; Sudhir Kakar, *The Inner World: A Psycho-Analytic Study of Childhood and Society in India* (New Delhi, 1981), 138; Bernard S. Cohn, *India: Social Anthropology of a Civilization* (Englewood Cliffs, 1971), 112–13; G. Morris Carstairs, *The Twice-Born: A Study of a Community of High-Caste Hindus* (Bloomington, 1961), 148–49.

13. A. K. Ramanujan, "The Indian 'Oedipus,' " in Arabinda Poddar, ed., *Indian Literature: Proceedings of a Seminar* (Simla, 1972), 127–37; Carstairs, *Twice-Born*, 69, 147.

14. Francine R. Frankel, *India's Political Economy, 1947–1977: The Gradual Revolution* (Princeton, 1978), 51; Salman Rushdie, *Midnight's Children* (New York, 1980), 272–73; Bernard S. Cohn and McKim Marriott, "Networks and Centres in the Integration of Indian Civilization," in Cohn, *An Anthropologist among the Historians and Other Essays* (Delhi, 1987), 81; Myron Weiner, "India: Two Political Cultures," in Lucian Pye and Sidney Verba, eds., *Political Culture and Political Development* (Princeton, 1965), 236.

15. Paul Scott, *The Day of the Scorpion* (New York, 1968), 396–411; Bayard Taylor, *A Visit to India, China, and Japan in the Year 1853* (New York, 1891), 64; Katherine Mayo, *Mother India* (New York, 1927), 215; Charles Allen, ed., *Plain Tales from the Raj* (New York, 1985), 187.

16. J. Bandyopadhyaya, *The Making of India's Foreign Policy* (Calcutta, 1970), 76–80; Charles Tilly, "Reflections on the History of European State-Making," in Tilly, ed., *The Formation of National States in Western Europe* (Princeton, 1975), 79.

17. Anand A. Yang, *The Limited Raj: Agrarian Relations in Colonial India, Saran District, 1793–1920* (Berkeley, 1989), 6, 93, 176, 228–29; Weiner, "India," 218; Ashis Nandy, *At the Edge of Psychology: Essays in Politics and Culture* (Delhi, 1980), 50, 56; idem, *The Intimate Enemy: Loss and Recovery of Self under Colonialism* (Delhi, 1983), 31–32.

18. Clifford Geertz, *The Interpretation of Cultures* (New York, 1973), 240; Howard Donovan to Secretary of State (SOS), August 3, 1947, Record Group (RG) 59, 845.00/8-2247, box 6071, National Archives (NA), Washington, D.C.

19. Tilly, "Reflections on the History of European State-Making," 37; David H. Bayley, "The Effects of Corruption in a Developing Nation," in Arnold J. Heidenheimer, ed., *Political Corruption* (New Brunswick, N.J. 1970), 521–33; S. Chandrasekhar, *American Aid and India's Economic Development* (New York, 1965), 27–28; Bowles, *Ambassador's Report*, 81.

20. Sarvepalli Gopal, ed. *The Selected Works of Jawaharlal Nehru* (*SWJN*), 1st ser., vol. 14 (New Delhi, 1982), 82, 215; ibid., vol. 15 (New Delhi, 1982), 32–33; ibid., 2d ser., vol. 1 (New Delhi, 1984), 152–53, 168–72.

21. Various letters to Nehru in All India Congress Committee (AICC) Papers, file G-8, part 1, 1946, Jawaharlal Nehru Memorial Museum and Library (NMML), New Delhi; P. E. Dustoor, *American Days: A Traveller's Diary* (Bombay, 1952), 238; Jawaharlal Nehru, *India's Foreign Policy* (New Delhi, 1961), 15; K. P. S. Menon Diary, entries for January 31, February 3, 1948, K. P. S. Menon Papers, NMML; John Frederick Muehl, *Interview with India* (New York, 1950), 201; *Times of India* (TOI), Bombay, December 22, 1953; January 24, 1954. The new government also tried to regulate the family at its most intimate place, through a birth control campaign. While the campaign was less than a triumph in its attempt to lower the birth rate, it institutionalized government involvement in family planning policy. See, for example, S. Chandrasekhar, *Population and Planned Parenthood in India*, rev. ed. (London, 1961); George B. Simmons, *The Indian Investment in Family Planning* (New York, 1971), David G. Mandelbaum, *Human Fertility in India: Social Components and Policy Perspectives* (Berkeley, 1974).

22. Chester Bowles, interview by Neal Gold, 1963, Chester Bowles Papers, box 396, folder 177, Yale University Library, New Haven, Conn.; Taya Zinkin, *Reporting India* (London, 1962), 205–6; *SWJN*, 1st ser., 14:304; Stanley Wolpert, *Nehru: Tryst with Destiny* (New York, 1996), 347; *TOI* (Bombay), January 1, 1954; *Hindustan Times* (*HT*), New Delhi, January 2, 1954; Partha Chatterjee, *Nationalist Thought and the Colonial World: A Derivative Discourse?* (London, 1986), 160.

23. *SWJN*, 1st ser., 14:107; 2d ser., 1:401–4; speech by G. L. Mehta, October 24, 1952, Harry S. Truman Papers, Official File (OF), box 220, Harry S. Truman Library (HSTL), Independence, Mo.; Sarvepalli Gopal, *Jawaharlal Nehru: A Biography*, vol. 3, *1956–1964* (New Delhi, 1984), 162–63; K. P. S. Menon, transcript, NMML; Wolpert, *Nehru*, 442.

24. Burton Stein, *Peasant State and Society in Medieval South India* (New Delhi, 1980), 8–9, 24; Jefferson Jones to Department of State (DOS), December 14, 1948, RG 59, Lot File 54D341, Records of the Office of South Asian Affairs, 1939–53, box 16, NA; "Centralization in the Government of India," February 16, 1950, ibid.; Congressional Briefing Book: India, August 18, 1961, John F. Kennedy Papers, President's Office Files (POF), Countries Series (CS), box 118a, John F. Kennedy Library (JFKL), Boston, Mass.

25. Muehl, *Interview with India*, 109; "Resolution of the Conference of the Presidents and Secretaries of the Provincial Congress Committees at Allahabad, February 1947," AICC Papers, file 6, 1947, NMML; Frankel, *India's Political Economy*, 17, 23–25, 103; Clifford Geertz, "The Integrative Revolution: Primordial Sentiments and Civil Politics in the New States," in Geertz, ed., *Old Societies and New States: The Quest for Modernity in Asia and Africa* (New York, 1963), 140; *Hindu* (Madras), September 29, October 2, 3, 9, 1961.

26. *TOI* (Bombay), November 2, 10, 1953, January 26, 1954; Congressional Briefing Book: India, August 18, 1961; Cohn, *India*, 54–57. The advertising of consumer goods also provided an opportunity for patriotic inspiration: "At tea-time all India relishes Parle's Gluco biscuits—the tempting proof of communal harmony." *TOI*, May 29, 1950.

27. Krishnalal Shridharani, *My India, My America* (Garden City, N.Y., 1943), 26–27; letter

from Ramachandran to the editor of the *Hindu*, February 1944, Papers of Krishnabal Nimb-kar, Bancroft Library, University of California–Berkeley; letters of entreaty to Nehru in AICC Papers, files 33 and G-8, 1946, NMML.

28. John B. Monteiro, "The Dimensions of Corruption in India," in Heidenheimer, *Political Corruption*, 220–29; Damodar Swarup Seth to Jawaharlal Nehru, June 23, 1948, G. D. Pant Papers, NMML; Seth to Nehru, July 7, 1948, ibid.; Nehru to Pant, January 7, 1952, ibid.

29. Ved Mehta, *A Family Affair* (New Haven, 1994).

30. *The Indian Situation: A Personal Note by Lord Ismay*, November 1, 1947, RG 59, 845.00/11-147, box 6071, NA.

31. *TOI* (Bombay), January 2, 1954; Mohammed Ayub Khan, *Friends Not Masters: A Political Autobiography* (London, 1967), 2.

32. L. B. Grafftey-Smith to Sir Percivale Liesching, November 21, 1950, Foreign Office (FO) 371, file 84257, document FL10118/151, Public Record Office (PRO), Kew, England; David E. Lilienthal, "Another 'Korea' in the Making?" *Collier's*, August 4, 1951, 23, 56–58; Donald Kennedy to George McGhee, August 7, 1951, RG 59, Lot File 54D341, box 22, NA; Richard Symonds, *The Making of Pakistan* (London, 1951), 98–103, 178; Khan, *Friends Not Masters*, viii–ix, 194–97.

33. Wolpert, Nehru, 413–19; M. J. Akbar, *The Siege Within: Challenges to the Nation's Unity* (London, 1985), 213–40; Prem Shankar Jha, *Kashmir 1947: Rival Versions of History* (New Delhi, 1996); Symonds, *Making of Pakistan*, 156–59; Lord Ismay to Commonwealth Relations Office (CRO), October 28, 1947, FO 371, file 63570, document 14516, PRO; minute by Peter Murray, November 3, 1947, FO 371, file 63570, document 14613, PRO; R. D. Gatewood to SOS, November 4, 1947, RG 59, 845.00/11-447, box 6071, NA; *SWJN*, 2d ser., 4:264–77, 283–86.

34. *SWJN*, 2d ser., 4:318–318b; Mushtaqur Rahman, *Divided Kashmir: Old Problems, New Opportunities for India, Pakistan, and the Kashmiri People* (Boulder, 1996), 82; Symonds, *Making of Pakistan*, 122; Charles W. Lewis, Jr., to SOS, November 8, 1947, RG 59, 845.00/11-847, box 6071, NA; Note on Visit to Abbottabad by C. B. Duke, December 29, 1947, FO 371, file 69702, doc. F67, PRO.

35. See *Foreign Relations of the United States* (*FRUS*), 1947, vol. 3, *The British Commonwealth; Europe* (Washington, D.C., 1972), 179–93; *FRUS* (1948), vol. 5, *The Near East, South Asia and Africa* (Washington, D.C., 1975), 265–485; memo for the President by Dean Acheson, July 5, 1949, Truman Papers, White House Central Files (WHCF), Confidential Files (CF), box 36, HSTL; background memoranda on visit to the United States of Liaquat Ali Khan, April 14, 1950, President's Secretary's File (PSF), box 182, HSTL; Sir Archibald Nye, "Review of Events in India, June–September Quarter," October 27, 1950, FO 371, file 84204, doc. FL1013/96, PRO.

36. J. Wesley Adams, interview by Richard McKinzie, December 18, 1972, HSTL; Robert Lovett to U.S. Delegation at UN General Assembly, November 11, 1948, *FRUS* (1948), 5:448–49; memo of conversation by Acheson, June 29, 1949, Acheson Papers, box 64, HSTL; memo of conversation by Acheson, January 9, 1950, Acheson Papers, box 66, HSTL; memo of conversation by Acheson, January 13, 1950, *FRUS* (1950), 5:1367–69; Sir Oliver Franks to FO, January 13, 1950, FO 371, file 84205, doc. FL1015/20; Philip Noel- Baker to Sir Alexander Cadogan, February 6, 1950, FO 371, file 84210, doc. FL1015/93; Sir F. Hoyer Millar to FO, February 10, 1950, FO 371, file 84210, doc. FL1015/90; Acheson to Ernest Bevin, February 14, 1950, FO 371, file 84211, doc. FL1015/98, all PRO; Ellsworth Bunker to SOS, June 2, 1958, Dwight D. Eisenhower Papers, Ann Whitman File (AWF), International Series (IS), box 27, Dwight D. Eisenhower Library (DDEL), Abilene, Kans.; J. K. Galbraith to Phillips Talbot, September 21, 1961, Kennedy Papers, POF, CS, Box 118a, JFKL; Kennedy to Jawaharlal Nehru, August 15, 1963, ibid.; Robert J. McMahon, *The Cold War on the Periphery: The United States, India, and Pakistan* (New York, 1994), 19 ff.

37. W. D. Allen to P. F. Falla, January 15, 1948, FO 371, file 69706, doc. F1085; minute by P. F. Grey, September 28, 1948, FO 371, file 69721, doc. 13613; M. E. Dening to J. W.

Nicholls, February 17, 1950, FO 371, file 84252, doc. FL10118/3, all PRO; National Intelligence Estimate (NIE)-41: "Probable Developments in the Kashmir Dispute to the End of 1951," September 10, 1951, Truman Papers, PSF, box 184, HSTL; William Pawley to George McGhee, September 24, 1951, *FRUS* (1951), 6:1863–64; DOS, "The Kashmir Dispute: Position Paper," December 10, 1956, released to author following Freedom of Information Act request.

38. Liaquat Ali Khan to Truman, September 7, 1949, Truman Papers, WHCF, box 36, HSTL; background memoranda on visit of Liaquat; C. L. Sulzberger, *A Long Row of Candles: Memoirs and Diaries* (Toronto, 1969), 524.

39. *SWJN*, 2d ser., 4:304–5; Michael Brecher, *The Struggle for Kashmir* (New York, 1953), 44; George Marshall to the Embassy in London, October 20, 1948, *FRUS* (1948), 5:431–32; Loy Henderson to SOS, August 15, 1949, *FRUS* (1949), 6:1732–33; memo of conversation by Secretary Acheson, October 12, 1949, RG 59, Lot File 54D341, box 19, NA; memo of conversation by Acheson, February 9, 1950, Acheson Papers, box 65, HSTL.

40. Background memoranda on visit of Liaquat Ali Khan; A. Z. Gardiner to DOS, June 29, 1956, *FRUS* (1955–57), vol. 8, *South Asia* (Washington, D.C., 1987), 86–90.

41. W. T. Fee, "Report on Projected Iron Manufacture in India," March 30, 1905, DOS, *Despatches of U.S. Consuls at Bombay*, 1888–1906 (microfilm), University of California-Berkeley Library; memo by Glenn E. McLaughlin and John Duvall, June 9, 1955, Records of the Council on Foreign Economic Policy (CFEP), Office of the Chairman (OC), Intelligence Reports Series (IRS), box 3, DDEL.

42. Dennis Merrill, *Bread and the Ballot: The United States and India's Economic Development* (Chapel Hill, 1990), 117–18; U.S. Embassy, New Delhi, to DOS, October 30, 1959, Records of CFEP, OC, IRS, box 6.

43. Documents concerning the abortive steel loan negotiations during 1955 are in Records of CFEP, OC, IRS, box 3. See also Merrill, *Bread and the Ballot*, 120–21; Herbert Hoover, Jr., to General Edgerton, June 6, 1955, *FRUS* (1955–57), 8:288–89; 248th meeting of the NSC, May 12, 1955, Eisenhower Papers, AWF, NSC Series, box 6.

44. For documents on the administration's response to the Indian loan request, see Records of CFEP, OC, Randall Series, box 6; and Merrill, *Bread and the Ballot*, 156–59.

45. Merrill, *Bread and the Ballot*, 176–77; John Kenneth Galbraith, *Ambassador's Journal: A Personal Account of the Kennedy Years* (Boston, 1969), passim; *Hindu* (Madras), October 28, 1961; Galbraith, "Proposal for Steel Mill in India Strikes Iron Resistance," *Washington Post*, August 18, 1963.

46. Galbraith, *Ambassador's Journal*, 175; Merrill, *Bread and the Ballot*, 200–201; Arthur M. Schlesinger, Jr., *A Thousand Days: John F. Kennedy in the White House* (Boston, 1965), 531; report to the President from the Committee to Strengthen the Security of the Free World: "The Scope and Distribution of United States Military and Economic Assistance Programs," March 20, 1963 (Washington, D.C., 1963), 5–6; U.S., House of Representatives, 88/1, Committee on Foreign Affairs, Hearings on the Foreign Assistance Act of 1963, April 5, 8, 9, 10; May 20–23, 1963 (Washington, D.C., 1963), 113–14, 118, 1119–21.

47. U.S. House of Representatives, 88/1, *Congressional Record*, vol. 109, 1963 (Washington, D.C., 1963), 9594–95, 13301; U.S. House, 88/1, *Congressional Record—Appendix* (Washington, 1963), A2107–8, A4595–97, A4781–83; U.S. Senate, 88/1, *Congressional Record*, vol. 109, 1963 (Washington, D.C., 1963), 9299, 13957–58, 15741.

48. U.S. House of Representatives, 88/1, *Congressional Record*, vol. 109, 1963, 15594–00, 16761; Chester Bowles, "New Delhi Diary," typescript, entry for August 28, 1963, Bowles Papers, box 392, folder 159; John F. Kennedy to Jawaharlal Nehru, September 4, 1963, Kennedy Papers, POF, CS, box 118a; memo for the President by R. W. Komer, November 12, 1963, ibid.; Merrill, *Bread and the Ballot*, 201; *India: A Reference Annual*, 1971–72 (New Delhi, 1971), 360; *India: A Reference Annual*, 1974 (New Delhi, 1974), 241.

49. Harrison article in U.S. House, 88/1, *Congressional Record—Appendix*, 1963, A3448–49.

4. Race

1. Helen Bannerman, *The Story of Little Black Sambo* (Marshall, Va., 1986); *Little Black Sambo*, illustrated by Suzanne (Racine, Wisc., 1950); Elizabeth Hay, *Sambo Sahib: The Story of Little Black Sambo and Helen Bannerman* (Edinburgh, 1981). Two new versions of the book appeared in 1996. *Sam and the Tigers* (New York, 1996), by Julius Lester and with illustrations by Jerry Pinkney, turns Sambo's story into an African-American folktale; Lester writes that the book's original "setting is fanciful and was never meant to be taken literally." Harper-Collins reissued Bannerman's text as *The Story of Little Babaji* (New York, 1996), illustrated by Fred Marcelino. The dust jacket asserts that the story "clearly takes place in India."

2. *The Compact Edition of the Oxford English Dictionary* (New York, 1971), 1875.

3. Chester Bowles, *Ambassador's Report* (London, 1954), 31; J. Saunders Redding, "Report from India," *American Scholar*, Autumn 1953, 441–49; log of Clifford Manshardt, February 22, 1952, Chester Bowles Papers, box 96, folder 280, Yale University Library, New Haven, Conn.; Pearl Buck, "Questions Indians Ask Me," *Asia and the Americas*, May 1946, 201–3; Bowles to John Foster Dulles, March 20, 1953, Bowles Papers, box 94, folder 243.

4. *The Random House Dictionary of the English Language* (New York, 1969), 1087. For the importance of skin color as a signifier of race, see Winthrop D. Jordan, *White over Black: American Attitudes toward the Negro 1550–1812* (Baltimore, 1969), 4; Kenneth J. Gergen, "The Significance of Skin Color in Human Relations," in John Hope Franklin, ed., *Color and Race* (Boston, 1968), 116–20; Harold R. Isaacs, "Group Identity and Political Change: The Role of Color and Physical Characteristics," ibid., 75–97.

5. Sander Gilman, *Difference and Pathology: Stereotypes of Sexuality, Race, and Madness* (Ithaca, 1985), 22–25; Tapan Raychaudhuri, *Europe Reconsidered: Perceptions of the West in Nineteenth Century Bengal* (New Delhi, 1988), 254.

6. Alain Corbin, *The Foul and the Fragrant: Odor and the French Social Imagination* (Cambridge, 1986), 39, 65, 144–46, 209–10; Constance Classen, David Howes, and Anthony Synnott, *Aroma: The Cultural History of Smell* (London, 1994), 161, 165–69; Gergen, "The Significance of Skin Color," 120.

7. Robin Jared Lewis, "The Literature of the Raj," in Robin W. Winks and James R. Rush, eds., *Asia in Western Fiction* (Honolulu, 1990), 53–58; Rudyard Kipling, "Beyond the Pale," in *Plain Tales from the Hills* (Oxford, 1987), 127–32. Henty's unwitting twentieth-century offspring was Harry Flashman, the notorious bully of *Tom Brown's Schooldays*, who is brought to life in the historical novels of George MacDonald Fraser. Flashman's dubious virtue is the bluntness with which he describes Indians, in contrast to the mannerly racism of Henty's heroes: "Universities?" says I. "Not for the niggers, surely?" George MacDonald Fraser, *Flashman in the Great Game* (New York, 1975). E. M. Forster's *A Passage to India* is also, in part, about racial difference. Forster's description of the "bridge party," to which English officials in Chandrapore invite Indians in order to prove them unfathomable, is among the most painful scenes in the literature of the raj. And when the Englishman Fielding attempts to defend Dr. Aziz, accused of having raped Adela Quested, he is condemned by his compatriots because "he had not rallied to the banner of race."

8. Journal of Thomas Tingey, December 26–28, 1795, Thomas Tingey Papers, Library of Congress (LC), Washington, D.C.; Robert Minturn, Jr., *From New York to Delhi* (New York, 1858), 96, 108, 114; Anna Harriette Leonowens, *Life and Travel in India* (Philadelphia, 1897), 314; William Fee to David J. Hill, September 14, 1899, *Despatches of U.S. Consuls at Bombay, 1838–1906* (microfilm), University of California–Berkeley Library; Frank Ilse to Fee, May 7, 1902, ibid.; Fee to Hill, March 21, 1900, ibid.

9. Joan M. Jensen, *Passage from India: Asian Indian Immigrants in North America* (New Haven, 1988), 13, 171, 246–69.

10. Emanuel Celler to President Truman, April 25, 1945, Harry S Truman Papers, President's Secretary's Files (PSF), box 180, Harry S Truman Library (HSTL), Independence, Mo.; Harold R. Isaacs, *Scratches on Our Minds: American Views of China and India* (New York, 1958), 285.

11. Frank Costigliola, "'Unceasing Pressure for Penetration': Gender, Pathology, and Emotion in George Kennan's Formation of the Cold War," *Journal of American History* 83, 4 (1997): 1323; Thomas Borstelmann, *Apartheid's Reluctant Uncle: The United States and Southern Africa in the Early Cold War* (New York, 1993), 40, 112; memo of conversation by Joseph S. Sparks, June 1, 1950, Record Group (RG) 59, 611.91/6-150, box 2857, National Archives (NA), Washington, D.C.; Chester Bowles to Stanley Andrews, December 1, 1952, Bowles Papers, box 93, folder 230; Chester Bowles, interview by Neal Gold, 1963, Bowles Papers, box 396, folder 179; John Foster Dulles telephone conversation with the president, August 1, 1953, Dulles Papers, Telephone Calls Series, box 10, Dwight D. Eisenhower Library (DDEL); Harris Wofford to President Kennedy, July 17, 1961, John F. Kennedy Papers, President's Office Files (POF), Special Correspondence (SC) Series, box 28, John F. Kennedy Library (JFKL), Boston.

12. Michael H. Hunt, *Ideology and U.S. Foreign Policy* (New Haven, 1987), 160–62. The argument that the language of development replaced that of race is not meant to exclude the possibility that such language carried several layers of meaning. As I argued in chapter 2, American perceptions of India's maturity and economics were linked by the language of development.

13. Thomas J. Noer, "New Frontiers and Old Priorities in Africa," in Thomas G. Paterson, ed., *Kennedy's Quest for Victory: American Foreign Policy, 1961–1963* (New York, 1989), 254.

14. Ibid., 254–56; Rupert Emerson, *Africa and United States Policy* (Englewood Cliffs, 1967), 24.

15. Richard D. Mahoney, *JFK: Ordeal in Africa* (New York, 1983), 20–24, 31–35; Thomas J. Noer, *Cold War and Black Liberation: The United States and White Africa, 1948–1968* (Columbia, Mo., 1985), 62–64.

16. Mahoney, *JFK*, 40, 164, 193; Noer, *Cold War and Black Liberation*, 65–66; Borstelmann, *Apartheid's Reluctant Uncle*, 76–77.

17. Borstelmann, *Apartheid's Reluctant Uncle*, 19, 39–41; Noer, *Cold War and Black Liberation*, 35; idem, "New Frontiers and Old Priorities," 276, 282–83.

18. Gerald Horne, *Black and Red: W. E. B. Du Bois and the Afro-American Response to the Cold War, 1944–1963* (Albany, 1986), 278–79; Mary Dudziak, "Desegregation as a Cold War Imperative," *Stanford Law Review* 41 (November 1988): 94–95, 101–13.

19. Elbert G. Mathews, "Regional Policy Statement: South Asia," October 9, 1950, Department of State (DOS), *Foreign Relations of the United States* (*FRUS*), 1950, vol. 5, *The Near East, South Asia, and Africa* (Washington, D.C., 1978), 248; Chester Bowles to Dean Acheson, December 6, 1951, *FRUS*, 1951, vol. 6, *Asia and the Pacific* (Washington, D.C., 1977), 2193; Dudziak, "Desegregation as a Cold War Imperative"; Emerson, *Africa and United States Policy*, 108.

20. Borstelmann, *Apartheid's Reluctant Uncle*, 199; Paul Gordon Lauren, *Power and Prejudice: The Politics and Diplomacy of Racial Discrimination*, 2d ed. (Boulder, 1996), 167–71; Mahoney, *JFK*, 241; Noer, "New Frontiers and Old Priorities," 275–78; idem, *Cold War and Black Liberation*, 139.

21. Emerson, *Africa and United States Policy*, 21, 24, 27–35; Borstelmann, *Apartheid's Reluctant Uncle*, 95–99; Mark Solomon, "Black Critics of Colonialism and the Cold War," in Thomas G. Paterson, ed., *Cold War Critics* (Chicago, 1971), 226–30; J. G. Parsons and S. K. C. Kopper to the Secretary of State (SOS), October 14, 1948, RG 59, 845.002/10-1448, box 6114, NA.

22. Jensen, *Passage from India*, 171.

23. John J. MacDonald to SOS, August 9, 1947, RG 59, 845.00/8-947, box 6071, NA; Chester Bowles to Howland Sargeant, December 24, 1951, Bowles Papers, box 96, folder 280; Bowles, *Ambassador's Report*, 216, 296–97, 319; DOS to Diplomatic and Consular Offices in India, January 20, 1956, *FRUS*, vol. 8 (1955–57), *South Asia* (Washington, D.C., 1987), 303; *Hindu* (Madras), November 19, 1961; Roshan Lal Sharma, *Holy Men and Holy Cows: The Adventures and Philosophies of an Americanized Hindu* (New York, 1968), 82, 108, 117, 124–27.

24. Jensen, *Passage from India*, 37; P. E. Dustoor, *American Days: A Traveller's Diary* (Bombay, 1952), 193; Ved Mehta, *Daddyji* (New York, 1972), 114–15.

25. "India: Problems and Prospects," October 5, 1949, RG 59, 845.002/10-549, box 6114, NA; Loy Henderson to Dean Acheson, September 6, 1951, *FRUS* (1951), 6:2180; Henderson to Acheson, January 29, 1951, ibid., 2094; Bowles to Acheson, October 28, 1952, *FRUS*, vol. 11 (1952–54), *Africa and South Asia* (Washington, D.C., 1983), 1672.

26. Bowles to Dulles, March 20, 1953; Charles Allen, ed., *Plain Tales from the Raj* (New York, 1985), 184–85, 199.

27. Merle Curti, "My Discovery of America in India," *American Scholar* 16, 4 (1947): 423; Hossain Shahid Faroqui, "In the Shadow of Globalism: The United States, South Asia, and the Cold War, 1939–1953" (Ph.D. diss., Cornell University, 1986), 138; Charles O. Thompson to SOS, August 24, 1948, RG 59, 711.45/8-2448, box 3233, NA; memo of conversation by Vincent Baker, October 26, 1951, *FRUS* (1951), 6:1892; memo of conversation by Henry C. Ramsey, September 20, 1955, RG 59, 611.91/9-2055, box 2562, NA; Frederick Jochem to G. Lewis Jones, December 15, 1950, RG 59, 611.91/12-1550, box 2857, NA.

28. Bowles to Dulles, March 20, 1953; Evan M. Wilson, interview by Richard McKinzie, July 18, 1975, HSTL; Sir Archibald Nye, "Political Report from India for the Period 11th/25th October," October 27, 1950, Foreign Office (FO) 371, file 84203, doc. FL1013/88, Public Record Office (PRO), Kew, England; memo of conversation between Vijayalakshmi Pandit and Philip Jessup, September 5, 1950, RG 59, Lot File 54D341, box 17, NA; *Times of India* (*TOI*), Bombay, December 7, 1950; Bowles, *Ambassador's Report*, 224; Bowles to Donald Kennedy, Bowles Papers, December 28, 1951, box 95, folder 265; J. LeRoy Davidson to Bowles, March 15, 1953, Bowles Papers, box 97, folder 304.

29. Jawaharlal Nehru, *India's Foreign Policy: Selected Speeches, September 1946–April 1961* (New Delhi, 1961), 2; DOS, evaluation of U.S.-India relations, 3d quarter, 1952, November 1, 1952, RG 59, 611.91/11-152, box 2858, NA; Redding, "Report from India," 443; Bowles to Dulles, March 20, 1953, op. cit.; memo by John Sherman Cooper, December 13, 1956, Dwight D. Eisenhower Papers, Ann Whitman File (AWF), International Series (IS), box 28, DDEL; address by G. L. Mehta at Annual Meeting of American Academy of Political and Social Science, Philadelphia, April 3, 1954, Dorothy Norman Papers, ser. 4, box 1, Syracuse University Library, Syracuse, N.Y.

30. MacDonald to SOS, August 9, 1947; Lauren, *Power and Prejudice*, 153, 167–71; Borstelmann, *Apartheid's Reluctant Uncle*, 69; Charles H. Heimsath and Surjit Mansingh, *A Diplomatic History of Modern India* (Bombay, 1971), 306; Parsons and Kopper to SOS, October 14, 1948.

31. *TOI* (Bombay), December 24, 1953; January 29, 1954; Sarvepalli Gopal, *Jawaharlal Nehru: A Biography*, vol. 3, *1956–1964* (New Delhi, 1984), 160; Nehru, *India's Foreign Policy*, 543, 545; *Hindu*, October 25, 1961.

32. Jawaharlal Nehru, note for Asaf Ali and K. P. S. Menon, January 22, 1947, K. P. S. Menon Papers, Correspondence File, Jawaharlal Nehru Memorial Museum and Library (NMML), New Delhi; John J. MacDonald to DOS, September 19, 1947, RG 59, 711.45/9-1947, NA; Howard Donovan to SOS, August 19, 1949, RG 59, 845.002/8-1949, box 6114, NA; *Statesman* (Calcutta), November 5, 1949; Sir Alexander Cadogan to FO, February 19, 1950, FO 371, file 84211, doc. FL1015/109, PRO.

33. Chester Bowles to Donald Kennedy, December 28, 1951, Bowles Papers, box 95, folder 265; Report of Jay [J.] Saunders Redding, September 30, 1952, ibid., box 111, folder 499; Ed Logue to Fraser Wilkins, December 8, 1952, ibid., box 107, folder 450.

34. Robert L. Hardgrave, Jr., and Stanley A. Kochanek, *India: Government and Politics in a Developing Nation*, 4th ed. (San Diego, 1986), 168–71; Bowles, *Ambassador's Report*, 37; Edward B. Harper, "A Comparative Analysis of Caste: The United States and India," in Milton Singer and Bernard S. Cohn, eds., *Structure and Change in Indian Society* (Chicago, 1968), 64, 68; Isaacs, "Group Identity and Political Change," 95; Philip Jessup to Chester Bowles, December 19, 1951, Bowles Papers, box 95, folder 262; Summary of Editorial Comment in Indian Press by Ernest H. Fisk, May 12, 1947, RG 59, 711.45/6-947, box 3323, NA; *TOI* (Bom-

bay), June 10, 1950; January 4, 1954; November 30, 1956; memo of conversation, October 8, 1957, *FRUS* (1955–57), 8:388.

35. Abbé J. A. Dubois, *Hindu Manners, Customs and Ceremonies*, 3d edit. (Oxford, 1905), 317; André Béteille, "Race and Descent as Social Categories in India," in John Hope Franklin, ed., *Color and Race* (Boston, 1968), 172–73; *TOI* (Bombay), May 17, 18, 31, 1950; November 13, 1953; *Hindu* (Madras), October 26, 1961; Isaacs, *Scratches on Our Minds*, 347.

36. Jawaharlal Nehru, *An Autobiography* (New Delhi, 1936), 17–26; M. K. Gandhi, *An Autobiography* (Ahmedabad, 1927), 36–91; Nayantara Sahgal, *Prison and Chocolate Cake* (New York, 1954), 144. Let it be said that Mohammad Ayub Khan, who would become Pakistan's prime minister in 1958, had a different impression at Sandhurst: "The British did not practise the colour bar in a blatant manner, as in some countries, but they were no less colour conscious. In those days [1926–27] anyone coming from a subject race was regarded as an inferior human being and this I found terribly galling." Mohammad Ayub Khan, *Friends Not Masters: A Political Autobiography* (London, 1967), 10.

37. Heimsath and Mansingh, *Diplomatic History*, 274, 309–10.

38. *Hindu* (Madras), November 7, 1961; Angus Ward to DOS, March 13, 1951, RG 59, 611.91/3–1351, box 2858, NA; Borstelmann, *Apartheid's Reluctant Uncle*, 118–19.

39. Isaacs, *Scratches on Our Minds*, 289–90.

40. Heimsath and Mansingh, *Diplomatic History*, 288–89, 310; Borstelmann, *Apartheid's Reluctant Uncle*, 119, 173–75; Sarvepalli Gopal, *Jawaharlal Nehru: A Biography*, vol. 2, *1947–1956* (New Delhi, 1979), 170; *TOI* (Bombay), December 24, 1953; DOS, "Semi-Annual Review of U.S.-Indian Relations," January–May 15, 1955, RG 59, 611.91/6-2155, box 2562, NA; George McTurnan Kahin, *The Asian-African Conference: Bandung, Indonesia, April 1955* (Ithaca, 1956), 75, 81.

41. *Hindu* (Madras), September 6, 16, 18, 1961; November 7, 1963; Isaacs, "Group Identity and Political Change," 95.

42. Heimsath and Mansingh, *Diplomatic History*, 289–90, 499–505; Noer, "New Frontiers and Old Priorities," 260–69; Mahoney, *JFK*, 34–156.

43. Arthur G. Rubinoff, *India's Use of Force in Goa* (Bombay, 1971), 30–35.

44. Ibid., 32, 47–48; Noer, *Cold War and Black Liberation*, 5–6.

45. Rubinoff, *India's Use of Force*, 47–61; *Hindu* (Madras), September 11, 1961.

46. Memo from Cooper, December 13, 1956; John Sherman Cooper to John Foster Dulles, December 11, 1955, Eisenhower Papers, AWF, IS, box 26; Dulles to Cooper, December 19, 1955, Dulles Papers, General Correspondence and Memoranda Series (GCMS), box 2, DDEL; DOS Position Paper, "Nehru Visit—December 16–20, 1956: The Goa Dispute," December 11, 1956, released to author following Freedom of Information Act (FOIA) request; memo of conversation with Prime Minister Nehru, December 19, 1956, Eisenhower Papers, AWF, IS, box 28.

47. Gopal, *Jawaharlal Nehru*, 3:197.

48. Rubinoff, *India's Use of Force*, 75–80.

49. *Hindu* (Madras), September 16, October 22, 23, 1961.

50. *Hindu* (Madras), October 21, 22, 24, 25, 29, 1961; Rubinoff, *India's Use of Force*, 80–83.

51. Arthur M. Schlesinger, Jr., *A Thousand Days: John F. Kennedy in the White House* (Boston, 1965), 526; *TOI* (Bombay), November 13, 15, 18, 1961; *Hindu* (Madras), November 13, 15, 18, 22, 1961.

52. *Hindu* (Madras), November 12, 25, 26, 28, 30, December 1, 4, 5, 6, 8, 11, 15, 16, 1961; John Kenneth Galbraith, *Ambassador's Journal: A Personal Account of the Kennedy Years* (Boston, 1969), 270–95; Schlesinger, *Thousand Days*, 522–26; Jawaharlal Nehru to John F. Kennedy, December 29, 1961, Kennedy Papers, POF, Countries Series (CS), box 118a.

53. *Hindu* (Madras), December 18, 20, 21, 1961; Rubinoff, *India's Use of Force*, 92–93. Nehru's desire to please the Africans was the explanation for the seizure of Goa given by G. L. Mehta, the former ambassador to the United States; Schlesinger, *Thousand Days*, 529.

54. Rubinoff, *India's Use of Force*, 95–96; *Hindu* (Madras), December 22, 1961.

55. Nehru to Kennedy, December 29, 1961; Kennedy to Nehru, January 18, 1962, Kennedy Papers, National Security Files (NSF), CS, box 111.

56. Nehru to Kennedy, December 29, 1961; Hugh Tinker, *Race, Conflict, and the International Order* (New York, 1977), 117.

57. Alan Roland, *In Search of Self in India and Japan* (Princeton, 1988), 17–54; Salman Rushdie, *Midnight's Children* (New York, 1980), 212.

5. Gender

1. William T. Moncrieff, *The Cataract of the Ganges: A Grand Romantic Melodrama* ([New York, 1823]). I am grateful to Faye Dudden for bringing the play to my attention.

2. Mrinalini Sinha, "Reading *Mother India*: Empire, Nation and the Female Voice," *Journal of Women's History* 6, 2 (1994), 6.

3. Joan W. Scott, *Gender and the Politics of History* (New York, 1988), 32.

4. Ibid., 48; Katherine Mayo, *Mother India* (New York, 1927); Sydney Greenbie, *The Romantic East* (New York, 1930), 15, 124; Richard Cronin, *Imagining India* (New York, 1989), 147.

5. Mayo, *Mother India*, 21; Wendell Thomas, *Hinduism Invades America* (New York, 1930), 98.

6. Mill quoted in Lloyd I. Rudolph, "Gandhi in the Mind of America," in Sulochana Raghavan Glazer and Nathan Glazer, eds., *Conflicting Images: India and the United States* (Glenn Dale, Md., 1990), 159; Mark Twain, *Following the Equator* (Hartford, 1897), 351; Henry M. Field, *From Egypt to Japan* (New York, 1877), 118–19.

7. Robert J. Minturn, Jr., *From New York to Delhi* (New York, 1858), 234; Jones quoted in Bernard Saul Stern, "American Views of India and Indians, 1857–1900" (Ph.D. diss., University of Pennsylvania, 1956), 119–20; Katherine Mayo, *The Face of Mother India* (New York, 1935), 38.

8. F. E. Cumming-Bruce to M. R. Metcalf, April 14, 1950, Foreign Office (FO) 371, file 83625, doc. FF10385/16, Public Record Office (PRO), Kew, England; Sir Archibald Nye to the Secretary of State for Commonwealth Relations, January 10, 1951, FO 371, file 92870, doc. FL1022/2, PRO; telephone call from Sherman Adams to John Foster Dulles, February 1, 1956, John Foster Dulles Papers, Telephone Calls Series, box 11, Dwight D. Eisenhower Library (DDEL), Abilene, Kans.; memo by Roger Hilsman, November 22, 1962, Roger Hilsman Papers, box 1, John F. Kennedy Library (JFKL), Boston.

9. Central Intelligence Agency (CIA), Situation Report (SR)-21, "India-Pakistan," September 16, 1948, President's Secretary's Files (PSF), box 260, Harry S. Truman Library (HSTL), Independence, Mo.; Loy Henderson to Dean Acheson, April 7, 1951, Department of State (DOS), *Foreign Relations of the United States* (*FRUS*), vol. 6, *Asia and the Pacific* (Washington, D.C., 1977), 2139–40; Eustace Seligman to John Foster Dulles, November 4, 1954, Dulles Papers, General Correspondence and Memoranda Series, box 3, DDEL; Dwight Eisenhower to Dulles, November 16, 1953, Record Group (RG) 59, 611.90D/11-1653, box 2857, National Archives (NA), Washington, D.C.

10. Harold Isaacs, *Scratches on Our Minds: American Views of China and India* (New York, 1958), 274–75, 359–60.

11. Lloyd I. Rudolph and Susanne Hoeber Rudolph, *The Modernity of Tradition: Political Development in India* (Chicago, 1967), 163–65; Charles Allen, ed., *Plain Tales from the Raj* (New York, 1985), 206; Mrinalini Sinha, *Colonial Masculinity: The 'Manly Englishman' and the 'Effeminate Bengali' in the Late Nineteenth Century* (Manchester, England, 1995), 15.

12. Ashis Nandy, *The Intimate Enemy: Loss and Recovery of Self under Colonialism* (New Delhi, 1983), 37–38; Veena Das, "The Imaging of Indian Women: Missionaries and Journalists," in Glazer and Glazer, eds., *Conflicting Images*, 211. See also Edward Said, *Orientalism* (New York, 1978), 1–28.

13. Stanley Wolpert, *A New History of India*, 3d ed. (New York, 1989), 239–42; Alan Roland, *In Search of Self in India and Japan* (Princeton, 1988), 19; Richard Cronin, *Imagining India* (New York, 1989), 148.

14. Emily S. Rosenberg, "Gender," *Journal of American History* 77, 1 (1990): 119; Tom Paine, "Common Sense," in Thomas G. Paterson, ed., *Major Problems in American Foreign Policy*, 3d ed. (Lexington, Mass., 1989), 1:30–33; Clyde Griffen, "Reconstructing Masculinity from the Evangelical Revival to the Waning of Progressivism: A Speculative Synthesis," in Mark C. Carnes and Clyde Griffen, eds., *Meanings for Manhood: Constructions of Masculinity in Victorian America* (Chicago, 1990), 189; Michael H. Hunt, *Ideology and U.S. Foreign Policy* (New Haven, 1987), 60–62, 66–67, 70, 75, 126, 142; Kristin L. Hoganson, *Fighting for American Manhood: How Gender Politics Provoked the Spanish-American and Philippines-American Wars* (New Haven, 1998), 9.

15. R. K. Gupta, *The Great Encounter: A Study of Indo-American Literature and Cultural Relations* (New Delhi, 1986), 16–17; Minturn, *From New York to Delhi*, 180, 206–7; William Butler, *The Land of the Veda* (New York, 1906), 19; Fairbank quoted in Nathan Glazer, "Introduction," in Glazer and Glazer, *Conflicting Images*, 14.

16. Susan Jeffords, *The Remasculinization of America: Gender and the Vietnam War* (Bloomington, 1989), xii; Krishnalal Shridharani, *My India, My America* (Garden City, N.Y., 1943), 198, 201.

17. Shridharani, *My India, My America*, 178; G. Morris Carstairs, *The Twice-Born: A Study of a Community of High-Caste Hindus* (London, 1957), 163; Roland, *In Search of Self*, 267; Rudolph and Rudolph, *Modernity of Tradition*, 215–16; Ashis Nandy, *At the Edge of Psychology: Essays in Politics and Culture* (Oxford, 1980), 37–38; Allen, *Plain Tales from the Raj*, 144. In 1948, the journalist John Frederick Muehl traveled in Maharashtra state with a circus troop. He noted that "the percentage of homosexuality in the troupe was enormous. . . . Indians are generally quite tolerant of inversions, and it was not at all uncommon to see two men keeping house together and behaving quite like a married couple." John Frederick Muehl, *Interview with India* (New York, 1950), 168.

18. Nandy, *Intimate Enemy*, 18–24.

19. Rudolph and Rudolph, *Modernity of Tradition*, 191–92, 214–5; Nandy, *Intimate Enemy*, 54; idem, *At the Edge of Psychology*, 74; M. K. Gandhi, *An Autobiography, or the Story of My Experiments with Truth* (Ahmedabad, 1927), 263–75. Note also Nehru's remark to a nationalist compatriot: "I find [Gandhi's] approach to events is rather feminine, if I may say so. That is to say it is intuitive and is more of a reaction than the result of logical reasoning." Quoted in M. O. Mathai, *Reminiscences of the Nehru Age* (New Delhi, 1978), 30.

20. Isaacs, *Scratches on Our Minds*, 293–94; Brisbane quoted in Joan Jensen, *Passage from India: Asian Indian Immigrants in North America* (New Haven, 1988), 272; Nayantara Sahgal, *Prison and Chocolate Cake* (New York, 1954), 16.

21. Jawaharlal Nehru to Frances Gunther, May 8, 1938, in Sarvepalli Gopal, ed., *The Selected Works of Jawaharlal Nehru* (*SWJN*), 1st ser., vol. 14 (New Delhi, 1982), 629; Sir Archibald Nye, "Review of Events in India, June-September Quarter," October 27, 1950, FO 371, file 84204, doc. FL1013/96, PRO; CIA, Situation Report (SR)-21, "India-Pakistan," September 16, 1948, PSF, box 260, HSTL; George Merrell to the Secretary of State (SOS), December 7, 1945, RG 59, 711.45/12-745, box 3323, NA.

22. Greenbie, *Romantic East*, 95; Das, "Imaging of Indian Women," 208–11.

23. Harland Wilson, "Kali—Dread Goddess of Life and Death," *Fate* 3, 2 (1950), 10–15.

24. Isaacs, *Scratches on Our Minds*, 280–81; *Gunga Din*, dir. George Stevens, RKO, 1939; *Indiana Jones and the Temple of Doom*, dir. Steven Spielberg, Paramount, 1984.

25. Milton Singer, *When a Great Tradition Modernizes: An Anthropological Approach to Indian Civilization* (Chicago, 1972), 19.

26. Saleni Hopkins, *Within the Purdah* (New York, 1898), 35; Mayo, *Mother India*, 25–28. G. M. Carstairs notes that while most young Indian children masturbate, the practice by older children or adults is "vehemently condemned"; see *Twice-Born*, 72. O. Mannoni once heard a French colonial official in Madagascar argue that blacks were inferior to whites be-

cause they masturbated to excess. As Mannoni observes, "the 'inferior' being always serves as a scapegoat; our own evil intentions can be projected on to him." O. Mannoni, *Prospero and Caliban: The Psychology of Colonization* (New York, 1956), 106.

27. Carstairs, *Twice-Born*, 73; Roland, *In Search of Self*, 261–62; Thomas, *Hinduism Invades America*, 76–77; Tapan Raychaudhuri, *Europe Reconsidered: Perceptions of the West in Nineteenth Century Bengal* (New Delhi, 1988), 300–301; Prakash C. Jain, "You Yanks Are Hypocrites," *The Saturday Evening Post*, June 30, 1961, 8–9; Deepak Lal, "Manners, Morals, and Materialism: Some Indian Perceptions of America and Great Britain," in Glazer and Glazer, *Conflicting Images*, 274.

28. Roshan Lal Sharma, *Holy Men and Holy Cows: The Adventures and Philosophies of an Americanized Hindu* (New York, 1968), 86; Shridharani, *My India, My America*, 77–78.

29. P. E. Dustoor, *American Days: A Traveller's Diary* (Bombay, 1952), 81–82; *Times of India* (*TOI*), Bombay, December 13, 1959; Sarvepalli Gopal, *Jawaharlal Nehru: A Biography*, vol. 2, *1947–1956* (New Delhi, 1979), 101, 226.

30. Geoffrey S. Smith, "Security, Gender, and the Historical Process," *Diplomatic History* 18, 1 (1994), 83; Loy Henderson to George McGhee, February 28, 1950, RG 59, Lot File 54D341, box 25, NA; John Kenneth Galbraith, *Ambassador's Journal: A Personal Account of the Kennedy Years* (Boston, 1969), 154.

31. Isaacs, *Scratches on Our Minds*, 246, 310; Phillips Talbot to Walter S. Rogers, August 19, 1947, Herschel V. Johnson Papers, box 5, HSTL; Stern, "American Views of India," 104. The bed of nails seems to me a somewhat different case. While snake charmers, rope trick artists, and riders of flying carpets are portrayed as generic Hindu men, only sadhus—holy men—lie on beds of nails. Could the image be a way of ridiculing, and thus subverting, swamis like Vivekananda, who, in the late nineteenth and early twentieth centuries, proved seductive of well-to-do American women? As Elizabeth Reed warned in 1914, "the insidious emissaries of the East have already penetrated our body politic." For a superb analysis of the holy man image, see Kirin Narayan, "Refractions of the Field at Home: American Representations of Hindu Holy Men in the Nineteenth and Twentieth Centuries," *Cultural Anthropology* 8, 4 (1993), 476–509. Reed is quoted on 494.

32. *TOI* (Bombay), November 15, December 4, 1953; Robert Trumbull, *As I See India* (New York, 1956), 122; C. L. Sulzberger, *A Long Row of Candles* (Toronto, 1969), 794; Stanley Wolpert, *Nehru: Tryst with Destiny* (New York, 1996), 374–75; Nina Padover to Dorothy and Ed Norman, October 23, 1949, Dorothy Norman Papers, ser. 1, box 1, Syracuse University Library, Syracuse, N.Y.; Sarvepalli Gopal, *Jawaharlal Nehru, A Biography*, vol. 3, *1956–1964* (New Delhi, 1984), 189–90. According to his personal secretary, Nehru had an active heterosexual social life. Mathai, *Reminiscences of the Nehru Age*, 201–11.

33. Report by H. M. Acting Consul General, San Francisco, on the State Visit by Pandit Nehru, to FO on November 28, 1949, FO 371, file 76097, doc. F17822, PRO. Let it be said that once danger had presented itself—in the form of the U.S.-Pakistan military agreement in early 1954—Nehru insisted that he welcomed the risk ("in some corner of my mind") because "there is a danger of our going soft. We are a rather soft people, and at the slightest opportunity we go soft again." At this point, he said, history would probably judge that "we lost our energy and vitality after independence and slipped back." For Indians, "the choice was either that [the threat] brought out our manhood, or we are just too weary and tired to carry out the things we are called upon to do." *TOI* (Bombay), January 23, 1954.

34. *TOI* (Bombay), December 14, 1953; DOS Position Paper, "Royal Government-Pathet Lao Settlement in Laos," November 11, 1956, released to author following Freedom of Information Act request; R. B. Smith, *An International History of the Vietnam War*, vol. 1, *Revolution versus Containment, 1955–1961* (London, 1983), 30–31; 180; Charles H. Heimsath and Surjit Mansingh, *A Diplomatic History of Modern India* (Bombay, 1971), 252–62, 283; *Hindu* (Madras), November 21, 1961.

35. Heimsath and Mansingh, *Diplomatic History*, 69–72; Gopal, *Jawaharlal Nehru*, 2:101; William Stueck, *The Korean War: An International History* (Princeton, 1995), 196; Loy Hen-

derson to SOS, July 13, 1950, *FRUS* (1950), vol. 7, *Korea* (Washington, D.C., 1976), 371; Henderson to SOS, January 31, 1951, *FRUS* (1951), vol. 7, *Korea and China* (Washington, D.C., 1983), 149–50; Henderson to SOS, February 21, 1951, ibid., 187–88; Warren Austin to SOS, May 22, 1951, ibid., 447; memo of conversation by William O. Hall, October 6, 1952, RG 59, Lot File 57D259, box 6, NA; Acheson to DOS, November 11, 1952, *FRUS* (1952–54), vol. 15, *Korea* (Washington, D.C., 1984), 599.

36. Gopal, *Jawaharlal Nehru*, 2:105; memo of conversation by Philip Jessup, December 4, 1950, *FRUS* (1950), 7:1376; Loy Henderson to SOS, July 13, 1950, ibid., 376; Alan Kirk to SOS, July 14, 1950, ibid., 376; Kirk to SOS, July 21, 1950, ibid., 44; Kirk to SOS, August 1, 1950, ibid., 513; Warren Austin to SOS, December 9, 1950, ibid., 1494; Ray L. Thurston to Harry Howard, December 29, 1950, RG 59, Lot File 54D341: Records of the Office of South Asian Affairs, 1939–53, box 18, NA; Dean Acheson to President Truman, November 20, 1952, *FRUS* (1952–54), 15:662–63; notes on a meeting held with the SOS, October 20, 1953, ibid., 1540.

37. Carstairs, *Twice-Born*, 46–47; *TOI* (Bombay), January 25, 1954, November 15, 1961.

38. Gopal, *Jawaharlal Nehru*, 2:109, 136, 226; Nehru to President Eisenhower, September 29, 1960, and Eisenhower to Nehru, October 2, 1960, Eisenhower Papers, Ann Whitman Files (AWF), International Series (IS), box 27, DDEL; J. Graham Parsons to Livingston Merchant, January 13, 1961, released to author following Freedom of Information Act request.

39. Loy Henderson to Dean Acheson, June 18, 1949, Loy Henderson Papers, box 8, Library of Congress (LC), Washington, D.C.; Ann C. Whitman to John Foster Dulles, August 30, 1956, John Foster Dulles Papers, Memoranda Series, box 5, DDEL; George McGhee, *Envoy to the Middle World: Adventures in Diplomacy* (New York, 1983), 47; Selig Harrison, "Nehru's Visit in Retrospect," *New Republic*, December 31, 1956, 7–8; Gopal, *Jawaharlal Nehru*, 3:190.

40. H. W. Brands, *The Specter of Neutralism: The United States and the Emergence of the Third World, 1947–1960* (New York, 1989), 128–32; "Indo-American Relations: Second Thoughts," *Eastern Economist* 26, 2 (January 13, 1956), 45–46; memo of conversations between Prime Minister Nehru and President Eisenhower, December 17–18, 1956, Eisenhower Papers, AWF, IS, box 28, DDEL; J. R. A. Bottomley to J. O. McCormick, September 18, 1956, FO 371, file 123588, doc. DL10345/24, PRO; *TOI* (Bombay), December 19, 1956; Gopal, *Jawaharlal Nehru*, 3:190.

41. Henry Fairlie, *The Kennedy Promise* (Garden City, N.Y., 1973), 185; Robert D. Dean, "Masculinity as Ideology: John F. Kennedy and the Domestic Politics of Foreign Policy," *Diplomatic History* 22, 1 (1998), 21–62; Gopal, *Jawaharlal Nehru*, 3:189–90; *Hindu* (Madras), November 9, 1961; Galbraith, *Ambassador's Journal*, 227; Arthur M. Schlesinger, Jr., *A Thousand Days* (Boston, 1965), 526.

42. Elbert G. Mathews, interview by Richard McKinzie, June 13, 1975, HSTL; Isaacs, *Scratches on Our Minds*, 276–77; James M. Langley to William Rountree, December 27, 1957, *FRUS* (1955–57), vol. 8, *South Asia* (Washington, D.C., 1987), 487.

43. McGhee, *Envoy to the Middle World*, 93; DOS, "Background Memoranda on Visit to the United States of Liaquat Ali Khan," April 14, 1950, RG 59, Lot File 54D341, NA; Sir Roger Makins to Sir Anthony Eden, October 28, 1954, FO 371, box 24, file 112307, doc. DY10345/6, PRO; Dulles to Eisenhower, July 8, 1957, microfilm, doc. 000863 in Declassified Documents Reference System Catalog, 15, 2 (March–April), 1989.

44. Paul Grimes, "In Pakistan: 'Maybe He Can Help Us,' " *New York Times Magazine*, November 27, 1960; President Eisenhower to Mohammed Ayub Khan, December 7, 1960, AWF, IS, box 38, DDEL; Mohammed Ayub Khan, *Friends Not Masters: A Political Autobiography* (New York, 1967), 59; Lyndon Johnson to President Kennedy, May 23, 1961, POF, Special Correspondence Series, box 80, JFKL.

45. Chester Bowles, "New Delhi Diary," entry for August 9, 1963, Chester Bowles Papers, box 392, folder 159, Yale University Library, New Haven, Conn.

46. Malcolm MacDonald, quoted in Taya Zinkin, *Reporting India* (London, 1962), 13; Henry Kissinger, *White House Years* (Boston, 1979), 848.

6. Religion

1. Robert Bellah, *The Broken Covenant: American Civil Religion in Time of Trial* (New York, 1975); Garry Wills, *Under God: Religion and American Politics* (New York, 1990), 116; Wilson's war message in Thomas G. Paterson, ed., *Major Problems in American Foreign Policy*, 2d ed. (Boston, 1984), 37–41; Roosevelt's war message in ibid., 209–10.

2. H. W. Brands, *The Devil We Knew: Americans and the Cold War* (New York, 1993); Townsend Hoopes, *The Devil and John Foster Dulles* (Boston, 1973); Michael Schaller, *The U.S. Crusade in China, 1938–1945* (New York, 1979); Chester L. Cooper, *The Lost Crusade: America in Vietnam* (New York, 1970); James Irving Matray, *The Reluctant Crusade: American Foreign Policy in Korea, 1941–1950* (Honolulu, 1985); Joshua Muravchik, *The Uncertain Crusade: Jimmy Carter and the Dilemmas of Human Rights Policy* (Lanham, Md., 1986); Steve Dryden, *Trade Warriors: USTR and the American Crusade for Free Trade* (New York, 1995); Stephen Whitfield, *The Culture of the Cold War* (Baltimore, 1991), 87.

3. David McClellan, *Dean Acheson: The State Department Years* (New York, 1976), 2–7; Dean Acheson, *Present at the Creation: My Years in the State Department* (New York, 1969), 360, 692–93.

4. Dean Rusk, as told to Richard Rusk, *As I Saw It* (New York, 1990), 23–25, 34–35, 41–42, 51, 60–61, 504.

5. Dulles's religious speeches in Henry P. Van Dusen, ed., *The Spiritual Legacy of John Foster Dulles* (Philadelphia, 1959), xiii, 42, 74–75, 122, 221–28; Mark G. Toulouse, *The Transformation of John Foster Dulles: From Prophet of Realism to Priest of Nationalism* (Macon, Ga., 1985), xxvi–xxvii, 215–20, 232, 250–54; George V. Allen, interview by Ed Edwin, March 7, 9, 1967, Columbia University Oral History Collection, New York.

6. Stanley Wolpert, *Jinnah of Pakistan* (New York, 1984); Omar Noman, *Pakistan: Political and Economic History Since 1947* (New York, 1990), 1–8, 33–35; Richard Symonds, *The Making of Pakistan* (London, 1950), 99–104.

7. Stephen A. Tyler, *India: An Anthropological Perspective* (Prospect Heights, Ill., 1986), 5; Alan Roland, *In Search of Self in India and Japan: Toward a Cross-Cultural Psychology* (Princeton, 1988), 299–300, 306–7; Milton Singer, *When a Great Tradition Modernizes: An Anthropological Approach to Indian Civilization* (Chicago, 1972), 316; *Times of India*, Bombay (*TOI*), May 28, 1950, December 29, 1953; B. N. Pandey, *Nehru* (London, 1976), 114; Department of State (DOS), "Biographic Reports on Prime Minister of India and Members of His Party," October 5, 1949, Record Group (RG) 59, FW845.02/10-549, box 6114, National Archives (NA), Washington, D.C.

8. Diana Eck, *Darśan: Seeing the Divine Image in India* (Chambersburg, Pa., 1985), 3–7.

9. Ibid., 5; Jawaharlal Nehru to Vijayalakshmi Pandit, June 5, 1930, Vijayalakshmi Pandit Papers, Correspondence File, Jawaharlal Nehru Memorial Museum and Library (NMML), New Delhi; Michael Brecher, *Nehru: A Biography* (London, 1959), 3–11. Nehru never lost his knack for giving darshan; see the account of his visit to Punjab in the summer of 1963 by Catherine A. Galbraith in *Harper's*, July 1965, 80.

10. *Statesman* (Calcutta), August 14, 1947.

11. K. P. S. Menon Diary, entry for January 1, 1947, K. P. S. Menon Papers, NMML; note from R. Dunbar to Eion Donaldson, December 5, 1946, Records of the Foreign Office (FO) 371, file 63528, doc. 911, Public Record Office (PRO), Kew, England; note by H. Hoyer Millar, December 21, 1946, FO 371, file 63528, doc. 907, PRO; John Foster Dulles to Dwight D. Eisenhower, March 14, 1955, RG 59, 611.91/1455, box 2562, NA; President's Talking Paper, Meeting with Krishna Menon, November 21, 1961, John F. Kennedy Papers, President's Office Files (POF), Countries Series (CS), box 118a, John F. Kennedy Library (JFKL), Boston; M. O. Mathai, *Reminiscences of the Nehru Age* (New Delhi, 1978), 55.

12. Memo of conversation by Loy Henderson, October 25, 1948, RG 59, Lot File 54D341: Records of the Office of South Asian Affairs, 1939–53, box 18, NA; Loy W. Henderson, interview by Richard D. McKinzie, June 14 and July 5, 1973, Harry S. Truman Li-

brary (HSTL), Independence, Mo.; Henderson to G. Lewis Jones, April 18, 1949, RG 59, Lot File 54D341, box 19, NA.

13. Frank Roberts to FO, March 1, 1951, FO 371, file 92884, doc. FL10345/2, PRO.

14. R. K. Gupta, *The Great Encounter: A Study of Indo-American Literature and Cultural Relations* (New Delhi, 1986), 19; Harold R. Isaacs, *Scratches on Our Minds: American Images of China and India* (New York, 1958), 265.

15. Ronald Inden, *Imagining India* (Oxford, 1990), 54; Gavin R. G. Hambly, "Muslims in English-language Fiction," in Robin W. Winks and James R. Rush, eds., *Asia in Western Fiction* (Honolulu, 1990), 35–41; Bernard Saul Stern, "American Views of India and Indians, 1857–1900" (Ph.D. diss., University of Pennsylvania, 1956), 121.

16. Price Collier, *The West in the East* (New York, 1911), 321; Isaacs, *Scratches on Our Minds*, 276–77.

17. *TOI* (Bombay), n.d. [August 1894].

18. Katherine Mayo, *The Face of Mother India* (New York, 1935), 1–3, 6, 30–31, 41; Herman Kulke and Dietmar Rothermund, *A History of India* (New York, 1986), 163–65.

19. Congressional Briefing Book: India, August 18, 1961, Kennedy Papers, POF, CS, box 118a, JFKL; Robert B. Minturn, Jr., *From New York to Delhi* (New York, 1858), 141; Henry M. Field, *From Egypt to Japan* (New York, 1877), 125, 140, 254–59; letter from a "woman friend" of Richard Sutton to Katherine Mayo, July 8, 1927, Katherine Mayo Papers, folder 37, box 5, Yale University Library, New Haven, Conn.; Isaacs, *Scratches on Our Minds*, 264. Joan Jensen notes that in the United States during the early twentieth century the word "Hindu was a common term of opprobrium." Joan M. Jensen, *Passage from India: Asian Indian Immigrants in North America* (New Haven, 1988), 214.

20. Abbé J. A. Dubois, *Hindu Manners, Customs and Ceremonies*, 3d ed. (Oxford, 1905), 4; Sara Bard Field, interview, Sara Bard Field Papers, Bancroft Library, University of California–Berkeley; Bayard Taylor, *A Visit to India, China, and Japan in the Year 1853* (New York, 1891), 84–85; Mayo, *Face of Mother India*, 29; idem, *Mother India* (New York, 1927), 179, 380; John Frederick Muehl, *Interview with India* (New York, 1950), 252; Hereward Carrington, "How to Practice Yoga," *Fate* 1, 4 (1949), 77–84.

21. Isaacs, *Scratches on Our Minds*, 344–45, 351–52, 354–55.

22. Wendy Doniger and Brian K. Smith, trans., *The Laws of Manu* (New York, 1991); Ramanujan quoted in Roland, *In Search of Self*, 251.

23. G. Morris Carstairs, *The Twice-Born: A Study of a Community of High-Caste Hindus* (Bloomington, 1961), 52–53; Field, *From Egypt to Japan*, 253; Muehl, *Interview with India*, 48–49.

24. Martin E. Marty, *Modern American Religion*, vol. 3, *Under God, Indivisible, 1941–1960* (Chicago, 1996), 118, 131–35, 151–52; Edwin S. Gaustad, ed., *A Documentary History of Religion in America since 1865*, 2d ed. (Grand Rapids, 1993), 488–93.

25. Richard Wightman Fox, *Reinhold Niebuhr: A Biography* (New York, 1985), 224–67.

26. J. J. Singh, "Prime Minister Liaquat Ali Khan," n.d., RG 59, Lot File 54D341, box 17; George McGhee, *Envoy to the Middle World: Adventures in Diplomacy* (New York, 1983), 97.

27. Salman Rushdie, *Midnight's Children* (New York, 1980), 343, 348; Mohammed Ayub Khan, *Friends Not Masters: A Political Autobiography* (London, 1967), 128; "Pakistan: A Leader Gets Things Done," *Newsweek*, April 18, 1960, 54–58; State Visit of Mohammed Ayub Khan, July 11–18, 1961, Kennedy Papers, POF, CS, box 123, JFKL; Richard Gookin to Evelyn Lincoln, July 11, 1961, ibid.

28. Isaacs, *Scratches on Our Minds*, 276; DOS, Office of South Asian Affairs, "Pakistan," May 23, 1952, RG 59, Lot File 54D341, box 22, NA; Embassy in Karachi to DOS, July 24, 1953, RG 59, 611.90D/7-2453, box 2857, NA.

29. Minute by Sir W. Jenkin, May 18, 1948, L/P & S/12/4646, Collection 48: India's Foreign Relations, India Office Library (IOL), London; minute by K. H. Jones, December 7, 1950, file 84204, doc. FL1013/96, FO 371, PRO; memo of conversation by John Frick Root, April 3, 1951, DOS, *Foreign Relations of the United States* (*FRUS*), 1951, vol. 6, *Asia and the Pacific* (Washington, D.C., 1977), 1689–92; Donald Kennedy to Chester Bowles, January 16, 1953, Chester Bowles Papers, box 95, folder 268, Yale University Library; Allen, interview.

30. Various minutes, October–November 1950, FO 371, file 84263, doc. FL10310/12, FO 371, PRO; memo from John Sherman Cooper, December 13, 1956, Dwight D. Eisenhower Papers, Ann Whitman File (AWF), International Series (IS), box 28, Dwight D. Eisenhower Library (DDEL), Abilene, Kans.

31. Minute by S. J. Olver, October 13, 1950, FO 371, file 84263, doc. FL10310/12, PRO; Arthur H. Dean to the Secretary of State (SOS), January 27, 1954, RG 59, 611.91/2-154, box 2858, NA; Carstairs, *Twice-Born*, 54; *TOI* (Bombay), December 2, 1956; Elbert Mathews to T. Eliot Weil, December 12, 1955, RG 59, 611.91/10-2755, box 2562, NA.

32. Tapan Raychaudhuri, *Europe Reconsidered: Perceptions of the West in Nineteenth Century Bengal* (New Delhi, 1988), 219–331.

33. Ellsworth Bunker to Dwight Eisenhower, December 7, 1959, Eisenhower Papers, AWF, IS, box 26, DDEL; memo of conversation by R. Smith Simpson and William J. Barnsdale, June 1, 1954, RG 59, 611.91/6-154, box 2859, NA.

34. Pearl S. Buck, "Questions Indians Ask Me," *Asia and the Americas*, May 1946, 202; *Statesman* (Calcutta), October 16, 1953; *TOI* (Bombay), December 9, 10, 1953.

35. Krishnalal Shridharani, "The Philosophic Bases of India's Foreign Policy," *India Quarterly* 14, 2 (1958), 196–202; S. Natarajan, "India's Foreign Policy," *TOI* (Bombay), December 2, 1953.

36. Ainslie Embry, *Imagining India: Essays on Indian History*, ed. Mark Juergensmeyer (New York, 1989), 16.

37. Howard Donavan to SOS, August 2, 1948, RG 59, 711.45/8-248, box 3233, NA.

38. Account of Krishna Menon's remarks at National Press Club luncheon by D. J. C. Crawley, July 14, 1955, FO 371, file 117283, doc. DL1022/17, PRO; memo of conversation by Joseph Sparks, September 21, 1948, RG 59, 711.45/9-2148, box 3233, NA; memo of conversation by William T. Turner, June 25, 1954, RG 59, 611.91/6-2554, box 2859, NA; Elbert Mathews to T. Eliot Weil, December 12, 1955, RG 59, 611.91/10-2755, box 2562, NA; NSC 5409, n.d. [February 19, 1954], *FRUS* (1952–54), vol. 11, *Africa and South Asia* (Washington, D.C., 1983), 1096–117.

39. B. A. B. Burrows to J. D. Murray, July 30, 1951, FO 371, file 93018, doc. FZ1023/23, PRO; minute by Ernest Bevin, June 26, 1949, FO 371, file 76093, doc. F10823, PRO; David D. Newsome to Avra M. Warren, May 27, 1950, RG 59, Lot File 54D341, box 24, NA; Horace A. Hildreth to SOS, December 2, 1953, RG 59, 611.90D/12-253, box 2857, NA.

40. G. W. Choudhury, *India, Pakistan, Bangladesh and the Major Powers* (New York, 1975), 100; minutes of US-UK Foreign Ministers meeting, January 31, 1956, *FRUS* (1955–57), vol. 21, *East Asian Security; Cambodia; Laos* (Washington, D.C., 1990), 171; Toulouse, *Transformation of John Foster Dulles*, 222–24.

41. Robert J. McMahon, *The Cold War on the Periphery: The United States, India, and Pakistan* (New York, 1994), 154–88; Choudhury, *India, Pakistan, Bangladesh*, 83; Memo of Discussion, 147th Meeting of the NSC, June 2, 1953, Eisenhower Papers, AWF, NSC Series, box 4, DDEL; "A Real Ally in South Asia?" *US News and World Report*, November 13, 1953, 44–46.

42. Memo of Discussion, 177th Meeting of the NSC, December 23, 1953, Eisenhower Papers, AWF, NSC Series, box 5, DDEL. See also chapter 1.

43. Memorandum for the NSC, May 22, 1959, White House Office Files, Papers of the White House Office of the Special Assistant for National Security Affairs (WHOSANSA), Policy Papers Subseries, Box 19, DDEL; Richard Rountree to SOS, May 21, 1961, Kennedy Papers, National Security Files, Trips and Conferences Series, box 242, JFKL.

44. *TOI* (Bombay), December 17, 1953; January 31, 1954; May 1, 1961; Choudhury, *India, Pakistan, Bangladesh*, 100; George V. Allen to John Foster Dulles, September 10, 1953, RG 59, 611.91/9-1053, box 2858, NA.

7. Class, Caste, and Status

1. Harold R. Isaacs, *Scratches on Our Minds: American Views of China and India* (New York, 1958), 388.

2. *Hindu* (Madras), October 26, 1961.

3. Gerald D. Berreman, "Stratification, Pluralism and Interaction: A Comparative Analysis of Caste," in A. V. S. de Reuck and Julie Knight, eds., *Ciba Foundation Symposium on Caste and Race: Comparative Approaches* (London, 1967), 45–73; Raymond Williams, *Keywords: A Vocabulary of Culture and Society* (New York, 1983), 60–69; Edward B. Harper, "A Comparative Analysis of Caste: The United States and India," in Milton Singer and Bernard S. Cohn, eds., *Structure and Change in Indian Society* (Chicago, 1968), 59.

4. Isaacs, *Scratches on Our Minds*, 387–88; Louis Dumont, *Homo Hierarchicus: The Caste System and Its Implications* (Chicago, 1980), 16–19; *Times of India* (*TOI*), Bombay, November 27, 1956; Hans Mattson to John Davis, March 30, 1883, *Despatches of U.S. Consuls in Calcutta, 1792–1906* (microfilm), University of California–Berkeley Library. On Turner and his influence see Patricia Nelson Limerick, *The Legacy of Conquest: The Unbroken Past of the American West* (New York, 1987).

5. Stephen A. Tyler, *India: An Anthropological Perspective* (Prospect Heights, Ill., 1986).

6. M. N. Srinivas, "Mobility in the Caste System," in Singer and Cohn, *Structure and Change*, 189–90; John Frederick Muehl, *Interview with India* (New York, 1950), 182.

7. Arjun Appadurai, "Putting Hierarchy in Its Place," *Cultural Anthropology* 3, 1 (1988), 36–49; Chester Bowles, interview by Neal Gold, 1963, Chester Bowles Papers, box 396, folder 178, Yale University Library, New Haven, Conn.

8. Krishnalal Shridharani, *My India, My America* (Garden City, 1943), 171; Tyler, *India*, 147–48; Sudhir Kakar, *The Inner World: A Psychoanalytic Study of Childhood and Society in India* (New Delhi, 1978), 123–24.

9. Michael Brecher, *Nehru: A Political Biography* (London, 1959), 2; Jawaharlal Nehru, *Toward Freedom* (Boston, 1958), 353.

10. Kakar, *Inner World*, 122–26.

11. Wendy Doniger and Brian K. Smith, trans., *The Laws of Manu* (New York, 1991); Ramanujan quoted in Alan Roland, *In Search of Self in India and Japan: Toward a Cross-Cultural Psychology* (Princeton, 1988), 251; Angelina M. Whitford, "Vaikom Road Satyagraha: Where Did it Lead?" (paper given at the 23d Annual Conference on South Asia, Madison, Wisc., November 4, 1994).

12. G. Morris Carstairs, *The Twice-Born: A Study of a Community of High-Caste Hindus* (Bloomington, 1961), 48; Roland, *In Search of Self*, 246.

13. R. Smith Simpson to Department of State (DOS), October 20, 1953, Record Group (RG) 59, 611.91/10-2053, box 2858, National Archives (NA), Washington, D.C.

14. Sydney Greenbie, *The Romantic East* (New York, 1930), 21; Deepak Lal, "Manners, Morals, and Materialism: Some Indian Perceptions of America and Great Britain," in Sulochana Raghavan Glazer and Nathan Glazer, eds., *Conflicting Images: India and the United States* (Glenn Dale, Md., 1990), 271–88.

15. Memo of conversation by Sheldon T. Mills, March 8, 1954, RG 59, 611.91/3-854, box 2858, NA.

16. Memo of conversation by T. Eliot Weil, November 6, 1950, RG 59, 611.91/11-650, box 2857, NA; Sarvepalli Gopal, *Jawaharlal Nehru: A Biography*, vol. 2, *1947–1956* (New Delhi, 1979), 189–90, 255; John Kenneth Galbraith, *Ambassador's Journal: A Personal Account of the Kennedy Years* (Boston, 1969), 157; Elbert G. Mathews, interview by Richard McKinzie, June 13, 1975, Harry S. Truman Library (HSTL), Independence, Mo.

17. Erving Goffman, *The Presentation of Self in Everyday Life* (Garden City, 1959), 55.

18. Benjamin Fleck to DOS, February 14, 1956, RG 59, 611.91/2-1456, box 2562, NA; Roland E. Wolseley to Chester Bowles, March 2, 1953, Bowles Papers, box 103, folder 381.

19. Memo of conversation by Dean Acheson, June 2, 1950, RG 59, 611.91/6-250, box 2859, NA.

20. Roland, *In Search of Self*, 66.

21. Jawaharlal Nehru, note for Asaf Ali and K. P. S. Menon, January 22, 1947, K. P. S. Menon Papers, Correspondence File, Jawaharlal Nehru Memorial Museum and Library (NMML), New Delhi; K. P. S. Menon, interview, NMML; Sarvepalli Gopal, ed., *The Selected Works of Jawaharlal Nehru* (*SWJN*), 2d ser., vol. 3 (New Delhi, 1985), 334; W. B. Smith to the

Secretary of State (SOS), March 20, 1948, *FRUS* (1948), vol. 5, *The Near East, South Asia, and Africa* (Washington, D.C., 1975), 499–500; *Hindustan Times* (*HT*), Calcutta, March 7, 1954.

22. *SWJN*, 2d ser., vol. 2 (New Delhi, 1984), 516–17, 631–32; ibid., vol. 3, 330; Ernest Fisk to Howard Donavan, August 25, 1947, RG 84, Foreign Service Posts of DOS: India, New Delhi Embassy, Confidential File, box 38, Washington National Records Center (WNRC), Suitland, Md.

23. *SWJN*, 1st ser., vol. 14 (New Delhi, 1982), 440–42, ibid., vol. 15 (New Delhi, 1982), 519, 562; ibid., 2d ser., vol. 1 (New Delhi, 1983), 471–76; Jawaharlal Nehru, *Speeches*, vol. 1 (New Delhi, 1949), 25–27; Jawaharlal Nehru, *India's Foreign Policy* (New Delhi, 1961), 12–13, 43.

24. Jawaharlal Nehru to M. C. Chagla, October 3, 1946, File 36, M. C. Chagla Papers, NMML; K. P. S. Menon Diary, entries for October 7, 1946, January 23, 1951, K. P. S. Menon Papers; SWJN, 2d ser., 1:542–43.

25. "Progress Report on U.S. Policy towards South Asia" (NSC 5409), March 30, 1956, DOS, *Foreign Relations of the United States* (*FRUS*), 1955–57, vol. 8, *South Asia* (Washington, D.C., 1987), 1–10; Mathews, interview.

26. New Delhi Embassy to DOS, April 28, 1959, Papers of the Council on Foreign Economic Policy (CFEP), Office of the Chairman (OC), Randall Series (RS), box 6, Dwight D. Eisenhower Library (DDEL), Abilene, Kans.

27. Memo of conversation by William L. S. Williams, June 26, 1950, RG 59, 611.91/6-2650, box 2857, NA; Prescott Childs to DOS, May 25, 1951, RG 59, 611.91/5-2551, box 2858, NA; Donald D. Kennedy to DOS, September 28, 1954, RG 59, 611.91/9-2854, box 2859, NA.

28. Abbé J. A. Dubois, *Hindu Manners, Customs and Ceremonies*, 3d ed. (Oxford, 1905), 322; Bernard Saul Stern, "American Views of India and Indians, 1857–1900" (Ph.D. diss., University of Pennsylvania, 1956), 124; Roland, *In Search of Self*, 26, 255.

29. O. Mannoni, *Prospero and Caliban: The Psychology of Colonization* (New York, 1956), 42–47. See also George Trumbull Ladd, *Intimate Glimpses of Life in India* (Boston, 1919), 62; Carstairs, *Twice-Born*, 50.

30. *Statesman* (Calcutta), October 17, 1949; Loy Henderson to SOS, April 12, 1950, RG 59, 611.91/4-1250, box 2857, NA; *TOI* (Bombay), May 20, 1961.

31. Memo of conversation by William L. S. Williams, May 2, 1950, RG 59, 611.91/5250, box 2857, NA; memo of conversation by George C. McGhee, October 26, 1950, 611.91/10-2650, ibid.; Chester Bowles, "New Delhi Diary," entry for September 3, 1963, Bowles Papers, box 392, folder 159.

32. *TOI* (Bombay), December 29, 1950; December 6, 1953; memorandum from the Indian Kisan Congress, May 31, 1949, Lot File 54D341, Box 16, RG 59, NA; Clifford Manshardt to Chester Bowles, June 12, 1952, Bowles Papers, Box 99, folder 327.

33. Galbraith, *Ambassador's Journal*, 126.

34. Dean Acheson to Loy Henderson, April 21, 1950, *FRUS* (1950), vol. 5, *The Near East, South Asia, and Africa* (Washington, D.C., 1978), 1464.

35. Jawaharlal Nehru to Asaf Ali, December 21, 1946, *SWJN*, 2d ser., 1:556–57; Nehru to chief ministers, October 2, 1949, Jawaharlal Nehru, *Letters to Chief Ministers 1947–1964*, vol. 1, 1947–1949 (New Delhi, 1985), 471; George Allen to John Foster Dulles, June 8, 1954, RG 84, Foreign Service Posts: India General Records, box 66, WNRC; Taya Zinkin, *Reporting India* (London, 1962), 212.

36. Dennis Merrill, *Bread and the Ballot: The United States and India's Economic Development* (Chapel Hill, 1990), 60–74; memo of conversation by P. L. Kelser, December 16, 1950, Dean Acheson Papers, box 65, HSTL; memo by J. Robert Fluker, January 15, 1951, *FRUS* (1951), vol. 6, *Asia and the Pacific* (Washington, D.C., 1977), 2085–87; "India's Request for Food Grains: Political Considerations," January 24, 1951, ibid., 2103–6; memo for President Truman by Acheson, February 2, 1951, Truman Papers, White House Central Files, box 38; "bulging file" is folder "Aid to India," Truman Papers, Official Files, box 1278; memo by Charles Murphy, February 6, 1951, David Lloyd Papers, Box 4, HSTL; Acheson to the em-

bassy in Egypt, March 28, 1951, and editorial note, *FRUS* (1951), 6:2132–33; U.S., House of Representatives, *Congressional Record* (Washington, D.C., 1951), 5651, 5842–43, 6182–84.

37. Robert J. McMahon, *The Cold War on the Periphery: The United States, India, and Pakistan* (New York, 1994), 101; memo of conversation by T. Eliot Weil, December 29, 1950, Acheson Papers, box 65; George McGhee to Acheson, January 25, 1951, RG 59, 611.91/1-2551, box 2858, NA; U.S. House, *Congressional Record* (1951), 5823–27.

38. Loy Henderson to SOS, April 22, May 7, 1951, *FRUS* (1951), 6:2150–51, 2158–59; U.S. Senate, *Congressional Record* (Washington, D.C., 1951), 5326; Merrill, *Bread and the Ballot*, 71.

39. McMahon, *Cold War on the Periphery*, 97; memo of conversation by Loy Henderson, February 20, 1951, *FRUS* (1951), 6:2127; report on interview with Prime Minister Nehru by Edgar A. Mowrer, March 22, 1951, Bowles Papers, box 98, folder 323; U.S. House of Representatives, *Appendix to the Congressional Record* (Washington, D.C., 1951), A1733; Gopal, *Nehru*, 2:137; Introduction of Daniel Patrick Moynihan by Loy Henderson, March 25, 1975, Loy Henderson Papers, box 8, Library of Congress (LC), Washington, D.C.

40. Dean Acheson to the embassy in India, January 24, 1951, *FRUS* (1951), 6:2090; *Washington Post*, April 1, 5, 22, May 1, 1951; U.S. House, *Congressional Record* (1951), 5615, 5618, 5741.

41. Loy Henderson to SOS, February 3, 1951, *FRUS* (1951), 6:2112; *Amrita Bazar Patrika* quoted in Office of Intelligence Research, "Foreign Reaction to the Question of Grain Shipments from the United States to India," May 16, 1951, Dorothy Norman Papers, ser. 1, box 1, Syracuse University Library.

42. *Statesman* (Calcutta), November 9, 1949; Douglas Ensminger, interview, 1971, Douglas Ensminger Papers, box 1, folder A.8, Yale University Library.

43. *TOI* (Bombay), May 22, 1953.

44. The President to the SOS, March 23, 1955, *FRUS* (1955–57), 8:278; H. W. Brands, *The Specter of Neutralism: The United States and the Emergence of the Third World, 1947–1960* (New York, 1989), 120, 138; *TOI* (Bombay), December 12, 15, 1959; May 14, 1961; Ellsworth Bunker to SOS, December 22, 1959, Dwight Eisenhower Papers, Ann Whitman File (AWF), International Series (IS), box 26, DDEL; John Kenneth Galbraith to SOS, December 7, 1962, John F. Kennedy Papers, National Security Files (NSF), Country Series (CS), box 111; Galbraith, *Ambassador's Journal*, 362.

45. Letter from Chester Bowles, n.d. [early 1953], Bowles Papers, box 112, folder 504; Bowles, "New Delhi Diary," July 22, 1963, Bowles Papers, box 392, folder 159; Bowles, *Ambassador's Report*, 32; M. V. Kamath, "Our Coca Cola Culture: An Indian View," *Current History* 31, 184 (1956), 321–27.

46. Memo of conversation by Clifford Manshardt, December 4, 1955, RG 59, 611.91/12-955, box 2562.

47. Memo of conversation by Peter Delaney, January 28, 1953, *FRUS* (1952–54), vol. 11, *Africa and South Asia* (Washington, D.C., 1983), 1822–24; memo of conversation by J. Robert Fluker, June 22, 1954, ibid., 1849.

Epilogue

1. Sarvepalli Gopal, *Jawaharlal Nehru: A Biography*, vol. 3, *1956–1964* (New Delhi, 1984), 266–71; Stanley Wolpert, *A New History of India*, 3d ed. (New York, 1989), 370.

2. *India Today (IT)*, June 1, 1998, 29.

3. Lloyd I. Rudolph, "Gandhi in the Mind of America," in Sulochana Raghavan Glazer and Nathan Glazer, eds., *Conflicting Images: India and the United States* (Glenn Dale, Md., 1990), 167; Diana L. Eck, " 'New Age' Hinduism in America," in ibid., 136; *New York Times (NYT)*, August 26, 1997.

4. *NYT*, June 7, 1998.

5. Zareer Masani, *Indira Gandhi: A Biography* (London, 1975), 157, 159, 164; Barbara Crossette, *India: Facing the Twenty-First Century* (Bloomington, 1993), 131; H. W. Brands, *India and the United States: The Cold Peace* (Boston, 1990), 179–80.

6. Brands, *India and the United States*, 150–52, 167–68.

7. *NYT*, May 27, 1989; June 21, 1995; *Washington Post* (*WP*), June 20, 1989; George Rosen, "The Indian Economy: Muddling Through in a Year of Turmoil," in Philip Oldenburg, ed., *India Briefing, 1991* (Boulder, 1991), 87–88.

8. Baldev Raj Nayar, "The Public Sector," in Leonard A. Gordon and Philip Oldenburg, eds., *India Briefing, 1992* (Boulder, 1992), 85, 93; *NYT*, November 12, 1998. Rajiv had nothing on his brother Sanjay, whom their mother groomed for political office before his death in an airplane accident in 1980. Salman Rushdie's analysis: "Mrs. Gandhi returned to power, with Sanjay at her right hand, so it turned out that there was no final morality in the affairs of state, only Relativity. I remembered Vasco Miranda's 'Indians variation' upon the theme of Einstein's General Theory: Everything is for relative. Not only light bends, but everything. For relative we can bend a point, bend the truth, bend employment criteria, bend the law. D equals mc squared, where D is for Dynasty, m is for mass of relatives, and c of course is for corruption, which is the only constant in the universe—because in India even speed of light is dependent on load shedding and vagaries of power supply." Salman Rushdie, *The Moor's Last Sigh* (New York, 1996), 272.

9. Pratap Bhanu Mehta, "India: The Nuclear Politics of Self-Esteem," *Current History*, December 1998, 403–6; *NYT*, May 12, 13, 29, 1998.

10. *NYT*, May 13, 31, 1998; *IT*, June 1, 1998, 28; *WP*, May 31, 1998.

11. *NYT*, September 21, 1995; May 8, June 25, 1996; May 29, 1998; *IT*, June 1, 1998, 28, 35–37. Pakistan's nuclear program began in the early 1970s as a quest for an "Islamic bomb," as then-president Zulfikar Ali Bhutto called it, a characterization readily believed by Western governments nervous at the prospect. By the time Pakistan made its tests, the government had grown testy at the thought that credit, or blame, for the achievement had to be shared. "Why do people talk about an Islamic bomb?" asked Information Minister Mushahid Hussain. "This is a Pakistani bomb. In the case of India, you don't talk of a vegetarian bomb" (*NYT*, June 7, 1998).

12. *WP*, May 17, 1998; *IT*, June 1, 1998, 28.

Index